Sport, Gender and Mega-Events

Emerald Studies in Sport and Gender

Series Editor

Helen Jefferson Lenskyj, University of Toronto, Canada.

Editorial Board: Doug Booth, University of Otago, New Zealand; Jayne Caudwell, Bournemouth University, UK; Delia Douglas, University of British Columbia, Canada; Janice Forsyth, University of Western Ontario, Canada; Tara Magdalinski, Swinburne University of Technology, Australia; Jaime Schultz, Pennsylvania State University, USA; Heather Sykes, University of Toronto, Canada; Beccy Watson, Leeds Beckett University, UK.

Emerald Studies in Sport and Gender promotes research on two important and related areas within sport studies: women and gender. The concept of gender is included in the series title in order to problematize traditional binary thinking that classifies individuals as male or female, rather than looking at the full gender spectrum. In sport contexts, this is a particularly relevant and controversial issue, for example, in the case of transgender athletes and female athletes with hyperandrogenism. The concept of sport is interpreted broadly to include activities ranging from physical recreation to high-performance sport.

The interdisciplinary nature of the series will encompass social and cultural history and philosophy as well as sociological analyses of contemporary issues. Since any analysis of sport and gender has political implications and advocacy applications, learning from history is essential.

Previous Volumes

Running, Identity and Meaning: The Pursuit of Distinction through Sport – Neil Baxter
Gender, Athletes' Rights, and the Court of Arbitration for Sport – Helen Lenskyj

Forthcoming Volumes

The Professionalisation of Women's Sport: Issues and Debates – Ali Bowes and Alex Culvin
Gender Equity in UK Sport Leadership and Governance – Philippa Velija and Lucy Piggott
Sport, Gender and Development: Intersections, Innovations and Future Trajectories – Lyndsay Hayhurst, Holly Thorpe, and Megan Chawansky
Women's Football in a Global, Professional Era – Alex Culvin and Ali Bowes

Sport, Gender and Mega-Events

EDITED BY

KATHERINE DASHPER

Leeds Beckett University, UK

United Kingdom – North America – Japan – India – Malaysia – China

Emerald Publishing Limited
Howard House, Wagon Lane, Bingley BD16 1WA, UK

First edition 2022

Reprints and permissions service
Contact: permissions@emeraldinsight.com

British Library Cataloguing in Publication Data
A catalogue record for this book is available from the British Library

ISBN: 978-1-83982-937-6 (Print)
ISBN: 978-1-83982-936-9 (Online)
ISBN: 978-1-83982-938-3 (Epub)

Printed and bound by CPI Group (UK) Ltd, Croydon, CR0 4YY

ISOQAR certified
Management System,
awarded to Emerald
for adherence to
Environmental
standard
ISO 14001:2004.

Certificate Number 1985
ISO 14001

INVESTOR IN PEOPLE

For Frank Brady

Contents

List of Figures and Tables   *xi*

List of Abbreviations   *xiii*

About the Contributors   *xv*

Acknowledgements   *xvii*

**Chapter 1   Introduction: Sport, Gender and
Mega-Events**   *1*
Katherine Dashper

Section 1: Problematising Gendered Bodies and Behaviours

**Chapter 2   Sex Testing in Sport Mega-Events: Fairness and the
Illusive Promise of Inclusive Policies – Situating Inter* and
Trans*Athletes in Elite Sport**   *33*
Anna Adlwarth

**Chapter 3   Ethical Relativism and Sport Mega-Event Gendered
Discourses: Uneasiness towards the Dominant Play of Women in
Sport**   *57*
Lindsey Darvin and Ann Pegoraro

Section 2: Masculinity, Sport and Mega-Events

Chapter 4   Not Feeling So Mega, but Still Being a Mega Star: Exploring Male Elite Athletes' Mental Health Accounts from a Gendered Perspective   *73*
Charlie Smith

Chapter 5   Security, Locality and Aggressive Masculinity: Hooliganism and Nationalism at Football Mega-Events   *91*
Jonathan Sly

Chapter 6   The Formula One Paradox: Macho Male Racers and Ornamental Glamour 'Girls'   *113*
Damion Sturm

Section 3: Gender, Disruption and Transformation at Mega-Events

Chapter 7   'Dare to Shine': Megan Rapinoe as the Rebellious Star of the FIFA Women's World Cup 2019   *133*
Riikka Turtiainen

Chapter 8   Who Owns the Ball? Gender (Dis)Order and the 2014 FIFA World Cup   *149*
Jorge Knijnik, Rohini Balram and Yoko Kanemasu

Chapter 9   I Gotta Feeling … Let's Turn to the People! The 2018 Football World Cup in Russia   *163*
Katarzyna Raduszynska

Section 4: Gender, Sport and Mega-Events: Moving towards Equality?

Chapter 10   Sport Mega-Events as Drivers of Gender Equality: Women's Football in Spain   *187*
Celia Valiente

Chapter 11   The Solheim Cup: Media Representations of Golf, Gender and National Identity   *201*
Ali Bowes and Niamh Kitching

Chapter 12   Flag before Gender Biases? The Case for National Identity Bolstering Women Athlete Visibility in Sports Mega-Events   *221*
Andrew C. Billings and Patrick C. Gentile

Chapter 13   Conclusions: Sport, Gender and Mega-Events: Looking to the Future   *239*
Katherine Dashper

Index   *247*

List of Figures and Tables

Figure 12.1.   Percentage of Women's Medals Won by
                Proportion of Received Clock-time.   232

Table 2.1.   Reviewed Articles by Themes.   41
Table 10.1.   Holders of Licences from the Royal Spanish
                Football Federation by Sex, 2009–2019.   191
Table 11.1.   Team Europe.   207
Table 11.2.   Team USA.   208
Table 12.1.   Clock-time for Women in the Summer
                Olympic Games (1996–2016).   229

List of Abbreviations

ASA	Athletics South Africa
CAS	Court of Arbitration for Sport
ESIM	Elaborated Social Identity Model of crowd behaviour
FA	Football Association (UK)
FBOs	Football Banning Orders
FWC	Football World Cup – FIFA Men's Football World Cup
IAAF	International Association of Athletics Federation, now World Athletics
IOC	International Olympic Committee
LET	Ladies European Tour (golf)
LPGA	Ladies Professional Golf Association
RCT	Role Congruity Theory
SRT	Social Role Theory
UEFA	Union of European Football Associations
USWNT	United States Women's National Team (soccer)
WWC	Women's World Cup – FIFA Women's Football World Cup
WWGR	Women's World Golf Rankings

About the Contributors

Anna Adlwarth works at Nord University in Norway as a PhD researcher in sociology, where she is located in the research group Sport and Society. She holds a master's degree in Gender Studies from the University of Graz (Austria) and a master's degree in Applied Linguistics from the University of Vienna.

Rohini Balram is a PhD student at the school of Education at Western Sydney University (Australia). Her research interest concentrates on gender, race and ethnicity, minority groups, sports, identity and the Indo-Fijian Diaspora.

Andrew C. Billings is the Ronald Reagan Chair of Broadcasting and the Executive Director of the Alabama Program in Sports Communication in the Department of Journalism and Creative Media at the University of Alabama (USA).

Ali Bowes is a Senior Lecturer in Sociology of Sport at Nottingham Trent University. She completed her PhD at Loughborough University. Her published work focusses primarily on qualitative investigations on elite and/or professional female athletes and elite women's sport cultures, including self and mediatised presentations, and considerations of national-level representation.

Lindsey Darvin is an Assistant Professor of Sport Management with the State University of New York (SUNY) College at Cortland. Her research examines sport industry gender equity, diversity, and inclusion rates while working to combat the underrepresentation of women leaders at the highest levels of sport competition and business.

Katherine Dashper is a Reader in the School of Events, Tourism and Hospitality Management at Leeds Beckett University, UK. Her research explores gender and identity in sport, leisure, and work. She also examines interspecies interactions in events, tourism and leisure. She has recently co-edited *Human, Horses and Events Management* (CABI, 2021).

Patrick Gentile is a Doctoral Student in Communication and Information Sciences at the University of Alabama (USA). His research interests include media perceptions of athletes based on race, ethnicity, nationality, gender, and language proficiency.

Yoko Kanemasu is an Associate Professor in Sociology at the University of the South Pacific. Her sport research centres around issues of power and domination. She has recently co-edited *Women, Sport and Exercise in the Asia-Pacific Region:*

Domination, Resistance, Accommodation (Routledge). Her other research interests include gender/sexuality, identity, migration and tourism.

Niamh Kitching is a Lecturer in Physical Education at Mary Immaculate College, University of Limerick. Her research interests include the sociology of sport and PE and gender and sport. Her published research focusses on female athletes and coaches and their presence, participation and presentation in sports and sports media.

Jorge Knijnik is an Associate Professor in the School of Education at Western Sydney University. He has recently published *The World Cup Chronicles: 31 Days that Rocked Brazil* (Fair Play publishing). He was recipient of the 'Building the Gender Equity' award presented by UN Women and the Brazilian Research Council.

Ann Pegoraro is the Lang Chair in Sport Management the University of Guelph and co-Director of EAlliance, the National Network for Research on Gender Equity in Canadian Sport. Her research examines the intersection of digital media and sport with a focus on gender and diversity.

Katarzyna Raduszynska is a theatre director, playwright and former actress. She is a multiple scholarship holder from Ministry of Culture and National Heritage in Poland and the Visegrad Fund. She is conducting a PhD at the Institute of Art of the Polish Academy of Sciences in Warsaw.

Jonathan Sly is a Lecturer in Sociology at Liverpool John Moores University. His research interests focus on contemporary manifestations of aggressive masculinity. This includes sports-related violence, subjective inter-personal violence and street culture in late-modern Britain, and the links between transgressive practices, social class and consumer culture.

Charlie Smith is an Associate Professor in Management and Organisation at the University of Leicester. Broadly, her research focusses on performance, well-being and individuals' lived experiences in work and sport. Being a keen Team GB amateur triathlete, she is acutely aware of the performative pressures of serious sport.

Damion Sturm is a Senior Lecturer in Sport Management at Massey University (Albany, New Zealand). With a specialisation in global media cultures (inclusive of sport, celebrity, fandom and events), his recent works are on the intersections of stardom, fan cultures, digital technologies, and sports as mega/media events.

Riikka Turtiainen is a Senior Lecturer and Adjunct Professor in Digital Culture at the University of Turku, Finland. Her research interests focus on sports and social media, particularly representations of female athletes. She has also studied digital embodiment and new aspects of exercise cultures and games.

Celia Valiente is a Professor of Sociology at the Department of Social Sciences of the Universidad Carlos III de Madrid, Spain. Her main research interests are the women's movement, gender-equality policies and gender in sports in Spain from a comparative perspective.

Acknowledgements

Many individuals contribute to the successful realisation of a project like this. The idea for this collection came from series editor Helen Lenskyj, Professor Emerita at University of Toronto, and Helen Beddow at Emerald. I appreciate their belief in the project and support in bringing it to fruition. I also thank the wider team at Emerald for a smooth and professional process.

I am grateful to all the authors for their hard work and the quality of their contributions. My colleagues at the School of Events, Tourism and Hospitality Management at Leeds Beckett University have provided a supportive working environment and special mention goes to Tom Fletcher for helping with some chapter reviews.

On a personal note, I am grateful for the support of my family and friends. This book would never have been completed without Ian's constant encouragement and practical and emotional support and, in a time of home-working during the COVID-19 pandemic, my animal companions – Charlie, Brie and Ruthie – have been invaluable in providing friendship and escapism.

Chapter 1

Introduction: Sport, Gender and Mega-Events

Katherine Dashper

Introduction

Sport mega-events form a regular part of life, providing a pinnacle for elite sports careers and moments of fun, excitement, pride and sometimes disappointment for fans around the world. Sport mega-events punctuate our lives in a regular, dependable pattern (notwithstanding major international crises, such as the impacts of the COVID-19 pandemic, see Chapter 13, Conclusions). Every four years we enjoy the Summer Olympic Games, followed two years later by the Winter Olympics. The same pattern is evident with the Fédération Internationale de Football Association (FIFA) Men's World Cup, followed two years later by the Women's World Cup. Regional multisport events follow a similar four-year pattern, such as the Commonwealth Games, Pan American Games and the Asian Games, while some events occur biennially, such as the Africa Cup of Nations and World Athletics Championships. Others occur annually, such as the Super Bowl, or even as a series of events, such as Formula 1. Sport mega-events have thus 'established an enduring presence, popularity and memorability in modern society' (Roche, 2008, p. 286), providing rhythm to global sporting and media calendars.

Sport is a central feature of contemporary societies, a ritualised, highly commercialised practice that is focused on the body (Horne & Manzenreiter, 2006). As such, it is a prime site for the production and reproduction of gendered identities, discourses and practices that can both constrain and empower groups and individuals. This book examines some of the complex, ambiguous issues around gender and sport mega-events, which are understood here as paradoxical phenomena that are simultaneously sites for traditional and restrictive gender performances *and* opportunities for disruption and even transformation of those same norms.

The book is, thus, a contribution to two fields. First, to the sociology of sport, a field which has long questioned the role of organised sport in perpetuating and amplifying traditional gender discourses that serve to marginalise and exclude many from full participation and recognition (Hargreaves, 1994; McDonagh &

Sport, Gender and Mega-Events, 1–29
doi:10.1108/978-1-83982-936-920211007

Pappano, 2007). Sport mega-events have been a prime site for these practices, in part due to their global mediatised nature that can transmit messages to billions of people around the world. However, with a few exceptions that tend to focus on the Olympic Games in particular (e.g. Lenskyj, 2013), sport sociologists have placed less focus on 'the mega-event phenomenon' (Roche, 2008) itself as a gendered entity and the ways in which these particular forms of sport spectacle lead to both restrictive and potentially transgressive gender practices. This book, thus, positions the mega-event phenomenon itself as an important factor in the ways in which gender is done, redone and potentially undone in the context of sport (Dashper, 2016). Second, the book is also a contribution to the field of critical event studies which attempts to include questions of power and representation in understanding the various roles planned events play in different communities (Spracklen & Lamond, 2016). However, there has been limited sustained focus on gender in relation to events (Dashper & Finkel, 2020), and certainly not in the context of mega-events, so this book helps extend understanding of the importance of gender and power to critical examinations of planned events.

Consequently, this book aims to draw together insights from a range of fields to question how sport mega-events are sites of struggle and contestation in terms of gender and identity, sometimes resulting in the entrenchment of restrictive and prohibitive gender norms and practices, but sometimes leading to change and transformation. The primary analytic focus for the book is gender, but gender can never be considered in isolation and chapters explore various ways in which gender intersects with other axes of power related to race, class and nationhood in and through sport mega-events. This introduction sets the scene for the discussions in subsequent chapters, by examining what sport mega-events are and their social, cultural, economic and political significance, and introducing some of the complex and fraught gender issues prevalent in organised sport within and beyond mega-events.

What Are Sport Mega-Events?

Competition is integral to contemporary forms of sport – between individuals, teams and nations. Elite sport is built around notions of excellence, where the best athletes compete for the number one position. As such, events are fundamental to the operation of high-level sport, and consequently in any given year, thousands of events occur across a broad range of sports. Events are temporal, occurring in a pre-defined time and space, with a clear beginning and end, and a programme of activities that is publicised in advance to allow participants – athletes and their support teams – and spectators to choose if they want to attend (Getz & Page, 2016). The field of events management/studies has contributed to understanding of the broad array of different types and scale of sport event, ranging from small, local sports tournaments where many elite athletes begin their competitive careers: to hallmark events associated closely with a specific place, such as the Wimbledon Tennis Championships; to major events, that are large in scale and attract widespread interest from athletes and spectators alike, like the Six Nations competition in rugby union; to so-called mega-events that have global impacts and reach and require substantial investment, like the Summer Olympic Games (Bowdin, O'Toole, Allen, Harris, & McDonnell, 2006; Dashper, Helgadóttir, & Sigurðardóttir, 2021).

Definitions are important for helping to describe a field and focus attention. The focus of this book is on sport mega-events, but the ways in which 'mega-events' are defined and distinguished from 'major events' and some 'hallmark events' are contested. Roche (2000, p. 1) described mega-events as 'large-scale cultural (including commercial and sporting) events, which have a dramatic character, mass popular appeal and international significance'. Building on this, Horne (2007) proposed that two factors are central to contemporary mega-events. First, they have significant consequences for the host city, region or nation. Second, they attract widespread media attention. Roberts (2004) also stressed the scale of mega-events, the importance of global media attention which facilitates the spreading of promotional messages worldwide (about the host, the sport, the organising body, etc.), and the fact that they are 'discontinuous' and, therefore, out of the ordinary, supporting Roche's (2003) argument that such events are important collective rituals that help mark the passing of time.

Müller (2015) argued that there is ambiguity around what make an event 'mega' and acknowledges that 'not all mega-events are "mega" in the same dimensions and to the same degree' (pp. 627–628). He identified four key dimensions that mega-events share:

(1) Visitor attractiveness – although Müller (2015) notes that it is impossible to accurately assess visitor numbers (ticket sales are one approach, but they likely over-estimate numbers as some people attend more than one session), mega-events are appealing to visitors from outside the local area who come to spectate and join in with the overall event atmosphere.

(2) Mediated reach – in line with numerous other scholars (e.g. Horne, 2007), Müller (2015) notes that an event cannot be considered 'mega' if it does not attract widespread, possibly global, media attention. The extent and reach of this will vary by event, but the mediated (re)production of events is an important contributor to their 'mega' scale and popularity.

(3) Cost – the first two factors focus on the output side of mega-events, but the input side is also important, that is, the significant costs of staging these tournaments. Direct costs include spending on infrastructure like venues, transport, and associated facilities, and staffing and logistics related to event operations, security etc. Müller (2015) also highlights the importance of opportunity costs related to hosting mega-events, where money that is spent on the event is not spent on other projects and needs. Mega-events are expensive.

(4) Urban transformation – a major theme of research on mega-events is their capacity to affect the host city or region, with large impacts on the built environment and the local population. Indeed, many cities and countries bid

to host mega-events in order to support urban transformation (Hiller, 2000; Smith, 2012). However, although mega-events are sold to populations as opportunities for positive transformation, they also frequently result in negative outcomes for local people, such as displacement, gentrification, and environmental damage (see Watt, 2013).

Müller's (2015) dimensions reflect many of the issues frequently identified in relation to the hosting of mega-events in terms of potential gains and losses. As large, complex, highly commercialised phenomena, mega-events pose complex logistical and strategic issues for hosts. Gursoy and Kendall (2006) illustrated the importance of local community support for ensuring the success of mega-events, and Lee Ludvigsen (2018) underscored the role of security and safety. Whitson and Horne (2006) suggested that the benefits of hosting mega-events are often overestimated, while costs are underestimated. Mega-events frequently exceed their original budgets – the 1976 Montreal Summer Olympics and the 1984 Sarajevo Winter Olympics exceeded initial budgets more than tenfold (Baade & Matheson, 2016). It took Montreal 30 years to pay off the debt incurred by cost overruns in 1976, and the cost overruns and debt of the 2004 Summer Olympics in Athens contributed to the Greek economic and financial crises of 2007–2012 (Flyvbjerg & Stewart, 2012). Yet many cities and nations still desire the prestige and global visibility that mega-event hosting can bring (Caiazza & Audretsch, 2015; Grix, 2012).

The enormous costs previously meant that hosting was dominated by nations in the Global North. However, as Lauermann (2019) notes, spiralling costs, questions about legacies and long-term benefits, and negative reactions from local communities have led to many of these nations stepping back from bids; between 2013 and 2018, 13 cities withdrew or cancelled plans to bid to host the Olympics, following negative referenda or in response to political pressures. In contrast, emerging nations are increasingly stepping up to host mega-events as part of strategies to project a global image and announce their position as major players on the international stage. As Black and Van Der Westhuizen (2004, p. 1200) argued, 'hosting major sports events is one of the few relatively accessible means through which developing nations may seek to enhance their global appeal'. Knott, Fyall, and Jones (2017) have suggested that, for emerging nations in particular, hosting sport mega-events remains an attractive proposition despite rising costs and global scandals related to event rights holders, like the International Olympic Committee (IOC) and FIFA. Drawing on the example of South Africa hosting the 2010 FIFA Men's World Cup, they suggested that mega-events create valuable nation-branding opportunities. It is the scale and global reach of mega-events that make them attractive propositions in this way, and mechanisms for the exercise of soft power (see also Grix & Brannagan, 2016).

Similarly, Black (2007) illustrated how sport mega-events provide unique opportunities to pursue what he calls 'symbolic politics' – a chance to reframe dominant narratives, to signal a change in direction and/or to reinforce key messages about a nation or a region. Drawing on three mega-events that all occurred in 2010 – the FIFA Men's World Cup in South Africa, the Commonwealth Games in Delhi in India, and the Winter Olympics in Vancouver in Canada – he argued that, despite some significant differences in context and circumstances of the hosts, all three locations sought to use mega-event hosting to signal their global significance as 'world-class' hosts, cities and nations.

Sport mega-events, thus, present (would-be) hosts with a complex mix of opportunities and costs. This leads Müller (2017) to position mega-events as paradoxical; they celebrate universal humanity (through ideals such as Olympism) yet clearly separate participants and spectators into distinct nations; they are heavily rule-bound, but there are frequent examples of rule-bending (not least in relation to use of performance-enhancing drugs); they claim to be based around inclusion and communal participation (e.g. through volunteering) but are also highly exclusive, focused on the very best of the best; they cause destruction – of neighbourhoods, communities, the environment – but they also create – new stadia, new images, new communities. This ambiguity is part of the enduring attraction of mega-events, as they 'spark the perhaps most fundamental of human paradoxes: a love-hate relationship. We love them, we love them not' (Müller, 2017, p. 238). The 'mega-event phenomenon' (Roche, 2008) is, thus, a complex and contradictory spectacle through which a variety of contemporary social, cultural and political issues play out on a global stage.

Roche (1994, p. 1) described mega-events as 'short-term events with long-term consequences for the cities that stage them'. However, the consequences of sport mega-events not only are relevant to host cities and nations but also affect a range of other groups, including event rights holders, sport governing bodies, sponsors, spectators, event staff and volunteers and, importantly, athletes. Much of the research that focuses on mega-events as important social, cultural, political and economic phenomena focuses more on issues related to event hosting, as outlined briefly above, more than on athletes and sport-related aspects of mega-events. Sport sociologists have explored many facets of the sport-related aspects of mega-events, but, with some exceptions, tend to place limited focus on the mega-event as a specific phenomenon. This collection seeks to combine focus of the sport aspects of mega-events – athletes, support teams, fans and spectators – with consideration of how the ambiguous, contradictory, highly commercialised and mediatised phenomena of mega-events provides a lens through to which to explore issues of gender and identity.

Billings and Wenner's (2017) definition is useful in relation to this broad conceptualisation of mega-events that includes focus on athletes and their supporters as integral to the mega-event phenomenon. They identified four key characteristics of sport mega-events:

(1) They represent the pinnacle of sport competition. Although some mega-events are technically open to amateurs, such as the Olympic Games, they represent the elite of athletic performance.
(2) They are regular and predictable occurrences. Sport mega-events are scheduled years in advance, often occurring at regular intervals (such as every one, two or

four years) and so are something that a range of stakeholders – from athletes, to spectators, to sponsors – can anticipate and plan for.

(3) They are opportunities for historical comparison. The format and regularity of sport mega-events allow for comparison across iterations of the same event, both year-to-year and across generations.

(4) They provide moments which transcend traditional meanings of sport. Just to compete at a mega-event is an enormous achievement for an athlete and is often the pinnacle of a sporting career. In such emotionally charged contexts, human stories often come to the fore, whether this be in personal or sometimes political terms.

For some, the only true 'mega' sports events are the Summer Olympic Games and the FIFA Men's World Cup. While these events certainly are 'mega' on every scale, to limit discussions of the ways in which gender is performed, negotiated and sometimes transformed through major events to just these two would be limiting, particularly given that one – the World Cup – is open only to male competitors. Rather, in this book a broader definition of mega-events is adopted that encompasses major events of different scale and magnitude. Black (2008) argued that only a handful of truly 'global cities' can credibly bid for 'first-order' events like the Summer Olympic Games and the FIFA Men's World Cup. He defined 'second-order' events as 'of international scope but lower-level participation and profile' (p. 468), like the Commonwealth Games and the Rugby World Cup, and 'third-order' events as 'of regional or continental scope' (p. 468), like the Asian or Pan American Games. The events discussed in this book encompass first-order mega-events (the Summer Olympics and the FIFA Men's World Cup), second-order mega-events (like the FIFA Women's World Cup and Formula 1) and third-order mega-events (like golf's Solheim Cup and the Union of European Football Associations [UEFA] European Championships). These mega-events of different scale and scope share the characteristics identified by Billings and Wenner (2017) and Müller (2015), and all are occasions through which gender identities are performed, (re)negotiated, and, at times, transformed.

Sport and Gender

Sport is a strongly gendered institution that was 'created by and for men' (Messner & Sabo, 1990, p. 9). Although girls and women have been playing a wide range of competitive sports for many years, the underlying norms, rules and expectations of what it means to be a 'real' athlete remain strongly masculine. This has implications for the ways in which sport mega-events have developed and how all athletes (and fans, officials and support teams) have been and continue to be represented.

The Olympic Games was initially founded by Pierre de Coubertin as a male-only event, where women's only role was as spectator, applauding male athletic achievement (Lenskyj, 2013). Although women now compete in a wide range of sports at the Olympics and at other mega-events, perceptions of women as lesser competitors, or as fit to occupy only supporting and decorative roles, continue (see Sturm, Chapter 6). The other 'first-order' mega-event, the FIFA Men's World Cup, is open only to male participants, although female football fans are increasingly claiming space within this masculine world (see Raduszynska, Chapter 9). The FIFA Women's World Cup has run eight times, since the inaugural event in China in 1991 (then called the FIFA Women's World Championship). Caudwell (2011) argued that while FIFA has been vocal about supporting women's participation in football, they have also been very forceful about keeping men's and women's football separate and differentiating between masculinity and femininity. As Caudwell (2011, p. 335) noted, for FIFA, in women's football, 'femininity is foremost'. Mega-events, thus, play a powerful role in helping to maintain gender differentiation and hierarchy in sport, although they may also provide opportunity to challenge current practices (see Darvin and Pegoraro, Chapter 3; Turtiainen, Chapter 7).

Organised sport has long been a site for the production and reproduction of particular forms of masculinity based around ideals of bravery, toughness, strength and dominance (Magnan, 2000). Connell's (1987) concept of hegemonic masculinity has been widely applied in studies of sport, as sport appears to offer many exemplars of hegemonic masculinity in action (Connell, 1990). For example, MacDonald (2014) illustrated how ice hockey in Canada acts as a site for socialisation of men and boys into the norms of hegemonic masculinity. Men's team sports in particular have been recognised as bastions of hegemonic masculinity, marginalising men who do not fit with this ideal (as well as women) and contributing to negative outcomes for many male athletes, in relation to injury and mental health problems (Anderson & Kian, 2012; Smith, Chapter 4). It is not just athletes who are affected by the hypermasculine norms of sport. Ncube and Chawana (2018) considered how fandom songs and seemingly harmless 'banter' amongst football fans in Zimbabwe illustrate some of the ways in which 'gender inequalities are produced and reproduced in patriarchal establishments' like sport (p. 82). In the context of mega-events, fan violence and hooliganism remain problems in relation to football (soccer), reflecting the ongoing significance of hypermasculinity to some fan cultures (see Sly, Chapter, 5).

Although sport remains a strongly masculine domain, celebrating strong, powerful male bodies, there have been shifts in the ways in which masculinity is performed and (re)produced in and through sport. Anderson's (2010) inclusive masculinity theory has been used to help explain some of these changes, which, in many contexts, appear to result in a wider range of 'acceptable' sporting masculinities and associated behaviours and practices (Dashper, 2012a; Gaston, Macgrath & Anderson, 2018). More male athletes are increasingly willing to be open about mental health challenges associated with being an elite athlete, admission of which would have been seen as unacceptable weakness in earlier years (see Smith, Chapter 4). However, despite these shifts 'the cultural marriage of men to sport' (Wenner & Jackson, 2009, p. 2) remains largely intact. Wenner's (1998) argument remains relevant, particularly in the context of sport mega-events:

[M]uch of the cultural power of sports is linked to its functioning as male rite of passage and the role sports spaces and places play as refuge from women. Sports explicitly naturalize 'man's place' in the physical. Implicitly, it also appropriates 'woman's place' as 'other', inherently inferior on the yardstick of the physical, and thus life. These dynamic elements allow sports to play a fundamental role in the construction and maintenance of patriarchy.

(p. 308)

The position of women in sport has long been contested (see Hargreaves, 1994, for a discussion of the historical development of women's roles in sport). In the twenty-first century, women remain on the margins in sport in relation to sports management (Burton, 2015), sports coaching (Lewis, Roberts, & Andrews, 2018), as sports journalists (Organista & Mazur, 2020), officials (Forbes, Edwards, & Fleming, 2015), fans and athletes (Pfister & Pope, 2018). Sport has been a key site of struggle over women's appearance and bodies. As Krane (2001, p. 116) has noted, 'sportswomen tread a fine line of acceptable femininity'. Women who become visibly strong and muscular as a result of their sporting practices have been ostracised and criticised for being 'unfeminine', and it is mainly feminine-looking athletes, competing in sports that are deemed feminine appropriate (such as tennis and gymnastics) that attract widespread attention and associated rewards of lucrative sponsorship and endorsement deals that can help support a professional career (Jones & Greer, 2011). Cohen (2013) discussed the example of Beth Tweddle, the first British female gymnast to win an Olympic medal, to illustrate some of the ambiguities that female athletes can face. Despite Tweddle's undoubted success in a feminine-appropriate sport, she received less media and popular attention than many less successful athletes, due in part to her strong, muscular body and powerful, technical style that positioned her outside the norms of sporting femininity in gymnastics. Such is the ambiguous status of female athletes in relation to their bodies and appearance that they frequently engage in impression management tactics to try and reconcile the perceived mismatch between themselves as competent elite athletes *and* feminine women (Bennett, Scarlett, Hurd Clarke, & Crocker, 2017).

Yet, idealised notions of sporting femininity are constantly shifting and are open to renegotiation and transformation. Combat sports offer an avenue through which normative ideas about sporting femininity are being challenged (Channon & Phipps, 2017). However, Hamilton's (2020) research on women in mixed martial arts suggests that, far from challenging gender norms, (hetero-sexual) women involved in this masculine domain actually 'overdo' gender, reflecting feelings of feminine insecurity. Washington and Economides (2016) examined how women participating in crossfit draw on post-feminist ideologies to expand possibilities for acceptable female sporting bodies, yet despite this they conclude that crossfit continues to 'mirror the hegemonic archetype of attractive and heteronormative femininity' (p. 143). In relation to mega-events, Toffoletti (2017) also draws on post-feminism to consider the emergence of new 'sexually empowered' female fandom to position (some) female football fans as 'active (rather than objectified or marginalised) participant[s] in the sporting crowd' (p. 469). However, Richards, Parry, and Gill's (2020) examination of female fandom in rugby league suggests that 'female fans' acceptance into sport fandom culture remains mostly contingent on adopting feminine roles and/or performances of fandom that do not encroach on the pre-existing masculine cultures' (p. 15). Whether as fans or athletes, women entering the masculine domain of organised sport do so under the proviso that they comply with the norms and expectations of these spaces, including in relation to acceptable gender roles and performances. Although gender is always subject to (re)negotiation, change is likely to be incremental rather than dramatic, as '[c]hallenges to the gender system modify rather than break it' (Westbrook & Schilt, 2014, p. 53). This does not mean that small changes are not significant, however, as 'seemingly small, mundane actions may begin to redo gender in ways that may, in concert with other actions, begin to "modify" the gender system' within and beyond sport and mega-events (Dashper, 2016, p. 364).

Most competitive sports are organised around binary sex categories and segregation between male and female participants. This helps reinforce the notion that men and women, masculinity and femininity, are complementary and opposite, yet inherently unequal (Schippers, 2007). Sport helps to naturalise differentiation between men and women, emphasising and celebrating the extremes of male bodies – primarily strength and speed (Kane, 1995). Female sports and athletes are frequently compared directly to their male peers, which at the elite level often makes female sporting achievements appear to be a lesser version of male excellence. However, not everyone fits within the rigid confines of a binary system of sex classification, and the position of transgender and nonbinary people in the world of competitive sport is highly ambiguous (see Anderson & Travers, 2017). Yet, binary sex segregation remains a persistent feature of organised sport, even though it has proven to be so contentious (Dashper, 2012b). Debates around what measures should be used to define sex have plagued elite sport organisations for decades, and the lack of a definitive answer about what makes an athlete 'female' (or 'male', but this is not up for debate in sporting organisations) indicates the problems of relying on these binary categories (see Adlwarth, Chapter 2). The high-profile case of South African athlete Caster Semenya has forced some of these issues onto the public stage, and the (mis)treatment of Semenya by the IOC and World Athletics (formerly International Association of Athletics Federations [IAAF]) has been beset by racist and sexist assumptions (Mahomed & Dhai, 2019). Mega-events are, thus, a highly visible site for struggle and contestation over sex and gender categories, bodies and acceptance.

This book focuses on gender in the context of sport mega-events, and subsequent chapters deliberately foreground gender analysis. However, gender is not the only, or always the most important, factor to consider in relation to any social practice and interaction, including sport mega-events. McDonald (2014, p. 151) argued that identity is 'concurrently the product of historically specific social relations' and urged researchers to draw on intersectionality to explore 'the ways in which interlocking forms of power produce difference'. Lenskyj's (2013) intersectional analysis of the Olympic Games considered the importance of transnational feminism for recognising the central role of colonialism and racism in women's oppression and for including the priorities, experiences and actions of women and women's organisations outside of Western countries in critiques of and efforts to transform the Olympic movement. Sykes (2017) also argued that mega-events cannot be understood without acknowledging their underpinning racial-colonial logics that shape discourses around gender, sexuality and diversity. Therefore, although the chapters in this collection deliberately foreground gender as the primary focus of analysis, the experiences of athletes, fans and other sport stakeholders are complex and gender always intersects with other axes of power, such as whiteness and sexuality in the case of US footballer Megan Rapinoe (see Turtiainen, Chapter 7), class and nationality in relation to football hooligans (see Sly, Chapter 5) or race and class in the experiences of local communities in host cities and nations (see Knijnik, Balram and Kanemasu, Chapter 8). Consequently, although all chapters in the book deliberately focus predominantly on gender as the primary frame of analysis, gender can never be analysed completely independently. All chapters, thus, recognise the value of intersectionality in any analysis of gender and sport mega-events and illustrate the various ways in which gender, race, class and nationhood intersect in the experiences, production and consumption of sport mega-events.

Sport Mega-Events, Gender and Mediatisation

Sport mega-events are global, highly mediatised spectacles. Sykes (2017, p. 6) argued that in the twenty-first century sport mega-events have developed through processes of globalisation and neoliberalism to become 'primarily a globalized media spectacle and transnational corporate business'. Lenskyj (2013) concurs, proposing that within what she terms the 'Olympic industry' sporting competition is but a part of a huge profit-making machine, supported by a largely uncritical mainstream media. For Roche (2008), the mediatisation of mega-events is key to their cultural and sociological significance. Most people will not attend a mega-event in person but will 'see' it through a range of media. Mega-events often have broader appeal and reach than regular sports programming. The 2016 Summer Olympic Games in Rio de Janeiro (Brazil) attracted global audiences of 3.6 billion (Statista, 2016), whereas the 2018 Winter Olympic Games in PyeongChang (South Korea) had a global cumulative audience of 1.92 billion (Lange, 2020). According to FIFA (2018), 3.57 billion viewers – more than half of the global population aged four and over – tuned in to the 2018 Men's World Cup in Russia. A record-breaking 1.12 billion viewers watched the 2019 FIFA Women's World Cup in France, with average live match audiences more than doubling from the 2015 mega-event in Canada (BBC, 2019). On a slightly smaller, but not insignificant, scale, an estimated 186 million people watched the 2021 Super Bowl (NRF, 2021). In many ways, it is these enormous, often global audiences that make mega-events 'mega' and enable their reach to be felt by people all over the world. This also positions media organisations as an extremely powerful stakeholder group in sport mega-events, with capacity to influence the development of those events and how global audiences perceive the events and participating athletes, with implications for gender (in)equality. As Kane (2013, p. 233) has argued, sport media is 'an especially effective tool for preserving male power and privilege'. The media – both traditional and new forms – thus play an extremely powerful role in (re)producing gendered discourses and practices in and through sport mega-events. As Rowe (2009) contends:

> In carrying messages about sport far beyond its restrictive origins, there is clear potential for media sports texts to perpetuate and reinforce ideologies of domination already present within the social institution of sport, and also to reproduce, exacerbate and amplify them through the presentation routines of the media sport spectacle.
>
> (pp. 548–549)

This is particularly significant in the context of the issues discussed in this book, as media representations of female sports and athletes contribute to the devaluing of women's athleticism through underreporting, trivialising, marginalising, infantilising and sexualising (Fink, 2015). Cooky, Messner, and Musto (2015) reported on a longitudinal study of televised coverage of women's sport in the United States that illustrates that, in the 25 years studied, there had been very little change in the (limited) amount of coverage devoted to women's sports and athletes. Similar findings have been reported in relation to print media coverage in the United Kingdom (Biscomb & Matheson, 2019) and Norway (Hovden & von der Lippe, 2019). The *type* of media coverage is also problematic, with numerous studies reporting how sports media both produces and reproduces gendered discourses associated with sport as discussed in the previous section, such as linkages between sport, (hyper)masculinity and violence, often infused with racial and/or class-based discourses (Rugg, 2019); associating female athletes with traditional feminine roles such as wife and mother, rather than elite athlete (Dashper, 2018); and although overt sexualisation of female athletes in traditional media is less common than in earlier periods (Cooky et al., 2015), it certainly has not disappeared (Smoot, 2017).

The so-called 'new' media may provide opportunity for alternative representations of athletes and sports that move beyond narrow gendered discourses that remain prevalent on traditional media platforms like television and print (Sanderson & Gramlich, 2016). Toffoletti (2016) suggested that the contemporary media landscape offers a somewhat contradictory space that often simultaneously marginalises and empowers female athletes. Drawing on third-wave feminism, post-feminism and neoliberal feminism, Thorpe, Toffoletti, and Bruce (2017) suggested that, while not erasing inequalities, social media may open up new possibilities for self-representation that may enable female athletes to position themselves as active, autonomous and visible (see also Turtiainen, Chapter 7).

However, social media also provides an environment where abuse and oppression can proliferate, as Litchfield, Kavanagh, Osborne, and Jones (2018) found in their netnographic analysis of comments posted on Twitter and Facebook about Serena Williams during the 2015 Wimbledon Championships. Social media provides an unregulated environment for virtual abuse and maltreatment of female athletes in ways that draw upon sexist, misogynistic, racist, and sometimes violent discourses (Litchfield, Kavanagh, Osborne, & Jones, 2016). Kavanagh, Litchfield, and Osborne's (2019) study suggests that social media now provides space for sexualisation and gender-based cyberhate directed at female athletes in ways that would not be acceptable on traditional media platforms. Increased media attention around mega-events may amplify abusive social media posts aimed at athletes.

Sport media, thus, offer opportunity both for amplifying limiting gender-based messages and for challenging them. Mega-events provide a rare opportunity for female sports and athletes to receive increased media attention (see Billings andand Gentile, Chapter 12; Bowes and Kitching, Chapter 11). This provides visible inspiration to girls and women around the world that may encourage increased sports participation and interest (see Valiente, Chapter 10). Xu, Billings, Scott, Lewis, and Sharpe (2019) analysed Australian prime time coverage of the 2016 Summer Olympic Games and found that networks devoted nearly equal clock time to male and female athletes. Yang, Hayes, Chen, Riot, and Khoo-Lattimore (2020) analysis of gendered representations of athletes on Twitter during the 2018 Commonwealth Games also found little difference in amount of coverage of male and female athletes. However, both these studies noted differences in the type of coverage male and female athletes received. Yang et al. (2020) noted subtle gendered connotations to the ways in which seemingly gender neutral words like 'dedicated' and 'hardworking' were applied, and Xu et al. (2019) found that male athletes were more likely to receive commentary and higher numbers of mentions, contributing to perceptions that the best athletes are men.

Media framing of sports and athletes during mega-events often repeats sexist tropes wherein male athleticism is valorised, celebrating physicality and athletic achievement, whereas coverage of female athletes is more likely to concentrate on personal characteristics and non-sport relationships (Quayle et al., 2019). Female athletes' achievements are often reported in highly ambivalent ways. For example, winning a silver medal was presented as 'losing' gold in both the British (Dashper, 2018) and Swedish press (Hellborg & Hedenborg, 2015), with these supposed failures being presented as due to personal shortcomings in the case of female athletes but due to external factors for male athletes. Litchfield and Kavanagh (2019) also reported ambiguous outcomes in their analysis of the official Twitter pages of 'Team GB' and the 'Australian Olympic Team' during the 2016 Olympic Games, reporting roughly equal amount of coverage, but some persistent differences in the ways in which female and male athletes are represented.

Although sport mega-events often provide opportunity for unprecedented media coverage for female sports and athletes, even if it is ambivalent, this increased interest does not last long after the event finishes, with traditional media outlets quickly returning to being 'a football-saturated boyzone' (O'Neill & Mulready, 2015, p. 652). Clearly media continue to play an extremely powerful role in shaping sport mega-events and disseminating associated gendered discourses. Changes in the media landscape open up spaces for alternative representations to contest limited frames that continue to dominate traditional media reporting, but this challenge is set within the constraints of long-established and persistent gender inequality in relation to sport and mega-events.

Gender Trouble and Sport Mega-Events

Sport mega-events are clearly important social, cultural, economic and political phenomena. They are heavily implicated in persistent gender inequality in and beyond sport, through processes of gender differentiation and hierarchy, exclusion, representation and discrimination. However, this does not mean that they have to remain mechanisms for the production and reproduction of gender inequality. There is also potential to challenge gender norms and create disruption and gender trouble (Butler, 1999).

The dominant response to gender inequality in sport and mega-events is the liberal feminist approach of advocating parity of participation between men and women. Yet, however parity is understood, gender inequality persists at mega-events, suggesting that liberal feminist goals of reform and assimilation may not be enough. For example, there has been a steady increase in the numbers of female athletes competing at the Summer Olympic Games. Out of 11,238 athletes competing at the 2016 Rio Games, 45% (5,059) were female, up from 34% at the 2000 Sydney Games, but this was still 1,120 fewer female than male athletes (O'Neill, 2020). The FIFA Men's World Cup in 2018 consisted of 32 national squads made up of 736 players, whereas the FIFA Women's World Cup in 2019 consisted of 24 national squads made up of 552 players (Christenson, Hills, Blight, Hulley-Jones, & Powell, 2018; FIFA, 2019). Parity can also be considered in relation to access to events and competitions. At the 2012 London Games, women's boxing first entered the Olympic schedule, which was seen as an important step towards equality and broadening notions of acceptable sporting femininity (Woodward, 2014). However, at the 2016 Rio Games, there was still considerable inequality in terms of medal opportunities, even though this was the closest to gender parity the Olympics has yet come: there were 161 events for men, 136 for women and 9 mixed (BBC, 2017). Gender marking is another measure that indicates lack of parity in status. The FIFA Men's World Cup is referred to by FIFA as simply 'the World Cup' whereas the women's event is 'the Women's World Cup', effectively marking the men's event as the real thing and the women's as a lesser supplement. On these and other measures, gender inequality persists in sport mega-events and, although improvements have been made, clear gender gaps persist. The liberal feminist goal of 'a level playing field' where women 'catch up' with men in sport is critiqued by Lenskyj (2013) who instead proposes problematising the playing field itself and questions if equal opportunity would really benefit women and marginalised groups.

One interesting challenge to masculine hegemony in mega-events is to disrupt the restrictive gender binary and strict sex segregation that differentiates male from female, leaving no space for anything or anyone else. McDonagh and Pappano (2007) have argued that sex segregation in sport is a crucial contributor to gender inequality as it helps naturalise hierarchical differences between males and females and reinforces the flawed assumption that sex is binary and that athletes can be definitively separated into one of the two mutually exclusive categories (see Adlwarth, Chapter 2). Sport mega-events are based almost exclusively on this binary segregation, with very few exceptions, but this does not necessarily have to be the way they are organised. One exception to this is equestrian sport, the only sport with no sex segregation at any level, from amateur to Olympics. Equestrian sport indicates that, in some sports, sex integration can work as both male and female equestrians perform well at elite-level sport. For example, the current Olympic champions (from 2016) are two men (in show jumping and eventing) and one woman (in dressage). The current World champions (from 2018) are all female. Even in an integrated context, both men and women perform well at the elite level of the sport. Although gender integration is not a panacea and other aspects of gender inequality persist in equestrian sport, it illustrates that in some cases, sex integration in competitive sport can be one way to begin to break down persistent barriers to equality and inclusiveness and reduce the salience of gender to athletes' identities (Dashper, 2012b; De Haan, Sotiriadou, & Henry, 2016). In so doing, equestrian sport challenges normative ideas about sex and gender in sport, and provides a visible alternative in the context of sport mega-events.

Equestrian sport provides a radical challenge to binary sex segregation in sport, as there is no differentiation by sex or gender within the organisation of the sport at any level, but other sports offer other, more limited, options for challenging hierarchical binary sex segregation. Mixed-doubles in tennis, competitive cheerleading and Nacra 17 in sailing all require teams of men and women together (Lake, 2016; Priyadharshini & Pressland, 2016). Some sports – including some martial arts and basketball – encourage male and female participants to train together, even if they do not compete against each other (Channon, 2014; Fink, La Voi & Newhall, 2016). Sex integration in any form begins to challenge gender norms and traditional ways of thinking about and understanding sport and athletes (Channon, Dashper, Fletcher, & Lake, 2016). While integration alone will not ensure equality, it does offer a potentially radical challenge to the ways in which gender is produced and reproduced at and through sport mega-events.

Sex integration may not be practical or desirable in all sports, but other forms of challenge and disruption can also cause gender trouble within the context of sport mega-events. This may be in the form of individual athletes challenging gender norms in relation to their self-presentation, such as the examples of US football star Megan Rapinoe (see Turtiainen, Chapter 6) or British boxer Nicola Adams (Dashper, 2018). It is not just athletes who can cause gender disruption and disorder in the context of mega-events. As large spectator events – including enormous, often global media audiences – fans and spectators have capacity to challenge gender norms. Raduszynska's (Chapter 9) discussion of fan performances at the 2018 FIFA Men's World Cup in Russia illustrates how mega-events can be occasions for joy and cohesion in ways that may disrupt expectations about a host nation (Russia, in this case) and a specific sport (the links between football, hypermasculinity and violence, including hooliganism remain strong, see Sly, Chapter 5). Local residents can also cause disruption and challenge, even in the face of the seemingly overwhelming might of 'informal empires' like FIFA and the IOC (Sykes, 2017). Local indigenous communities may provide powerful opposition to sport mega-events in ways that force some renegotiation around mega-event norms and practices (O'Bonsawin, 2010; Knijnik, Balram, and Kanemasu, Chapter 7).

Another subversive challenge comes from mega-events that do not operate according to the norms of elite sport, like the Gay Games, the largest lesbian, gay, bisexual, trans, queer (LGBTQ+) sport and cultural event in the world. Founded in 1982, the Gay Games was built on principles of inclusiveness, participation and the idea of 'personal best' and so in many ways was the antithesis to mainstream mega-events like the Olympics which focus on elite performance (Lenskyj, 2013). Although the event's principles may have become diluted over time as the event has become more commercialised and assimilated with other mega-events, the Gay Games continues to offer 'alternative, diverse, even radical and always inclusive ways of expressing sporting communities, identities and practices' (Symons, 2014, p. 318).

Successful challenge remains difficult, set within the context of the restrictive power structures of sport and mega-events, supported by global media corporations and sponsors. Yet, as some of the chapters in this book illustrate, although such challenge is extremely tough, it is not impossible. Challenge and transformation may come from a variety of angles and surprising quarters. Some of this challenge may be based upon incremental changes in access and representation, akin to liberal feminist goals, and although this is unlikely to lead to radical change, it can enable important shifts that can contribute to greater gender equality (see Valiente, Chapter 10). Alternatively, challenge may come from changes in athlete behaviour, such as increasing openness from male athletes to discussing mental health vulnerabilities (see Smith, Chapter 4). Fans may also instigate change, reconfiguring mega-events as celebrations and opportunities for unity (see Raduszyńska, Chapter 9). Perhaps most surprisingly, marginalised groups may, occasionally, take on the power and might of global organisations like FIFA and win, as Knijnik, Balram and Kanemasu illustrate in their discussion of the *Baianas* in relation to the Men's World Cup in Brazil 2016 (see Chapter 8).

These examples indicate that change and challenge are possible. Although mega-events are conservative entities that reflect their masculine, racial-colonial histories and the deeply ingrained gender norms of elite sport, they are not immune to challenge and change.

Theorising Gender and Sport Mega-Events

The chapters presented in this book adopt a range of theoretical positions to consider different issues related to gender and sport mega-events. Theoretical pluralism can inspire different views on complex issues like gender inequality, thus helping to develop new insights and practices (Crăciun, 2019). As Griffiths (1997) argued:

> ... all problems cannot be studied fruitfully using a single theory. Some problems are large and complex and no single theory is capable of encompassing them, while others, although seemingly simple and straightforward, can be better understood through the use of multiple theories.
>
> (p. 372)

Gender (in)equality, in and beyond sport, can be considered a 'large and complex' problem, and so multiple theoretical positions can be useful to try to examine and understand it more fully. Theoretical approaches are adopted on the basis of a range of measures including appropriateness, fruitfulness, context, the potential to lead to new insights and the epistemological positioning of the researchers. In this section, some of the main theoretical positions adopted by contributors to this book are introduced briefly. This is not an exhaustive discussion of any of these theoretical positions, which are developed further in subsequent chapters, but is intended to help guide readers through the rest of the book. However, while each chapter addresses the importance of gender to sport mega-events in different ways and from a variety of theoretical positions, they all consider how the paradoxical phenomenon of mega-events plays an important role in both reinforcing and challenging normative gender discourses, ideologies and practices.

All contributors adopt theoretical positions that can be considered broadly feminist in their examinations of gender and sport mega-events. As Birrell (2000, p. 61) noted, although there is a multitude of feminisms, they all share the 'main purpose to theorize about gender relations within our patriarchal society as they are evidenced by, played out in, and reproduced through sport and other body practices'. However, while all feminist approaches share a starting point that women are oppressed within current gender orders and a commitment to changing and challenging this, they do not all agree on how oppressive relations and practices are (re)produced or what real change would look like. A dominant way of theorising 'progress towards gender equality' is the liberal feminist approach, discussed briefly above. Based upon belief in social and legal reform as a way of levelling the gendered playing field, liberal feminist approaches reject biological reasons for women's lack of involvement or achievement in sport, assuming that it is social and cultural factors that are holding women back and, thus, reform will help gradually improve women's representation (Hargreaves, 1994). Such an approach is evident in Valiente's (Chapter 10) discussion of women's involvement in football in Spain, wherein increased visibility for women's sport is taken as progress that will lead towards greater equality. However, Valiente illustrates some of the limitations of the liberal feminist approach to change, as within Spain structural inequalities contribute to women's continued marginalisation in football, through things like low wages and poor working conditions, and ideological belief in the primacy of men's football is apparent in the ways in which men's football was given priority to reopen long before women's following restrictions owing to the COVID-19 pandemic. Valiente, thus, illustrates many of the limitations of liberal feminist approaches to change as they fail to identify, let alone challenge, the established masculine principles of sport, largely accepting the values of mainstream sport and failing to relate inequality to wider economic, social, cultural and political issues (Hargreaves, 1994). Liberal feminist approaches are attractive to many stakeholders in sport, as they do not advocate radical change, yet it is this that limits the potential of such theoretical positions to really question how sport mega-events contribute to and reinforce gender inequality.

Another strong critique of liberal feminism is that it tends to assume 'women' are a homogenous group, based on the experiences of mainly white, Western, middle-class, able-bodied, cis-gender women. Black feminists have long challenged this, illustrating how binary understandings of gender based on a simple dichotomy between (white) 'men' and (white) 'women' fails to account for the dynamism of identities and the complex and multiple ways in which gender intersects with race, ethnicity and other axes of power. Brown's (2018) discussion of both postcolonial and Black feminisms shows how such approaches allow for more complex examinations of gender and sport. Postcolonial feminism disrupts Western feminist discourses that render 'other women' as marginal and homogenous, and instead foregrounds issues of representation and location, theorising difference in terms of fluidity, hybridity and multiplicity (Brown, 2018). Black feminism is also intersectional, recognising multiplicity of identities, being explicitly anti-racist as well as anti-sexist and foregrounding Black women's experiences and voices (Brown, 2018). In this collection, Adlwarth (Chapter 2) engages with these critiques through her critical evaluation of sex testing in sport mega-events being built upon norms that exclude and marginalise all those who do not conform to narrow binary racist and neo-colonial gender norms that disproportionately affect women of colour and from the Global South, while also problematising her position as a white, Western cis-gender woman researching and potentially reproducing these power discourses. Knijnik, Balram and Kanemasu (Chapter 8) also draw on Black feminism in their examination of the disruptive actions of the *Baianas*, Black women descended from slaves in Brazil. Their analysis illustrates the power of intersectional approaches, informed by postcolonial and Black feminist insights, to foreground the experiences of those usually marginalised and disenfranchised, both through sport mega-events and academic research.

Postcolonial and Black feminisms, while placing emphasis on different issues of power and representation, both illustrate the fruitfulness of intersectional approaches to the study of gender and sport mega-events. Other axes of power are also relevant to critical evaluation of sport, gender and mega-events, and although he does not position his research as explicitly intersectional, Sly's (Chapter 5) examination of aggressive masculinity and hooliganism considers the intersections of gender, nationality and class. Bowes and Kitching (Chapter 11) and Billings and Gentile (Chapter 12) also do not position their theoretical frameworks as explicitly intersectional but focus on various ways in which gender and nationality intersect in and through sport mega-events. Intersectional approaches, thus, make extremely important contributions to understanding of sport mega-events, and, as the chapters in this book illustrate, can take numerous forms to examine different axes of power.

Third-wave feminism, postfeminism and neoliberal feminisms represent another important shift in feminist approaches to understanding sport. Thorpe et al. (2017) provide an overview of the similarities and differences between these theoretical positions that all seek to recognise the shifting landscape in which sport and women athletes operate in neoliberal, consumerist times. In this collection, Turtiainen (Chapter 7) engages with these ideas in her examination of the social media self-presentation of US footballer Megan Rapinoe during the 2019 FIFA Women's World Cup. Turtiainen's analysis reveals some of the contradictory aspects of these contemporary feminisms which recognise women's ability to be agentic and claim strong and powerful identities but at the same time are tied to consumerist logics that continue to privilege white Western norms. As Turtiainen suggests, feminism within neoliberal times provides space for (some) women to reimagine their sporting identities in ways that begin to challenge and disrupt normative ideas about sporting femininities, but this challenge is muted somewhat by its reliance on individualising norms of late capitalism that fail to offer a radical critique of the ways in which sport and mega-events are constituted.

Some research on sporting masculinities can also be considered feminist, through centralising gender inequality and looking for ways to address it. Within sport studies more broadly, and in numerous chapters in this collection, Connell's (1987) concept of hegemonic masculinity has been widely used, as discussed above. Connell's (1987) theorisation of gender power relations, and the multiplicity of masculinities, has proven fruitful for researchers over the last 30 years. In this collection, Smith (Chapter 4) and Sturm (Chapter 6) both draw on Connell's work to examine the ways in which sporting masculinities continue to define and constrain acceptable gender performances for men, often with negative consequences for male athletes and fans, limiting potential for change and transformation (see also Sly, Chapter 5). Although Connell's theories have been subject to critique and development for being overly negative or for inadequately theorising marginalised masculinities and femininities (e.g. see Connell & Messerschmidt, 2005; Howson, 2006), they remain relevant to the field of critical masculinities studies within and beyond sport, as chapters in this book illustrate (Messerschmidt, 2019).

There are, thus, multiple feminisms that focus on different causes and outcomes of gender inequality in sport and suggest different ways to contest and alter current practices. The chapters in this book adopt different theoretical positions and, thus, foreground different issues and strategies for change. What they share in common is a feminist recognition of the prevalence of continued gender (and other forms of) inequality in and beyond sport, and a commitment to identify approaches, strategies and opportunities for challenge and transformation.

Conclusion

The remainder of the book is split into four sections which consider some of the many issues raised in the previous sections of this chapter, and the wider literature on sport, gender and mega-events, drawing on a broad range of mega-events of different scale and type.

Problematising gendered bodies and behaviours introduces some of the core complex issues that underpin considerations of gender, sport and mega-events. The two chapters in this section explore different ways in which sport mega-events are mechanisms for defining and controlling sex, gender and gender performances, often leading to marginalisation and exclusion and focused particularly on the bodies and behaviours of athletes who differ from the sporting masculine ideal. Anna Adlwarth begins by discussing the problematic issue of sex regulation in Chapter 2. She provides a critical synthesis of research on sex testing and regulation in relation to the policies of the IOC and IAAF (now World Athletics) and the consequences of this for trans*women and women with inter*sex variations specifically. She argues that policies in this area are dominated by medico-scientific approaches that fail to engage with feminist and queer insights, undermining notions of 'fairness' in elite sport. In this context, where these policies are underrun with racist and neo-colonial underpinnings, it is mainly women from the Global South who lose out and are subject to humiliating, often career-ending speculation and interventions. Adlwarth considers the implications this has for the illusive promise of fair and inclusive policies at sport mega-events.

In Chapter 3, Lindsey Darvin and Ann Pegoraro discuss the treatment of women and men athletes in the sports media and the ways in which female athletes are held to different, and in many ways, unattainable standards of accountability. Drawing on the example of the US Women's National Team (USWNT) during the 2019 FIFA Women's World Cup, they argue that when women display 'dominant play' – be that in terms of sporting success and competitive dominance, or in relation to athletes' actions and reactions to that success – they are judged harshly as not conforming to standards of acceptable femininity, even though that very behaviour is celebrated when enacted by men athletes. Darvin and Pegoraro conclude that sport mega-events provide valuable opportunities for increased media and popular interest in women's sports and athletes, but also increase the likelihood for negative reactions and criticism.

Section 2, *Masculinity, sport and mega-events*, turns attention to the masculine norms and standards that shape sport mega-events. In Chapter 4, Charlie Smith discusses the increasing openness of elite male athletes to discussing mental health issues, despite seeming incongruence between acknowledging these difficulties and the masculine sporting norms of strength and toughness. Drawing on public testimonies from athletes competing in a wide range of elite sports, Smith suggests this represents a positive step towards normalising discussions about mental health in sport and wider society, challenging stigma and possibly encouraging others to speak out and seek help themselves. Although this is a progressive step and suggests some acceptance of more feminised traits of discussing emotions and mental health problems, Smith notes that the ways in which athletes talk about recovery remain tied to masculine sporting norms that emphasise self-control and heroism in relation to (male) mega-event athletes.

In Chapter 5, Jonathan Sly focuses on fans and the persistent problems of violence and hooliganism surrounding some sport mega-events, particularly men's football. Drawing on ethnographic data collected at the 2016 UEFA Championships in France and 2018 FIFA Men's World Cup in Russia, Sly explores some of the reasons why some football mega-events suffer serious problems of hooligan violence, while others pass off relatively peacefully. Focussing on the well-established hooligan cultures of England and Russia, he traces the subcultural norms of hypermasculine aggression and nationalism that underpin hooligan violence around these two national sides. Sly argues that policing and security concerns, location of the event and geo-political relations between nation states all play a role in determining whether hooligan violence occurs or not. However, he suggests that it is also important to take into account subcultural norms, practices, gendered discourses and antagonisms between football hooligan groups in order to understand hooliganism and inform preparations for football mega-events in efforts to try and reduce, even eliminate, fan violence.

Attention then turns in Chapter 6 to Formula 1, an event built on gendered ideas of 'glamour', as Damion Sturm discusses the gendered tensions that play out in this mega-event space. As a media spectacle, Formula 1 builds on images of hegemonic masculinity tied to technical sophistication, risk-taking and jet-setting lifestyles, positioning men as heroic, active and brave. Traditional and, in many ways, outdated notions of femininity position women in mostly supportive and decorative roles, as the symbolic 'prize' for the masculine heroes. Sturm considers how shifts in gender relations and ideas about masculinity and femininity are changing the sport and providing some new opportunities and spaces for different gender performances to emerge. However, he concludes that Formula 1 as a mega-event may have a limited shelf life unless it becomes more environmentally, economically and socially sustainable, including embracing more equitable and contemporary gender relations, performances and practices.

Section 3, *Gender, disruption and transformation at mega-events*, considers different ways in which mega-events can become sites of challenge and change. In Chapter 7, Riikka Turtiainen examines the self-representation of US national soccer player, Megan Rapinoe, 'the respected rebel of the FIFA Women's World Cup France 2019' (p. 136). Turtiainen explores Rapinoe's Instagram posts during the 2019 mega-event, within a post-feminist and neoliberal context. Rapinoe is a divisive figure who refuses to conform to traditional notions of sporting femininity and is 'an unapologetic activist-athlete' who uses her considerable platform to support marginalised groups, such as LGBTQ+ youth and #blacklivesmatter. Her appearance and openly gay identity are transgressive in the traditional world of elite sport, and her unapologetic stance is reflective of a postfeminist sensibility of female empowerment. Rapinoe also embraces neoliberal opportunities to promote her brand, partners and products, indicative of some of the complexities and ambiguities inherent in contemporary feminism. Turtiainen concludes that Rapinoe's self-presentation and gender performance during the 2019 FIFA

Women's World Cup – on and off the pitch – was highly disruptive to traditional gender norms of sporting femininity within mega-events.

In Chapter 8, Jorge Knijnik, Rohini Balram and Yoko Kanemasu present an 'off-field' case study of gender disorder catalysed by the 2014 FIFA Men's World Cup in Brazil. The 'Copa' was a mega-event that permeated every single aspect of life in football-crazy Brazil. Knijnik, Balram and Kanemasu focus on gendered resistance provided by *Baianas* (Black Brazilian women descended directly from African slaves) who challenged FIFA guidelines that banned them from selling street food near the stadiums – the official 'FIFA zone' – in Salvador, the 'more African' city in Brazil. Drawing on the concept of 'everyday resistance', Knijnik, Balram and Kanemasu explore the Baianas' collective strategy to fight FIFA's attempts to ban them from their livelihoods and consequently from gaining any benefit from Brazil hosting the mega-event. The Baianas won, and FIFA had to back down and allow them to sell acarajés in the 'FIFA zone', a surprising example of the effectiveness of everyday resistance to enable marginalised groups to take on powerful elites, such as FIFA. The actions of the Baianas before and during the mega-event can, thus, be understood 'as a collective, repeated practice of disrupting the geopolitical, gender, class and racialised relations of power that subordinate them as Black working-class women of a postcolonial society' (p. 151).

In Chapter 9, Katarzyna Raduszynska turns a performance lens on fan experiences at the 2018 FIFA Men's World Cup in Russia. With a background in theatre, Raduszynska draws on McKenzie's (2002) theory of performance to explore the ways in which the World Cup in Russia was a moment of transition and transgression. She considers how the pre-event international environment was hostile to Russia, but the experiences of the World Cup itself challenged these views and resulted in moments of creativity, efficiency and collaboration. Based on ethnographic immersion in fan culture at five cities in Russia, she presents numerous examples of transformation performed by fans of different nationalities that illustrate how such mega-events can be sites of transformation, even if only temporarily, within the broader masculine world of sport.

Section 4, *Gender, sport and mega-events: Moving towards equality?*, considers ways in which sport mega-events may provide opportunity for progress in terms of representation, participation and gender equality. In Chapter 10, Celia Valiente uses the example of women's football in Spain to argue that sport mega-events can be drivers for gender equality. Sport mega-events have led to improvements in women's professional football in Spain, through the relaunch of women's football leagues, the establishment of women's teams by major men's football teams, and various other measures, such as including women players' names on their shirts to foster recognition and fan involvement. Another positive impact of sport mega-events, like the FIFA Women's World Cup, is that they provide inspiration and role models for girls and women, helping to challenge beliefs that football is a man's game and contributing to increases in sporting participation. However, the limitations of this liberal feminist aspiration that increased visibility of role models will lead to greater gender equality is evident through practices related to pay and working conditions for female professional players, and continued lack of women in football management. Valiente argues that in Spain gender inequality in sport remains pervasive, but sport mega-events play an important role in moving towards greater equality.

In Chapter 11, Ali Bowes and Niamh Kitching discuss media representations, national identity and golf in the Solheim Cup, golf's mega-event for women. The Solheim Cup is a replica of the men's Ryder Cup and represents the pinnacle of professional women's golf, so provides opportunity for critical examination of media representations of elite women golfers. In comparison to many other sports, golf is claimed to be relatively free of nationalistic sentiments, with golfers playing on global tours considered borderless athletes. However mega-events – the Olympics, the Ryder Cup and the Solheim Cup – are exceptions to this with their national or supra-national representation. Bowes and Kitching apply a critical feminist theoretical framework to analysis of British print media coverage of the 2019 Solheim Cup, identifying positive shifts in media representations of women's sport. They argue that national and supra-national identity are important in deprioritising gender in media representations of women's sport and suggest that international sport mega-events open up space for more coverage of women's sports and athletes where the salience of gender is reduced and sporting identity and performance takes precedence.

Chapter 12 continues this theme, with Andrew Billings and Patrick Gentile's discussion of the ways in which sport mega-events provide opportunities for more progressive media coverage of female sports and athletes, where 'wrapping women's sport in a national flag' (p. X) results in different, less-gendered representations. They argue that it is the atypicality of sport mega-events that makes them advantageous vehicles for advancing gender equality in terms of visibility, but perhaps less so in relation to 'more troubling dialogue-oriented terrain' (p. 219). Using the Summer Olympic Games and the FIFA World Cup as exemplars, they argue that the importance of national identity at these mega-events blunts many of the common gender tropes often used in everyday sports media. Although they note this is not a panacea for solving gender inequality in sport and media, Billings and Gentile suggest that the 'flag over gender' model during sport mega-events, wherein nationality seems to take precedence over other markers of identity, including gender, means that 'women athletes manage to move from being bit players to starring roles when donning the colours and flag of their home nation' (p. 230).

In Chapter 13, the final chapter, Katherine Dashper considers some of the future challenges facing sport mega-events and highlights areas for further research and potential transformation in the ever-changing context of sport mega-events.

References

Anderson, E. (2010). *Inclusive masculinity: The changing nature of masculinities.* London: Routledge.

Anderson, E., & Kian, E. M. (2012). Examining media contestation of masculinity and head trauma in the National Football League. *Men and Masculinities, 15*(2), 152–173.

Anderson, E., & Travers, A. (Eds.). (2017). *Transgender athletes in competitive sport.* Abingdon: Routledge.

Baade, R. A., & Matheson, V. A. (2016). Going for the gold: The economics of the Olympics. *Journal of Economic Perspectives, 30*(2), 201–218.

BBC. (2017). 100 women: Do the Olympics have a gender gap? *BBC News.* Retrieved from https://www.bbc.co.uk/news/world-41272613. Accessed on February 9, 2021.

BBC. (2019, October 18). Women's World Cup 2019: FIFA reports record-breaking viewing figures. *BBC Sport.* Retrieved from https://www.bbc.co.uk/sport/football/50096999#:~:text=A%20record%2Dbreaking%201.12%20billion,World%20Cup%2C%20a%20Fifa%20report&text=The%20USA%20lifted%20their%20fourth,doubled%20from%20Canada%20in%202015. Accessed on February 8, 2021.

Bennett, E. V., Scarlett, L., Hurd Clarke, L., & Crocker, P. R. (2017). Negotiating (athletic) femininity: The body and identity in elite female basketball players. *Qualitative Research in Sport, Exercise and Health, 9*(2), 233–246.

Billings, A. C., & Wenner, L. A. (2017). The curious case of the mega-sporting event: Media, mediatization and seminal sports event. In L. A. Wenner & A. C. Billings (Eds.), *Sport, media and mega-events* (pp. 3–18). Abingdon: Routledge.

Birrell, S. (2000). Feminist theories for sport. In J. Coakley & E. Dunning (Eds.), *Handbook of sports studies* (pp. 61–76). London: Sage.

Biscomb, K., & Matheson, H. (2019). Are the times changing enough? Print media trends across four decades. *International Review for the Sociology of Sport, 54*(3), 259–281.

Black, D. (2007). The symbolic politics of sport mega-events: 2010 in comparative perspective. *Politik, 34*(3), 261–276.

Black, D. (2008). Dreaming big: The pursuit of 'second order' games as a strategic response to globalization. *Sport in Society, 11*(4), 467–480.

Black, D., & Van Der Westhuizen, J. (2004). The allure of global games for 'semi-peripheral' polities and spaces: A research agenda. *Third World Quarterly, 25*(7), 1195–1214.

Bowdin, G., O'Toole, W., Allen, J., Harris, R., & McDonnell, I. (2006). *Events management.* Abingdon: Routledge.

Brown, L. E. C. (2018). Post-colonial feminism, black feminism and sport. In L. Mansfield, J. Caudwell, B. Wheaton, & B. Watson (Eds.), *The Palgrave handbook of feminism and sport, leisure and physical education* (pp. 479–495). London: Palgrave Macmillan.

Burton, L. J. (2015). Underrepresentation of women in sport leadership: A review of research. *Sport Management Review, 18*(2), 155–165.

Butler, J. (1999). *Gender trouble: Feminism and the subversion of identity* (2nd ed.). New York, NY: Routledge.

Caiazza, R., & Audretsch, D. (2015). Can a sport mega-event support hosting city's economic, socio-cultural and political development? *Tourism Management Perspectives, 14*, 1–2.

Caudwell, J. (2011). Gender, feminism and football studies. *Soccer & Society, 12*(3), 330–344.

Channon, A. (2014). Towards the "undoing" of gender in mixed-sex martial arts and combat sports. *Societies, 4*(4), 587–605.

Channon, A., Dashper, K., Fletcher, T., & Lake, R. J. (2016). The promises and pitfalls of sex integration in sport and physical culture. *Sport in Society, 19*(8–9), 1111–1124.

Channon, A., & Phipps, C. (2017). Pink gloves still give black eyes: Exploring 'alternative' femininity in women's combat sports. *Martial Arts Studies, 3*, 24–37.

Christenson, M., Hills, D., Blight, G., Hulley-Jones, F., & Powell, J. (2018). Your complete guide to all 736 players at the 2018 World Cup. *The Guardian*. Retrieved from https://www.theguardian.com/football/ng-interactive/2018/jun/05/world-cup-2018-complete-guide-players-ratings-goals-caps. Accessed on January 9, 2021.

Cohen, R. L. (2013). Femininity, childhood and the non-making of a sporting celebrity: The Beth Tweddle case. *Sociological Research Online, 18*(3), 178–187.

Connell, R. W. (1987). *Gender and power: Society, the person and sexual politics*. Stanford, CA: Stanford University Press.

Connell, R. W. (1990). An iron man: The body and some contradictions of hegemonic masculinity. In D. Karen & R. E. Washington (Eds.), *Sociological perspective on sport: The games outside the games* (pp. 141–149). New York, NY: Routledge.

Connell, R. W., & Messerschmidt, J. W. (2005). Hegemonic masculinity: Rethinking the concept. *Gender & Society, 19*(6), 829–859.

Cooky, C., Messner, M. A., & Musto, M. (2015). "It's dude time!" A quarter century of excluding women's sports in televised news and highlight shows. *Communication & Sport, 3*(3), 261–287.

Crăciun, I. C. (2019). Positive aging theories and views on aging. In I. C. Crăciun (Ed.), *Positive aging and precarity* (pp. 17–34). Cham: Springer.

Dashper, K. (2012a). 'Dressage is full of queens!' Masculinity, sexuality and equestrian sport. *Sociology, 46*(6), 1109–1124.

Dashper, K. (2012b). Together, yet still not equal? Sex integration in equestrian sport. *Asia-Pacific Journal of Health, Sport and Physical Education, 3*(3), 213–225.

Dashper, K. (2016). Strong, active women: (Re)doing rural femininity through equestrian sport and leisure. *Ethnography, 17*(3), 350–368.

Dashper, K. (2018). Smiling assassins, brides-to-be and super mums: The importance of gender and celebrity in media framing of female athletes at the 2016 Olympic Games. *Sport in Society, 21*(11), 1739–1757.

Dashper, K., & Finkel, R. (2020). "Doing gender" in critical event studies: A dual agenda for research. *International Journal of Event and Festival Management*. doi: 10.1108/IJEFM-03-2020-0014

Dashper, K., Helgadóttir, G., & Sigurðardóttir, I. (2021). *Horses, humans and events management*. Boston, MA: CABI.

De Haan, D., Sotiriadou, P., & Henry, I. (2016). The lived experience of sex-integrated sport and the construction of athlete identity within the Olympic and Paralympic equestrian disciplines. *Sport in Society, 19*(8–9), 1249–1266.

FIFA. (2018, December 21). More than half the world watch record-breaking 2018 World Cup. Retrieved from https://www.fifa.com/worldcup/news/more-than-half-the-world-watched-record-breaking-2018-world-cup#:~:text=A%20combined%203.572%20billion%20viewers,the%202018%20FIFA%20World%20Cup. Accessed on February 8, 2021.

FIFA. (2019). Final squad lists for FIFA Women's World Cup France 2019™ announced. Retrieved from https://www.fifa.com/womensworldcup/news/final-squad-lists-for-fifa-women-s-world-cup-france-2019tm-announced#:~:text=A%20total%20of%20552%20players,on%20the%20world's%20greatest%20stage. Accessed January 9, 2021.

Fink, J. S. (2015). Female athletes, women's sport, and the sport media commercial complex: Have we really "come a long way, baby"? *Sport Management Review*, *18*(3), 331–342.

Fink, J. S., LaVoi, N. M., & Newhall, K. E. (2016). Challenging the gender binary? Male basketball practice players' views of female athletes and women's sports. *Sport in Society*, *19*(8–9), 1316–1331.

Flyvbjerg, B., & Stewart, A. (2012). *Olympic proportions: Cost and cost overrun at the Olympics 1960–2012*. Said Business School Working Papers. Oxford: University of Oxford.

Forbes, A., Edwards, L., & Fleming, S. (2015). 'Women can't referee': Exploring the experiences of female football officials within UK football culture. *Soccer and Society*, *16*(4), 521–539.

Gaston, L., Magrath, R., & Anderson, E. (2018). From hegemonic to inclusive masculinities in English professional football: Marking a cultural shift. *Journal of Gender Studies*, *27*(3), 301–312.

Getz, D., & Page, S. (2016). *Event studies: Theory, research and policy for planned events* (3rd ed.). Abingdon: Routledge.

Griffiths, D. (1997). The case for theoretical pluralism. *Educational Management & Administration*, *25*(4), 371–380.

Grix, J. (2012). 'Image' leveraging and sports mega-events: Germany and the 2006 FIFA World Cup. *Journal of Sport & Tourism*, *17*(4), 289–312.

Grix, J., & Brannagan, P. M. (2016). Of mechanisms and myths: Conceptualising states' "soft power" strategies through sports mega-events. *Diplomacy and State-craft*, *27*(2), 251–272.

Gursoy, D., & Kendall, K. W. (2006). Hosting mega events: Modeling locals' support. *Annals of Tourism Research*, *33*(3), 603–623.

Hamilton, J. (2020). Undoing gender or overdoing gender? Women MMA athletes' intimate partnering and the relational maintenance of femininity. *Sociology of Sport Journal*, *37*(4), 1–9.

Hargreaves, J. (1994). *Sporting females: Critical issues in the history and sociology of women's sport*. Abingdon: Routledge.

Hellborg, A. M., & Hedenborg, S. (2015). The rocker and the heroine: Gendered media representations of equestrian sports at the 2012 Olympics. *Sport in Society*, *18*(2), 248–261.

Hiller, H. H. (2000). Mega-events, urban boosterism and growth strategies: An analysis of the objectives and legitimations of the Cape Town 2004 Olympic Bid. *International Journal of Urban and Regional Research*, *24*(2), 449–458.

Horne, J. (2007). The four 'knowns' of sports mega-events. *Leisure Studies*, *26*(1), 81–96.

Horne, J., & Manzenreiter, W. (2006). An introduction to the sociology of sports mega-events. *The Sociological Review*, *54*(2_suppl), 1–24.

Hovden, J., & von der Lippe, G. (2019). The gendering of media sport in the Nordic countries. *Sport in Society*, *22*(4), 625–638.

Howson, R. (2006). *Challenging hegemonic masculinity*. Abingdon: Routledge.

Jones, A., & Greer, J. (2011). You don't look like an athlete: The effects of feminine appearance on audience perceptions of female athletes and women's sports. *Journal of Sport Behavior*, *34*(4), 358–377.

Kane, M. J. (1995). Resistance/transformation of the oppositional binary: Exposing sport as a continuum. *Journal of Sport & Social Issues, 19*, 191–218.

Kane, M. J. (2013). The better sportswomen get, the more the media ignore them. *Communication & Sport, 1*(3), 231–236.

Kavanagh, E., Litchfield, C., & Osborne, J. (2019). Sporting women and social media: Sexualization, misogyny, and gender-based violence in online spaces. *International Journal of Sport Communication, 12*(4), 552–572.

Knott, B., Fyall, A., & Jones, I. (2017). Sport mega-events and nation branding. *International Journal of Contemporary Hospitality Management, 29*(3), 900–923.

Krane, V. (2001). We can be athletic and feminine, but do we want to? Challenging hegemonic femininity in women's sport. *Quest, 53*(1), 115–133.

Lake, R. J. (2016). 'Guys don't whale away at the women': Etiquette and gender relations in contemporary mixed-doubles tennis. *Sport in Society, 19*(8–9), 1214–1233.

Lange, D. (2020, November 26). Global TV audience/viewership of Olympic Winter Games 2010–2018. *Statista*. Retrieved from https://www.statista.com/statistics/531768/global-audience-of-the-winter-olympic-games/. Accessed on February 8, 2021.

Lauermann, J. (2019). The urban politics of mega-events: Grand promises meet local resistance. *Environment and Society, 10*(1), 48–62.

Lee Ludvigsen, J. A. (2018). Sport mega-events and security: The 2018 World Cup as an extraordinarily securitized event. *Soccer and Society, 19*(7), 1058–1071.

Lenskyj, H. J. (2013). *Gender politics and the Olympic industry*. Basingstoke: Palgrave.

Lewis, C. J., Roberts, S. J., & Andrews, H. (2018). 'Why am I putting myself through this?' Women football coaches' experiences of the Football Association's coach education process. *Sport, Education and Society, 23*(1), 28–39.

Litchfield, C., & Kavanagh, E. (2019). Twitter, team GB and the Australian Olympic team: Representations of gender in social media spaces. *Sport in Society, 22*(7), 1148–1164.

Litchfield, C., Kavanagh, E. J., Osborne, J., & Jones, I. (2016). Virtual maltreatment: Sexualisation and social media abuse in sport. *Psychology of Women Section Review, 18*(2).

Litchfield, C., Kavanagh, E., Osborne, J., & Jones, I. (2018). Social media and the politics of gender, race and identity: The case of Serena Williams. *European Journal for Sport and Society, 15*(2), 154–170.

MacDonald, C. A. (2014). Masculinity and sport revisited: A review of literature on hegemonic masculinity and Men's Ice Hockey in Canada. *Canadian Graduate Journal of Sociology & Criminology, 3*(1).

Mahomed, S., & Dhai, A. (2019). Global injustice in sport: The Caster Semenya ordeal–Prejudice, discrimination and racial bias. *SAMJ: South African Medical Journal, 109*(8), 548–551.

Mangan, J. A. (2000). *Athleticism in the Victorian and Edwardian public school: The emergence and consolidation of an educational ideology* (2nd ed.). Abingdon: Routledge.

McDonagh, E., & Pappano, L. (2007). *Playing with the boys: Why separate is not equal in sports*. Oxford: Oxford University Press.

McDonald, M. G. (2014). Mapping intersectionality and whiteness: Troubling gender and sexuality in sport studies. In J. Hargreaves & E. Anderson (Eds.), *Routledge handbook of sport, gender and sexuality* (pp. 151–159). Abingdon: Routledge.

McKenzie, J. (2002). *Perform or else: From discipline to performance*. New York, NY: Routledge.

Messerschmidt, J. W. (2019). The salience of "hegemonic masculinity". *Men and Masculinities, 22*(1), 85–91.

Messner, M. A., & Sabo, D. F. (1990). Introduction: Toward a critical feminist reappraisal of sport, men, and the gender order. In M. A. Messner & D. F. Sabo (Eds.), *Sport, men, and the gender order* (pp. 1–16). Champaign, IL: Human Kinetics.

Müller, M. (2015). What makes an event a mega-event? Definitions and sizes. *Leisure Studies, 34*(6), 627–642.

Müller, M. (2017). Approaching paradox: Loving and hating mega-events. *Tourism Management, 63*, 234–241.

Ncube, L., & Chawana, F. (2018). What is in a song? Constructions of hegemonic masculinity by Zimbabwean football fans. *Muziki, 15*(1), 68–88.

NRF. (2021). 2021 Super Bowl: Over 185 million estimated viewers: Holidays and season trends, Super Bowl. National Retail Federation. Retrieved from https://nrf.com/insights/holiday-and-seasonal-trends/super-bowl. Accessed on February 8, 2021.

O'Bonsawin, C. M. (2010). 'No Olympics on stolen native land': Contesting Olympic narratives and asserting indigenous rights within the discourse of the 2010 Vancouver games. *Sport in Society, 13*(1), 143–156.

O'Neill, A. (2020, July, 15). Number of athletes at the summer Olympics by gender 1896–2016. *Statista*, Retrieved from https://www.statista.com/statistics/1090581/olympics-number-athletes-by-gender-since-1896/. Accessed on February 9, 2021.

O'Neill, D., & Mulready, M. (2015). The invisible woman? A comparative study of women's sports coverage in the UK national press before and after the 2012 Olympic Games. *Journalism Practice, 9*(5), 651–668.

Organista, N., & Mazur, Z. (2020). "You either stop reacting or you don't survive. There's no other way": The work experiences of polish women sports journalists. *Feminist Media Studies, 20*(8), 1110–1127.

Pfister, G., & Pope, S. (Eds.). (2018). *Female football players and fans: Intruding into a man's world*. London: Springer.

Priyadharshini, E., & Pressland, A. (2016). Doing femininities and masculinities in a 'feminized' sporting arena: The case of mixed-sex cheerleading. *Sport in Society, 19*(8–9), 1234–1248.

Quayle, M., Wurm, A., Barnes, H., Barr, T., Beal, E., Fallon, M., ... Wei, R. (2019). Stereotyping by omission and commission: Creating distinctive gendered spectacles in the televised coverage of the 2015 Australian Open men's and women's tennis singles semi-finals and finals. *International Review for the Sociology of Sport, 54*(1), 3–21.

Richards, J., Parry, K. D., & Gill, F. (2020). "The guys love it when chicks ask for help": An exploration of female rugby league fans. *Sport in Society*, 1–18.

Roberts, K. (2004). *The leisure industries*. London: Palgrave.

Roche, M. (1994). Mega-events and urban policy. *Annals of Tourism Research, 21*(1), 1–19.

Roche, M. (2000). *Mega-events and modernity*. London: Routledge.

Roche, M. (2003). Mega-events, time and modernity: On time structures in global society. *Time & Society, 12*(1), 99–126.

Roche, M. (2008). Putting the London 2012 Olympics into perspective: The challenge of understanding mega-events. *Twenty-First Century Society, 3*(3), 285–290.

Rowe, D. (2009). Media and sport: The cultural dynamics of global games. *Sociology Compass, 3*(4), 543–558.

Rugg, A. (2019). Civilizing the child: Violence, masculinity, and race in media narratives of James Harrison. *Communication & Sport, 7*(1), 46–63.

Sanderson, J., & Gramlich, K. (2016). "You Go Girl!": Twitter and conversations about sport culture and gender. *Sociology of Sport Journal, 33*(2), 113–123.

Schippers, M. (2007). Recovering the feminine other: Masculinity, femininity, and gender hegemony. *Theory and Society, 36*(1), 85–102.

Smith, A. (2012). *Events and urban regeneration: The strategic use of events to revitalise cities*. London: Routledge.

Smoot, R. N. (2017). Olympic athletes or beauty queens? The sexualization of female athletes. *Augsburg Honors Review, 10*(1), 9.

Spracklen, K., & Lamond, I. R. (2016). *Critical event studies*. Abingdon: Routledge.

Statista. (2016, August 18). Olympic Games TV viewership worldwide 2002–2016. Retrieved from https://www.statista.com/statistics/287966/olympic-games-tv-viewership-worldwide/#:~:text=The%20most%20recent%20summer%20games,the%20opening%20ceremony%20in%202016. Accessed on February 8, 2021.

Sykes, H. (2017). *The sexual and gender politics of sport mega-events: Roving colonialism*. Abingdon: Routledge.

Symons, C. (2014). The gay games: A beacon of inclusion in sport? In J. Hargreaves & E. Anderson (Eds.), *Routledge handbook of sport, gender and sexuality* (pp. 318–327). Abingdon: Routledge.

Thorpe, H., Toffoletti, K., & Bruce, T. (2017). Sportswomen and social media: Bringing third-wave feminism, postfeminism, and neoliberal feminism into conversation. *Journal of Sport & Social Issues, 41*(5), 359–383.

Toffoletti, K. (2016). Analyzing media representations of sportswomen—Expanding the conceptual boundaries using a postfeminist sensibility. *Sociology of Sport Journal, 33*(3), 199–207.

Toffoletti, K. (2017). Sexy women sports fans: Femininity, sexuality, and the global sport spectacle. *Feminist Media Studies, 17*(3), 457–472.

Washington, M. S., & Economides, M. (2016). Strong is the new sexy: Women, CrossFit, and the postfeminist ideal. *Journal of Sport & Social Issues, 40*(2), 143–161.

Watt, P. (2013). 'It's not for us' regeneration, the 2012 Olympics and the gentrification of East London. *City, 17*(1), 99–118.

Wenner, L. A. (1998). In search of the sports bar: Masculinity, alcohol, sports, and the mediation of public space. In G. Rail (Ed.), *Sport and postmodern times* (pp. 302–332). Albany, NY: SUNY Press.

Wenner, L. A., & Jackson, S. J. (2009). Sport, beer and gender in promotional culture: On the dynamics of a holy trinity. In L. A. Wenner & S. J. Jackson (Eds.), *Sport, beer and gender: Promotional culture and contemporary social life* (pp. 1–32). New York, NY: Peter Lang Publishing.

Westbrook, L., & Schilt, K. (2014). Doing gender, determining gender: Transgender people, gender panics, and the maintenance of the sex/gender/sexuality system. *Gender & Society, 28*(1), 32–57.

Whitson, D., & Horne, J. (2006). Underestimated costs and overestimated benefits? Comparing the outcomes of sports mega-events in Canada and Japan. *The Sociological Review, 54*(2_suppl), 73–89.

Woodward, K. (2014). Legacies of 2012: Putting women's boxing into discourse. *Contemporary Social Science, 9*(2), 242–252.

Xu, Q., Billings, A. C., Scott, O. K., Lewis, M., & Sharpe, S. (2019). Gender differences through the lens of Rio: Australian Olympic primetime coverage of the 2016 Rio Summer Olympic Games. *International Review for the Sociology of Sport, 54*(5), 517–535.

Yang, E. C. L., Hayes, M., Chen, J., Riot, C., & Khoo-Lattimore, C. (2020). A social media analysis of the gendered representations of female and male athletes during the 2018 Commonwealth Games. *International Journal of Sport Communication, 1*(aop), 1–26.

Section 1
Problematising Gendered Bodies and Behaviours

Chapter 2

Sex Testing in Sport Mega-Events: Fairness and the Illusive Promise of Inclusive Policies – Situating Inter* and Trans*Athletes in Elite Sport

Anna Adlwarth

Introduction

In order to discuss gender and sport mega-events, we need to acknowledge the fact that almost all sports competitions are organised in binary sex categories, based on the assumption that there are only two sexes and that these are mutually exclusive, especially when it comes to physical prowess and athletic ability. In the two-sex model, the concept of the women's category in elite sport is particularly fragile, which becomes apparent when looking at attempts to regulate it to ensure 'fair competition'. This is because the binary categorisation of sex assumes that all women are physically inferior to all men (Cahn, 1994; Messner, 1988). Consequently, the women's category is understood as a 'weaker' category with poor(er) athletic performance. Therefore, so-called sex verification tests are used to 'prove' the sex of female athletes and their eligibility to compete in 'the right' category. Since the 1920s (Pieper, 2016), sex testing has been carried out by the International Olympic Committee (IOC) and World Athletics (formerly the International Association of Athletics Federation, IAAF).[1] Sex testing is still practised by these governing bodies in relation to sport mega-events today. While these tests initially attempted to ensure that 'men in disguise' could not participate as women in sports events, they actually exclude, humiliate and discriminate against athletes who do not fit into the gender binary created by the two-sex model (Moi, 2005).

The matter is even more complicated because sex is not as dimorphic as is often assumed, and science cannot 'prove' sex that easily (Fausto-Sterling, 2000). This becomes apparent when we look at the history of sex testing, where the 'sex markers' being tested varied due to whatever was considered up to date in the medico-sciences at the time. Several of the tests have since proved to be medically inaccurate and ethically flawed (Sullivan, 2011). The current practice of sex testing is based on testosterone levels. Female athletes with 'too much'

Sport, Gender and Mega-Events, 33–55
doi:10.1108/978-1-83982-936-920211008

testosterone are required to artificially regulate their testosterone. This concerns two groups of athletes in particular: trans*women and women with inter*sex variations (women with differences in sex development).[2] Trans*people are people who do not identify with the sex assigned to them at birth and deliberately undergo a change of sex and/or gender. Inter*sex people have 'conditions' that do not fit the medico-scientific two-sex model, e.g. 5α reductase deficiency, an autosomal defect on a chromosome other than the X or Y chromosome, or Androgen Insensitivity Syndrome, which occurs when a person's body cells are unable to respond to androgen hormones (ISNA, 2008).

Looking at the history of sex testing, it becomes apparent that the two main sports bodies that determine the rules and regulations concerning the eligibility criteria for the female category are the IOC and the IAAF (Pieper, 2016; Sullivan, 2011), both of which organise sport mega-events, such as the Olympic Games and the World Athletics Championships. These mega-events are of high cultural importance and winning a medal in one of the competitions brings considerable status (Coalter, 2008). When it comes to research on gender and sport mega-events, it is therefore important to uncover any discrimination of athletes against the background of a sex/gender categorisation that restricts participation to athletes with normative, 'normalised' gendered bodies. With an empirical focus on the IOC and IAAF regulations, the following literature review endeavours to synthesise critical voices and research exploring the current knowledge about sex testing and sex categorisations in sport mega-events.

Particularly, with regard to a critical intervention towards shifting the discourse about sex testing and sex regulation in sport mega-events, it seems important as a starting point to map the different considerations in the debate about the integration of trans*women and women with differences of sexual development (DSD) in elite sports and sport mega-events.[3] This is important because although the issue is constituted interdisciplinarily, the medico-sciences, feminist and queer studies and sport philosophers and sociologists introduce seemingly incommensurable perspectives. Basing their insights mostly on scientific evidence, sport policymakers appear confident of having found a solution that meets the requirements of providing fair and equal competition. As the current policies affect the professional careers, health and bodily integrity of athletes, the normative impact that scientific hierarchies have on this needs to be critically reflected upon (Karkazis & Jordan-Young, 2018). The research question guiding my exploration is, accordingly, how the current sex regulation practices contribute to reifying the Western notion of binary sex – particularly in reference to the concept of fairness in competition at sport mega-events.? While current policies have far-reaching consequences, and the sciences do not agree on the handling of the issue, reaching consensus with 'inclusive policies' seems impossible. Drawing on this insight, I also aim to explore whether the promise of inclusive policies is illusive.

In the subsequent parts of this chapter, I will first of all provide an overview of the history of sex testing and introduce the most recent debate from June 2020. Following this, I present my methodological approach. The literature is mapped by breaking down the current perspectives into themes, which I then discuss. The chapter concludes with a critical evaluation of future perspectives.

Author's Position

Considering my own standpoint in this chapter, it can be noted that I am a white, European cis-woman working in academia. Reflecting on this, I acknowledge the risk of a reproduction of and/or contribution to a neo-colonial fetishism and exploitation of gender nonconforming individuals and non-normative bodies. I also understand – and take into account – that matters of gender identity are not abstract but real and painful everyday struggles that are complex and intersect. In addition, it is notable that apart from my privileged standpoint as a white European academic, I also identify as a queer advocate whose understanding of the world is shaped by post-structuralist and (post-)constructivist theories (Asdal, 2005; Barad, 2003; Butler, 1993; Foucault, 1976, 1978; Harraway, 1985). Consequently, my critical review of the literature is shaped by these premises.

In opposition to the ruling knowledge paradigm of sex as a biological binary, which is dominating the current debate concerning sex regulation, I accordingly take on the conception that dichotomous sex is a construct, rooted in a Western notion of science which emerged with the enlightenment and brings forth sexed bodies as a result (Butler, 1993; Foucault, 1978). This scientific tradition is also deeply entrenched in a racial and colonial binary logic (Sommerville, 1994). Hence, from my point of analysis, the debate does not only involve conflicting theoretical perspectives, but moreover, brings to light a differing ontology or onto-epistemology of sex. That is, completely different understandings of reality, the essence of sex and what and how we know about both.

From my queer theoretical perspective, I furthermore apply terms like 'woman' with an inherent critique. For instance, when I later in the chapter refer to Ewa Kłobukowska not passing female gender verification but giving birth later in life, the aim is to expose that gender verification tests fail in a binary understanding of sex. However, I do not agree with the notion that giving birth is the ultimate proof of womanhood – and thus binary sex (Costello, 2014).

The History of Sex Testing in Sport Mega-Events

The issue of the 'femaleness' of women athletes became a topic of discussion even before women were admitted to sport mega-events such as the Olympic Games, and there is evidence of sex testing as early as the 1928 Olympic Summer Games (Pieper, 2016). However, routine sex tests of female athletes were not introduced until the European Athletic Championships in 1966. The early gender verifications constituted a physical examination by a team of doctors, known as 'nude parades', where the presence of female genitalia and secondary sexual characteristics constituted the selected sex marker and object of testing. However, what exactly was considered as 'anatomical maleness and femaleness is unclear' (Rupert, 2011, p. 347).

For the 1968 Olympics, the IOC introduced the Barr body test – a sex chromosome test focussing on XX chromosomes. This change of procedure depicts the medico-scientific shift from the idea of determining sex by genitalia to determining sex by chromosomes. However, the Barr body test was not failproof, in that women could fail the test and men could pass it due to various flaws in the attempt to determine sex by XX chromosomes (for a detailed explanation, see Rupert, 2011; Sullivan, 2011, p. 404f). Scholars repeatedly pointed out these flaws, especially when errors appeared that affected the lives of individuals (Rupert, 2011; Sullivan, 2011). For instance, Polish sprinter Ewa Kłobukowska failed the Barr body test in 1968, despite having passed the physical examination the previous year. The test showed that she had one chromosome too many and was therefore 'declared unfit' to be a woman. Later in life, Kłobukowska gave birth to a healthy baby (Molnar & Kelly, 2013, p. 160). Following Kłobukowska, Spanish hurdler Maria José Martínez-Patiño failed the test at the 1985 World University Games and was disqualified, again despite having passed another sex test two years earlier. Later, it was shown that Patiño was androgen insensitive and was reinstated in 1988 after legally campaigning against the IAAF's ruling. Patiño was the first athlete to protest against the testing/ruling. The publicity involved in her case prompted the IAAF to hold workshops on the matter and eventually to abandon mandatory sex tests altogether (Pieper, 2016).

Although the IAAF suspended obligatory sex testing in 1992, the IOC continued to test until 1999. However, another shift in the conception of sex determination took place when sex chromatin testing was replaced by the polymerase chain reaction test. Instead of focussing on XX chromosomes, these tests focussed on the genetic makeup of the Y chromosome:

> Up to this point female athletes had to prove they were 'female' according to the IOC definition of what constitutes female at that time (XX). Now, female competitors were asked to prove that they were 'not male' (XY).
>
> (Sullivan, 2011, p. 406)

This time, more scientists and medical specialists protested against the testing due to its medical and ethical flaws. Following the IAAF, the IOC suspended mandatory sex testing in 1999, although the option to test on a case-by-case basis remained. Referring to the time of mandatory sex testing, Rupert (2011, p. 360) concluded that:

> Over 10 000 female athletes were sex tested between 1966 and 1998 and not one male imposter was discovered despite the fact that a number of women like Ewa Kłobukowska 'failed'. Based on the chromosome- and gene-based tests, an estimated 27 women competing between the 1980s and 1990s (about 1/400) were XY DSD. This is a frequency 50 to 100 times greater than would be expected based on population frequencies. Elite athletes are a highly self-selected population and the overrepresentation of XY

women amongst Olympians suggests that the genotype does contribute to athletic performance. Without knowing which sports the XY women were competing in, the nature of this advantage (whether it was physiological, psychological, or sociocultural or some combination of these) cannot be determined.

Mandatory sex testing was in part also terminated in favour of the case-by-case basis option after a 'biological passport' was introduced by the World Anti-Doping Agency (WADA). According to this, athletes had to undergo regular doping controls that included urinary samples. The delivery of the samples was to be observed by doping officers who had (and still have) to indicate if a female athlete had a 'deviating' female physique, such as an enlarged clitoris (Jordan-Young, Sönksen, & Karkazis, 2014). Again, sporting bodies seemed to fall back on the visibility of sex. In the following years of hormonal screening, the regular doping controls were expanded to screening for high testosterone.

The Current Debate on Sex Testing and Fairness in Sport Mega-Events

As shown above, the various sex tests mainly affected females showing anomalies related to the sex marker of the test in question. However, as trans*athletes additionally challenged the eligibility policies for the women's category, in 2003 the IOC drew up new guidelines for the participation of trans*athletes in the so-called Stockholm Consensus. According to this, in order to be eligible, athletes had to: (1) have completed sex reassignment surgery, including gonadectomy and surgery of the external genitalia, (2) have their gender confirmed legally and (3) have undergone hormonal therapy for a sufficient amount of time. A two-year waiting period between gonadectomy and eligibility was also suggested. However, as Sullivan (2011) pointed out, no reason was given as to why two years were regarded as crucial. Furthermore, almost no attention was paid to trans*men (Sullivan, 2011).

In 2015, the IOC eligibility regulations for trans*athletes were changed again when the IOC admitted that legal proof of gender discriminated against athletes from countries in which a change of gender might be illegal. Furthermore, they renounced obligatory sex reassignment surgery for healthy athletes. The new regulations thus state that trans*women can compete in the women's category as long as they do not renounce their female gender identity within four years. Furthermore, for a period of at least 12 months before competing, and for the period of eligibility, they have to prove a testosterone level below 10 nmol/litre (IOC, 2015). Trans*men, on the other hand, are able to participate without restriction. In the meantime, the IAAF recommends a threshold of 5 nmol/litre for eligibility (World Athletics, 2019).

A deliberate medical change of sex, which is often desired by trans*persons in contrast to people classified as inter*sex, is at present usually achieved by hormone therapy, and/or surgery (WPATH, 2012).[4] Consequently, the issue of the eligibility of trans*women in sport mega-events was tackled in terms of the regulation of hormone levels, i.e. androgens like testosterone. Although the IAAF adopted the Stockholm Consensus, it used it as a guiding document for new policies on gender verification for inter*sex athletes (Bavington, 2019). This merging of inter* and trans* issues gave the go-ahead for yet another shift in sex determination. Since the 2000s, the governing bodies have tested 'suspicious athletes' on the grounds of hormonal sex, where the predestined new sex marker is testosterone.

> The IAAF Policy on Gender Verification outlined a process to broadly address the problem of gender ambiguity in women's events. This process, which included a comprehensive medical evaluation conducted by a team of experts, was the same for athletes who had conditions that led their bodies to naturally produce high levels of testosterone and transgender women taking testosterone suppressants as part of their medical transition. In both cases the problem had to be resolved through medical and surgical interventions. [...] By aligning intersex female athletes with transgender women on the basis of hormonal characteristics, it made possible the notion that all women should be made hormonally similar to compete in the female category.
>
> (Bavington, 2019, p. 193f)

From 2011, the IAAF and IOC resumed sex verification tests, this time based on androgens.[5,6] Consequently, those included in the new regulations were 'females with hyperandrogenism' (IAAF, 2011; IOC, 2012). Even though the medical term hyperandrogenism includes a range of conditions that do not necessarily need medical attention, such as polycystic ovary syndrome, sports policies only use hyperandrogenism to refer to high testosterone and tissue sensitivity in female athletes (Jordan-Young et al., 2014; Karkazis & Jordan-Young, 2018).[7] According to these new regulations, athletes diagnosed with hyperandrogenism were required to undergo medical treatment. Thus, for the first time in the history of sex verification, healthy bodies were required to undergo artificial regulation in order to correspond to a supposedly 'natural' sex.

In 2015, following an appeal from Indian sprinter Dutee Chand, the IAAF regulations were suspended by the Court of Arbitration for Sport (CAS). Chand had previously been declared ineligible for the women's category due to her testosterone levels and was asked to withdraw from competition or medically lower her testosterone (Karkazis & Carpenter, 2018). The CAS (2014) ruled in favour of Chand, but nevertheless enabled the IAAF to reinstall the regulations if it could present evidence showing a performance advantage for women with naturally high testosterone. In 2018, the IAAF returned to the CAS with revised regulations that only covered a subset of track events (400m, 400m hurdles, 800m, 1500m, the mile). Although the IAAF did not succeed in showing the claimed performance difference, the CAS terminated the suspension in favour of the new regulations (Karkazis & Carpenter, 2018; Sönksen, Bavington, Boehning, Cowan, & Guha, 2018).

The IAAF's new regulations came into effect in May 2018 and stipulate a testosterone level of 5 nmol/L. Furthermore, the new regulations narrow down the athletes affected to women with DSD and certain androgen sensitivity.[8] Karkazis and Carpenter (2018, p. 581) conclude that:

> ...[t]his focus is reinforced by an apparent exemption of other causes of hyperandrogenism from this regulation [and] while a range of medical diagnoses may lead to higher natural testosterone in women, intersex variations are explicitly included whereas non-intersex diagnoses are explicitly excluded.

In other words, women who have naturally high testosterone above the threshold level and are not classified with DSD are not required to lower their levels medically, whereas athletes classified with DSD are.

When the new regulations came into effect in April 2018, South African track and field athlete Caster Semenya and Athletics South Africa (ASA) appealed against them. Already in 2009 Semenya had been declared 'suspicious' due to the combination of her strong performance and physical appearance (Pieper, 2016), but was later reinstated. Her 2018 legal challenge was rejected by the CAS in May 2018 (CAS, 2018). However, the CAS admitted to flaws in the system that were discriminatory to individuals (The Guardian, 2019; see also Conclusion). Semenya appealed the ruling of the CAS to the Swiss Federal Supreme Court, but lost her appeal in September 2020 when the Swiss Court decided that the CAS decision cannot be challenged. Semenya can now appeal to the European Court of Human Rights; however, as things stand at present, she will not be able to compete at the Tokyo 2020 summer Olympics, which are planned to take place in 2021 (Ingle, 2020).

Methods

In this section I describe the literature review process and the subsequent sampling of texts. I also clarify my position as a researcher and reader of the current knowledge on sex testing, gender and fairness in sport mega-events.

The sample of articles referred to above is based on an integrative review approach (Torraco, 2005). In an initial bibliographic screening and in order to retrieve the relevant literature, I first identified the literature on which the IOC and IAAF based their policies. At the same time, I identified perspectives discussing the policies and their research grounds. This was also checked against relevant online academic databases, namely Scopus, PubMed and SPORTDiscus for 'sex testing', 'gender verification', 'Olympics', 'sport', 'fairness', 'sex segregation', 'equality', 'transgender', 'intersex' and 'sex regulation'. However, as my aim was to identify novel and critical texts, and not carry out a systematic review of the literature, a manual reference screening and a screening of full-text journal databases proved more relevant and effective for completing the search. Concerning a discussion of the current debate, it seemed appropriate to concentrate on papers published after 2003 because it was in that year that the most recent debate on hormonal sex testing commenced with the Stockholm Consensus (see above, The Current Debate on Sex Testing and Fairness in Sport Mega-Events). This left me with 50 articles. I decided to approach the reading in stages and began with an initial reading of abstracts, followed by a second stage of reading full-text articles. Before defining the final selection for an in-depth analysis, I started to organise the literature in themes to map the complexity of the debate. Initially these themes consisted of: (1) medico-scientific basis of eligibility regulations, (2) critique within the medico-sciences and bio-ethics and (3) theoretical and philosophical considerations.

Analysis

Following the second stage of reading, I identified two articles that present the medico-scientific basis of the regulations and 15 articles for an in-depth analysis of recent critique, using a content analysis strategy (Mayring, 2014). Like this, I identified the following themes and articles to guide my exploration of the research question, as detailed in Table 2.1.

Concerning the analysis of the literature, it is important to stress that trans*-women and women with DSD are affected differently by the regulations. While trans*women would usually already have undergone hormone therapy and may, due to their own notion of gender, approve or even advocate the regulations, it is possible that women with DSD will be unaware of their 'condition'. Thus, the fact that trans*women deliberately change sex positions them differently to those who identify with the female sex ascribed to them at birth. Moreover, changing sex is a financial burden and it is mostly athletes from the Global North who have come out as trans*, whereas those identified as women with DSD are almost exclusively from the Global South (Bavington, 2019; Karkazis & Jordan-Young, 2018). Thus, while the regulations on eligibility for the women's category discriminate against all women who do not happen to comply with the 'standards of femaleness' set by the IOC or IAAF, the regulations relating to women with DSD seem more problematic and complex.[9] In my analysis of the medico-scientific research and the current regulations, as well as the ethical considerations and the question of racism, I refer to women with DSD, although when it comes to the questions of fairness and 'what is a woman', I draw on texts concerned with all aspects of gender nonconformity.

Medico-scientific Foundation and (Bio)ethical Considerations of the Current Regulations

The claim that high testosterone levels lead to a performance advantage in female athletes has been repeatedly objected to (Jordan-Young et al., 2014; Karkazis & Jordan-Young, 2018; Sönksen et al., 2018; Tannenbaum & Bekker, 2019). The

Table 2.1. Reviewed Articles by Themes.

Theme	Articles
Medico-scientific foundation of the current regulations	Eklund, E., Berglund, B., Labrie, F., Carlström, K., Ekström, L., & Hirschberg, A. (2017). Serum androgen profile and physical performance in women Olympic athletes. *British Journal of Sports Medicine, 51*(17), 1301–1308.
	Bermon, S., & Garnier, P. (2017). Serum androgen levels and their relation to performance in track and field: Mass spectrometry results from 2127 observations in male and female elite athletes. *British Journal of Sports Medicine, 51*(17), 1309–1314.
(Bio)ethical critique of the regulations and their foundation	Jordan-Young, R., Sönksen, P., & Karkazis, K. (2014). Sex, health, and athletes. *British Medical Journal, 384*, g2926.
	Karkazis, K., & Carpenter, M. (2018). Impossible "choices": The inherent harms of regulating women's testosterone in sport. *Bioethical Inquiry, 15*(4), 579–587.
	Sönksen, P. H., Bavington, L. D., Boehning, T., Cowan, D., & Guha, N. (2018). Hyperandrogenism controversy in elite women's sport: An examination and critique of recent evidence. *British Journal of Sports Medicine, 52*(23), 1481–1482.
	Tannenbaum, C., & Bekker, S. (2019). Sex, gender, and sports. *British Medical Journal, 364*.
Hyperandrogenism as a sport policy term and its relation to race and gender	Karkazis, K., & Jordan-Young, R. (2018). The power of testosterone: Obscuring race and regional bias in the regulation of women athletes. *Feminist Formations, 30*(2), 1–39.

Table 2.1. *(Continued)*

Theme	Articles
	Magubane, Z. (2014). Spectacles and scholarship: Caster Semenya, intersex studies, and the problem of race in feminist theory. *Sings: Journal of Women in Culture and Society, 39*(3), 761–785.
	Pieper, L. P. (2014). Sex testing and the maintenance of Western femininity in international sport. *The International Journal of the History of Sport, 31*(13), 1557–1576.
Fairness, sex segregation and the level playing field	Behrensen, M. (2013). In the halfway house of ill repute: Gender verification under a different name, still no contribution to fair play. *Sport, Ethics and Philosophy, 7*(4), 450–466.
	Cavanagh, S. L., & Sykes, H. (2006). Transsexual bodies at the Olympics: The International Olympic Committee's Policy on Transsexual Athletes at the 2004 Athens Summer Games. *Body & Society, 12*(3), 75–102.
	Dworkin, S. L., & Cooky, C. (2012). Sport, sex segregation, and sex testing: Critical reflections of this unjust marriage. *The American Journal of Bioethics, 12*(7), 21–23.
	Sykes, H. (2006). Transsexual and transgender policies in sport. *Women in Sport & Physical Activity Journal, 15*(1), 3–13.
The concept and renegotiation of fairness	Bianchi, A. (2017). Transgender women in sport. *Journal of the Philosophy of Sport, 44*(2), 229–242.
	Coggon, J., Hammond, N., & Holm, S. (2008). Transsexuals in sport-

Table 2.1. *(Continued)*

Theme	Articles
	fairness and freedom, regulation and law. *Sports Ethics and Philosophy, 2*(1), 4–17.
	Gleaves, J., & Lehrbach, T. (2016). Beyond fairness: The ethics of inclusion for transgender and intersex athletes. *Journal of the Philosophy of Sport, 43*(2), 311–326.
	Teetzel, S. (2014). The onus of inclusivity: Sport policies and the enforcement of the women's category in sport. *Journal of the Philosophy of Sport, 41*(1), 113–127.

reintroduction of the IAAF's eligibility criteria for women with DSD in 2018 is based on two studies: Eklund et al. (2017) and Bermon and Garnier (2017), both of which set out to examine the relationship between endogenous androgens and athletic performance using a cross-sectional design. However, both approaches have been criticised for their failure to prove a significant performance difference in women with high testosterone levels or to show causality between high testosterone and enhanced athletic performance overall (Karkazis & Carpenter, 2018; Sönksen et al., 2018; Tannenbaum & Bekker, 2019). Sönksen et al. (2018) conclude that:

> The IAAF was tasked by CAS with providing sufficient evidence that female athletes with androgen levels in the so-called male range have a competitive advantage over their peers, comparable to that men have over women previously identified as 10%–12% [2; Para 526]. These studies do not provide this evidence. Both papers provide some new data but do not directly tackle the issues articulated by the CAS.

Additionally, Bermon and Garnier's (2017) study was funded by the IAAF and WADA (Sönksen et al., 2018). As these studies form the basis for regulations that require healthy athletes to medically regulate their bodies in order to be eligible for competition, there could be a conflict of interest, especially as Sönksen et al. (2018) also pointed to methodological flaws in Bermon and Garnier's (2017) analysis, such as the fact that the analysis concentrated on derived fT (free testosterone) and not on total endogenous blood testosterone, which the hyper-androgenism rules actually refer to. Furthermore, the validity of calculating as a method, rather than measuring seems dubious. In the next section, I highlight several of the critical voices identified in the debate and begin with the ethical critique of the suggestions for medical interventions for women with DSD.

As Jordan-Young et al. (2014) specify in their reaction to the 2014 IOC 'hyperandrogenism – policies' (IOC, 2014), two-thirds of the women who medically lower their testosterone experience serious side effects, such as 'diuretic effects that cause excessive thirst, urination, and electrolyte imbalances; disruption of carbohydrate metabolism (such as glucose intolerance or insulin resistance); headache; fatigue; nausea; hot flushes; and liver toxicity' (Jordan-Young et al., 2014, p. 2). Additionally, there is a risk of liver damage, the disruption of other necessary steroid production and serious cortisol deficiency. That is, athletes who undergo hormone treatment may suffer from serious (long-term) side effects that not only damage their health but also influence their athletic performance.

In addition to testosterone levels, the policies on hyperandrogenism focus on physiological androgen sensitivity. However, as Tannenbaum and Bekker (2019) problematise, physiological androgen sensitivity cannot be retrieved in the form of data in the laboratory. Whenever 'suspicious cases' with high endogenous testosterone appear, the IAAF thus falls back on the initially abandoned practices of physical examination, chromosomal testing and imaging of sex organs, including gynaecological assessment and an assessment of muscularity, body hair, voice, breast and clitoral size. Apart from being humiliating procedures, 'testing on suspicion' and subjectively judging gender to determine sex are highly problematic, in that they fall back on cultural ideas of femininity. Karkazis and Carpenter (2018, p. 583) stress this normative judgement of gender as follows:

> Relying on suspicion as a basis for investigation effectively legitimizes widespread surveillance of all women athletes by instructing national federations as well as doctors, doping officials, and other official personnel to scrutinize women athletes' perceived femininity. This can include appearance, gender expression, and sexuality. Who is understood to be suspicious is tied to subjective and cultural expectations regarding which bodies and modes of gender expression are appropriate or even valorized by adherence to traditional or normative aesthetics of femininity.

Taking the risk of long-term side effects, humiliating physical inspections and a corresponding climate of fear and suspicion (Karkazis & Carpenter, 2018) into account, much of the critical literature on sex testing in sport mega-events questions how such regulations can be defended ethically by sporting bodies, when the aim is to secure fair elite sport competitions. This becomes evident when looking at the options that are left for the affected athletes, as Karkazis and Carpenter (2018) do in their critical discussion of the 2018 IAAF rules. The direct consequence for an athlete who does not submit to assessment – if suspected – is the end of her career in the women's category. Although no-one is obliged to be assessed, the options that are left would effectively lead to the end of their career.

Additionally, if an athlete decides to appeal, she must be willing and able to pay for a legal challenge against the IAAF, and besides exposing herself to public judgement of her sex and gender identity, she must also consider that, while the case is active, she may be barred from competing in sport mega-events.

In their analysis, Karkazis and Carpenter (2018) point out that these circumstances challenge the postulate of informed consent regarding the regulation requirements. This applies particularly to athletes from resource poor regions who are economically dependent on their competitive careers. Hence, athletes may consent to harmful procedures without considering the short- and long-term consequences in order to maintain their own, their families' or even their communities' livelihoods.

The solution offered by the sporting bodies is to compete in the men's category or in a third category. As there is no third gender category in sport mega-events at present, this is not a practical option. Karkazis and Carpenter (2018) argue that it is ethically questionable to force women who identify as such into categories other than female. Consequently, these measures represent a public judgement and a punishment for athletes who refuse to medicalise their bodies (Karkazis & Carpenter, 2018). Participation in a different category than that for which the athlete has trained and taken part in the past may furthermore destroy her career. As female athletes still struggle for recognition, equal competition and remuneration (Hovden, 2012), we can only imagine the kinds of struggles that participants in 'a third category' would have to face. Suggestions like a third category should therefore be rejected until they have been thoroughly thought through. There is also a need for more research on the inclusion of more categories, or other novel ways of organising competitions in sport mega-events.

Hyperandrogenism, Race and Gender

The new hyperandrogenism-rules almost exclusively affect female athletes of colour from the Global South (Karkazis & Jordan-Young, 2019).[10] Drawing on the Colonial/Modern Gender System, Pieper (2014) explores how the notion of verifying gender medically is based on Eurocentric, colonialist concepts of dimorphic sex and racial classifications that promote and privilege white Western femininity in sport. In her historical analysis, she shows how European colonisers perceived and depicted Black people as animalistic and inferior and Black women as masculine or non-gendered (Pieper, 2014).

The reintroduction of sex testing based on testosterone, which targets a very specific population of inter*sex variations in women, was a reaction to the physical appearance of individual athletes like Semenya and Chand. Arguably, this is no coincidence. Magubane (2014), who looks at the ontology of inter*sex, points out that the Black inter*sex body has not had to undergo the same history of medical normalisation as white inter*sex bodies. As being classified as either male or female was a white privilege in the first place, the white citizen was obliged to conform to the dichotomic sex/gender system, if necessary by means of surgical correction. However, no-one cared to align the black body in the same way. In fact, 'the lack of social and biological differentiation between men and women marked blacks as blacks while also indexing their fundamental difference from and inferiority to whites' (Magubane, 2014, p. 770). According to Pieper (2014), the Colonial/Modern Gender System continues to organise not only society, but also elite sport and mega-events such as the Olympic Games. Based on these deep rooted racial and gendered stereotypes, the victorious black female runner still triggers white Western anxiety. Following this logic, Eurocentric sport governing bodies identify the untamed black body as problematic and ineligible (Pieper, 2014). Furthermore, by framing deviant bodies as unhealthy, the 'modern' Global North offers its help to medically fix 'the problem'.

Karkazis and Jordan-Young (2018) set out to answer the question of how and why women of colour from the Global South are the sole targets of the hyper-androgenism regulations. In order to do this, they analyse the multi-layered perspectives of 'T-talk', a term used by the authors to circumscribe 'the web of direct claims and indirect associations that circulate around testosterone as a material substance and a multivalent cultural symbol' (Karkazis & Jordan-Young, 2018, p. 1):

> [...]racial hierarchies are often not explicit nor are they rational and ordered; they are chaotic and camouflaged, but operate foundationally. Thus, we must look to the way that the T regulation and its enforcement alchemizes ideas about gender, race, and 'advantage' through sideways moves, indirect logics, resonances, reinforcements, and disavowals, relying on images and aesthetics as much as words, and on the wide circulation of unspoken tropes of gender, race and modernity or civilization. [Only then one can see, that via] T talk, sex biology is reshaped from messy distributions into clean dimorphism, which is reintroduced as the natural state of human biology; a racialized aesthetic of gender is made to appear 'normal/natural' and biological, not cultural; 'sex testing' is disavowed and repackaged as a health intervention 'for the good of the athlete'; and the operations of power and harm in the regulation are inverted – the least advantaged are figured as 'unfairly advantaged', and the extraordinary harms of interventions are framed as beneficial.
>
> (pp. 9, 11)

T-talk frames testosterone as a male attribute that is not only 'unnatural' in women but also 'harmful' to women. The people identified as 'suffering' from high T are untreated women from the Global South. By offering treatment – provided in specialist centres established in the Global North – a 'regime of care' comes into effect. Through this, 'T-talk' perpetuates the colonial and Eurocentric order as explored by Pieper (2014) and Magubane (2014).

In my review of the literature, I observed a lack of research on the affected female athletes themselves and their experiences and an overall lack of research perspectives from the Global South on sex testing and sport mega-events. In my aim for the synthesis of critical literature, I became moreover aware, that I, by following current academic publishing hierarchies and logics, reproduce the very same by drawing exclusively on Western academic library catalogues. Admitting that I failed to (cannot?) solve this problem in this chapter, this must be addressed in future research. Furthermore, it calls for a literature review from a solely postcolonial perspective, which is important particularly in view of the historical analysis of Magubane (2014), which clearly emphasises the necessity of such a research tradition on matters of gender.

The Level Playing Field

In the current debate, the attempt to prevent men in disguise from participating in the women's category has been replaced by the idea of preventing women with 'a male advantage' from competing against those who do not have this perceived biological advantage. Sykes (2006) and Cavanagh and Sykes (2006) refer to this idea as the advantage theory. The advantage theory is based on medico-scientific discourses on the endocrinological and morphological benefits of trans*athletes and discourses on the fairness of competition and the safety of the competitors. Quoting the UK Women's Sport Foundation, Sykes (2006, p. 8) summarises that the advantage theory relies on beliefs about trans*women benefitting from '[p] revious muscular development[, h]igh testosterone levels[, g]reater muscle to fat ratio[, g]reater heart and lung capacity [and the t]endency to greater aptitude in motor skills'. That is, 'Anyone exposed to testosterone before puberty will be a good athlete [and all] males are better athletes than all females'. The perpetuation of this belief has the consequence that:

> There is an incompatibility between conventional ideas about genetic women and femininity, and the idealized muscular Olympic body. Because muscles and muscularity (key ingredients of the most valorized Olympic bodies) have been gendered masculine, there is a psychic need to regulate female bodies entering into the masculinized arena of sport.
>
> (Cavanagh & Sykes, 2006, p. 83)

As shown above, the merging of medical discourses on trans* and inter*-athletes initiated the hormonal screening of the latter and hence rigidified the myth of women with DSD having the same 'advantages' as trans*women, that is 'biological men'. The advantage theory has thus also been shown to apply to discourses referring to inter*athletes (Jordan-Young et al., 2014; Karkazis & Carpenter, 2018).

However, many of the authors behind the reviewed literature argue for the inclusion of trans* and inter*athletes based on scientific evidence that their bodies do not disrupt the (alleged) level playing field (Behrensen, 2013; Dworkin & Cooky, 2012; Sykes, 2006; Teetzel, 2014). This argument thus follows the logic that the rationality of the regulation of the women's category is based on socio-cultural beliefs about the performance abilities of the female and male body, particularly regarding muscularity and sex hormones. These beliefs are inter-twined with the heteronormative notion that women are physically inferior to men (Cahn, 1994; Messner, 1988). This notion has been repeatedly challenged and it has been shown that there is an overlap in male and female sports per-formance and that women have been actively prevented from winning over men, either by preventing them from competing against men or limiting or cutting back their competition formats (Dworkin & Cooky, 2012). Consequently, sex segre-gation per se is challenged, and the suggestion has been made that sex segregation may very well inflict performance differences (Gleaves & Lehrbach, 2016) and thus reify the dominant gender model in sport mega-events. According to Sykes (2006), gender nonconforming bodies in sport mega-events thus provoke anxieties about 'bodily deterioration'. She continues to explain that:

> ...[the advantage theory] serves to preserve the cultural fantasy of binary gender categories and, therefore, the logic of women's and men's sport by disavowing that gender identities are ongoing, unstable achievements that are not always intelligible within stable binary categories.
>
> (p. 9)

Taking these insights into consideration, the conception of fairness in sport per se needs to be questioned. Accordingly, every potential physical advantage or disadvantage depends on the discipline and individual factors. For example, tallness and long limbs may be advantageous for basketball players but would be disadvantageous for weightlifters. Thus, every athlete benefits from congenital advantages or suffers from congenital disadvantages. An often cited example is Michael Phelps' above-average wingspan, his size 14 feet and the fact that he is double jointed, all of which give him an advantage that his competitors lack and are unable to achieve naturally (Bianchi, 2017). While he is praised as lucky, female athletes with such biological advantages are regarded as cheats. Further-more, socioeconomic factors affect an individual's performance, just as testos-terone levels, weight or height do, as Dutee Chand herself pointed out in her letter to the CAS (2014, p. 9):

> I was born a woman, reared up as a woman, I identify as a woman and I believe I should be allowed to compete with other women, many of whom are either taller than me or come from more privileged backgrounds, things that most certainly give them an edge over me.

That is, professional sport does not only ignore but also celebrate a broad spectrum of biological and socioeconomic inequalities, which means that from the beginning the level playing field is not that level after all. Consequently, the question emerges as to why gendered advantages 'should be singled out as a congenital inequality that [are] deeply problematic' (Behrensen, 2013, p. 459).

The Promise of Fairness and Inclusive Policies

Gleaves and Lehrbach (2016) criticise that most social scientists and humanists argue for the equal treatment of all athletes solely against medico-scientific reasoning, i.e. as long as the argument for equality only relies on medico-scientific findings and conclusions, it simply reproduces the medico-scientific discourse and does not really examine the problem as a cultural one. Accordingly, what they call the physical equivalence argument provides no ethical justification for the inclusion of trans* and inter*athletes. The argument reasons for inclusion by proving – regardless of the conceptual evidence – that the athletes do not have an advantage over their competitors. Consequently, the argument relies on the very same strategy that it tries to dismiss, since athletes who do not meet the biological norms of their gender have to prove that they fit in. According to Gleaves and Lehrbach (2016), it is thus rather the conceptualisation of fairness in sport that needs to be renegotiated.

Taking this into consideration, Teetzel (2014) points out that the entire debate is hampered by a lack of consensus on the meaning of fairness in sport. Overall, institutional fairness clashes with the right of the individual's freedom, which is based on the notion of giving women as a 'disadvantaged group' (Gleaves & Lehrbach, 2016) 'fair' access to competition. Accordingly, Coggon, Hammond, and Holm (2008) evaluate justifications of sex discrimination in sport. Although they dismiss some of the justifications as unreasonable, they do not succeed in overcoming sex discrimination: '[…] it is surely better to have an imperfect system that fits more happily in a world that is also imperfect than a philosophical perfect system that disadvantages 50 per cent of the population in the present (imperfect) world' (Coggon et al., 2008, p. 10).

While, according to Teetzel (2014), playing by the rules in order to play the game seems to be a logical requirement, she points out that a rule is not automatically fair and she suggests that from a social justice perspective there is an obligation to question and break unjustified rules. However, members of minority groups may struggle to have their voices heard. Moreover, there are several ways to evaluate whether a rule is morally acceptable. According to her, sporting bodies could move towards a focus on the equality of conditions instead of the equality of results, but they should assess the desire for a fair system against economical and practical considerations (Teetzel, 2014). On this matter, Bianchi (2017) suggests drawing on McKinnon's theory of luck and credit (McKinnon, 2013) for inclusive policies. Bianchi's suggestion builds on the idea of implementing a 'luck scale', 'which would be developed by geneticists, physiologists, kinesiologist etc. in order to gage any unfair genetic advantage […]. The luck scale could be used to mitigate a variety of genetic endowments if certain features are recognized as contributing to unfair advantages in sport' (236f). However, combining fairness with other considerations (Teetzel, 2014) would only seem to perpetuate the current sex binary paradigm, as Bianchi's possible solution and Coggon, Hammond, and Holm's (2008) analysis make abundantly clear.

Gleaves and Lehrbach (2016) depart from the usual premise of sport being about skilfulness by dismissing this interpretation as the (sole) meaning of sport as a relatively new one and calling for a shift of the emphasis away from physical equivalence to other meaningful values of sport – hence going 'beyond the idea of fairness' (p. 323). In their approach they draw on meaningful narratives of sport, 'that sport is about telling ourselves a meaningful story about ourselves' (p. 318). They conclude that:

> …rather than including transgender and intersex athletes on the contingent fact that they do not upset the comparative test by having unfair advantages, a stronger rationale starts from the premise that sport is about meaningful narratives, that one of those narratives is a gendered narrative, that transgender and intersex athletes are not only participating in that gendered narrative, but significantly enriching and improving it, and that transgender and intersex athletes have as great a right to express gendered narratives as any athletes.
>
> (p. 321)

Accordingly, every athlete should be allowed to participate in their favoured gender category. Furthermore, they suggest that mixed-gender and gender-segregated competitions do not rule each other out.

Conclusion

In this chapter, I have mapped the various critical research approaches concerning sex regulation in sport mega-events. Criticism is rich and comes from various research traditions and fields. Some researchers base their critique against medical interventions on medico-scientific evidence themselves and argue for inclusion by virtue of showing that inter* and trans*athletes have no biological advantage. Others again suggest that this does not solve the problem as it is a cultural one, in that there is a desire for a clear gender binary that is projected on regulating biological sex. From their perspective, the concept of fairness in elite sport and sport mega-events needs to be renegotiated, as science cannot provide an answer to the dilemma. All of these approaches scrutinise the requirement for the medical regulation of healthy bodies on ethical and moral grounds. However, the practice of sex segregation per se is deeply intertwined or even underlies the whole matter (Behrensen, 2013; Coggon et al., 2008; Dworkin & Cooky, 2012; Gleaves & Lehrbach, 2016; Teetzel, 2014). That is, if there was no sex segregation to start with, no athlete would be discriminated against on the grounds of not fitting into the gender binary. Still, some researchers argue in favour of sex segregation because to them it still seems the best way of giving women as a group a chance to participate in organised elite sports (Behrensen, 2013; Coggon et al., 2008).

In this chapter I have also argued that many of the different perspectives are incommensurable. For instance, there is a discrepancy between essentialist and constructivist traditions, and, hence, gender mainstreaming and deconstructive approaches are contradictory in nature. Accordingly, these perspectives are hard to unify in one and the same policy. After the current debate attracted international media attention and individual athletes have appealed against the IAAF and IOC policies, the sporting bodies were prompted to move towards more inclusive policies. But science, policymakers and jurisdiction seem to face exactly the insurmountable problem of unifying various insights and objectives. That is, if policymakers want to establish equal opportunities for male and female athletes, they must also acknowledge the binary sex system. Hence, they cannot at the same time fall back on the deconstructivist notion of dichotomous sex/gender being a social construct, a differentiation that deconstructivism aims to break down. Accordingly, allegedly inclusive policies will always be at the expense of at least one interest group.

In its own ruling against the appeal of Caster Semenya in 2019, the CAS recognised that the current solutions are not fair but in fact discriminate against individuals, like Semenya, but that '[...] such discrimination is a necessary, reasonable and proportionate means of achieving the [...] objectives of preserving the integrity of female athletics [...]' (The Guardian, 2019).

However, critical research from fields other than the medico-sciences is scarcely, if at all, recognised by policymakers or the jurisdiction but is rather dismissed as opinion (Karkazis & Jordan-Young, 2018), i.e. policies solely rely on medico-scientific evidence, even though that very issue points to the fact that the solution is not to be found in the medico-sciences. In fact, I suggest that it is not gender non-conforming athletes, bodies or identities that constitute the issue but an essentialist, racial-colonial Western notion of science that brought forth a binary understanding of the world in the first place. In order to find solutions that do not involve medical interventions and that bypass the current sex testing regime, more research is hence needed on the ontology of sex and gender. This becomes particularly evident in the Black African notion of the ontology of inter*sex as shown by Magubane (2014). Consequently, this literature review calls for more postcolonial research to unfold the inherent racial gender binary logics of the sex regulations.

In order to move the debate about the inclusion of inter* and trans*athletes in elite sport and sport mega-events forward, I suggest that inclusiveness only comes with a change of paradigm, since the scientific traditions cannot overcome their disaccord on the question of 'What is a woman?' While at this juncture this seems insuperable in policymaking, the topic will nevertheless become increasingly important in sport mega-events in the years to come. It is therefore vital that academic research rethinks its epistemologies and ontologies concerning sex, gender, fairness and sporting competition.

Notes

1. At the end of 2019, the IAAF was renamed *World Athletics*. In this chapter I use the former name and its abbreviation IAAF.
2. Differences in sex development, in short DSD, is another term used for inter*sex variations. Some people prefer DSD to inter*sex if they do not identify as gender fluid, while others prefer inter*sex, because DSD pathologises their 'condition' (especially as DSD is sometimes also used as 'disorder in sex development'). In their latest regulations, the IAAF and IOC decided to use the term women with DSD.
3. From now on, I use the term women with DSD.
4. As trans*people do not identify with the sex ascribed to them at birth, they may wish to undergo a change of sex during life. However, not all trans*people wish to undergo surgery or medical intervention and may be content with a legal change of sex (which in most countries can only be achieved through medical intervention).
5. Regulations Governing Eligibility of Females with Hyperandrogenism to Compete in Women's Competition.
6. Regulations on Female Hyperandrogenism.
7. Which affects, depending on source, 5%–10% of women worldwide.
8. The IAAF added this to its 2018 regulations: 'Eligibility Regulations for the Female Classification (Athletes with Difference of Sex Development)'.
9. The establishment of the current eligibility criteria for the women's category is interdependent between IAAF and IOC. The key texts identified refer to either the IAAF or IOC regulations. For a precise overview of this interdependency, see Bavington (2019).
10. As shown above, in 2018, the rules were changed to specifically target *women with DSD and androgen sensitivity*. However, I still refer to the rules as hyperandrogenism rules because the 2018 rules draw on the (sporting bodies) concept of hyperandrogenism.

References

Asdal, K. (2005). Returning the kingdom to the king. A post-constructivist response to the critique of positivism. *Acta Sociologica, 48*(3), 253–261.

Barad, K. (2003). Posthumanist performativity: Toward an understanding of how matter comes to matter. *Signs, 28a*(3), 801–831.

Bavington, D. L. (2019). Sex control in women's sport: A history of the present regulations on hyperandrogenism in female athletes. In V. Krane (Ed.), *Sex, gender, and sexuality in sport. Queer inquiries* (pp. 181–202). New York, NY: Routledge.

Behrensen, M. (2013). In the halfway house of ill repute: Gender verification under a different name, still no contribution to fair play. *Sport, Ethics and Philosophy, 7*(4), 450–466.

Bermon, S., & Garnier, P. (2017). Serum androgen levels and their relation to performance in track and field: Mass spectrometry results from 2127 observations in male and female elite athletes. *British Journal of Sports Medicine, 51*(17), 1309–1314.

Bianchi, A. (2017). Transgender women in sport. *Journal of the Philosophy of Sport*, *44*(2), 229–242.

Butler, J. (1993). *Bodies that matter: On the discursive limits of "sex"*. New York, NY: Routledge.

Cahn, S. (1994). *Coming on strong: Gender and sexuality in twentieth century women's sport*. New York, NY: Free Press.

CAS. (2014). Dutee Chand V. Athletics Federation of India (AFI) & the International Association of Athletics Federations (IAAF). Retrieved from https://www.doping.nl/media/kb/3317/CAS%202014_A_3759%20Dutee%20Chand%20vs.%20AFI%20%26%20IAAF%20%28S%29.pdf. Accessed on January 30, 2020.

CAS. (2018). CAS 2018/O/5794 & CAS 2018/O/5798. Caster Semenya v. IAAF & Athletics South Africa v. IAAF. Retrieved from https://www.tas-cas.org/fileadmin/user_upload/CAS_Award_-_redacted_-_Semenya_ASA_IAAF.pdf. Accessed on January 21, 2020.

Cavanagh, S. L., & Sykes, H. (2006). Transsexual bodies at the Olympics: The International Olympic Committee's Policy on Transsexual Athletes at the 2004 Athens Summer Games. *Body & Society*, *12*(3), 75–102.

Coalter, F. (2008). Sport-in-development: Development for and through sport? In M. Nicholson & R. Hoye (Eds.), *Sport and social capital* (pp. 39–67). London, New York: Routledge.

Coggon, J., Hammond, N., & Holm, S. (2008). Transsexuals in sport-fairness and freedom, regulation and law. *Sport, Ethics and Philosophy*, *2*(1), 4–17.

Costello, C. (2014). Not a "medical miracle": Intersex reproduction and the medical enforcement of binary sex and gender. In M. Gibson (Ed.), *Queering motherhood: Narrative and theoretical perspectives* (pp. 63–80). Bradford, ON: Demeter Press.

Dworkin, S. L., & Cooky, C. (2012). Sport, sex segregation, and sex testing: Critical reflections of this unjust marriage. *The American Journal of Bioethics*, *12*(7), 21–23.

Eklund, E., Berglund, B., Labrie, F., Carlström, K., Ekström, L., & Hirschberg, A. (2017). Serum androgen profile and physical performance in women Olympic athletes. *British Journal of Sports Medicine*, *51*(17), 1301–1308.

Fausto-Sterling, A. (2000). *Sexing the body. Gender politics and the construction of sexuality*. New York, NY: Basic.

Foucault, M. (1976). *Histoire de la sexualité I. La volonté de savoir*. Paris: Gallimard.

Foucault, M. (1978). *Dispositive der Macht. Über Sexualität, Wissen und Wahrheit*. Berlin: Merve.

Gleaves, J., & Lehrbach, T. (2016). Beyond fairness: The ethics of inclusion for transgender and intersex athletes. *Journal of the Philosophy of Sport*, *43*(2), 311–326.

Harraway, D. (1985). Manifesto for cyborgs: Science, technology, and socialist feminism in the 1980s. *Socialist Review*, *80*, 65–108.

Hovden, J. (2012). Discourses and strategies for the inclusion of women in sport–The case of Norway. *Sport in Society*, *15*(3), 287–301.

IAAF. (2011). Regulations governing eligibility of females with hyperandrogenism to compete in women's competition. Retrieved from https://www.sportsintegrityinitiative.com/wp-content/uploads/2016/02/IAAF-Regulations-Governing-Eligibility-of-Females-with-Hyperandrogenism-to-Compete-in-Women%E2%80%99s-Competition-In-force-as-from-1st-May-2011-6.pdf. Accessed on June 29, 2020.

IAAF. (2018). Eligibility regulations for the female classification (athletes with differences of sex development). Retrieved from https://www.worldathletics.org/news/press-release/eligibility-regulations-for-female-classifica. Accessed on June 29, 2020.

Ingle, S. (2020). Caster Semenya's Olympic hopes fade as runner loses testosterone rules appeal. *The Guardian*. Retrieved from https://www.theguardian.com/sport/2020/sep/08/caster-semenya-loses-appeal-against-world-athletics-testosterone-rules. Accessed on September 29, 2020.

IOC. (2012). IOC regulations on female hyperandrogenism. Retrieved from https://stillmed.olympic.org/Documents/Commissions_PDFfiles/Medical_commission/2012-06-22-IOC-Regulations-on-Female-Hyperandrogenism-eng.pdf. Accessed on June 29, 2020.

IOC. (2014). IOC regulations on female hyperandrogenism. Retrieved from https://stillmed.olympic.org/Documents/Commissions_PDFfiles/Medical_commission/IOC-Regulations-on-Female-Hyperandrogenism.pdf. Accessed on June 29, 2020.

IOC. (2015). IOC consensus meeting on sex reassignment and hyperandrogenism. November 2015. Retrieved from https://stillmed.olympic.org/Documents/Commissions_PDFfiles/Medical_commission/2015-11_ioc_consensus_meeting_on_sex_reassignment_and_hyperandrogenism-en.pdf. Accessed on June 21, 2020.

ISNA. (2008). Intersex conditions. Retrieved from https://isna.org/faq/conditions/. Accessed on June 20, 2020.

Jordan-Young, R., Sönksen, P., & Karkazis, K. (2014). Sex, health, and athletes. *British Medical Journal, 384*, g2926.

Karkazis, K., & Carpenter, M. (2018). Impossible "choices": The inherent harms of regulating women's testosterone in sport. *Bioethical Inquiry, 15*(4), 579–587.

Karkazis, K., & Jordan-Young, R. (2018). The power of testosterone: Obscuring race and regional bias in the regulation of women athletes. *Feminist Formations, 30*(2), 1–39.

Magubane, Z. (2014). Spectacles and scholarship: Caster Semenya, intersex studies, and the problem of race in feminist theory. *Sings: Journal of Women in Culture and Society, 39*(3), 761–785.

Mayring, P. (2014). *Qualitative content analysis: Theoretical foundation, basic procedures and software solution*. Klagenfurt: ssoar.

McKinnon, R. (2013). Getting luck properly under control. *Metaphilosphy, 44*(4), 496–511.

Messner, M. (1988). Sport and male domination: The female athlete as contested ideological terrain. *Sociology of Sport Journal, 5*(3), 197–211.

Moi, T. (2005). *Sex. Gender and the body: The student edition of what is a woman?* Oxford: Oxford University Press.

Molnar, G., & Kelly, J. (2013). *Sport, exercise and social theory: An introduction*. London: Routledge.

Pieper, L. P. (2014). Sex testing and the maintenance of western femininity in international sport. *International Journal of the History of Sport, 31*(13), 1557–1576.

Pieper, L. P. (2016). 'Preserving la difference': The elusiveness of sex-segregated sport. *Sport in Society, 19*(8–9), 1138–1155.

Rupert, J. L. (2011). Genitals to genes: The history and biology of gender verification in the Olympics. *CBMH/BCHM, 28*(2), 339–365.

Somerville, S. (1994). Scientific racism and the emergence of the homosexual body. *Journal of the History of Sexuality, 5*(2), 243–266.

Sönksen, P. H., Bavington, L. D., Boehning, T., Cowan, D., & Guha, N. (2018). Hyperandrogenism controversy in elite women's sport: An examination and critique of recent evidence. *British Journal of Sports Medicine, 52*(23), 1481–1482.

Sullivan, C. F. (2011). Gender verification and gender policies in elite sport: Eligibility and "fair play". *Journal of Sport & Social Issues, 35*(4), 400–419.

Sykes, H. (2006). Transsexual and transgender policies in sport. *Women in Sport & Physical Activity Journal, 15*(1), 3–13.

Tannenbaum, C., & Bekker, S. (2019). Sex, gender, and sports. *British Medical Journal, 364*, l1120. doi:10.1136/bmj.l1120

Teetzel, S. (2014). The onus of inclusivity: Sport policies and the enforcement of the women's category in sport. *Journal of the Philosophy of Sport, 41*(1), 113–127.

The Guardian. (2019, May 1). 'IAAF rules necessary to preserve integrity of female athletics,' says Cas on Caster Semenya [video file]. *The Guardian*. Retrieved from https://www.theguardian.com/sport/2019/may/01/caster-semenya-loses-landmark-legal-case-iaaf-athletics. Accessed on January 15, 2020.

Torraco, R. J. (2005). Writing integrative literature reviews: Guidelines and examples. *Human Resource Development Review, 4*(3), 356–367.

World Athletics. (2019). World athletics eligibility regulations for transgender athletes. Retrieved from https://www.worldathletics.org/search/?q=transgender. Accessed on June 21, 2020.

WPATH. (2012). Standards of care for the health of transsexual, transgender, and gender-nonconforming people. Retrieved from https://www.wpath.org/media/cms/Documents/SOC%20v7/Standards%20of%20Care_V7%20Full%20Book_English.pdf. Accessed on January 15, 2020.

Chapter 3

Ethical Relativism and Sport Mega-Event Gendered Discourses: Uneasiness towards the Dominant Play of Women in Sport

Lindsey Darvin and Ann Pegoraro

Introduction

Over the past few decades, women have made significant inroads in the field of sport with more opportunities to participate than ever before (Women's Sport Foundation, 2018). In the United States, participation rates at present have experienced increases of roughly 1000% compared with the late 1970s. While the participation rates of women in sport have increased substantially, the coverage and exposure of this same population throughout the mainstream media remains drastically low. The lack of coverage is often due to masculine privilege and stereotypical norms associated with the industry by stakeholders, fans and viewers alike (Darvin & Demara, 2020). However, in one arena, women's sport mega-events, the coverage of women's teams and female athletes approaches that of their men counterparts.

For the 2019 FIFA Women's World Cup, Fox Sports, the broadcast partner for the United States, covered the United States Women's National team (USWNT) games on television, live streaming and used their social platforms to produce pre-game and post-game content. For the USWNT first game, a 13-0 win over Thailand, Fox Sports social platforms received over 7 million views, a 528% increase over numbers for the 2015 Women's World Cup. Their live Twitter show, FIFA Women's World Cup Now, saw a 49% increase in daily viewership over the same show for the Men's 2018 World Cup (Sporttechie, 2019). With all of these eyes on the women's event, discussion of the harmful gendered and stereotyped opinions of the behaviours, appearance, and dominance of women athletes and teams was heightened in this mega-event environment. With increased visibility and international viewership often comes a chance for increased scrutiny of women in sport.

Overall, sport is one of the most masculine practices present in today's society. Masculinity in sport is often celebrated and provides men with ample opportunities to display their masculine strengths, while women are largely forced to tirelessly maintain their femininity (Darvin & Sagas, 2017). From an occupational standpoint, women are found in more traditionally feminine roles within sport

Sport, Gender and Mega-Events, 57–70
Copyright © 2022 by Emerald Publishing Limited
All rights of reproduction in any form reserved
doi:10.1108/978-1-83982-936-920211009

organisations (e.g., lower level coaching, lower level administration), while men maintain the majority of leadership positions both in coaching (e.g., head coach) and administration (e.g., general manager, athletic director) (Acosta & Carpenter, 2014; Burton, 2015; Darvin, Pegoraro, & Berri, 2018). This male privilege extends past the specific types of positions that men and women occupy in sport. The emphasis on masculinity in sport serves to exclude feminine attributes from entering the sphere and affirms men's power not only over sport but also over women.

It has been asserted that sports 'actively construct boys and men to exhibit, value, and reproduce traditional notions of masculinity' (Anderson, 2009, p. 4). More specifically, sport operates as a space to define and reproduce hegemonic masculinity. Within this space, heterosexual and physically dominant forms of masculinity have maintained male dominance through the suppression and subordination of women and femininity. Historically, sport has always been framed in a masculine context, to the distinct benefit of (some) male participants, as organisations consistently place a great deal of emphasis on sport's ability to transform boys into men and men into gods. This gendered nature of sport extends past the sport organisation and seeps into the mainstream media. According to Jarratt (1990), women athletes fight an uphill battle to gain recognition for their athletic accomplishments. Just as Jarratt (1990) attested to roughly 30 years ago, this uphill battle has continued for women athletes as they attempt to gain additional media coverage opportunities for their sporting achievements.

The general public's negative perceptions regarding women athletes have made it difficult for large portions of present-day society to accept that women have the ability to successfully compete in sport. Shaping the general public's perceptions of women athletes is partially the role of the mainstream media, but the media has been lacking in sufficient and thoughtful coverage. For example, in a study conducted by Cheska (1981), when a basketball game was announced on television, the general public felt differently about the score based solely on the gender of the team competing. The score was 41-40, and when the audience was informed that this score referred to a female team, they attributed the lack of scoring to a lack of basketball skill (Cheska, 1981). Conversely, when the audience was informed that the score referred to a male team, they attributed the lack of scoring to successful and well-executed defending (Cheska, 1981). Although this example is roughly 40 years old, it provides evidence to support the deep-rooted notion that the coverage of women athletes is not only substantially lower than the coverage of men athletes but also lower in quality. This pattern is still evident today (Cooky, Messner, & Musto, 2015).

In an attempt to off-set these gendered associations, sport mega-events such as the FIFA Women's World Cup and the Olympic Games provide a much-needed opportunity for women athletes to receive higher levels of visibility. This visibility and the increased marketing efforts for the mega-events provide the public with some of the most consistent opportunities to view women's sporting events, either in person or virtually. With an improved chance that individuals will view women's sport during sport mega-events comes the increased possibility that an individual will then view or attend a future women's sport contest as well (Darvin & Sagas, 2017). Previous research has determined that once an individual views at least one half of a professional women's sporting event, they are twice as likely to view another women's sporting event in the future (Darvin & Sagas, 2017). Results further indicated that individuals who had never viewed a professional women's sporting event were significantly more likely to state that they would not seek to view one in the future, due to low event expectations (Darvin & Sagas, 2017). Therefore, the importance of increased coverage of women's sporting events, such as that which has been experienced during sport mega-events, will likely continue to increase fandom and viewership numbers into the future.

That being said, with this increased visibility during mega-events, there is also an increased likelihood that an intensified level of critique of women athletes and teams will ensue. For that reason, this chapter will lay the groundwork for a critical discussion of the perceptions of women athlete behaviours, specifically within a highly visible, international, sport mega-event setting. This will be accomplished via a review of previous research on women athletes in the media, along with a critical analysis of the perceptions of the 'dominant play' of women athletes in mega-events, through the application of ethical relativism, gender stereotypes, role congruity theory (RCT) and social role theory (SRT).

Women Athletes in the Media

In contrast to the gains made in sport participation for women athletes, media coverage of women's sports has long been inequitable and often inferior in comparison to men (Cooky et al., 2015). Previous research suggests that women's sport receives just 2% of total sport media coverage (Cooky et al., 2015), despite women making up 40% of all sport participants in North America (Kane, 2013). When women athletes do receive coverage by traditional media outlets, their portrayal is often quite gendered. As noted by Mean and Kassing (2008, p. 127), 'gender remains the primary categorization of women athletes, reproducing female athletes as women who play sport rather than as athletes first and foremost'. Traditional media often portray women athletes as girlfriends, wives or mothers, with visuals and stories focussing on their femininity as opposed to their athletic abilities and achievements. While Cooky et al. (2015) suggested that sexualised coverage of women athletes is dissipating, they also noted that media outlets often cover women's sports in a manner that conforms to conventional gender norms (e.g., increased media coverage of 'gender-appropriate' sports like tennis).

When researchers have focussed on traditional media coverage for men and women athletes (Lebel, Pegoraro, & Harman, 2018), they often conclude that women athletes are predominately depicted in feminine ways, including frequent mentions of their families or personal lives, while men athletes are often portrayed as more powerful and dominant (e.g., Knight & Giuliano, 2002, 2003). Much of this research has focussed on how mass media visually portrays women athletes in both broadcast media and photographs (e.g., Angelini, MacArthur, & Billings, 2012; Billings & Angelini, 2007; Fink & Kensicki, 2002; Hardin, Lynn, & Walsdorf, 2005; Jones, 2006). Researchers have demonstrated that the portrayal of women athletes can have substantial social and economic outcomes in terms of both the general acceptance of women athletes in society and their marketability as elite athletes (Kim, Walkosz, & Iverson, 2006). While this body of research has predominantly focussed on traditional media, the rise of digital platforms has brought with it a slew of new challenges, including new outlets for reactions to women during athletic competitions. New research is needed to examine this.

The growing popularity of social media platforms and their widespread adoption by athletes have made women athletes more visible and subject to public discussion (Allison & Pegoraro, 2018). Although some women's sports enjoy measures of popularity and material reward, mass media attention to women's sport remains persistently low (Bruce, 2016; Cooky et al., 2015). Social media has expanded the number and type of people able to create and disseminate information about women's sports. Social media has been an important space for fans of women's sports, where the very fact of being neglected in the mainstream generates tight bonds among members of the online women's sports community (Creedon, 2014). Social media generate a 'particularly potent sense of coherence and community on the Internet for fans of women's sports' (Van, 2014, p. 441).

As these digital media opportunities have increased, many hoped women's representation in sport might showcase more of their athletic abilities and strength; but the results of this remain mixed. While the digital media landscape has in some cases provided an outlet for strong female sport brands, it has also reflected deeply ingrained female stereotypes and, at times, revealed an ugly, vicious and patriarchal digital culture (e.g., Clavio & Eagleman, 2011; Hum, Chamberlin, Hambright, & Bevan, 2011; Kane, LaVoi, & Fink, 2013; Lebel & Danylchuk, 2014). As noted by Allison and Pegoraro (2018, p. 213), 'Few studies have focused on how social media users construct and communicate the meanings they attach to women athletes, and none examine responses to women's transgression on social media'.

The experiences of women athletes and teams in the mainstream media, along with the perceptions of women athletes by the general public, are largely influenced by both socialised and implicit barriers. These prevailing barriers or frameworks associated with the obstacles faced by women athletes and teams include gender stereotypes, RCT and SRT. These frameworks detail the background and rationale for the development of hurdles and biased opinions faced by women athletes when compared to their men counterparts. Gender stereotyping has influenced not only the performance and behaviour expectations of girl and women athletes but also the perception of this population during and throughout highly visible sport mega-events.

Barriers for Women in Sport

Gender Stereotypes in Sport Media

Within the sport media context, it can be argued that a lack of coverage of women teams and athletes has served to further hinder societal opinions and subsequent expectations of women in sport. More specifically, it can be argued that the perceived lack of interest in women's athletics is the result of social practices that have been carried out by particular institutions, such as the mainstream media. If an audience is not provided an opportunity to view women athletes as often as men athletes through media outlets, the stereotypical and socialised opinions regarding women athlete behaviour and ability will be difficult to change.

Additionally, the perceived lack of viewer interest of women in sport has developed through gender stereotyping and discrimination. Gender stereotyping in the mainstream media has predominantly been equated to the sexualisation and objectification of women athletes; and young girls are often socialised into performing within the sport context in manners that reinforce femininity (e.g., low levels of contact, minimal arguing with officials, not too physical), while young boys are often socialised into performing acts that reinforce their masculinity (e.g., tackling, hitting, explosive remarks, in-game fighting) (Darvin & Sagas, 2017).

While men in professional sport overtly cultivate their public images and pursue endorsements for commercial gain, women athletes are often perceived more negatively for similar behaviours. As a result, women are often held more accountable to expectations of being an inspiration for others, such as acting in nurturing ways and pursuing sport for motivations beyond fame and fortune (Crosby, 2016; Douglas, 2014). Any perceived transgression or negative behaviour may thus be perceived as more severe for women than men as this is viewed as a violation of gender norms, as well as social and/or legal structures (Brazeal, 2013; Brown, Billings, Mastro, & Brown-Devlin, 2015; Douglas, 2014).

Compton (2013) looked at the case of the University of New Mexico soccer player Elizabeth Lambert, who rose to brief fame and notoriety, becoming a household name in 2009 for a rough play during which she pulled an opponent to the ground by her hair during a soccer match. This action was perceived as well outside the bounds of acceptable play, even though men routinely use similar levels of force in soccer, and Lambert was ultimately suspended from the team. In a study of Lambert's image repair after the incident, Compton (2013) concluded that different standards trigger disapproval for men and women; 'when a female takes it too far in a soccer game, it becomes national news' (p. 263).

The emergence of social media and its widespread adoption by athletes has made women athletes and their activities both inside and outside of sport more visible and therefore increasingly subjected to public discussion. Although some women's sports enjoy some degree of popularity and material reward, media attention to women's sport continues to remain persistently low (Bruce, 2016; Cooky et al., 2015). Social media have expanded the attention from fans, and a broader number and range of people can now create and disseminate information about women's sports. Social media has been an important space for fans of women's sports and generates a strong sense of community for fans of women's sports (Van, 2014). That being said, social media can also turn into a mob mentality and provides for essentially an 'open season' attitude amongst some users. While few studies have looked at how social media users construct and communicate meanings they attach to women athletes and any behaviour considered contrary to social norms (e.g., Allison & Pegoraro, 2018; Allison, Pegoraro, Frederick, & Thompson, 2019), there are prevailing frameworks that assist in our understanding of the reactions to the dominant play of women athletes.

Role Congruity and Social Role Theory

In conjunction with the existence of gender stereotyping in sport, previous investigations of media coverage have uncovered two dominant recurring themes in relation to women athletes and teams including (1) that the amount of coverage devoted to women athletes, teams, and sporting events is drastically lower than the amount of coverage men athletes, teams, and sporting events receive (e.g., Cooky et al., 2015), and (2) when women athletes do receive media coverage, they are often portrayed in ways that work to emphasise their femininity rather than their athletic achievements (Darvin & Sagas, 2017). The emphasis placed on portraying women athletes and teams in a manner that is feminine often results in stereotypical expectations of the behaviour of women athletes (Darvin, 2020; Hancock & Hums, 2016; Schull & Kihl, 2018). This stereotyping can be associated with the theoretical frames of RCT and SRT. These two frameworks detail the rationale behind stereotyped and implicit associations of women in male-dominated spaces such as sport (Darvin, 2020; Hancock & Hums, 2016; Schull & Kihl, 2018).

RCT suggests that women who display more masculine behaviours and mannerisms fail to align with prescribed gender roles (Darvin, 2020; Eagly & Karau, 2002). In addition to the tenets and application of RCT to women athletes in sport media, SRT is an additional framework that is often utilised when examining and exposing discrimination and bias towards women in male-dominated environments (Darvin, 2020; Eagly & Wood, 2011; Hancock & Hums, 2016; Schull & Kihl, 2018). SRT combines a variety of disciplinary accounts that aim to solve the profound question of behavioural differences and similarities between men and women and boys and girls (Eagly & Wood, 2011). SRT establishes that

> … sex differences and similarities in behaviour reflect gender role beliefs that in turn represent people's perceptions of men's and women's social roles in the society in which they live.
>
> (Eagly & Wood, 2011, p. 459)

As a result, stereotypes, or gender role beliefs, often form as people are observing the behaviours of men and women. From these observations, individuals infer that the sexes possess corresponding characteristics and behaviours that are natural to their biological makeup (Eagly & Carli, 2003).

These gender roles are incredibly powerful, as they appear to reflect innate attributes associated with the sexes that make these stereotypes appear natural while also inevitable (Darvin, 2020; Eagly & Wood, 2011). In turn, those gender role beliefs fuel gender identities that often motivate an individual to respond via self-regulatory processes (Darvin, 2020; Witt & Wood, 2010). A critical point of emphasis for women athletes and teams as it relates to the tenets of SRT stems from the use of one's gender identity as a standard against which to regulate one's behaviour (Witt & Wood, 2010). As such, the pressure and expectation of conforming to one's gender identity for women athletes can have negative effects on individuals who are thought to lack the stereotypical qualities essential to maintain the status quo in a given society.

SRT has been utilised most frequently within the male-dominated environment (e.g., the sport industry) discourse as a way to frame the biological and psychological socialisation processes that have influenced the division of labour and subsequently the discrimination faced by minority individuals (Eagly & Carli, 2003). SRT is largely concerned with the occupations and roles women and men maintain within society as it applies to the influence of socialisation. The interesting facet of this framework centres upon the merge of both biology and psychology.

Women, who are biologically the child bearers in a society, often assume positions that tend to be associated with emotional labour, such as caregiving, raising children, and working within the home. These associations subsequently influence the behaviours that are expected to be displayed by women, such as increased levels of empathy and emotional intelligence, regardless of context. Men, on the other hand, who do not bear children and are not deemed implicitly responsible for roles that require emotional labour, are permitted and expected to behave in ways that do not lend themselves towards high levels of empathy. With this aspect of biology in mind, a distinct division of behaviour and expectations for men and women emerged throughout society, which has led to both implicit and explicit biases. Within sport, and specifically for athletes and teams, the outcome of such a distinct separation of the sexes often manifests itself in discriminatory perceptions and evaluations of women participants if they do not display signs of empathy and caring during an athletic pursuit.

Ethical Relativism

The gender role beliefs ingrained within present society are arguably deeply connected to the ethical considerations associated with one's behaviour and attitude. Said differently, the behaviours of women athletes and teams are often judged based on whether or not those women are acting and behaving in accordance with ways that are stereotypically feminine. Based on these socialised gender role norms, men athletes and teams are often expected and permitted to display hypermasculine and dominating behaviours while their women counterparts are expected to tone down their masculinity in similar contexts. The perceptions of any misalignments often lend themselves to more advanced criticism of the ethical or unethical conduct of women athletes. These critiques may be heightened within international mega-event competition, given that cultural inconsistencies lend themselves to a diverse range of opinions as to the correct or incorrect behaviours of women athletes and teams.

These associations generate an additional barrier to equity throughout sport as discriminatory judgements are defended based upon individual conclusions of what is morally correct or incorrect in a sport competition context for women. While this is often the case when women athletes perform in ways that are not considered feminine or empathetic, the theory of ethical relativism calls into question the development of those associations while also elaborating on the cultural distinctions that appear to rationalise the critiques themselves.

The theory of ethical relativism argues that each individual determines what is true and therefore each point of view is equally valid (Lumpkin, 2016). This theory operates under the premise that cultural norms often differ and the morals associated therein tend to evolve as a particular society changes over time. Ethical relativism holds that in the process of deciding whether an action is morally right or wrong, one must reflect on the ethical norms of the society in which the action took place. From a sport competition perspective, this would also mean that one must take into account the ethical and cultural norms of the nation and/or society from which the team originates and represents. For example, an action that may be considered morally wrong in one society or nation may be considered morally right or at least acceptable in another. The tenants of ethical relativism would largely manifest themselves when comparing the differing levels of opportunity, support, and acceptance of women and girls in sport among a variety of nations.

When it comes to female involvement in sport, whether based on participation or fandom, some nations have maintained cultural preferences that limit or have previously altogether banned women and girl athletes and spectators. Iran banned women from attending soccer matches from 1981 to 2019, and Saudi Arabia allowed women to attend a soccer match for the first time in 2018. In some of these more extreme examples, ethicists may reject the tenets of ethical relativism, claiming instead that regardless of cultural norms there are certain fundamental underlying moral principles that should not differ by country.

Beyond the extreme examples, additional factors in particular contexts may generate a similar disagreement with the tenets of ethical relativism. Specifically, gender stereotyping may influence the presumed fundamental underlying moral principles that society at large has adopted over time. Throughout the sport industry, social norms largely dictate the opportunities, access, and behaviours that are offered or expected of a variety of diverse athlete groups. Ethical relativism, however, asserts that there is no universal code of what is ethically right and wrong (Lumpkin, 2016). Instead, each culture offers its own perspective on morality and the behaviours that are deemed permissible within that domain (Lumpkin, 2016). If the actions of women athletes are analysed in relation to ethical relativism, one would need to consider the cultural norms of the nation of origin prior to providing judgement.

Gendered Evaluations of Dominant Play

A distinct example of an application of ethical relativism in sport, and a subsequent impact on implicitly biased perceptions of women athletes and teams, came during the 2019 FIFA Women's World Cup. During this international sport mega-event, the United States Women's National Team (USWNT) undoubtedly dominated play in record setting fashion. The USWNT scored the most goals by a team during any FIFA World Cup (26), their top players – Megan Rapinoe and Alex Morgan – combined for 12 of these goals and the most of any team duo for

2019, and the USWNT pushed their FIFA World Cup Championship total to 4, the most of any nation. While the USWNT was dominant overall during their pursuit of the 2019 Women's World Cup, as the favourite team entering the mega-event they were under intense media scrutiny both abroad and at home in the United States. During their early round games, several specific 'incidents' garnered a lot of media attention and distinct criticism towards the women athletes.

First, the USWNT beat the Thailand National Women's Soccer Team by a score of 13-0. The USWNT's lopsided win over Thailand in the opening game received a lot of media attention for the score and what it showed about the inequity in women's soccer, as well as how the US players celebrated every goal. These celebrations included actions of excitement, exuberant displays, and joyful interactions as the players would run around the field in search of teammates to embrace. While these were all highly common actions for the sport and within the North American soccer culture, media and social media users criticised their behaviour as unsportsmanlike and ultimately as unladylike, with calls for 'decency' and 'respect' (White, 2019). As international criticism heightened, criticism at the national level within the United States followed. For example, an online feud between Megan Rapinoe and US President Trump resulted in her now famous 'how do you like me now' goal scoring pose with her arms outstretched and head pointing up towards the sky. After a video circulated of Rapinoe stating she would not go the 'F$%ing White House' when the team won the World Cup, a war of Twitter words erupted with President Trump calling her out and teammate Ali Krueger doubling down on not visiting the White House. Rapinoe responded by striking a pose after scoring a goal in the quarterfinals versus host nation France – a pose that could be construed as 'how do you like me now' or perhaps even a middle finger like gesture to naysayers alike (see Turtiainen, Chapter 7). This was instantly turned into a meme on social media (Moran, 2019).

Overall, the media and social media reaction to the dominant play of these United States women athletes on an international scale was highly toxic (Vertelney, 2019). The USWNT was described as 'classless', 'disgraceful' and 'villains' following their overwhelming victory. While women athletes typically compete at a national level within more consistent cultural associations regarding sporting behaviours, international sport mega-events can generate an added layer of cultural inconsistencies. These inconsistencies lend themselves to additional barriers and critiques of women athletes, as they are not only misaligned with stereotypical feminine behaviours but also may partake in actions that misalign with cultural standards of a particular competing nation. Men athletes, on the other hand, are at less risk of the same cultural critiques, as sport has historically been celebrated as a hypermasculine pursuit regardless of the nation. Through a combination of stereotyped gendered roles and the visibility of athletes during international sport mega-events, the judgements and critiques of women athlete behaviours and actions may be largely based on flawed perceptions of what is ethically right or wrong in a particular sporting context. Application of the theory of ethical relativism allows for a more well-rounded understanding of these added barriers for women athletes on an international scale. In the example of the US women's soccer team at FIFA (2019), given that this mega-event was an international competition, criticisms were often based on culturally charged beliefs regarding how women athletes should compete and behave. The claim that these women athletes were somehow unethical through their dominant display runs counter to the same cultural benefits that men athletes are awarded simply because men are less likely to be implicitly and culturally associated with empathy, modesty and caregiving.

Under the tenants of ethical relativism, the argument would be that each culture and sub-culture differs and therefore the actions of a group, or sport team, within a specific culture should be judged based on their own forms of socialisation. The USWNT behaviours may misalign more severely with the cultural norms of nations where women have not been provided the same sporting opportunities for as long a time period. While the United States has a sport culture for women that still lags behind that of the men's, the development and support of women in sport within US society is often considered near the top of the pack internationally.

Scoring 13 goals in a mega-event World Cup setting, the highest level of competition for a group of soccer players, is exceptional and not to be compared with any other sport competition setting. That being said, the added visibility associated with a sport mega-event, combined with the fact that the event itself was international, provides evidence to support the notion that women athletes have to overcome an additional barrier related to the ethics of dominating an opponent. If women athletes do not show empathy for an opponent, it is clear that they run the risk of being judged as out of alignment with their perceived gender role. As a result, even in a setting that provides a great opportunity for increased visibility for women in sport, incredible challenges still remain to overcome the largely implicit gender role beliefs that exist both within specific societies and on a global scale.

Conclusion

The perceptions and expectations of women athletes and teams throughout society have been consistently limited by traditional gender norms. These socialised gender beliefs influence the implicit roles, behaviours, and appearance of women throughout society, but are heightened in male-dominated spaces such as sport. Traditional gender roles have a variety of impacts on women athletes and teams, such as inconsistencies with player behaviour and team actions when compared with their men counterparts. Perceptions of how women athletes compete and subsequently celebrate their success are often measured against gender role norms rather than sporting culture norms and the behaviour exhibited by their men counterparts.

Overall, a combination of the frameworks introduced in this chapter (gender stereotypes, RCT, SRT, ethical relativism) within the scope of sport mega-events and the US women's national soccer team example suggests that the actions of women athletes are often implicitly placed within a highly critiqued state and that their sporting behaviours are debated more harshly than their men counterparts. Not only may women fall subject to any perceived misalignment with femininity, detailed via SRT and RCT, but under the tenets of ethical relativism these women athletes may also be critiqued based on a misalignment with subjective, culturally derived moral norms and codes of appropriate behaviour. While the dominant play of women in a sport context may not align with stereotypical expectations of empathy and caregiving for women, those perceived misalignments do not warrant the claims or suggestions that women athletes are behaving in a manner that is unethical. Instead, it is important for viewers to consider the implicit biases they may base their critiques upon when it comes to competitive women's sport, especially within the international mega-event context which brings together athletes, coaches, media, and spectators from all over the world.

References

Acosta, R. V., & Carpenter, L. J. (2014). *Women in intercollegiate sport: A longitudinal, national study thirty-seven year update 1922–2014.* Accosta-Carpenter.

Allison, R., & Pegoraro, A. (2018). Abby Wambach: G.O.A.T. (Greatest of All Time) or just a goat? In A. Billings (Eds) *Reputational challenges in sport* (pp. 210–226) New York, NY: Routledge.

Allison, R., Pegoraro, A., Frederick, E., & Thompson, A. (2019). When women athletes transgress: An exploratory study of image repair and social media response. *Sport and Society.*

Anderson, E. D. (2009). The maintenance of masculinity among the stakeholders of sport. *Sport Management Review, 12*(1), 3–14.

Angelini, J. R., MacArthur, P. J., & Billings, A. C. (2012). What's the gendered story? Vancouver's prime time Olympic glory on NBC. *Journal of Broadcasting & Electronic Media, 56*(2), 261–279.

Billings, A. C., & Angelini, J. R. (2007). Packaging the games for viewer consumption: Gender, ethnicity, and nationality in NBC's coverage of the 2004 Summer Olympics. *Communication Quarterly, 55*(1), 95–111.

Brazeal, L. (2013). Belated remorse: Serena Williams' image repair rhetoric at the 2009 U.S. Open. In J. R. Blaney, L. Lippert, & J. S. Smith (Eds.), *Repairing the athlete's image: Studies in sports image restoration* (pp. 239–252). Lanham, MD: Lexington Books.

Brown, K. A., Billings, A. C., Mastro, D., & Brown-Devlin, N. (2015). Changing the image repair equation: Impact of race and gender on sport-related transgressions. *Journalism & Mass Communication Quarterly, 92*(2), 487–506.

Bruce, T. (2016). *Terra ludus: A novel about media, gender and sport.* Springer.

Burton, L. J. (2015). Underrepresentation of women in sport leadership: A review of research. *Sport Management Review, 18*(2), 155–165.

Cheska, A. T. (1981). Games of the native North Americans. In R. F. G. Lüschen, G. H. Sage (Eds.), *Handbook of social science of sport* (pp. 49–77). Stipes.

Clavio, G., & Eagleman, A. N. (2011). Gender and sexually suggestive images in sports blogs. *Journal of Sport Management, 25*(4), 295–304.

Compton, J. L. (2013). Unsports(wo)manlike conduct: An image repair analysis of Elizabeth Lambert, the University of New Mexico, and the NCAA. In J. R. Blaney, L. Lippert, & J. S. Smith (Eds.), *Repairing the athlete's image: Studies in sports image restoration* (pp. 253–264). Lanham, MD: Lexington Books.

Cooky, C., Messner, M. A., & Musto, M. (2015). "It's dude time!" A quarter century of excluding women's sports in televised news and highlight shows. *Communication & Sport, 3*(3), 261–287.

Creedon, P. (2014). Women, social media, and sport: Global digital communication weaves a web. *Television & New Media, 15*(8), 711–716.

Crosby, E. D. (2016). Chased by the double bind: Intersectionality and the disciplining of Lolo Jones. *Women's Studies in Communication, 39*(2), 228–248.

Darvin, L. (2020). Voluntary occupational turnover and the experiences of former intercollegiate women assistant coaches. *Journal of Vocational Behavior, 116*, 103349.

Darvin, L., & Demara, E. H. (2020). The emergence, experiences, and empowerment of women administrators, coaches, and athletes. In T. Moeke-Pickering, S. Cote-Meek, & A. Pegoraro (Eds.), *Critical reflections and politics on advancing women in the academy* (pp. 87–104). Hershey, PA: IGI Global.

Darvin, L., Pegoraro, A., & Berri, D. (2018). Are men better leaders? An investigation of head coaches' gender and individual players' performance in amateur and professional women's basketball. *Sex Roles, 78*(7–8), 455–466.

Darvin, L., & Sagas, M. (2017). Objectification in sport media: Influences on a future women's sporting event. *International Journal of Sport Communication, 10*(2), 178–195.

Douglas, D. D. (2014). Forget me…not: Marion Jones and the politics of punishment. *Journal of Sport and Social Issues, 38*(1), 3–22.

Eagly, A. H., & Carli, L. L. (2003). Finding gender advantage and disadvantage: Systematic research integration is the solution. *The Leadership Quarterly, 14*(6), 851–859.

Eagly, A. H., & Karau, S. J. (2002). Role congruity theory of prejudice toward female leaders. *Psychological Review, 109*(3), 573.

Eagly, A. H., & Wood, W. (2011). Feminism and the evolution of sex differences and similarities. *Sex Roles, 64*(9–10), 758–767.

FIFA. (2019). *2019 Women's World Cup*. FIFA. https://www.fifa.com/tournaments/womens/womensworldcup/france2019.

Fink, J. S., & Kensicki, L. J. (2002). An imperceptible difference: Visual and textual constructions of femininity in Sports Illustrated and Sports Illustrated for Women. *Mass Communication & Society, 5*(3), 317–339.

Hancock, M. G., & Hums, M. A. (2016). "A leaky pipeline?" perceptions of barriers and supports of female senior-level administrators in NCAA division I athletic departments. *Sport Management Review, 19*(2), 198–210.

Hardin, M., Lynn, S., & Walsdorf, K. (2005). Challenge and conformity on "contested terrain": Images of women in four women's sport/fitness magazines. *Sex Roles, 53*(1–2), 105–117.

Hum, N. J., Chamberlin, P. E., Hambright, B. L., Portwood, A. C., Schat, A. C., & Bevan, J. L. (2011). A picture is worth a thousand words: A content analysis of Facebook profile photographs. *Computers in Human Behavior, 27*(5), 1828–1833.

Jarratt, E. H. (1990). Feminist issues in sport. *Women's Studies International Forum, 13*(5), 491–499.

Jones, A. H. (2011). Visual and verbal gender cues in the televised coverage of the 2010 Winter Olympics. *International Journal of Interdisciplinary Social Sciences*, *6*(2), 199–216.

Kane, M. J. (2013). The better sportswomen get, the more the media ignore them. *Communication & Sport*, *1*(3), 231–236.

Kane, M. J., LaVoi, N. M., & Fink, J. S. (2013). Exploring elite female athletes' interpretations of sport media images: A window into the construction of social identity and "selling sex" in women's sports. *Communication & Sport*, *1*(3), 269–298.

Kim, E., Walkosz, B. J., & Iverson, J. (2006). USA Today's coverage of the top women golfers, 1998–2001. *The Howard Journal of Communications*, *17*(4), 307–321.

Knight, J. L., & Giuliano, T. A. (2001). He's a Laker; she's a "looker": The consequences of gender-stereotypical portrayals of male and female athletes by the print media. *Sex Roles*, *45*(3), 217–229.

Knight, J. L., & Giuliano, T. A. (2003). Blood, sweat, and jeers: The impact of the media's heterosexist portrayals on perceptions of male and female athletes. *Journal of Sport Behavior*, *26*(3).

Lebel, K., & Danylchuk, K. (2014). Facing off on Twitter: A generation Y interpretation of professional athlete profile pictures. *International Journal of Sport Communication*, *7*(3), 317–336.

Lebel, K., Pegoraro, A. & Harman, A. (2018). The impact of digital culture on women in sport. In D. Parry, C. Johnson, & S. Fullagar (Eds.), *Digital dilemmas: Transforming gender identities and power relations in everyday* life (pp.163–182). Palgrave Macmillan.

Lumpkin, A. (2016). *Modern sport ethics: A reference handbook*. Santa Barbara, CA: ABC-CLIO.

Mean, L. J., & Kassing, J. W. (2008). "I would just like to be known as an athlete": Managing hegemony, femininity, and heterosexuality in female sport. *Western Journal of Communication*, *72*(2), 126–144.

Moran, L. (2019, June 29). Megan Rapinoe's World Cup goal celebration is now a Donald Trump-trolling meme. *Huffington Post*. Retrieved from https://www.huffingtonpost.com.au/entry/megan-rapinoe-goal-celebration-troll-donald-trump_n_5d173b48e4b082e55369a4b1?ri18n=true. Accessed on January 30, 2020.

Schull, V. D., & Kihl, L. A. (2018). Gendered leadership expectations in sport: Constructing differences in coaches. *Women in Sport and Physical Activity Journal*, *27*(1), 1–36.

Sporttechie. (2019, June 28). Favored USWNT and France to set digital, social and ticketing FIFA WWC records while Fox sports simulcasts on Mega-Zilla. Retrieved from https://sportstechie.net/favored-uswnt-and-france-to-set-digital-social-and-ticketing-fifa-wwc-records-while-fox-sports-simulcasts-on-mega-zilla/. Accessed on January 30, 2020.

Van, P. (2014). Changing the game: The role of social media in overcoming old media's attention deficit toward women's sport. *Journal of Broadcasting & Electronic Media*, *58*(3), 438–455.

Vertelney, S. (2019, June 13). Disgraceful? Classless? That's exactly what the reaction to USWNT's 13-0 win has been. *Goal.com*. Retrieved from https://www.goal.com/en-us/news/disgraceful-classless-thats-exactly-what-the-reaction-to/1k24v7d9vkawf1sgd-brucrmmk5. Accessed on January 11, 2019.

White, J. (2019, June 12). FIFA Women's World Cup 2019: USWNT beat Thailand 13-0 to provoke criticism for 'running up the score'. Retrieved from https://www.scmp.com/sport/football/article/3014136/fifa-womens-world-cup-2019-uswnt-beat-thailand-13-0-provoke. Accessed on January 30, 2020.

Witt, M. G., & Wood, W. (2010). Self-regulation of gendered behavior in everyday life. *Sex Roles*, *62*(9–10), 635–646.

Women's Sport Foundation. (2018). Chasing equity executive summary. Retrieved from https://www.womenssportsfoundation.org/articles_and_report/chasing-equity-the-triumphs-challenges-and-opportunities-in-sports-for-girls-and-women/

Section 2
Masculinity, Sport and Mega-Events

Chapter 4

Not Feeling So Mega, but Still Being a Mega Star: Exploring Male Elite Athletes' Mental Health Accounts from a Gendered Perspective

Charlie Smith

Introduction

Competing and performing at mega-events is what an elite athlete strives, trains and lives for. These events are emotionally charged and filled with devotion, celebration and expectation, yet paradoxically, even when the greatest success is achieved, athletes can find themselves emotionally distressed when competing at them (Howells & Lucassen, 2018). Given the factors that are entangled within high-performance sport and its commoditisation, such as injuries, perfectionist personalities and enforced pressures to win (Baum, 2005; Mummery, 2005), elite athletes are often susceptible to mental health problems, such as depressive behaviour and suicidal ideation (Reardon et al., 2019). The expectation is that female athletes are normally more open about their mental health issues and display greater tolerance towards societal stigmas attached to their experiences, compared to males who are less likely to express their concerns and seek help (Oliffe & Phillips, 2008; Poucher, Tamminen, Kerr, & Cairney, 2019). Recently, however, there has been an increasing number of male athletes disclosing details of their dark times in the media (Souter, Lewis, & Serrant, 2018), despite the prevalent view that men are less likely to disclose or seek help for psychological problems as it could lead to them being perceived as weak (Souter et al., 2018).

This chapter focusses on male elite athletes' discussions of their mental health in and around mega-events and explores how their accounts incorporate and challenge gendered norms concerning stoicism and 'mental toughness', concepts which have been the key foci of research on this topic thus far (e.g. Gucciardi, Hanton, & Flemming, 2017). After considering literature on elite sport, mental health and toughness, the findings show that male athletes are increasingly challenging mental health stigmas by demonstrating stereotypically feminine traits of seeking help. However, their overall approach to recovery and their

Sport, Gender and Mega-Events, 73–90
Copyright © 2022 by Emerald Publishing Limited
All rights of reproduction in any form reserved
doi:10.1108/978-1-83982-936-920211010

discussion of it remain tainted with a masculinised guise of toughness that is partly engrained within the process and identity of being a mega-event athlete.

Sport and Mental Health

There has been burgeoning interest in athletes' mental health with key campaigns and debates such as the Independent's *Sporting Mind Series* presenting five key threats to sportspeople's mental well-being. Another recent campaign is the Football Association's (FA) (2019) collaborative work with *Heads Together*. The project entitled 'Heads up' seeks to normalise discussion of mental health by helping everyone feel equally comfortable talking about it as they are football. Sadly, many of these campaigns are situated alongside fatal cases of depression (Wolanin, Gross, & Hong, 2015), with athletes such as Ellie Soutter (snowboarder) and Kelly Catlin (cyclist) recently taking their own lives. Following such tragedies, there has been an increase in elite athletes' disclosures and discussions of their mental illness (Kennedy & Scott-Bell, 2018), with individuals such as Ian Thorpe (swimmer) and Freddie Flintoff (cricket player) just two of many notable examples. To address this issue researchers have begun examining mental health among athletes in more depth (e.g. Poucher et al., 2019). Emanating from research is the idea that sport is a crucial arena where masculine hegemony is constructed and maintained and often quite aggressively (Bryson, 1987). More recently Messner's (2018) study of rugby players demonstrates how they ensure they play when injured and suppress empathy for others and themselves. Studies such as these have highlighted the creation of an environment whereby the stigmas around psychiatric illness are fundamentally antithetical to the athletic ideal (Baum, 2005). Since the initial theorisation and use of masculine hegemony, however, the concept has developed in both theory and practice, more generally and in sport specifically. A relevant development for this chapter is the idea of 'inclusive masculinity' whereby femininity becomes less stigmatised and the narrow set of behaviours and activities once valued by men expands (Anderson & McCormack, 2018; Anderson & McGuire, 2010). These developments imply that men have more social freedom to express whatever form of masculinity they desire in social settings (Anderson & McCormack, 2018; Anderson & McGuire, 2010).

In terms of the prevalence of mental health problems in athletes, there are often comparisons made between the extent of their suffering and the rest of society. On this issue, Gouttebarge et al. (2019) have recently calculated that the level of mental health symptoms and disorders in athletes could be higher than the general population, even when taking into account substantial under reporting, they suggest the figures show that 16–34% of athletes are suffering. Foskett and Longstaff (2018) have provided a less optimistic picture and demonstrate that of 143 elite athletes recruited in their study, 47.8% showed signs of anxiety and depression, with a split of 17.3% of male athletes and 39.3% of female athletes reporting distress. There are multiple aspects of being an elite athlete and competing at mega-events that present considerable risks, making these individuals vulnerable candidates for experiencing mental health difficulties (Biggin,

Burns, & Uphill, 2017). Beyond hefty physiological demands there are personal attributes such as perfectionism, extreme focus and necessary unwavering commitment that threaten individuals' mental health (Biggin et al., 2017; Newman, Howells, & Fletcher, 2016). These risks further increase when an athlete is injured, facing involuntary career termination, overtraining, nearing retirement or experiencing performance difficulty (Rice et al., 2016), all elements prevalent within the spectacularism of mega-events. Unsurprisingly Wolanin et al. (2015) have therefore found a significant relationship between Olympic athletes, their performance and depression symptoms. Research also shows there is a normalisation of negative emotions and depressive behaviours when returning home following Olympic and major event participation (Howells, 2016; Howells & Lucassen, 2018).

The Nuance of Suffering in Sport: 'Mental Toughness' and Masculinity

The picture surrounding mental health in sport becomes more complicated when the concept of 'mental toughness' is introduced. This concept is positively associated with perseverance, an important factor contributing to elite sport performances (Gucciardi, Peeling, Ducker, & Dawson, 2016), but also traditionally a beneficial indicator and facilitator of mental health (Gucciardi et al., 2017). 'Toughing it out' has long been a prized trait amongst athletes and particularly amongst males (Malcom, 2006). For example, as Addis and Mahalik (2003) note, male athletes who can suppress the experience of intense physical pain and injuries are often applauded for their commitment and mental toughness, and thus meet societal expectations of being a 'real man' and a 'warrior' (Adams, Anderson, & McCormack, 2010). Being a 'real man' also reflects stressed male values such as 'courage, inner direction, certain forms of aggression, autonomy, mastery, technological skill, group solidarity, adventure and considerable amounts of toughness in mind and body' (Sexton, 1969, p. 4). As part of this ideal, men are generally expected to reject or avoid any behaviours that are stereotypically feminine (Mankowski & Smith, 2016), such as discussing their perceived weaknesses or mental health issues. If expected orthodox scripts of masculinity are unfulfilled, then athletes disclosing mental health problems can be subordinated through physical dominance and ridicule by fellow athletes, team members and spectators (Adams et al., 2010). The reluctance to seek professional help is therefore one of the biggest challenges, and especially for men, when suffering with mental health issues (Gulliver, Griffiths, & Christensen, 2012), permeating a culture of loneliness and potentially the loss of lives. This chapter therefore takes growing concerns and interest in elite male athletes' mental health and explores how their discussions are placed alongside traditional notions of masculine hegemony and stoicism in sport.

Methods and Approach to the Study

An interpretative analysis is used to explore elite male athletes' direct speech in publicly available online news articles speaking out about their mental health experiences before, during and after mega-events or major championships in their sport. Online news accounts have been chosen as they often provide a means of converting individuals' private life experiences into public ones (Dumitriu, 2015). The chapter adopts the World Health Organisation's (2014) definition of mental health as: 'A state of well-being in which every individual realises his or her own potential, can cope with the normal stressors of life, can work productively and fruitfully and is able to make a contribution to his or her community'. Following this open definition, there are no strict criteria on the mental health conditions imposed herein, although for the most part athletes refer to depression and anxiety. Athletes from all 33 Olympic sports (originally scheduled for 2020, but which has become 2021) were included in the dataset as the early analysis illustrated that they often spoke about the general practice of being an elite athlete and its pressures, rather than specific issues arising from their sport. Whilst a mega-event was considered broadly in combination with a major championship within each respective sport, it was also apparent that many of the athletes spoke about their challenges and threats to well-being *around* mega-events too, such as their preparation and feelings afterwards, thus suggesting these times sometimes caused them more distress than competing itself. Therefore, it was decided that more would be learnt about athletes' discussions of their mental health by leaving the inclusion criteria broad and including those who compete at the highest level as a professional (e.g. nationally, internationally). Whilst it might be expected that those partaking in team sports have differing mental health concerns, the analysis does not differentiate between different sports as all the athletes wrote and spoke out alone and their individual experiences were the focus of the analysis. Accounts were searched for via Google's news domain, inserting the names of all sports with terms such as 'mental illness', 'mental health', 'depression' and 'anxiety'. It is important to note that whilst several Black and minority athletes are quoted in the findings, their accounts demonstrated no different or specific demands compared to their white counterparts. Overall there were 65 male cases considered across all sports.

Conceptually this work draws on theories of gender relations, performativity (e.g. Butler, 1988), and hegemonic masculinities (e.g. Connell, 1995) to research how gender is presented in male athletes' accounts of mental well-being and understand how they perform, present and contest their experiences as gendered subjects. Understanding athletes' experiences was paramount and therefore the emphasis in the analysis was on their intentional discussion of mental health (including sometimes 'depressive talk') and the performative aspects of their narratives, rather than searching for any kind of validation of their behaviours. As from Butler's (1988) work, their speech has been understood as a 'repeated stylisation of the body', that denotes masculine and stereotypically feminine ways of talking, with gender being a part of the mobilisation of their identity. These framings of gender performativity were supplemented with Hochschild's (1979) work on emotion management to understand how athletes use emotional rules to determine what they feel they can or cannot display in relation to being a mega-event athlete or inhabiting its settings, guided by idioms such as 'what men and boys do' (Paechter, 2006).

The first round of analysis involved reading and rereading each individual's account and demonstrated that athletes would discuss their symptoms and feelings, presenting transitory moments or 'breaking points' that lead to their recovery. Therefore, Lazarus and Folkham's (1984, p. 141) definition of 'coping strategies' was also incorporated as: 'constantly changing cognitive and behavioural efforts to manage specific external and/or internal demands that are appraised as taxing or exceeding the resources of the person'. For the second stage of the analysis, each athlete's case was imported into the qualitative software NVivo and coded on the basis of the aforementioned conceptual categories. This included how they performed gender, what they actually feel and what they think they are supposed to feel, and how they coped with their feelings. The findings of the research are presented next and show that whilst mega-events produce a set of masculinised subcultural norms and values that exist within an environment associated with mental toughness, there is a growing shift in athletes' accounts that moves towards a stereotypically feminine re-evaluation of mental health in elite sport for all, even though discussion of recoveries still had masculinised underpinnings. The data are presented as relatively lengthy direct quotations with little interruption or discussion from the author so the reader can gain an in-depth understanding of each athlete's personal narrative and experience. The quotes and cases presented have been chosen as exemplars across the broadest range of sports. There are four key findings sections including: mental health suffering as the antithesis of sport, athletes displaying vulnerability, sport as a coping mechanism and athletes' role model stance on discussing mental health.

Mental Health Suffering as the Antithesis of Sport

It has been argued already that men are often less likely to express troubles and discuss sensitive issues than women (Smith, Mouzon, & Elliott, 2018), but it was clear from the outset that elite male athletes wanted to challenge this social norm via sharing their stories of mental health suffering. Whilst doing this, athletes explicitly recognised the tensions between being a sportsman and showing poor mental health, or even being depressed, confirming what is known already about the masculinised sport setting. This meant they felt they could not show any weakness and were compelled to present as 'mentally tough' as doing otherwise was antithetical to the sport and masculinised ideal:

> Being a professional sportsman, we don't really believe in any weaknesses for a start, yet alone mental weaknesses because it's not the done thing, is it?
>
> (Jack Green, Hurdler)

> I think sport inherently probably doesn't encourage people to come out and talk about it [mental health]. It's definitely getting better, but I think the nature of it is... quite a macho environment.
>
> (David Kettle, Hockey player)

> As sportspeople, you pride yourself on being mentally strong and ruthless, all the attributes that lead to competitive performance. But when you have a weakness in you, you don't really want to open up to it. You always want to show that you are strong.
>
> (Monty Panesar, Cricket player)

Athletes thus often spoke about occasions when they felt they had to hide their pain. In the cases below, this was not only through assumed expectations from being an elite athlete but also because of the incompatibility between 'being a champion' and mental health suffering:

> When I was in my early 20s and relocating to Italy to start the racing season, I'd find myself crying alone in my room. I'd gone from being around my family and friends all the time to committing to this pretty intense sport. It was lonely and isolating. But I definitely wasn't sharing that with anybody because there's a level of hardness you think you're expected to have to be a "great champion".
>
> (Taylor Phinney, Cyclist)

> I was so drained. People think I should be fine. I'd played at the Olympics and the European Under-21 Championship. Played in the Premier League. On good money. But it didn't feel like that...I didn't tell anyone.
>
> (Marvin Sordell, Football player)

> I went to Beijing, 19 years old, young Louis Smith, got the first ever erm Olympic medal there, the first medal for GB in 100 years... I had kids waiting outside my house and people recognised my name, I think people can look at successful people and think everything in their lives is perfect...I think men try to be proud and almost to the point where they try to be in denial and it's wrong, it just boils over.
>
> (Louis Smith, Gymnast)

> As athletes a lot of the times, on both sides, men and women, we are treated like superheroes who are indestructible. But you don't see the layers to it. Success doesn't make you immune to depression.
>
> (Kevin Love, Basketball player)

Much like Lopez and Levy (2013) found, the male athletes included herein spoke about the implications of showing their weakness, being afraid they would lose their funding or be dropped from the team if they disclosed their problems. They recognised the need to hide their pain, even if they did not agree with doing so:

> I'm one of the athletes that was never able to say anything because I was scared of not being selected for the team which then leads to losing funding.
>
> (Dan Keatings, Gymnast)

> To open up and be vulnerable with a teammate or a coach or a family member, sometimes it can feel like they're going to possibly use that against you, or it sort of cheapens your bravado or your confidence in the future.
>
> (Alex Deibold, Snowboarder)

> On tour it's kind of a dog-eat-dog world, you don't want to show weakness to anyone else, you don't want to say you're struggling because they're trying to take food off your plate and you're trying to take food off theirs.
>
> (Liam Broady, Tennis player)

Despite the negative implications of being 'found out' and disclosing their mental health issues, critically their accounts began opening up space for challenging the expectation of 'toughness' in sport and with masculinity more broadly. This was often through athletes' indication that sport is not immune to mental health problems and that they are just as likely to suffer as anyone else in society. Athletes tried to make discussion of mental health issues more humanised and challenged the social guidelines that 'manning up' is the right behaviour to deal with these problems:

> I think, if you're a man, there's a sense you have to be strong and deal with things on your own, 'man up' and get on with it. But we're all the same, really. Most people have mental health issues at some time or another.
>
> (Liam Pitchford, Table Tennis player)

> A lot of sportsmen get depression, all sorts of mental health issues.
>
> (James Haskell, Rugby player)

> People talk about the poker face in sports, but it's so much more than not showing pain on the bike. You have this idea that you're not allowed to show weakness anywhere. It becomes a liability. I

think the reality is that our individual issues might be different, but
we're all in this one together, we're all fighting something.

(Bobby Lea, Cyclist)

Displaying Vulnerability

As part of telling their stories, athletes often outlined the symptoms they experienced in considerable detail which enabled them to show the depth and breadth
of their issues. They openly displayed emotion, which is something usually
considered a more traditionally feminine practice, with males normally being
expected to supress their feelings. When sharing their emotions, they presented
depressive emotions that are often considered powerless, uncontrolled and contrary to masculinised norms (Emslie, Ridge, Ziebland, & Hunt, 2006). The athletes also displayed some emotions stereotypically associated with females, such
as stating that they cried in public. The causes of their suffering were multiple and
reflected what is already known on athlete depression (Reardon et al., 2019).
Sport-specific reasons associated with suffering included performance pressures,
expectations of success from their home nation governing body, injury, retirement, isolation at mega-events, deselection, being unprepared for success and
guilt at the privileges they derived from being a mega star. The accounts below
had a depressive emphasis, with athletes often cruelly emphasising their
shortcomings:

I remember going into a black hole for five days because it wasn't
good enough. It wasn't a world record.

(Michael Jamieson, Swimmer)

The enormity of it all just kind of tipped me over the edge. I felt
lost, I felt lonely, I felt suffocated. That whole period – topped up
with the attention from social media – I just spiralled out of
control and got myself in a really dark place that was difficult to
get out of.

(Nile Wilson, Gymnast)

Golf and I always had a rocky relationship, but it became more
hostile during my time as a professional. Each shot had a price tag,
and any failure on the course led to me berating myself.

(Lucas Glover, Golfer)

You have to be at your best for that 52 seconds out of four years,
otherwise you're kind of out of luck, you don't make the spot.
That one race every four years, you have to be perfect.

(Matt Grevers, Swimmer)

> I got asked to go to the parade and I was like, 'What for? I didn't
> f———— medal. How could I show my face?' Every
> championships I've been to I've medalled. I felt ashamed, like
> I'd let down everyone. I just bottled things up and that's the
> problem.
>
> > (David Weir, Wheelchair athlete)

There were more extreme versions of these performance expectations, as Eddie
Hall (Strongman) put it harrowingly bluntly: *If I don't win, I want to die.* In these
accounts talking about performances, the athletes displayed masculinised
toughness but were frustrated at not being able to live up to the ideal of being
autonomous and able to master their own craft and destinies.

Whilst athletes demonstrated vulnerability due to their perceived failure of
meeting performance expectations, they also presented feelings of hopelessness
and confusion at their emotions, with some expectation that they knew they were
not supposed to feel this way in their roles. This challenged masculinised agendas
on mental health which normally suggest a more informed understanding and
knowledge about themselves and their health:

> I'm the most competitive guy you'll ever meet, but suddenly I'd
> lost something inside. I didn't want to be there anymore. I felt
> myself going further and further down a hole. I felt trapped in my
> own life, and totally alone.
>
> > (Liam Pitchford, Table Tennis player)

> If you were to base success on external things, it was the most
> successful season any snooker player had had. Even winning
> tournaments isn't solving my problems, what is it, why am I
> feeling like this?
>
> > (Ronnie O'Sullivan, Snooker player)

> There is something wrong, but you don't know what it is. And you
> start an internal process, thinking you feel bad, but you do not
> know why. You have some tests, and everything is fine, but you
> don't feel well, and you enter a loop in which you end up feeling
> very empty.
>
> > (Andres Iniesta, Football player)

> You used to love this game. You still love training, trying to
> master your craft. Why are you not enjoying what you used to
> thrive on?
>
> > (Moises Henrique, Cricket player)

It was common for athletes to discuss 'breaking points', when they felt they could not go on suffering, having exhausted their own resources in trying to cope with their pain, before turning to professional help, and sometimes doing so in an emergency. This often led to accompanying statements of suicidal ideation and behaviour. Masculinised norms and behaviours were challenged here by openly talking about the intention to take their own lives publicly. Suicide is often labelled as a silent killer and not something either gender – especially males – normally talks to others about:

> As dramatic as it sounds now, I remember being on the bathroom floor with a handful of pain meds thinking about swallowing them all.
>
> (Brandon Hudgins, Runner)

> Back in 2008 [following the Olympics] I knew, at some point, I needed to deal with my depression. That cloud was growing and after London 2012 it was uncontrollable. In early 2014, when I was injured, I missed training for four weeks. I didn't leave the house. I remember planning a way out and thinking if I'm going to do this what do I need to get in order?
>
> (Michael Jamieson, Swimmer)

> I remember sitting in my room for like 4 or 5 days not wanting to be alive, not talking to anybody and erm you know that was a struggle for me but that also was a sign and for me I reached that point where I finally realised I couldn't do it alone.
>
> (Michael Phelps, Swimmer)

Sport as a Coping Mechanism

Despite athletes often emphasising their breaking points and evident need for help as they could not cope alone, their accounts also implied that they were reluctant to take up the support of others. As Oliffe and Phillips (2008) state, when an individual first recognises symptoms of a mental health problem, their response is often one of self-care involving medium to long-term self-monitoring and treatment, prior to seeking professional medical help, with this trajectory often exacerbated in males. The athletes' narratives exhibited a range of coping behaviours (Lazarus & Folkman, 1984; Oliffe & Phillips, 2008) that were often solitary and closely reflected their persona associated with preparation and performances in sport and mega-events. Behaviourally this was evident through immersing themselves in training and competition routines, often hiding within their performances and pushing on in a masculinised way, even though they recognised their struggles:

> I don't have many memories of that time, I just remember getting up, eating breakfast, going to the track, doing my training, coming home, eating, resting and going back to the track ... I felt like it was Groundhog Day.
>
> (Aled Sion Davies, Shot-putter)

> They weren't with you when you burst into tears in the middle of practice and you didn't know why. And despite that, you kept pushing. They weren't there every time your fiancé [sic] helped calm you down night after night when the pressure seemed to consume you, but you kept pushing. They don't understand you couldn't smile through the latter half of the season because the anxiety and pressure were eating at you, but you still kept pushing.
>
> (Kyle Guy, Basketball player)

> After the Commonwealth Games in 2014 I realised that something wasn't quite right, I kind of addressed it a little bit through professionals, but just carried on and didn't really seek any help outside of that.
>
> (David Kettle, Hockey player)

> Six and a half hours a day I was in a place I would not swap for the world - inside the boundary ropes in countries like India, Australia and the West Indies. For the other nine hours when I wasn't asleep, I was thinking 'I don't want to be here'.
>
> (Steve Harmison, Cricket player)

> I said to myself 'If you take the easy way out, if you don't go onto the pitch, then you'll always do that'. I stayed on the pitch and after a few minutes I made a save from [Francesco] Cozza. We won the game 1-0 and it was like electroshock therapy for me.
>
> (Gianluigi Buffon, Football player)

Whilst some athletes hid in their training and competition to forget their pain, others used their suffering as a means of motivation and progression within their sport by improving their performances:

> Obviously, it hurts when I don't get picked. But my mindset is always to make sure my performance doesn't dip and to make sure I'm always performing at an elite level.
>
> (Danny Cipriani, Rugby player)

> I worked on training myself to identify what things would stress me out at 4 a.m. and try to make sure those were done the day before.
>
> (Phil Gaimon, Cyclist)

This sporting mindset was also an integral part of athletes' recovery narratives. Hence there was considerable similarity with learning and skill acquisition processes in sport more generally that require dedicated effort, commitment and patience. Despite it being seen thus far that male athletes are trying to challenge masculine hegemony towards mental health stigmas in sport by speaking out, as they began to talk about their recovery there was a switch in their narratives that aired a more controlled and masculinised manner. This was exemplified in an autonomous approach that was already prevalent in their existing sport regime and routines:

> Not every day is easy. You still come across humps but every year I'm getting new tools to be able to handle and deal with them and learning new things all the time.
>
> (Lewis Hamilton, Racing driver)

> You have got to take one step at a time and be patient with the whole process and eventually have the faith that things will get better.
>
> (Monty Panesar, Cricket player)

> I have probably gone through 3 different stages of depression after Olympic Games and then erm you know for me that was a sign that something in my life wasn't going right. I had to figure out what it was and what I was going to take on and what I was going to try and tackle.
>
> (Michael Phelps, Swimmer)

Athlete Role Models and Recovery: "It's OK, Not to Be OK"

Whilst athletes discussed masculinised sport techniques to help them with their mental well-being, they continued to recognise the potentially 'unhealthy' and 'dysfunctional' relationship between their mental health and sport (Doherty, Hannigan, & Campbell, 2016). The prominent physical and mental toughness that exists in their everyday practice and performances was challenged by labelling it as an emotional problem and their accompanying admission of need for help (Addis & Mahalik, 2003). However, there was still an element of being a 'warrior' as the hegemonic masculinity of fighting to feel better and regain control remained an undercurrent. Their accounts reflected a heroic struggle from which they felt they emerged a stronger person, including after their recovery and then sharing the story of their suffering (Emslie et al., 2006). As has been argued thus far, sharing pain, showing vulnerability or asking for help is often perceived as a stereotypically feminine trait, one that these athletes' narratives challenged via the very act of speaking out. However, despite this, these statements on their recovery were often of a masculinised performative and authoritative nature:

> I wanted to be that success story, [someone] who people could lean on, knowing that even peers and colleagues of mine who hadn't come out with it or didn't know much about it have probably had it and we don't know.
>
> (Mardy Fish, Tennis player)

> There are times when I'm struggling, but if I speak out and somebody sees my story, they can maybe do something with it. I'm just trying to spread a little light to it because I know it's such a tough subject to speak on and a lot of people don't want to talk about it. So, if somebody can maybe use me or talk with me, it can be positive.
>
> (Isiah Wilkins, Basketball player)

> All the experiences you have become about how you can pass your learnings on and how you can positively help other people.
>
> (Danny Cipriani, Rugby player)

Adopting this performative approach and encouraging others to seek help implied these athletes would gain themselves by giving someone else the strength to address their own issues. Speaking out about their mental health struggles therefore also bought them extra media coverage. This is similar to Dumitriu's (2015) argument that once an athlete's sporting performance or career stops bringing them media coverage then speaking about their private life (and sharing issues such as mental health difficulties) can secure them alternative advantages, including further coverage.

As part of this encouragement towards others seeking help, the athletes also emphasised how communicating about their pain was uncomfortable, but something they considered necessary as it could eventually prove beneficial for themselves (Friesen et al., 2013):

Hang in there. Keep looking for help...you're definitely not alone. Talk about it, people want to hear because everyone wants to share deep down. Talk about it, but also understand that also that this is potentially the beginning of something that will change lives forever.

(Jonny Wilkinson, Rugby player)

It's ok to talk, don't be ashamed, don't be embarrassed. You'll always get some people who mock you, but those people are cowards and should be ashamed of themselves. Make sure you talk. Once I started talking things seemed a lot clearer and there are people there who will help you.

(Chris Kirkland, Football player)

The quicker you open up the quicker you will get the support and the help.

(Monty Panesar, Cricket player)

Despite being open about their mental health problems and encouraging others to do the same, struggling was often labelled as a form of strength reflecting the persona of a mega-event athlete. By speaking out these athletes demonstrated their struggles, but they persevered and overcame them to emerge victorious and did so through highlighting their integrity and honesty both inside and outside of sport and supporting less fortunate others through inspiration and unselfish deeds (Barney, 1985; Gammon, 2014). Rather than continuing in pain silently and being applauded for doing so, these athletes suggest a different kind of toughness beyond physiological traits where they are instead praised and supported for speaking out. The values underpinning this approach to recovery are still imbued with classic sporting behaviour and masculine toughness via a strong commitment to overcome adversity and eventually successfully reach the goal of recovery with perseverance.

This performative masculinity in athletes' accounts is also evident via the authoritative tone of their speech towards getting help. They challenged masculine norms by emphasising an alternative and allowable set of feeling and talking rights around male athletes' mental health suffering and framed speaking out as a strength:

If a guy who thought he could walk through walls can say, 'I feel like shit here, I'm crying every night, I'm swear sick of hating myself and I need to see someone,' then there's no reason why anyone else can't. It doesn't mean that you're weak. It means you're swear clever. You can either sulk and die or go do something about it.

(Ricky Hatton, Boxer)

My advice to anyone suffering from mental health issues – and specifically athletes who can relate – is this: Ask for help. Stop trying to deal with these serious matters alone. You're not alone. Believe me.

(Steve Smith, American Football player)

I want to make people believe they can beat this sickness (of depression). I was really at the bottom of the ocean, I was touching the rocks. It was deep, really deep. But I came up again.

(Daniel Chaves, Runner)

Conclusions

This chapter began from the premise of an increase in high-profile male athletes openly discussing their experiences of mental illness, despite its incongruence with the masculinised image of sportsmen as tough and strong individuals. The fact these athletes are speaking out about their mental well-being and suffering broadly challenges the masculinised toughness in sport and by expressing these views it could also prove inconvenient for those governing sport who could be duty bound to address it (Hassan, 2013). The narratives studied herein are an attempt to start normalising conversations about mental health more generally in society as these athletes' accounts can act as important resources for identity stories that others can draw on (Dumitriu, 2015). By persuading others in the general population (Donaldson, 1993) these athletes may continually challenge hegemonic versions of male toughness and shame around mental health in sport via normalising discussion of it. By speaking out in a stigmatised arena about their mental health issues, these athletes have been exceptional beyond their normalised sporting excellence through discussing honestly and with integrity issues that they recognise could potentially threaten their sporting lives and careers. Literature on the legacy of the Olympic Games and other mega-events is well established but often focusses on economic and political gains and whilst in-depth discussions of mental health in sport are still in their infancy, work such as that herein exemplifying lived and real experiences may start extending the social gains and effects of such events beyond increasing sport participation.

Overall male athletes displayed and described their emotions in their narratives and often emphasised the need for help that is sometimes considered more of a feminine trait. However, when they spoke about their recovery, it was often tainted with a masculinised performative agenda, commonly associated with sporting behaviour and outcomes emphasising self-control and being a heroic mega star. These male athletes have been able to begin improving their mental well-being, but this pursuit is in its early stages and still located within a society and setting that places considerable weight on mental toughness associated with sport. Reading these narratives has emphasised further that there are clear aspects of sport that threaten athletes' mental well-being and which reinforce existing stigmas. Whilst institutional provisions are beginning to increase (for example, each UK sport governing body is required to have designated safeguarding staff) (Grey-Thompson, 2017), athletes in their narratives continued to reiterate points such as 'the more we talked', suggesting more room for communal and shared spaces within these institutionalised settings.

The majority of these athletes were sharing their mental health narratives after much suffering, often suggesting they had felt this way for a long time. There remains a prevalent culture of silence around mental health suffering before and during mega-events as none of these athletes mentioned raising their concerns at the time of their experiences, either within their informal circles or more publicly in media narratives such as those presented herein. Therefore, whilst there is progress in bringing these concerns into the public domain and challenging mental toughness, to some extent, the effects and impacts from this are considerably watered down as the performative and masculinised culture of sport upholds within these events. This chapter has focussed on the increase in male athletes' disclosures that are beginning to challenge ideas of stoicism, resilience and mental toughness (Doherty et al., 2016) and owing to space limitations has not included females' accounts. Future research should therefore compare how females discuss and present their mental health in conjunction with sports and mega-events.

References

Adams, A., Anderson, E., & McCormack, M. (2010). Establishing and challenging masculinity: The influence of gendered discourses in organized sport. *Journal of Language and Social Psychology, 29*(3), 278–300.

Addis, M., & Mahalik, J. (2003). Men, masculinity and the contexts of help seeking. *American Psychologist, 58*(1), 5–14.

Anderson, E., & McCormack, M. (2018). Inclusive masculinity theory: Overview, reflection and refinement. *Journal of Gender Studies, 27*(5), 547–561.

Anderson, E., & McGuire, R. (2010). Inclusive masculinity theory and the gendered politics of men's rugby. *Journal of Gender Studies, 19*(3), 249–261.

Barney, R. (1985). The hailed, the haloed, and the hallowed: Sport heroes and their qualities – an analysis and hypothetical model for their commemoration. In N. Muller & J. Ruhl (Eds.), *Olympic scientific congress sport history*. Eugene, OR: University of Oregon.

Baum, A. (2005). Suicide in athletes: A review and commentary. *Clinical Sports Medicine, 24*(4), 853–869.

Biggin, I., Burns, J., & Uphill, M. (2017). An investigation of athletes' and coaches' perceptions of mental-ill health in elite athletes. *Journal of Clinical Sport Psychology, 11*(2), 126–147.

Bryson, L. (1987). Sport and the maintenance of masculine hegemony. *Women's Studies International Forum, 10*(4), 349–360.

Butler, J. (1988). Performative acts and gender constitution: An essay in phenomenology and feminist theory. *Theatre Journal, 40*(4), 519–531.

Connell, R. (1995). *Masculinities*. Cambridge: Polity Press.

Doherty, S., Hannigan, B., & Campbell, M. (2016). The experience of depression during the careers of elite male athletes. *Frontiers in Psychology, 7*(1069), 1–11.

Donaldson, M. (1993). What is hegemonic masculinity? *Theory and Society, 22*(5), 643–657.

Dumitriu, D. L. (2015). The face management challenges of sport celebrity. *Management Dynamics in the Knowledge Economy, 3*(1), 79–97.

Emslie, C., Ridge, D., Ziebland, S., & Hunt, K. (2006). Men's accounts of depression: Reconstructing or resisting hegemonic masculinity. *Social Science & Medicine, 62*(9), 2246–2257.

Foskett, R., & Longstaff, C. (2018). The mental health of elite athletes in the United Kingdom. *Journal of Science and Medicine in Sport, 21*(8), 765–770.

Friesen, A., Lane, A., Devonport, T., Sellars, C., Stanley, D., & Beedie, C. (2013). Emotion in sport: Considering interpersonal regulation strategies. *International Review of Sport and Exercise Psychology, 6*(1), 139–154.

Gammon, J. (2014). Heroes as heritage: The commoditization of sporting achievement. *Journal of Heritage Tourism, 9*(3), 246–256.

Gouttebarge, V., Castaldelli-Maia, J., Gorczynski, P., Hainline, B., Hitchcock, M., Kerkhoffs, G., … Reardon, C. (2019). Occurrence of mental health symptoms and disorders in current and former elite athletes: A systematic review and meta-analysis. *British Journal of Sports Medicine, 53*(11), 700–706.

Grey-Thompson, T. (2017). *Duty of care in sport; independent report to government.* Duty of Care Review.

Gucciardi, D., Hanton, S., & Flemming, S. (2017). Are mental toughness and mental health contradictory concepts in elite sport? A narrative review of theory and evidence. *Journal of Science and Medicine in Sport, 20*(3), 307–311.

Gucciardi, D., Peeling, P., Ducker, K., & Dawson, B. (2016). When the going gets tough: Mental toughness and its relationship with behavioural perseverance. *Journal of Science and Medicine in Sport, 19*(1), 81–86.

Gulliver, A., Griffiths, K., & Christensen, H. (2012). Barriers and facilitators to mental health help-seeking for young elite athletes: A qualitative study. *BMC Psychiatry, 12*(157), 1–14.

Hassan, D. (2013). Introduction: What makes a sporting icon? *Sport in History, 33*(4), 417–426.

Heads Together. (2019). Heads up: Changing the conversation on mental health. Retrieved from https://www.headstogether.org.uk/heads-up/. Accessed on January 7, 2020.

Hochschild, A. (1979). Emotion work, feeling rules and social structure. *American Journal of Sociology, 85*(3), 551–575.

Howells, K. (2016). 'Super-human' athletes are at risk from the post-Olympic blues – here's why. Retrieved from http://theconversation.com/super-human-athletes-are-at-risk-from-the-post-olympic-blues-heres-why-64266. Accessed on June 29, 2019.

Howells, K., & Lucassen, M. (2018). 'Post-Olympic blues': The diminution of celebrity in Olympic athletes. *Psychology of Sport and Exercise, 37*(1), 67–78.

Kennedy, I., & Scott-Bell, A. (2018). Team GB star's death and the pressured world of elite sport. Retrieved from http://theconversation.com/team-gb-stars-death-and-the-pressured-world-of-elite-sport-100791. Accessed on December 3, 2019.

Lazarus, R., & Folkman, S. (1984). *Stress, appraisal, and coping.* New York, NY: Springer.

Lopez, R., & Levy, J. (2013). Student athletes' perceived barriers to and preferences for seeking counselling. *Journal of College Counselling, 16*(1), 19–31.

Malcom, N. (2006). "Shaking it off" and "toughing it out": Socialization to pain and injury in girls' softball. *Journal of Contemporary Ethnography, 35*(5), 495–525.

Mankowski, E., & Smith, R. (2016). Men's mental health and masculinities. *Encyclopedia of Mental Health, 3*(1), 66–74.

Messner, M. (2018). Male athletes, injuries and violence. In R. Washington & D. Karen (Eds.), *Sport, power and society; institutions and practices* (pp. 397–408). New York, NY: Routledge.

Mummery, K. (2005). Depression in sport. *The Lancet, 366*(1), 536–537.

Newman, H., Howells, K., & Fletcher, D. (2016). The dark side of top level sport: An autobiographic study of depressive experiences in elite performances. *Frontiers in Psychology, 7*(868), 1–12.

Oliffe, J., & Phillips, M. (2008). Men, depression and masculinities: A review and recommendations. *Journal of Men's Health, 5*(3), 194–202.

Paechter, C. (2006). Masculine feminities/feminine masculinities power, identities and gender. *Gender and Education, 18*(3), 253–263.

Poucher, Z., Tamminen, K., Kerr, G., & Cairney, J. (2019). A commentary on mental health research in elite sport. *Journal of Applied Sport Psychology, 9*(1), 1–23.

Reardon, C., Hainline, B., Aron, C., Baron, D., Baum, A., Bindra, A., … Engebretsen, L. (2019). Mental health in elite athletes: International Olympic Committee consensus statement. *British Journal of Sports Medicine, 53*(11), 667–699.

Rice, S., Purcell, R., De Silva, S., Mawren, D., McGorry, P., & Parker, A. (2016). The mental health of elite athletes: A narrative systematic review. *Sports Medicine, 46*(9), 1333–1353.

Sexton, P. (1969). *The feminized male.* New York, NY: Random House.

Smith, T., Mouzon, D., & Elliott, M. (2018). Reviewing the assumptions about men's mental health: An exploration of the gender binary. *American Journal of Men's Health, 12*(1), 78–89.

Souter, G., Lewis, R., & Serrant, L. (2018). Men, mental health and elite sport: A narrative review. *Sports Medicine, 4*(57), 1–8.

Wolanin, A., Gross, M., & Hong, E. (2015). Depression in athletes: Prevalence and risk factors. *Current Sports Medicine Reports, 14*(1), 56–60.

World Health Organisation. (2014). Mental health: A state of well-being. Retrieved from http://www.who.int/features/factfiles/mental_health/en/. Accessed on March 12, 2019.

Chapter 5

Security, Locality and Aggressive Masculinity: Hooliganism and Nationalism at Football Mega-Events

Jonathan Sly

Introduction

When it comes to international football mega-events, the issue of fan violence between opposing groups of spectators is frequently outlined by governing bodies, law enforcement agencies and the media as a prominent organisational concern. It was during the run-up to the 1966 World Cup Finals, held in England, that the label 'hooligan(s)' was first used to describe disorderly fans by the UK popular press, and 50 years later at the UEFA European Football Championship tournament held in France (2016), the issue of hooliganism was still high on the agenda, with the eventual outcome being one of the most disorderly football mega-events in recent years. (Football) 'hooliganism' is a global phenomenon that can be seen to mutate and adapt alongside changes related to both the sport of football and to the particular societies in which the game is played. When such highly gendered violence takes place around the competitive matches of national teams, the issue of nationalism comes to the fore, alongside that of aggressive masculinity.

Some international football mega-events have previously been championed by the world's media for passing off peacefully, whereas at others it has been the events on the stands and in the streets surrounding stadia that overshadow those on the pitch. Academic research exploring why this might be the case has highlighted issues of policing, security and locality as key explanations as to why football hooligan violence flares up at some sporting mega-events and not at others (e.g. Stott, 2014; Stott & Pearson 2006, 2007; Stott & Reicher, 1998). Other recent works have emphasised the role of supporter nationalism and geopolitical relations between nation states as primary indicators of the potential for football fan disorder to occur when particular national sides face off (e.g. Kozon, 2018).

Sport, Gender and Mega-Events, 91–111
Copyright © 2022 by Emerald Publishing Limited
All rights of reproduction in any form reserved
doi:10.1108/978-1-83982-936-920211011

This chapter builds on these findings through a case study of interactions between Russian and English supporters at the 2016 UEFA European Championships (France) and the 2018 FIFA World Cup Finals (Russia). The work uses a mixture of empirical observational data gathered at both football tournaments, interviews with English and Russian hooligan groups and secondary data analysis of online media coverage. The findings add to previous literature about hooligan fan violence at sport mega-events, and illuminate the importance of emic sub-cultural developments, alongside issues of event security and locality, in advancing theoretical explanations as to why some international football mega-events pass off relatively peacefully, and others suffer serious problems of hooligan violence.

The chapter considers how the continuous interactions between local-national-structural forces and individual agency can give rise to and strengthen specific forms of (hyper-)masculine gender identities that are flourishing in increasingly ambivalent and volatile contemporary societies, such as England and Russia, and that have very real consequences both inside and outside of the sporting sphere.

Masculinity, Football and Violence

The associations between collective male-on-male violence and ball games has a history that long pre-dates the inception of football as a codified sport. Within many early forms of folk football that were played in early modern Europe prior to the 1800s, the distinction between player and spectator was rarely clear-cut, and organised competitive ball games were often just an excuse for the inhabitants of one village to go and fight with those of another (Marsh, 1994). It was not until the industrialised Victorian era, in Britain at least, that formal rules of 'fair-play' were drafted for ball sports, dislocating much of the more unacceptable violent behaviour from the fields of play to the spectator stands. As Dunning, Murphy, and Williams (1988, p. 01) state 'there has never been a period in the history of modern soccer when spectator disorderliness on a greater or lesser scale has been entirely absent from Britain'. Such violence, however, despite being omnipresent, changes dramatically in both form and scale depending on the specific time period, contemporary social events and location.

Turning to the evolution of football hooliganism in England, it was not until the early to mid-1960s that we see the origins of a specific quasi-organised, almost exclusively male, subculture focused on intentionally seeking violent confrontation with rivals emerge at domestic football matches. This mirrored other social developments that were taking place at this time both in the sport of football and in wider British society. How football hooliganism evolves can thus be seen to be heavily influenced by changing social attitudes and male class-cultural gender identities over time (Armstrong, 1998), along with developments in leisure opportunities, the political and economic climate, differing supporter demographics, stadium developments and shifting security practices, new technologies and many other socio-historical factors.

Football Hooliganism: An English Disease?

The expansion of the football hooligan subculture in England from the 1960s onwards was initially highly localised. Minimal crowd violence or disorder occurred around fixtures of the England national team, primarily as few supporters had the economic means to follow either their domestic club side or the national team abroad until the late 1970s. As a result, matters of nationalism played little direct role in the negotiation and formulation of the English hooligan's individual or collective identity. Therefore, in the context of England international football fixtures prior to the late 1970s, the idea of one hooligan group 'teaming up' with another to go and fight with a greater foe on foreign shores was not commonplace.

The UK media has played an important role in both influencing and documenting English football hooligan culture, and Stott and Pearson (2007) discuss how, by the 1980s, the hooligan phenomenon had attracted the applied media label 'the English disease'. The first widely reported incident of disorder involving English football supporters abroad was the second leg of the 1974 UEFA Cup Final in Rotterdam, Netherlands, when numerous incidents of hooligan violence occurred between fans of Tottenham Hotspur and Feyenoord of Rotterdam (Stott & Pearson, 2007). This event helped fuel the popular media narrative of hooliganism being a phenomenon exported to the continent by English thugs, despite, on this occasion, Dutch hooligans being equally complicit (Stott & Pearson, 2007). Certainly, elements of English hooligan culture were adopted, both intentionally and otherwise, from the 1970s onwards by football hooligan 'firms' in other European countries, but the suggestion that violence at and around football matches did not exist in other national contexts until English fans began to follow their club sides and national team abroad is largely a media-induced fallacy. Rather, as Dunning, Murphy, Waddington, and Astrinakis (2002) suggest, football hooliganism is a historical–social phenomenon that has existed in some form or another, and in varying degrees of prevalence, in many countries long before the 'tabloidisation' of the UK popular press.

Fan Violence at Football Mega-Events

Football-related violence is thus a phenomenon that has existed historically in many national contexts where the sport is played professionally, though widespread instances of hooliganism at international matches and football mega-events were not prevalent until large numbers of fans began to travel abroad for matches at the end of the 1970s. Largely as a result of cheaper travel options, many more football supporters began to follow both the successful domestic club teams and national sides abroad to international football matches, European club competitions and ultimately to international mega-events (Malinowski, 2002). Pennant and Nicholls (2006) state that although there were two instances of disorder at England away games in 1975, it was not until the very late 1970s that prominent English hooligan groups began to take a collective interest in following their national team at home and abroad.

The Belgium vs England game in Turin at the European Championships in 1980 marked the first time that English hooligans were involved in violence at a football mega-event outside of the United Kingdom, with fighting occurring both before and during the game between groups of travelling English fans, Belgian supporters and Italian locals (Pennant & Nicholls, 2006). English hooligans struck again the following year at a World Cup qualifying match in Basil, Switzerland, and by the time the World Cup Finals tournament was held in Spain in the summer of 1982, the number of travelling England supporters, both hooliganism-inclined and otherwise, had grown significantly (see Williams, Dunning, & Murphy, 1984) – a pattern that would continue at European football mega-events throughout the remainder of the 1980s, the 1990s and 2000s.

Football Hooliganism at Mega-Events: Policing and Policy

Since the time of John Williams' detailed ethnographic account of disorder involving England fans at Spain 1982 (Williams et al., 1984), Clifford Stott and his colleagues' work on policing large football events, and Geoff Pearson's on matters of 'anti-hooligan' policy and legislation, have led the field. Principally they have focused on the combined issues of policing football crowds, collective supporter identities and shifting inter-group dynamics, as well as the impact of recent legislative policy measures, such as Football Banning Orders (FBOs), that are aimed at addressing the 'hooligan problem' both in England and at sport mega-events abroad.

Stott's work uses the 'Elaborated Social Identity Model' (ESIM) of crowd behaviour in order to understand collective supporter conflicts, set within the context of large football events (e.g. Stott, Hutchinson, & Drury, 2001; Stott, Livingstone, & Hogget, 2008). He argues that the constant interplay between the associated media coverage of disorderly events, hostile rival fan groups, aggressive local youths and the police can help explain the presence – or absence – of violent fan behaviour at different football matches and tournaments. For Stott and his colleagues, if fans perceive the atmosphere around a game to be hostile, then they may develop elements of a collective identity close to a persecution complex. Regardless of how many of the fans present had any prior intention of seeking disorder, supporters will become more likely to react aggressively to any inter-group action that they collectively perceive as hostile, and thus *actual* violence has more chance of occurring.

Geoff Pearson assesses the effectiveness of the mass use of FBOs for reducing hooligan violence at football mega-events through a number of detailed ethnographic works conducted with England fans at major tournaments, alongside Clifford Stott (e.g. Stott & Pearson, 2006, 2007). Stott and Pearson (2006) examine the case of the European Championship tournament jointly hosted by Holland and Belgium in 2000, stating that out of the 965 England supporters arrested during the disorder, only 30 had previously been identified as 'known' hooligans. They state that 'it is unclear how a strategy based exclusively upon controlling the movement of "known hooligans" can actually prevent [violent] incidents from occurring' (2006, pp. 245–246), and see 'low profile', information-led policing, 'where officers interact with fans in a friendly manner and on the basis of fans' actual behaviour rather than their reputation' (2006, p. 248), as being the most effective policing and policy-based strategies for reducing the risk of major disorder occurring at football mega-events, and for minimising the impact that smaller incidents of competitive hooliganism amongst 'high risk' fans may have on the overall success of the sporting occasion.

Whilst the use of the ESIM approach to understanding collective human behaviours has led to some important changes in the policing of many (often potentially volatile) crowd events in recent years (at both football events and protests), Stott and Pearson (2007) are aware of the pitfalls of attempting to use this model to explain all hooligan action at professional football events. As Armstrong (1998) and Giulianotti and Armstrong (2002) have discussed previously, ever since the increased 'fortification' of English league stadia in the 1980s, quasi-organised football hooligan groups or 'firms' have fought their subcultural battles with rivals in increasingly obscure and 'hidden' urban landscapes, where the police are unlikely to be present or to be able to respond quickly.

Garland and Rowe (2000) have also discussed how the increasing use of CCTV cameras both at football stadia and in town and city centres across the United Kingdom has resulted in the further displacement of incidents of hooliganism, as the cameras act as a contemporary panoptic in regulating the behaviour of those most dedicated to the hooligan 'scene' when they attend matches. The majority of the more serious and longer lasting violent incidents that took place over the course of my own research into contemporary English hooliganism in the twenty-first century (Sly, 2019) occurred in hyper-displaced, often impoverished, urban locales of contemporary Britain, with ever smaller contingents of the most dedicated semi-organised hooligans taking part in the violence. These incidents sometimes occurred whilst the match took place several miles away, and even occasionally on non-match days (Sly, 2019). Such hyper-displacement of football-related disorders in the English domestic leagues is in part testament to the success of the increased policing and legal measures aimed at combatting hooliganism in England in the twenty-first century. However, these authoritarian strategies can also be viewed as in some ways responsible for increasing the organisation and co-operation of a small number of highly dedicated rival *firms* domestically, some of whom are also occasionally 'active' on the international hooligan scene.

Football Hooliganism at Mega-Events: Subcultural Violence and Nationalism

One must look beyond an analysis of the behaviour of the crowd if we are to seek to understand what motivates the minority of 'hardcore' hooligan participants who look for competitive disorder with rival fans at football mega-events. There is a key distinction of both identity and patterns of behaviour between the young men who self-identify as football hooligans and go to matches with their peers to engage in violent conflict, and the 'carnival' (Pearson, 2012) or 'hoolifan' supporters (King & Knight, 1999) of clubs and national teams, who do not intentionally seek out violence at matches, but believe some violent actions to be legitimate in certain circumstances, such as if one were to be attacked by rival hooligan fans or the police (Stott & Pearson, 2007).

Looking at the motivations of those supporters who *do* self-identify as football hooligans, and who deliberately attend matches in groups intent on seeking disorder with rivals, it becomes apparent that both the individual and collective identities of such fans are key components in explanations of any subsequent violent behaviour. In the context of England international fixtures, structural socio-historical factors out of which local-regional rivalries are born frequently transgress some – but not all – international fan rivalries. Certain collectives within domestic hooligan factions will use their discretion, subcultural knowledge, 'street' credibility and contacts, to either team up with or fight with other like-minded, sub-culturally respected hooligan peers against any identifiable, albeit often temporary, 'foreign' foe. Therefore, it is here that we see the issue of nationalism come to the fore in influencing motivations for violence at England's international matches.

The size of the hooligan collectives that band together for international matches at sport mega-events, as well as the hostility displayed towards rivals, will differ greatly across space and time, and will principally depend upon the opposing nation and the set of supporters that one is facing. Sometimes international hooligan fan rivalries can be historical-geographical, such as England vs Scotland or Wales, or the Netherlands vs Belgium, but on many occasions the geo-political relations between nation states, both historic and contemporary, also come into play in the negotiation of nationalist hostilities. Historic and contemporary geo-political relations between nation states are potential 'red flags' for the likelihood of disorder occurring between supporters of opposing national sides at sporting events. For example, Kozon (2018) discusses the complex geo-political relations between the Russian Federation and Poland that underscored much of the hostilities between the supporters of these national sides at the mega-event Euro 2012. A second round Group fixture, uneventful on the pitch, resulted in large-scale disorder between hooligan fans in the streets around the stadium.

In order to understand some of the reasons behind the recent presence – and absence – of fan violence at football mega-events involving Russian and English supporters in 2016 and 2018, one must consider the recent historical development of the domestic hooligan scenes in both nations.

Football Hooliganism in the Russian Federation – A Short History

In an extremely simplistic summary of the evolution of football hooligan culture in contemporary Russia, the phenomenon can be loosely segregated into three identifiable time periods, where both the types of violent behaviours that occurred and the subculture that existed around them fluctuated greatly in response to broader socio-political developments. This combined with a significant shift in the psycho-social understanding of post-soviet Russian masculinity and ingrained *habitus* (Bourdieu, 1984) of Russian hooligan fans.

The first stage relates to supporter disorder that occurred during the time of the USSR. The first organised supporter movements and forms of terrace disorder that developed in the USSR did so in a similar way to that of other 'Eastern Bloc' socialist nations in the same time period, such as Poland (Kossakowski, 2017) and (what was then) Czechoslovakia (Duke & Slepicka, 2002). Fans of the more successful teams in the larger Soviet cities such as Moscow, Leningrad and Kiev first began to imitate perceived styles of English, Italian and even South American football supporters (Brimson, 2003). This was done by beginning to openly show club colours at matches, grouping together on the terraces and chanting, and singing in particular quasi-organised areas of the stadium. In an era of communism where displaying any type of partisan support for one's team could be treated by the authorities as an act of political dissent in itself, the early pioneers of football fan culture in the Soviet Union were perceived as troublesome rebels from the get-go, as any active support for one's football club was vigorously discouraged by the communist State. Travelling to away games was initially an infrequent activity, but a practice which began to spread during the 1980s (Brimson, 2003), and with the arrival of two sets of partisan fans at matches came spontaneous bouts of open hostility towards authority figures and each other.

Early forms of terrace hooliganism in the USSR can be likened to the unorganised forms of spectator disorder that took place in England pre-1960s, as the majority of trouble was often a spontaneous reaction to events on the pitch, but as more away supporters began to travel the Soviet Union in the 1980s, unplanned and impulsive fights took place between ad hoc opposing fan collectives. A Spartak Moscow supporter cited in Brimson (2003, p. 200) states that; 'in many towns and cities in Russia, Muscovites were less than welcome and would often come under attack from local youths while the police stood by and watched'. Most of the disorder or instances of deviancy labelled as 'hooliganism' at this time in the Soviet Union were expressions of communal dissent against both footballing and State authority figures. Although the State-controlled media did their best to play down any displays of public unrest, the few written fan accounts which do exist from this period, penned by Russian supporters 'active' on the scene at the time, proclaim that a football hooligan subculture was growing in the late USSR (Brimson, 2003).

The second, more violent and chaotic, subcultural stage of Russia hooliganism developed in various degrees of prevalence between the years of perestroika at the end of the 1980s, prior to the collapse of the Soviet Union, and the early 2000s in post-soviet Russia. The socio-economic chaos and political turmoil in the wake of the collapse of the USSR was reflected on the football terraces of the newly formed Russian Federation. Initially there was a decline in match attendances, away support, and thus incidents of competitive hooligan violence. This was until around the 1994/95 season when supporters at the two most successful clubs in the country, who had also been some of the most active on the football terraces before the fall, formed the first named hooligan groups in Russia, with the *Red-Blue Warriors* at CSKA and *Flints Crew* at Spartak Moscow (Brimson, 2003). By the end of the 1990s the Russian fan scene had a thriving hooligan culture similar in size to that of the Western European nations. Smaller provincial clubs began to form hooligan gangs, and smaller fringe groups appeared alongside the already established firms in the country's larger cities. Quasi-organised gang fights involving quick-to-hand weapons such as bottles and stones became common (Brimson, 2003), and the first football 'casuals', alongside other subcultural fashions such as punks and skinheads, appeared on Russian terraces. Looking to the West for inspiration in behavioural fashions and styles of violence, by the turn of the Millennium Russia had one of the most chaotically violent and rapidly evolving hooligan subcultures in Europe.

The third stage relates to the emergence of 'Russian Style' hooliganism. In the early to mid-2000s the first 'fair fights' between organised hooligan groups occurred in certain regions of Eastern Europe. Early accounts of such disorder in these years became apparent when numerous poor-quality videos first emerged, displaying grainy images of roughly evenly numbered groups of opponents fighting without weapons in secluded locations. Fair fights, also known as 'forest fights' (because of their commonly secluded locations), became the most widely used English language expressions to describe the new form of hooliganism emerging from Eastern Europe. Each European language will often have their own term to describe this form of football-related disorder, such as *ustawki* (arrangements/arranged fights) in Polish, and *okolofutbola* (around football/what happens around football) in Russian.

The chaotic levels and forms of hooligan violence which took place in the Russian Federation in the 1990s and early 2000s were later argued to have no place in the country's drive toward political and social stability in the mid- to late 2000s, where the dominant popular political mantra became heavily focused on the nationalist rhetoric of the United Russia Party (Muller, 2009). After the political and economic free-for-all which took place across the former Soviet Union during the process of separatism, ruling politicians in the Russian Federation attempted to assert a degree of stability through economic and social policies which positioned the 'new' Russian citizen as the epitome and embodiment of a newfound, or regained, might of the Russian nation.

It is difficult to assess the degree to which the changing political narrative of the State impacted upon the coinciding shift in the style of hooligan violence which occurred 'around football' (*okolofutbola*) in the mid- to late 2000s. By the time FIFA announced that Russia would host the 2018 World Cup Tournament on 2 December 2010, materials posted online by Russian contributors to Central and Western European administrated hooligan websites had taken on an increasingly nationalist tone. With the 'fair fight' style of competitive hooliganism now spreading into other areas of Europe from the East, Russian participants eschewed some of the more 'just' practices within this scene, such as not kicking someone repeatedly in the head whilst on the floor, or allowing individual participants to quit mid-fight, as is still seen in other examples of European 'fair fight' cultures (Sly, 2019). Instead, Russian hooligans took pride in the more violent videos being circulated online, where victory for one side would only be declared by those officiating after the majority of one group of participants appeared to be laid upon the floor. 'Death is the only reason to stop the fight' was one phrase openly joked about amongst Russian hooligan participants and commentators online.

The rawness and seeming brutality of football-related violence emerging out of the Russian Federation had originally been initiated primarily to make hooligan confrontations 'fairer' to avoid the loss of life or serious injury. However, this more brutal version of the pre-arranged, equal numbers, no weapons form of hooligan violence sweeping Europe at this time rapidly earned itself the label 'Russian Style'.

The Presence and Absence of Fan Violence at Football Mega-Events: A Case Study of England and Russia

With the development of the 'Russian Style' hooligan subculture taking on an increasingly politico-nationalist narrative in the early 2010s, the Russian national football team qualified for the European Championships mega-event held in France in 2016, and was subsequently drawn to face England in the opening Group match. Hooligan fans of both the English and Russian national teams had clashed nine years previously in Moscow, prior to a European Championship qualifying match in 2007, and supporters from a number of English domestic clubs who had visited the Russian Federation during the 2000s and early 2010s in the UEFA Europa and Champions League competitions reported a number of violent incidents and attacks by local hooligan groups. There was an emerging discourse being formulated on the English hooligan scene that the new Russian Federation, like a number of other post-socialist European nations, was becoming a 'difficult' place for away fans to visit – particularly if you were English. This was coupled with another counternarrative emerging out of the rapidly developing Russian hooligan subculture that the football hooligan scene in England was 'finished', and that Russian hooligan groups were now the 'top boys' of an economically united but increasingly politically polarised 'new' Europe.

The self-projected (hyper-)masculine image of the contemporary Russian football hooligan can be seen to be a product of the continuous interplay between emic subcultural actions and wider structural forces. The contemporary narratives and performances that are 'released' by Russian hooligan groups into the wider European and global online subcultural domains often mirror the masculine values idealised by the contemporary Russian State (see Foxall, 2013; Muller, 2009). The carefully edited use of social media imagery and videography, coupled with the (hyper)masculine nationalist ideological narrative of the supremacy of hooligan groups in the Russian Federation over those of 'Western' European nations, holds distinct comparisons with the nationalised, militarised and sexualised narratives of masculinity found in mainstream political discourse of the United Russia Party and Kremlin rhetoric under President Vladimir Putin (Foxall, 2013; Verkhovsky, 2007).

During the build-up to the UEFA European Championship tournament in 2016, as part of a more prolonged online campaign to disseminate gendered ideological values and nationalist propaganda, one prominent Russian hooligan firm – the 'Gladiators' of Spartak Moscow – published a short video clip on YouTube, with the simple title in English 'Eastern Europe – Beautiful Thing'

(2016). The video was one of a series of short Internet clips that presented the contemporary Russian football hooligan as dominant and superior to current Western European football 'lads', due to their alleged commitment to peak physical performance through fighting abilities, as well an imagined racial and ethnic 'purity'. Accompanied by the text (in English) 'Defend Europe' and dramatic emotive music, the video depicts a small group of the Spartak Gladiators firm walking slowly through a secluded wooded or parkland area. Dressed in similar black t-shirts that host nationalist slogans, as the group turn to face the camera the lead male – a well-known 'top boy' of the Gladiators firm – removes his t-shirt to reveal his athletic physique, before kissing an Orthodox Christian cross hanging around his neck and putting a personalised gum-shield sporting his nickname – 'Killer' – into his mouth. The group begin to raise their fists (which are bound by hand wraps or Mixed Martial Arts gloves) and bounce on the spot as if they are warming up for a physical confrontation.

As well as the staged, symbolic and performative nature of this expression of hyper-masculine nationalist identity, the main purpose of the short series of video clips featuring the football hooligans from Spartak Moscow was not to taunt or de-masculinise domestic rivals from other dominant Russian hooligan firms, but to disseminate their ideological propaganda virally beyond the Russian Federation and its close neighbours, particularly throughout the 'Western' online world. The choice of YouTube is of note here, rather than the use of any of the Russian language social media sites such as VK.com. Russian hooligans claimed their national subculture to be the 'strongest' in Europe – typical taunts that one might expect between football hooligan groups – but these taunts were set within a broader ethno-nationalist and hyper-sexualised ideological framework proclaiming that these young Russian men were the last bastion of 'true' white, straight, Christian masculinity. Offensive views proliferated Internet discussion forums and social media platforms – platforms which help to sustain the existence of late-modern hooligan subcultures globally (see Sly, 2019) – in the run up to the France 2016 tournament. This set the scene not just for a confrontation between fans of the England and Russia national teams, but for an (imagined) clash of 'styles' of (hyper-)masculinity between imagined versions of 'Eastern' and 'Western' Europe. This visceral battle, based upon the antagonistic hyper-masculine gendered identities of English and Russian hooligans, would be enacted through street contestations between the proponents of 'Russian Style' and the originators of the 'Old Skool' typologies of hooligan violence.

The violent events that occurred around the England vs Russia match between 9 and 11 June in Marseille, and then between 14 and 15 of June in Lille, were well publicised through both mainstream media and social media platforms internationally. Images of athletic, semi-organised Russian hooligan groups, prepared with hand wraps, balaclavas and gum shields, 'steaming in' to much larger groups of English football 'casuals' in a flurry of punches and kicks before hurriedly moving on towards their next set of 'targets', were broadcast globally through predominantly Western media platforms, introducing audiences around the world to their first taste of the brutality of *Russian Style* hooliganism. The (Western) media laid the blame largely at the feet of their latest hooligan folk devil, the

'Beast from the East'. However, in a bid to advance understanding of the violence that occurred at the Euro 2016 tournament – as well as why the World Cup in Russia in 2018 remained largely absent of such trouble – some of the less well publicised events that occurred before, during and after the European Championships mega-event must also be examined.

Framing the analysis within the broader thematic contours of this chapter, the data presented here document certain events that took place at and between each tournament, not covered by the mainstream media. The following sections of this chapter draw principally upon ethnographic data collected by the author at both mega-events, formal and informal interviews with hooligan groups and an extensive digital library of secondary data, gathered from subcultural social media platforms and internet forums as part of a larger project into contemporary football hooliganism globally.

UEFA Championships, France, 2016

The first fan violence that took place at the UEFA Championships mega-event in France in 2016 did so two nights before the England vs Russia game in Marseille, when English 'carnival fans' (Pearson, 2012) were attacked by local hooligans from Olympique Marseille (OM). An attack by 60–70 hooligans on groups of English supporters drinking in bars around the Vieux Port (Old Port) area led to an elaborated social identity of the persecuted (Reicher, 2001) forming amongst some of England's travelling fans the evening before the tournament's first match. The initial attack by OM fans can be seen to have led to an evening of escalating disorder between small groups of English fans, French locals and riot police.

The first hooligan disorder that involved both English and Russian fans occurred at around 5.30 p.m. on June 10th as a small group of roughly 25 hooligans from Torpedo Vladimir – a third-tier club from the provincial city of Vladimir, 200km east of Moscow – fought with a mixed ad hoc collective of English hooligans. This collective, upon witnessing the Torpedo firm fighting with a much smaller group of Wigan Athletic (a third-tier English club) hooligans, came to the defence of their fellow countrymen, running out from one of the bars on the Vieux Port promenade throwing glass bottles and chasing the Russian fans off in the direction of the nearby Vieux Port Metro Station. French riot police showed up on the scene and the mixed collective of English hooligans, now also joined by some carnival fans, threw glass bottles and metal chairs at the police. Some young English hooligans were later arrested in relation to this incident upon their return to the United Kingdom.

The violence that took place the evening before the match followed a similar pattern; small firms of provincial Russian domestic clubs and a larger group of locals supporting Olympique Marseille appeared at repeated intervals, in different areas, before attacking, fighting with and eventually being chased off by larger ad hoc collectives of English hooligan groups, with some carnival fans in tow. Once again, the groups of English fans were active in hunting down any hooligan rivals as the night unfolded and more groups of known English hooligans arrived into town. The fact that on both evenings it had been an opposing national group who had made the first move in attacking English fans meant that there was a hastily implemented truce amongst the various English hooligan groups. As a result, Marseille did not witness any of the low-level intra-national hooligan violence that permeates many England national team fixtures abroad.

On the evening of Friday 10 June 2016 two English and Russian hooligan groups fought each other outside O'Quinze bar close to the Marseille Vieux port. Prior to this fight, I had heard small groups of active, many well known, English hooligans discussing Russian hooligan fans in a particularly derogatory manner. Formulated as a counter-narrative to the Russian taunts of English hooligans being 'old and past it', English fans developed a discourse that de-masculinised the new Russian subculture as not being 'real' hooliganism, due to the hyper-rationalised organised conflicts that characterise the 'Russian Style' hooligan scene. Derogatory jokes which questioned the sexuality of Russian football hooligans were widely disseminated by English fans, due to the often shirtless dress code of many of their domestic hooligan encounters and their perceived obsession with a commitment to peak physical performance – including the suggested widespread use of anabolic steroids amongst Russian hooligan firms. The counter-accusation of English hooligan fans all being junkies, due to the common heavy use of alcohol and cocaine amongst English hooligan firms (see Ayres & Treadwell, 2012), was one rebuttal that I heard several times asserted by Russian hooligan fans.

Following this incident of hooliganism at O'Qunize – a fight which lasted several minutes before the riot police arrived and fired tear gas into the middle of brawling fans as both groups then moved in opposite directions away from the scene – another narrative was developing amongst some English hooligans on the ground. Speaking to a small group of known hooligan fans from English non-league club Tamworth, who were present at the fight with some Lincoln City supporters, 33-year-old Danny said:

> Game as f**k they were! There was only 25 of them [sic]. They come down 'ere, fair-play to them, the Russians. I don't know what they was thinking [sic]. There was only 25 of them [sic], loads of English, but game as f**k they were.

Pointing out how many English fans were involved whilst discussing the incident, the comments of Danny (a seasoned traveller at England's away games as well as his domestic non-league club) demonstrated a begrudging level of respect that was slowly developing amongst England's travelling hooligan contingent about the fighting abilities of the Russian fans. It seemed that the narrative projected about the Russian hooligans by the England lads on the ground was beginning to change.

The many incidents of violence that took place between English, Russian and local French hooligans continued to shape the subcultural narratives presented online through new media and also slowly impacted events on the ground. After the initial fights between small groups of fans the day before the match, many smaller groups of English fans began to join forces in larger heterogeneous consortiums of hooligans in anticipation of the arrival of more Russian firms on the day of the match. It was observable that such collectives were again ad hoc, and despite grouping together in large numbers outside pubs, the English groups became fragmented once disorder with rivals erupted, in an overt display of the behavioural disparity between the highly motivated football 'hooligan' and 'carnival' fans. This was seen to particularly be the case in Lille on June 15th when many more England fans arrived in the city who had not been present on June 10 and 11 in Marseille. Gaining their knowledge of the disorderly events predominantly from the mainstream UK media about England fans being continually attacked by Russian supporters, many English and Welsh hooligan groups arrived into the city of Lille with a distinct intent not to fight with one another but to group together to attack the Russian firms. These hastily implemented collectives of hooligan fans from both England and Wales resulted in a reverse situation in Lille where the England fans were the main instigators of the violence and many non-hooligan Russian fans became caught in the crossfire.

In analysing the many incidents of violence which took place over the first week of the Euro (2016) tournament, incidents too numerous and complex to describe here in full, several key theoretical themes emerge related to aggressive nationalism and fan violence at sport mega-events.

The observational data discussed so far from Euro (2016), as well as the absence of such widespread disorder at the World Cup (2018), do initially support the theoretical ideas of Clifford Stott and colleagues who have used the Elaborated Social Identity Model of crowd behaviour to explain the likelihood of fan disorder at football mega-events (e.g. Stott, 2014; Stott, Livingstone & Hoggett, 2008; Stott & Pearson, 2006, 2007; Stott & Reicher, 1998). The lack of coordination, communication and organisation of the French police at Euro (2016) contrasted with the observable 'firm but fair' approach of the Russian authorities at the World Cup (2018), and influenced the capacity of the tournament security authorities to either escalate or diffuse any low-level conflict as it began to unfold amongst fans. However, the ESIM alone is not sufficient for outlining the motivations of the most dedicated hooligan fans, and therefore further theoretical tools are needed to assess the root causes of hooligan violence at sport mega-events and beyond.

In this exploration of contemporary football hooligan identity and motivations in England and Russia specifically, it has been noted how individual agency can intersect with broader ideological and social-structural forces. The recent social history of, and geopolitical relationships between, nation states at the time may influence individual and group hooligan motivations to travel to mega-events and seek disorder with rivals to both a greater and lesser degree. With ultranationalism being a central pillar of the contemporary 'Russian Style' subculture, alongside the (hyper-)masculine ideals of a certain type of 'toughness', white ethnicity and heterosexuality, the forms of taunts between Russian and English hooligan fans online developed into opposing emic discourses that began to frame the fixture in France (2016) as a battle between the new 'Russian Style' and 'Old Skool' styles of hooligan violence. Many Russian groups who were present in France eschewed their domestic 'Russian Style' rules of not using weapons in fights and instead sought to take the English groups on in a more 'Old Skool' style of violent disorder. This resulted in a severe escalation of levels of violence at the Euro (2016) mega-event, as two English supporters experienced life-changing injuries after being kicked unconscious in Marseille and numerous Russian hooligans received treatment in French hospitals for deep cuts and other wounds obtained after being hit with glass bottles.

The debate around the extent to which digital technological platforms and online media may influence the *actual* levels of violence that take place around football has been addressed previously (see Fafinski, 2007). Opinion is divided on the reliability and credibility of the written accounts and information about football hooligan cultures available online (Hopkins & Hamilton-Smith, 2014; Poulton, 2008), so I will stop short of claiming that any form of (social)media-amplification occurred at Euro (2016). Much of the new media content that appeared online in the immediate aftermath, particularly from individuals claiming to be Russian hooligans involved in the violence, aligned with the ideological narratives and subcultural discourses disseminated by Russian hooligan groups online prior to the event.

For example, the carefully edited video footage that was posted to YouTube filmed by a Russian hooligan participant wearing a Go-Pro camera as he was fighting, selectively edited out footage of an incident where England supporters were chasing after a Russian group, and framed the violent incident to appear as if it were completely dominated by Russian aggression. Similarly, when an England fan posted mobile phone footage of one of the main Russian hooligan firms present appearing to retreat from an advancing English group on the small side road 'Rue Fort Notre Dame' in Marseille, Russian supporters responded with photographs taken from their own 'front line' of members of the advancing English group overtly carrying weapons, arguing that the English hooligan's use of weapons was unmasculine and that any Russian weapon use in the fights in France was only in response to being confronted with weapons by English fans. One anonymous supporter of Spartak Moscow commented upon this particular incident online (Okolofutbola.TV, 2016, p. 6.20) stating that:

> The most interesting and the most memorable, I think, was this lane of one of the streets adjacent to the Port. The English thus were attacking from the side of the Port. Russian United forces which had considerably thinned out by this time, were going from the other side. With a lot of shoving, the battle was going backwards and forwards, 'toe-to-toe' for around 15 minutes I think... There were a lot of injuries, cuts, shrapnel wounds of all kinds. One guy by the end of it had a leg of a chair pulled from his legs.

Glathe and Varga (2018) have written previously on Russian hooligan fans' use of social media to spread right-wing political ideology and demasculinise and exclude 'Others' in Russian society. Here similar tactics were seen to be used for negotiation and dissemination of competing ideological narratives of both English and Russian hooligan scenes. Such selective readings and interpretations of events are not unique to the recounting of hooligan incidents in order to taunt rivals online, but are seen to run deep in the (hyper-)masculine psyche in any recollection of previous violent incidents. These selective readings of history attempt to satisfy a narcissistic desire to present oneself as 'heroic' in the face of danger for the purposes of psycho-social identity performance and self-understanding, as well as conscious displays of (sub)cultural capital. As Winlow and Hall (2009, pp. 291–292) state in their critical analysis of the role of memory, humiliation and trauma in the lives of violent men:

> ...what actually occurred need be of no more significance than what actually might have occurred. [...] in any localised culture dominated by a strong and insistent visceral habitus, the individual will tend to select in the imagination specific alternative events and reactions that reflect idealized, competent forms of masculine identity and performance.

In the case of the Russian hooligans' collective memories of the violence against English supporters in France, matters of ultranationalism are seen to intertwine with culturally idealised understandings of aggressive masculinity, as illuminated in the following two quotations taken from a popular online social media platform run by Russian football hooligans (Okolofutbola.TV), where a Lokomotiv Moscow hooligan from the 'Vikings' firm, comments upon one incident in Marseille on 11 June 2016:

> There were about twenty of us, and we turned out to be... I suppose many have seen the video... so not by our own wish we appeared to be surrounded by much superior forces of English so to say hooligans, who managed to lock us in one of the backstreets in one moment, but we nevertheless managed to force them back. Because of the Russian spirit I suppose and the strength of our fists, our will. Everybody saw it I think, that was cool.
>
> (2016, p. 3.48)

The interplay between nationalism and aggressive masculinity is evident in the following quotation from an anonymous hooligan of the 'Yaroslavka' firm of CSKA Moscow:

> The average Russian hooligan... Our lads spend most of their time in gyms and in the forests fighting. Those who keep a healthy lifestyle are doubly stronger. The English are not like this, so in this case there were 200 professionals against 2000 amateurs, and that's why the victory was ours with the better hand... All the lads got together, never mind the colors and the clubs they are supporting. Everybody was acting as one united, so to say, powerful fist. How

good it worked out, I think everybody already knows, the entire world, certainly all of Europe.

(2016, p. 9.18)

FIFA Men's World Cup, Russia, 2018

The issue must be addressed as to why the football World Cup held in Russia only two years later passed off without major incident, when once again the national sides of England and Russia were both present at the tournament – although this time not playing against one another – as well as small groups of hooligan fans.

The matter of the much more effective model of policing implemented by Russian police forces, private security personnel and state security services at the World Cup in 2018, has already been mentioned and certainly played a key role in defusing any minor incidents before they developed. The Russian authorities also came down more severely on any local hooligans in host cities whom they believed may look for competitive violence with visitors, whilst at the same time being observably tolerant of the rowdy behaviour of English carnival fans.

Another altogether simpler and more practical matter of tournament geography, time free from work and travel costs for many English hooligans prevented them from attending the 2018 tournament. This is an uninteresting reason for the absence of hooligan violence at a sport mega-event, but is a significant factor that may prevent large numbers of, particularly young, domestically active, hooligan participants from travelling to tournaments that are geographically distant. Many of the Russian hooligans who attended the European Championships in 2016 had their travel funded by certain football clubs, Ultras fan groups or the Russian supporters union, which is a common practice in many European nations – institutions funding the travel of fans. However, for many young working-class English supporters who would have liked to have attended the 2018 World Cup, the financial costs of getting to a sport mega-event in Russia as opposed to France made it impossible for them to attend in person.

For example, in order to attend England's opening Group game in Volgograd, a small group of Leicester City and Birmingham City hooligan participants with whom I had been conducting research domestically for another project, travelled from London to Riga in Latvia, Riga to Tallinn in Estonia, Tallinn to St. Petersburg in Russia, St. Petersburg to Volgograd, and then had to stay around 30km away in the city of Volzhskiy for two nights. The financial cost of travelling to Volgograd directly, or staying in a hotel in the host city, was far too much for the young men in this group. Subsequently, after travelling such a distance over a period of a week, any desire to search for disorder with local Russian rivals was greatly diminished. Moreover, upon coming into contact with small groups of Russian hooligans on the day of the match, some Russian fans were seen to extend a hand of friendship and wished instead to drink beer with the small number of English lads rather than to fight them.

The small numbers of English fans who travelled to the World Cup in 2018 reinforced the discourse put forward by Russian hooligan groups that after experiencing the 'superiority' of 'Russian Style' over 'Old Skool' hooliganism at the European Championships in 2016 few, if any, international hooligan firms would travel to Russia intent on trouble. Such reluctance to travel to Russia was not something I experienced in conducting my research with English youth firms, but the lack of any serious opposition for local Russian firms at 'their' mega-event helped to support this Russian narrative. The matter of nationalism trumping football hooligan rivalry amongst Russian thugs was also witnessed at the World Cup in Russia in 2018. When some young local fans in St Petersburg sought conflict with visiting supporters, other Russian hooligans stepped in to verbally reprimand the group of youths, declaring that, after all the negative geopolitical pressure on Russia pre-tournament, hosting a peaceful and successful mega-event would be an important opportunity to prove international political and media objectors in the 'West' wrong, by demonstrating Russian national organisation and public hospitality on the international stage (see also Raduszynska, Chapter 9).

Discussion

In moving towards a summary of the data presented here from both tournaments, some important conclusions emerge in relation to nationalist fandom at sport mega-events and aggressive masculinity, both inside and outside of the sporting sphere. In his comparative analysis of the football hooligan cultures that exist around six domestic clubs in London, Barcelona and Rotterdam, Ramón Spaaij (2006, p. 228) states that locality 'is never an inert primitive or a given, which pre-exists whatever arrives from outside itself'; locality 'has always had to be produced, maintained nurtured deliberately'. Spaaij uses Back et al.'s (2001) approach to understanding racism in football to explain variations in cross-cultural hooligan behaviour through exploring the constant interplay between time-space-place and symbolic or ritual hooligan group-action. In this sense, Spaaij (2006) emphasises that although there are some similarities transnationally, football hooliganism is a phenomenon with distinct differences across geographical location and time. The case study data presented here of the interactions between English and Russian hooligan fans at both the France UEFA Championships (2016) and the Russia World Cup (2018) demonstrate the importance of systematically analysing and understanding these differences for informing the organising and policing of football mega-events. These continuously evolving interactions between local-national-structural forces and individual agency can give rise to and strengthen specific forms of (hyper-)masculine gender identities.

Football hooliganism is perhaps best understood as a cultural landscape for those who identify with an aggressive supporter collective or 'firm' to attempt to negotiate a particular (hyper-)masculine identity for themselves and their group, in conjunction with broader social events that take place within the immediate locale or region, on a national or increasingly international and virtual (online) scale. The masculine gendered performances found enacted on the football terraces of each society in which the sport is played reflect the broader gendered norms of wider communities (Armstrong, 1998; King, 2002). We see some of the more aggressive aspects of certain (hyper-)gendered identities enacted within football hooligan subcultures globally. This chapter illustrates how the football hooligan 'scene' developed in 1960s England in relationship with, and in some ways response to, the spatial-regional rivalries found in localised social antagonisms and historic industrial conflicts. Thus, due to the enhanced geographic and cultural immediacy of the English domestic hooligan rivalries, it is only in the face of a greater external threat that we see otherwise rival domestic hooligan groups standing together on the international stage. In the Russian hooligan scene, the hyper-masculine ultranationalist identities of the 'Okolofutbol'shchiki', and how they are performed internationally, provide an example of a form of (hyper-)masculine, (hyper-)nationalist identity reflective of the scars of the broader socio-economic and political climate of the Russian Federation.

Russian football hooliganism and the forms of (hyper-masculine) gendered identities continually negotiated and enacted by hooligan groups are largely reflective of the broader gendered ideals held in esteem by the contemporary Russian state, intersecting with recent political-economic, social and military policies that place a new found nationalism and imagined 'might' of the Russian Federation at the core of their ideological apparatus. The case study events documented at the Euro (2016) and World Cup (2018) mega-events, as well as recent domestic developments in hooligan culture in contemporary England, Russia and beyond, demonstrate some of the complex processes involved in the way aggressive masculinities are moulded and performed by young men, both in their immediate environments and internationally.

Crucially, the rise of digitally enabled technologies has paved the way for new versions of masculine antagonisms between gendered cultures internationally. The analysis of hyper-gendered identity formation and the corresponding motivations for engaging in the inter-personal violence outlined here, suggest that hegemonic gendered values of nation states (Connell, 1995) intersect with more localised class-cultural habits and traits (Bourdieu, 1984) that find common ground with opposing hyper-gendered ideologies virtually and internationally, whilst at the same time attempting to distinguish themselves from them. This suggests the need for continued academic examination of football hooligan cultures. Further exploration is needed of different versions of aggressive gendered identities that exist globally in the myriad of our complex late-modern societies if we are to understand the reasons for displays of (hyper-)masculine nationalisms, aggression and violence at sport mega-events, both within and beyond football.

Conclusion

This chapter has drawn on ethnographic study of interactions between English and Russian hooligan fans at the UEFA European Championships 2016 and the FIFA World Cup 2018 in order to explore some of the reasons why some international football mega-events pass off peacefully, whereas others suffer serious problems of hooligan violence. The findings build on previous academic research into fan violence at sport mega-events, through illuminating the importance of the sometimes-overlooked emic subcultural developments across the football hooligan scene internationally. The work suggests that whilst policing and security concerns, the location of the tournament, and geo-political relations between nation states may all play a role in determining whether violence occurs between supporters of national teams, any existing or emerging subcultural antagonisms between football hooligan fan groups must also be taken into account by tournament organisers when considering preparations for sport mega-events. The widespread fan violence that occurred around matches in France in 2016 compared to the almost complete absence of disorder at Russia 2018 is testament to the importance of acknowledging and understanding emic subcultural developments, alongside issues of event security and locality, in assessing the likelihood of potential fan disorder and violence at international sport mega-events.

References

Armstrong, G. (1998). *Football hooligans: Knowing the score*. Oxford: Berg.

Ayres, T. C., & Treadwell, J. (2012). Bars, drugs and football thugs: Alcohol, cocaine use and violence in the nighttime economy among English football firms. *Criminology and Criminal Justice, 12*(1), 83–100.

Back, L., Crabbe, T., & Solomos, J. (2001). *The changing face of football: Racism, identity and multiculture in the English game*. Oxford: Berg.

Bourdieu, P. (1984). *Distinction: A social critique of the judgment of taste*. London: Routledge.

Brimson, D. (2003). *Euro Trashed: The rise and rise of Europe's football hooligans*. London: Headline.

Connell, R. W. (1995). *Masculinities*. Cambridge: Polity.

Duke, V., & Slepicka, P. (2002). Bohemian rhapsody: Football supporters in the Czech Republic. In E. Dunning, P. Murphy, I. Waddington, & A. Astrinakis (Eds.), *Fighting Fans: Football hooliganism as a world phenomenon* (pp. 49–61). Dublin: University College Dublin Press.

Dunning, E., Murphy, P., Waddington, I., & Astrinakis, A. (2002). *Fighting fans*. Dublin: University College Dublin Press.

Dunning, E., Murphy, P., & Williams, J. (1988). *The roots of football hooliganism: An historical and sociological study*. London: Routledge.

Eastern Europe. (2016). Eastern Europe – Beautiful thing. Retrieved from http://www.youtube.com/watch?v=QFNj3H8L7P8. Accessed on June 19, 2019.

Fafinski, S. (2007). In the back of the net: Football hooliganism and the internet. In Y. Jewkes (Ed.), *Crime online*. Cullompton: Willan Publishing.

Foxall, A. (2013). Photographing Vladimir Putin: Masculinity, nationalism and visuality in Russian political culture. *Geopolitics, 18*, 132–156.

Garland, J., & Rowe, M. (2000). The hooligan's fear of the penalty. *Soccer and Society, 1*(1), 144–157.

Giulianotti, R., & Armstrong, G. (2002). Avenues of contestation. Football hooligans running and ruling urban spaces. *Social Anthropology, 10*(2), 211–238.

Glathe, J., & Varga, M. (2018). Far-right fan culture in Russia: The politicisation of football hooligans on Russian social media. *Journal Fur Entwicklungspolitik, 34*(2), 20–49.

Hopkins, M., & Hamilton-Smith, N. (2014). Football banning orders: The highly effective cornerstone of a preventative strategy? In Hopkins & Treadwell (Eds.), *Football hooliganism, fan behaviour and crime* (pp. 222–247). London: Palgrave Macmillan.

King, A. (2002). *The end of the terraces: The transformation of English football in the 1990s* (2nd ed.). London: Leicester University Press.

King, M., & Knight, M. (1999). *Hoolifan: Thirty years of hurt*. London: Mainstream Publishing.

Kossakowski, R. (2017). From communist fan clubs to professional hooligans: A history of polish fandom as a social process. *Sociology of Sport Journal, 34*(3), 281–292.

Kozon, M. J. (2018). 'Derby of a 'difficult' history: The Poland-Russia match at Euro 2012. *Soccer and Society, 9*(5–6), 745–765.

Malinowski (2002). 'Hooligans'. Three-Part Series. BBC. [DVD off-air].

Marsh, P. (1994). Trouble on the terraces [DVD off-air].

Muller, M. (2009). *Making great power identities in Russia: An ethnographic discourse analysis of education at a Russian elite university*. Zurich: LIT.

Okolofutbola, T. V. (2016). Euro 2016/Russian hooligans in France. Retrieved from http://www.youtube.com/watch?v=wRopBwFFe0c. Accessed on February 15, 2021.

Pearson, G. (2012). *An ethnography of English football fans: Cans, cops and carnivals*. Manchester: Manchester University Press.

Pennant, C., & Nicholls, A. (2006). *30 Years of hurt; the history of England's hooligan Army*. London: Pennant Books.

Poulton, E. (2008). Toward a cultural sociology of the consumption of "fantasy football hooliganism". *Sociology of Sport Journal, 25*, 331–349.

Reicher, S. (2001). Crowds and social movements. In M. Hogg & S. Tindale (Eds.), *The Blackwell handbook of social psychology: Group processes* (pp. 232–258). Oxford: Blackwell.

Sly, J. (2019). *Revisiting Football Hooliganism Inside-Out: An exploration of the transformation of football disorder in England*. Unpublished doctoral thesis. University of Leicester.

Spaaij, R. (2006). *Understanding football hooliganism: A comparison of six Western European football clubs*. Amsterdam: Vossiuspers UvA.

Stott, C. (2014). Policing football 'hooliganism': Crowds, context and identity. In M. Hopkins & J. Treadwell (Eds.), *Football hooligans, fan behaviour and crime* (pp. 248–272). London: Palgrave Macmillan.

Stott, C., & Pearson (2006). Football banning orders, proportionality, and public order policing. *The Howard Journal, 45*(3), 241–254.

Stott, C., & Pearson (2007). *Football hooliganism: Policing and the war on the English 'disease'*. London: Pennant Books.

Stott, C., & Reicher, S. (1998). How conflict escalates: The inter-group dynamics of collective football crowd 'violence'. *Sociology, 32*(2), 353–377.

Stott, C., Hutchinson, P., & Drury, J. (2001). "Hooligans" abroad? Inter-group dynamics, social identity and participation in collective "disorder" at the 1998 World Cup Finals. *British Journal of Social Psychology, 40*, 359–384.

Stott, C., Livingstone, A., & Hogget, J. (2008). Policing football crowds in England and Wales: A model of 'good practice'? *Policing and Society, 18*(3), 258–281.

Verkhovsky, A. (2007). The rise of nationalism in Putin's Russia. *Helsinki Monitor: Security and Human Rights, 2*, 126–137.

Williams, J., Dunning, E., & Murphy, P. (1984). *Hooligans abroad: The behaviour and control of English fans in continental Europe*. London: Routledge and Kegan Paul.

Winlow, S., & Hall, S. (2009). Retaliate first: Memory, humiliation and male violence. *Crime, Media, Culture, 5*(3), 285–304.

Chapter 6

The Formula One Paradox: Macho Male Racers and Ornamental Glamour 'Girls'

Damion Sturm

Introduction

Formula One offers an interesting terrain to explore the gendered tensions that play out in a mega-event/motorsport space. Indeed, despite some recent progressive transformations, Formula One's long-standing intertwining of 'glamour' and hi-tech racing has arguably reflected and projected a set of 'traditional' gendered dynamics seemingly out of step with most contemporary mega-events. This chapter will outline some of these problematic gendered assumptions, representations and relationships. Despite revisions to contemporary masculinities and transformations within contemporary motorsport, hegemonic depictions of drivers as 'real men' exhibiting bravado, machoism and risk-taking still prevail in Formula One. In contrast, women are predominantly limited to subsidiary and largely ornamental roles, and it is argued here that despite feminist challenges to stereotypes and inequalities, Formula One has generally privileged appearance-based roles for females. More recently, while positive progressive changes have created greater opportunities for women in the sport, females seemingly still function in a decorative rather than driving capacity. The chapter begins by considering the construction of Formula One as an event, both in terms of its mega-event status and its recasting as media event and spectacle, before turning to Formula One's evocation as a 'glamorous' event.

Formula One as Mega-Event

Formula One is viewed as the pinnacle of auto racing (if not all motorsport), with expensive, sophisticated and hi-tech machines raced at global locations (23 races are planned for 2021). This generates widespread media and audience interest, as well as substantial funding from large transnational corporations who adorn the cars and drivers with their sponsors' logos (Sturm, 2014). Thus, Formula One is clearly a major sporting event while thematically being underpinned by varying elements of commercialisation, corporatisation, innovative mediation, prestige

Sport, Gender and Mega-Events, 113–130
Copyright © 2022 by Emerald Publishing Limited
All rights of reproduction in any form reserved
doi:10.1108/978-1-83982-936-920211012

and popular status that, collectively, make it a significant contemporary global sporting competition. Nevertheless, ascribing its precise event 'status' remains vexed.

Roche (2000) asserts that, '"mega-events" are large-scale cultural (including commercial and sporting) events which have a dramatic character, mass popular appeal and international significance' (p. 1). Sturm (2014) posits that Formula One would appear to fit Roche's (2000) criteria 'through its sheer scale, global exposure, elite positioning, vast commercial and corporate interests, and the mass media attention that it garners' (p. 69). Focusing on the scope, scale and reach of events, Roche (2000, 2017) notes that oscillating local and global dimensions may influence aspects such as media coverage, commercial investment, global interest or attention and tourism. Moreover, due to the contested distinctions, definitions and categories when considering whether an event is either mega, major, hallmark or special (Hall, 1992; Horne, 2007, 2010; Muller, 2015), where Formula One precisely 'fits' remains debatable. For example, Roche (2017) identifies Formula One as a 'special event', asserting that such events 'can address and be influential in both national and international-level visitor markets and media' (p. 4), which many localities explicitly buy into for self-promotional purposes when taking on Formula One host nation status (John & McDonald, 2020). In contradistinction, Hall (1992) applies 'hallmark' to linking or identifying an event with a location, seemingly supported by Lowes' (2002) reference to IndyCar racing as a hallmark event. Nevertheless, Lowes (2004) subsequently refers to the (Formula One) Australian Grand Prix as a major event while, somewhat confusingly, Formula One is classed as a mega event (Lowes, 2018), with little explanation for if or why he sees a distinction between a one-off event and the series, nor any broader rationale for his terminology.

Regardless, in terms of the significance and appeal of Formula One, its 'mega' component appears irrefutable. Currently Formula One is disseminated to approximately 400 million television viewers across 185 countries (Sylt, 2018), with broadcast rights for television (and streaming services) worth approximately $600 million annually (Saward, 2013). Moreover, the sport cost over US$2 billion per season in the 2000s (Sturm, 2014), with localities paying over US$400 million annually to obtain host-nation status (Lefebvre & Roult, 2011). The sport has also expanded beyond its European origins to Asia and the Middle East (Bromber & Krawietz, 2013; Silk & Manley, 2012), progressively rising from approximately 16 races in the 1990s to between 19 and 23 races in recent times.

Horne (2010) draws upon elements of Roche's (2000) criteria to construct a taxonomy of mega events based on their scope, scale and reach, while also considering the impacts and legacies of mega-events in terms of their cultural, economic and political significance for host localities, both pre- and post-event (see also Muller, 2015). As such, Formula One does not adhere to Horne's (2010) 'first-order' mega-events, which is solely restricted to the Summer Olympic Games and Men's Football World Cup. Arguably, Formula One would be best situated amidst Horne's (2010) 'second-order' mega-events, which includes other World Championships and World Cups in relation to international athletics, rugby, cricket and the Winter Olympics. Problematically, whether Formula One is classed as a first- or second-order mega-event, this status may not be sustainable long term due to continued high costs, the unpredictable impact of COVID-19 on global travel and a renewed scrutiny surrounding the environmental impact of motorsport (Miller, 2017; Smith, 2019; Sturm, 2018).

Formula One as Media Event and Spectacle

Originating in 1950, Sturm (2014) suggests that Formula One was repackaged 'as an event *for* the media' (p. 69) in the 1980s to help streamline what had largely been a haphazard and disjointed series with fluctuating numbers of teams and cars per race. The notion of media events was first traced by Dayan and Katz (1992) as a recurrent series of ritual-like events that comprised "contests, conquests and coronations" (inclusive of sport). Subsequent revisions have reconsidered media events as potentially either disruptive and sites of planned/unplanned protests (e.g. Couldry, Hepp, & Krotz, 2010; Spracklen & Lamond, 2016), or the domain of the more mundane, commercial and everyday workings of popular culture reproduced through traditional, digital and social media (Fox, 2016; Frosh & Pinchevski, 2017; Mitu & Poulakidakos, 2016; Ytreberg, 2017). Indeed, the overtly mediatised nature of most contemporary events means that often they are re-conceptualised and re-packaged as a set of mediated experiences for attendees via collective and individualistic forms of connectivity, co-creation and personalisation (Andrews & Ritzer, 2018; Hudson & Hudson, 2013; Hutchins, 2016; Koivisto & Mattila, 2020). In this way, many sport and non-sport events construct image-based realities (Baudrillard, 2002) and become heavily reliant upon producing consumable media content while, potentially, reducing events to an 'app', digital experience or as shareable social media content (Benigni, Porter, & Wood, 2014; Bustard, Bolan, Devine, & Hutchinson, 2019; Hoksbergen & Insch, 2016; Thompson, Martin, Gee, & Guerin, 2017).

Kellner (2003) posits that there has been a significant temporal and cultural shift from media events to media spectacles, noting how events are often usurped by and reshaped through the media as spectacles. Kellner (2003) suggests, media spectacles 'involve an aesthetic dimension and are often dramatic…They are highly public social events, often taking a ritualistic form to celebrate society's highest values…media spectacles are increasingly commercialized, vulgar, glitz, and…important arenas of political contestation' (p. 76). Collectively, sport events often reflect, embed and project many of the tapestries of history, tradition, myth and ritual permeating the select sports being re-orientated as spectacles. Kellner is also cognisant of the convergence of media, technologies, entertainment and commercialisation required to continually reproduce the event as spectacle. Therefore, these media transformations predominantly comprise the spectacular, seductive and sensationalised when representing events, using dazzling representations and excessive displays to amplify the projection and circulation of images (Kellner, 2003).

As media spectacles, motor-racing events are carefully crafted to furnish forms of sensory engagement with media representations of speed, risk, drivers and machines that are often beyond our real-world experiences or opportunities (such as driving at over 200mph in hybrid-rocket cars). For example, Sturm (2017) analyses how the Monaco Grand Prix and Indianapolis 500, both iconic events on the global motor-racing calendar, are transformed through re-presentations of immediacy, liveness and close proximity to the racing action in what, at times, can otherwise become processional or monotonous motorsport events (Sturm, 2017). Fundamentally, Formula One as media spectacle strives to balance how to render experiential elements for live in situ spectators and from pseudo-participatory driver perspectives, while informing, entertaining and retaining the large global media audience (Sturm, 2014). Collectively, televisual techniques re-present speed and danger through 20–30 diverse camera placements and perspectives (e.g. trackside, helicopters, cranes, wall mounted), with rapid transitions and frequent intercutting between dramatic angles, long shots and close-proximity framing (Sturm, 2017). There is often also a video game aesthetic to the televised coverage (Sturm, 2019b) with all cars carrying two to three on-board cameras which provide a 'dazzling' array of visual information and pseudo-participatory perspectives to relay the driving experience from an illusory shared racer's perspective (Sturm, 2014).

More broadly, the mediatisation of sport events is well established, particularly in terms of how sport has been both integrated with and transformed through the spectacle (Cairns, 2015; Frandsen, 2020; Sturm, 2021; Wenner & Billings, 2017), as well as serving an inherent promotional function around placemaking and city-branding for the host cities and nations (Chalip & Fairley, 2019; John & McDonald, 2020; Lowes, 2018). A final core component to Formula One as media spectacle is the concerted construction of what Sturm (2014) refers to as a *glamorous and hi-tech global spectacle of speed*. Collectively, this media focus merges and repackages Formula One's global, commercial and mediatised dynamics around technology and 'glamour'. Problematically, traditional notions of gender are evoked and codified as glamour, with Formula One's media spectacle punctuated by gendered stereotypes, relationships and representations.

Formula One as a (Gendered) 'Glamorous' Event

Premised on a mix of speed, expense and the exotic, notions of 'glamour' seem to crystallise around three core components. First, projections of affluence and a jet-setting orientation associate 'glamour' with the expensive and consumeristic lifestyles promoted by the sport as it travels to an array of global locations. Nowhere is this more striking than at the Monaco Grand Prix which projects 'an assemblage of iconic global images that are suggestive of wealth, prestige, elitism and symbols of excess (for example, celebrities, yachts, fashion, jewellery and stereotypically beautiful females)' (Sturm, 2017, p. 177). The gendered inferences often drawn upon to extol Monaco's glamourous appeal will be returned to.

The second link to glamour emphasises the expense and technical sophistication of the hybrid racing cars, which remain both incomparable to even top-end sports road cars and inaccessible to audiences due to their costs and capabilities (Fleming & Sturm, 2011). Hence, 'glamour' is often ascribed onto the cars as something beyond our means and comprehension. Nevertheless, gender too pervades in this technological space; presenting 'active' men as 'active' drivers and women often as ornamental props for men and their hi-tech cars.

Finally, as intimated above, it is difficult to untangle glamour in Formula One from a preconceived (and admittedly dated) set of gendered relations and performances. Indeed, arguably glamour and gender have been the default representational regime underpinning many popular narratives of the sport. For example, Noble and Hughes (2004) infer that Formula One's glamour relates to 'impossibly fast cars driven by brave and handsome young men of all nationalities in a variety of exotic backdrops throughout the world, with beautiful women looking on adoringly' (p. 25). While technologies and locations are alluded to, the gendered clichés and assumptions are pronounced in such stereotypical depictions. Men are heroic and risk-takers in their hi-tech driving pursuits, seemingly embodying Formula One's glamour via the associated luxurious lifestyle of world travel, wealth and excesses. Conversely, the relatively few women in Formula One have been marginalised and subjugated; their 'glamour' residing in a decorative capacity to adorn the cars and symbolically become trophies for these macho racers. As Turner (2004) succinctly and dismissively asserts, 'it is the ultimate male fantasist's sport: fast cars, expensive kit, global jet-setting and beautiful women with spray-on smiles' (p. 205).

Such an outdated 'tradition' and approach to the framing and encoding of gender seems at odds with how one expects a contemporary mega-event to function. Despite incremental improvements, Formula One's gendered dynamics are clearly defined, and the sport is almost exclusively a male preserve. All teams are run by male owners, team principals or technical directors, with men occupying most of the roles either within teams or within the press covering races. Not surprisingly, all the drivers are currently also men, with only five women having ever competed in Formula One; the last in 1992, interspersed with minor female test driver roles. In the foreseeable future, while a rhetorical and progressive push for a female driver will remain ever-present, Formula One is likely to continue to consist of only male drivers due to gendered stereotypes, phrased as concerns over fitness, skill and safety, remaining pervasive in the sport, while sponsors seem unwilling to invest in a female driver (Matthews & Pike, 2016; Pflugfelder, 2009; Turner, 2004). Thus, as Lenskyj (2013) reminds us, even attempts at greater inclusion or for goals of numeric gender equality (e.g. an equal distribution of female drivers on the grid) are arguably fraught and futile without the systemic and structural overhaul of a sport so overwhelmingly steeped in masculine values and privileges. This is highly unlikely to occur within Formula One anytime soon. Our attention now turns to unpacking some of these tensions, assumptions and representations of gender that circulate within Formula One.

Macho Racers

Formula One is steeped in traditional views of masculinity, aligning to a vision and version of hegemonic masculinity (Connell, 1995; Connell & Messerschmidt,

2005) that emphasises and embellishes masculine attributes such as bravado, technical mastery and risk-taking (Messner, 1992; Shackleford, 1999). Heroic deeds and mythic depictions of masculinity are also to the fore, particularly at Monaco, with Sturm (2017) asserting that 'the treatment of the sport seems meant to facilitate heroic understandings of these racing men as the noble drivers who "vanquish" opponents and "conquer" Monaco's narrow streets through the exceptional display of skill' (p. 178). Thus, connotations of masculine mastery abound, with these male drivers demonstrating their skill and bravado to supposedly 'tame' the challenging circuit. Moreover, Kennedy (2000) likens the Formula One driver to a 'knight going into battle', asserting that the 'symbolic armour and vehicle for the warrior hero is provided by the helmet, protective clothing and racing car' (p. 65). Much of this approach points to the traditional, dominant and often problematic nature of hegemonic masculinity which, subject to refinements, tends to espouse that 'real men' combine elements of heroism, aggression, bravery, toughness and strength while being men of action rather than emotions or words (Connell, 1995; Connell & Messerschmidt, 2005; Messner, 1992).

Subsequent revisions and re-conceptualisations of masculinities have challenged the dominant hegemonic model over time. Thus, 'new men' and 'new lads' (Whannel, 2002) were popular re-presentations of the 1990s and 2000s, suggesting a more sensitive, well-groomed and nurturing side to men ('new men'), which included forms of vanity, exhibitionism and narcissism via the 'metrosexual' (Coad, 2008), through to 'new lads' who were less concerned with their own appearance while favouring hedonism, excess and the renewed objectification of women (Whannel, 2002). More recently, inclusive masculinity (Anderson, 2009; Anderson & McCormack, 2018) promulgates the influence of homosexuality for shaping how men enact and perform their masculinities in relation to other men, notably with contemporary rhetoric promoting inclusivity, diversity and greater acceptance, or at least tolerance, of same-sex relations. However, by neglecting different contexts and scenes for male interrelations, Pringle (2018) suggests that inclusive masculinity arguably overestimates the significance of homosexuality alone, particularly by overlooking how relations with females also inform and influence masculinities.

Intriguingly, despite four decades of critical research, masculinity/masculinities still remains contested, complex and confusing as a concept. For example, Crocket, Pringle, and Puddle (in press) question whether the notion of masculinity:

> Should be tied to male *and* female bodies, refers to something fluid and fractured *rather* than solid and identifiable; affirms *or* rejects the concept of a gender binary, is a performance *rather* than an identity category, and whether theories of masculinities should be underpinned by feminist ideals *or* not.
>
> (n.p.)

While the above challenges are not easily resolved and remain pertinent to analyses of masculinity/masculinities, notions of flexible masculinity (Gee, 2014; Gee & Jackson, 2017) potentially yield useful insights by asserting that masculinities are fluid and adaptable, reading and reacting to contemporary contexts and constraints to enact performances of masculinities in often multiple and modified ways.

Similar transformations have emerged within Formula One to permit a softening of male driver images and representations, such as Lewis Hamilton's ever-changing fashion and style on social media, or Daniel Riccardo's often jocular and self-deprecating interviews. Additionally, more drivers are demonstrating inclusive or flexible masculinity through some of their displays and performances, albeit against a backdrop of commodified and corporate masculinity unduly influenced by teams and/or sponsors via the branded displays or overtly manufactured driver personas (Fleming & Sturm, 2011). However, the lack of any publicly acknowledged gay or trans Formula One drivers (or for any other men in significant positions of power in the sport) suggests disruptive unpackings of masculinities, or progressive notions of gender more broadly, are still a long way off (Anderson & McCormack, 2018; Crocket et al., in press). Fundamentally, Formula One has stubbornly and steadfastly clung to displays of 'bravado-exhibiting male racing drivers in a fashion that is cartoonish in its perpetuation of old stereotypes' (Fleming & Sturm, 2011, p. 169). Hence, variations of hegemonic masculinity remain the dominant framework, with Formula One allegedly the domain of and for 'real men'.

The history of motorsport has invariably been linked with masculine traits, with Matthews and Pike (2016) noting that 'the motor car emerged from an industrial yet elitist, masculine dominated Western culture. Males were often those who manufactured early motor cars' (p. 1546), while 'motoring was associated with mechanical engineering, speed and bravery; traits not ascribed to women of the time' (p. 1546). Additionally, Wagg (in press) provides a sketch of early motor-racing, including key developments around risk and safety in Formula One from its origins in 1950 through to present day. Specifically, Wagg (in press) showcases the pioneering male drivers, the grave risks and dangers encountered, as well as the assemblage of wealthy, entrepreneurial and 'playboy' characteristics (e.g. enjoying the companionship of glamorous females away from racing) associated with these 'real men'.

Poignantly, while steeped in risks, Formula One's too frequent driver fatalities ushered in a raft of safety features that, since the mid-1960s, have made the sport relatively safe in contemporary times. Thus, while masculine bravado and risk-taking are entrenched as endemic to Formula One, and while the spectre of death (Baudrillard, 2002) may loom over the sport due to wheel-to-wheel racing at speeds in excess of 200mph, ironically Formula One has become relatively safe and sanitised. Indeed, there have only been four driver fatalities in nearly 40 years – Gilles Villeneuve at Zolder (Belgium) in 1982, Roland Ratzenburger and Ayrton Senna in separate incidents at Imola in 1994, and most recently Jules Bianchi in Japan in 2015. In 2020, with his car split in half by barriers and engulfed in flames, Romain Grosjean had a fortunate escape at Bahrain (Morlidge, 2020).

Other contemporary transformations have blunted the need for machoism, bravado, mastery and risk-taking in Formula One. A raft of regulations, including the ban on re-fuelling in 2009 (on the grounds of safety) and the new 'hybrid' technology era since 2014, requires drivers to manage, conserve and preserve their cars in a manner that seemingly is at odds with 'racing'. Indeed, the contemporary state of Formula One led seven-time world champion Lewis Hamilton to decry Formula One as being 'too easy' for young drivers, while bemoaning the lack of effort, risk or fear for drivers (Hamilton, 2019). Finally, further encroaching into Formula One's space is the appeal of eSports and sim-racing which, through their rapid progression, development and commercialisation, are offering an alternative 'virtual' motorsport avenue replete with championships and ratification by official organisations (Robeers & Sharp, 2020; Sturm, 2019b).

Hence, despite mythological media representations of the drivers as hegemonic and heroic 'real men', the once sacred space for displays of masculine bravado, mastery and risk-taking is being largely negated in contemporary Formula One racing. Of course, forms of technical mastery and control are still evinced in both the design of and servicing of these cars (Shackleford, 1999), and through the exclusivity of male-only racers driving these machines (Baudrillard, 2002). Our attention now turns to the interrelationship, positioning and role of women in Formula One which offers a further layering to the workings of gender.

Ornamental Females

With men as the alleged bravado-infused and risk-taking drivers, the technical experts, the team leaders, and as the owners and controllers of the sport, the relatively few women in Formula One have overwhelmingly been cast in a supporting role. Pflugfelder (2009) asserts that 'in most racing series, women support male drivers and are relegated to the stands or garages. The typical position of women in racing is that of the wife or girlfriend of the male driver' (p. 414). Problematically, throughout the history of Formula One, women have primarily functioned as adornments or trophies for the men and their cars; most overtly via grid girls dressed in revealing lycra suits, mini-skirts or bikinis adorned with sponsors' logos. While Formula One may have removed the grid girls in 2018 (Jakubowska, 2018; Tippet, 2020), persistent sexism and a lack of opportunities have long pervaded.

Formula One is arguably trapped in a time warp of still encountering and negotiating with second-wave feminism which, fundamentally, seeks forms of equality, equal opportunity and fairer (media) representation for female athletes and for women in sport more broadly (Cooky, Messner, & Musto, 2015; Hargreaves, 1994; Jeanes et al., 2020). Many of these battles for access and forms of equality have already been waged in a range of other sports since the 1960s and 1970s, even including other motorsports. Problematically, when compared to Formula One, female drivers have had greater prominence in other series such as

IndyCar and Le Mans (Pflugfelder, 2009). Regrettably, the sparse and largely unsuccessful driving history of only five female Formula One drivers paints a forlorn picture of limited opportunities and sponsorship while attempting to qualify poor cars (Matthews & Pike, 2016). As such, female Formula One drivers total a mere 15 race starts and one 'half' point, scored back in 1975.

Broader second-wave feminist (and increasingly post-feminist) analyses have also explored the forms of marginalisation, trivialisation, sexualised representations and other narrowly conceived frameworks that often lead to the poor treatment of women's sport and/or female athletes (Bernstein, 2002; Bruce, 2013; Dashper, 2018; Fuller, 2006). Jakubowska (2018) observes that sociocultural changes have 'influenced the perception of women's roles and their representations. As a consequence, and according to the second wave of feminism, sexualised images of women are perceived as imposed by men and maintain male domination by women's objectification' (p. 126). Clearly this has implications for the presence of grid girls and the subsequent divisive debate that erupted after their ban, which will be returned to shortly. However, elements of misogyny and the subsidiary roles accorded for women have also influenced the explicitly gendered terrain of Formula One.

Recently, while a handful of female drivers have been signed up by teams, they have been relegated to testing or 'development' roles. For example, Susie Wolff joined Williams in 2012 as their development and test driver, becoming the first female driver to run in a practice session since 1992 at the 2014 British Grand Prix. Nevertheless, Wolff retired from all racing in 2015, reportedly inferring that she realised no racing opportunity was going to materialise: 'I wanted and fought very hard to make it on to that starting grid but the events at the start of this year and the environment in F1 the way it is, it isn't going to happen' (Weaver, 2015, para. 8). Wolff also allegedly stated,

> Do I think F1 is ready for a competitive female racing driver who can perform at the highest level? Yes. Do I think it is achievable as a woman? Most definitely. Do I think it will happen soon? Sadly no.
>
> (Weaver, 2015, para. 10)

Similarly, with four years previous IndyCar experience, Simona de Silvestro became an affiliated driver for Sauber in 2014 before a financial 'contractual' dispute (in lower teams most race and test drivers are 'pay-drivers', providing forms of finance that pay for the opportunity to drive) ended her 2015 race prospects (Anderson, 2014). Otherwise, only a few females have actually driven in official testing capacities, notably Katherine Legge in 2005 and Tatiana Calderón in 2018, both moving on to other series as Formula One drives were unlikely.

The crash and subsequent death of María de Villota arguably did little to advance the prospects of future female drivers. Already slated as a paying test driver with no acknowledged track record of any motorsport success, de Villota had a bizarre accident in straight line testing for the Marussia team in 2012.

Seemingly stopped, de Villota then accelerated into the back of a team transporter at helmet level between 30 and 40mph (Tremayne, 2012); de Villota would lose her right eye and later die from associated complications in 2013 (Wagg, in press). For different reasons, the hiring of Carmen Jorda by the Lotus and then Renault team as a development driver between 2015 and 2017 was also criticised. Essentially, Jorda paid for the opportunity while primarily being utilised for her appearance (Newbold, 2015). Notably, with a highest finish of 28th in three previous seasons in the GP3 series, there was the broader perception that 'without any on-track success, it's tough to take her seriously as a driver when her official website gallery is basically a supermodel photo shoot that sometimes incorporates a fire suit' (Carmen, 2015, para. 9). Jorda was never used in any meaningful driving capacity by the teams; rather, although not explicitly sexualised, Jorda would be positioned prominently in sponsored team gear to ensure that she regularly featured on global race telecasts. Thus, Jorda seemingly had an ornamental 'development driver' role with Lotus and Renault geared towards a media emphasis on her appearance rather than driving ability.

Of course, there have been more progressive steps for women within the sport. Monisha Kaltenborn was the first female team principal (e.g. the boss or leader in charge of the team) for Sauber from 2012 until 2017, while Claire Williams was deputy-principal of the Williams F1 team alongside her father, Frank Williams, from 2015 to 2020. However, both women generally oversaw struggling, lower order teams and left due to Sauber's new technical partnership with Alfa Romeo and Williams' change of ownership. Collectively, across the last 5 to 10 years, more females are taking on diverse roles within teams – such as race strategists, engineers, designers, aero dynamists, mechanics etc. – albeit Formula One remains an overwhelmingly male sport in terms of team compositions and global fan bases (Sturm, 2014).

Consequently, most women in Formula One tend to work in catering and the public relations sector for teams, such as media-, sponsor- or driver-liaison. Here, again, 'feminine' qualities seem to be a pre-requisite within the male world of Formula One. In her interview with Michael Schumacher's media manager Sabine Kehm, Turner (2004) alleges 'she admits that feminine "charm" can be a powerful negotiating tool in Formula One. Sabine is slim and blonde. She fits the F1 criteria perfectly' (p. 159). Additionally, Matthews and Pike (2016) observed that British television reporter Lee McKenzie was often the only woman working trackside at most Formula One events, noting '"It is still very much a man's world", she says. 'There are about two hundred guys to every woman. The only girls there are models or girlfriends. It is very chauvinistic"' (p. 1541). Most major media networks covering Formula One do now have female presenters or reporters in the field. Nevertheless, despite some signs of improvement, there still seems to be a gendered construction of women as facilitators, sexy props or adornments for the male drivers and world of Formula One.

At its most blatant, grid girls were an overt signifier of Formula One's gendered relations via its myopic sexualised representation of 'glamour' in relation to females (Tippet, 2020). Originating in the 1960s and initially linked to sponsors rather than the teams (Jakubowska, 2018), grid girls have always filled a decorative, ornamental or sexualised function within the sport and in relation to men more broadly. Thus, young and conventionally 'beautiful' women are photographed either sprawled over the cars for publicity, on the pre-race formation grid beside the cars and drivers or posing for 'sexy' photos with the drivers (and attendees at some races). From the late 2000s, a 'guard of honour' was provided for the top three drivers 'from the track to the podium by up to 100 female models applauding them, or in other supporting roles' (Matthews & Pike, 2016, p. 1545). Elements of diversity have also been notable, with 'local' grid girls of different nationalities and ethnicities in all locations, such as Brazil, China, Hungary, Italy, Japan and Malaysia. Nevertheless, these potentially 'progressive' politics are essentially versions of 'stylized exoticism' (Silk & Manley, 2012, p. 475) that offer symbolic novelty and seductive images of the 'other', with Formula One presenting a selective line-up of young females in the host nation's sexualized attire as stereotypical projections of localized beauty and as an 'exotic' prize (Sturm, 2014).

It has been suggested that the prominence of stereotypically beautiful women (e.g. grid girls and driver partners and/or wives), operated, symbolically at least, as part of the 'spoils of victory' for the winning driver via their explicitly sexualised representations dismissively codified as glamour. Kennedy (2000) notes in her narrative analysis of the 1996 Monaco Grand Prix,

> The role of 'beautiful women' in providing that glamour is evident, and the plentiful camera shots of (mainly blonde haired) women among the spectators at balconies or employees of the racing teams (holding placards with the driver's name inscribed) testify to their importance in creating the atmosphere. The narrative function of closure provided by the 'beautiful women' is clear….they are part of the prize for the victorious hero driver.
>
> (p. 65)

Moreover, with reference to Monaco, often the global telecast will pick out or linger on the celebrated, the bikini-clad and the beautiful, inferring their central role in contributing to its allegedly glamorous spectacle (Sturm, 2017).

Nevertheless and perhaps unsurprisingly, with an obvious disconnect from the sport and in the context of the #MeToo movement against female sexual harassment, grid girls were banned by Formula One management in 2018 for being 'at odds with modern societal norms' (F1, 2018, para. 3). Jakubowska (2018) and Tippet (2020) provided separate analyses of the mediated representations and reactions to the banning of grid girls which both suggested revolved around exploitation versus empowerment debates. On one side, proponents lauded the ban in relation to second wave feminism perspectives. Tippet (2020) argues that the overt sexualisation and objectification of grid girls offered up to male audiences essentially reinforced forms of male entitlement, asserting that,

> Photographs of male race car drivers and male motor sports enthusiasts with grid girls surrounding them denotes a broader

message that is recurrent in society; men hold positions of power, whilst women are there to decorate and adorn their positions of authority. Women are thus consistently constructed in promotional modelling as complimentary to men.

(p. 197)

Collectively, such practices were deemed to be unnecessary and outdated, with opponents critical of the explicitly sexualised ornamental function that grid girls played as sexy props and in subsidiary roles in support of men (Jakubowska, 2018; Tippet, 2020).

Conversely, the often more vocal counterarguments posed by traditional fans and the grid girls themselves bemoaned forms of political correctness as well as the lost opportunity to provide 'glamour' or to be paid for such promotional work. Specifically, Jakubowska (2018) and Tippet (2020) noted the barbed attacks on second-wave feminism and accusations that female opponents were being 'feminazis', 'killjoys' and 'traditionalists' imposing their views and values unnecessarily, even though it was Formula One Management who took the decision to ban grid girls. Here, post-feminism and neoliberal sensibilities were being espoused (Thorpe, Toffoletti, & Bruce, 2017; Toffoletti & Thorpe, 2018), with individuated agency reflecting if and how women self-portray, self-objectify and self-sexualise (Carah & Dobson, 2016; Sturm, 2019a). Moreover, the prevalence of provocative sexual agency and hetero-sexy practices is conceived to potentially be empowering for the women involved, while generating promotional and commercial opportunities (Gill, 2016), which was clearly evident in many of the grid girl responses (Tippet, 2020).

More broadly, such post-feminist sensibilities could be expanded to some of the other roles long held by females in Formula One; for example, those who can capitalise on 'feminine charm' in public relations roles (Turner, 2004). Furthermore, it could be argued that, despite her appearance-based 'development driver' role, Formula One availed Carmen Jorda a platform for enhancing her global and media profile, while engaging in entrepreneurial strategies of the self (Sturm, 2019a; Toffoletti & Thorpe, 2018). Nevertheless, the clear demarcation of often subsidiary and subservient roles seemingly determined and assigned by 'gender' is suggestive of a somewhat outdated approach to femininities (and gender relations more broadly) historically ensconced within Formula One.

Conclusion

It is perhaps astonishing in 2021 to still be conceiving of significant 'real-world' male domains as masculine fantasies (Fleming & Sturm, 2011). Indeed sport, like most areas of socio-cultural life, has needed to undergo revision to redress unfair gendered practices, barriers and inequality. Of course, not all spheres of sport or social life have been rectified, while any impulse to pursue a strand of post-feminism that suggests feminism is 'won', 'over' or that 'equality for all' exists seems wide of the mark (see critiques in Gill, 2016; Tippet, 2020). And, yet,

Turner's (2004) statement that Formula One 'is the ultimate male fantasist's sport' (p. 205) still seemingly rings true given the myopic infatuation with technology, elitism, bravado and gendered divisions codified via notions of glamour and reinforced through Formula One's media spectacle. Nevertheless, some of Formula One's myths, traditions and popular media narratives are gradually shifting, or are not as symbolically powerful as they were once supposed.

Formula One's mega-event status may have a limited shelf-life if it cannot find ways to be more economically, environmentally and socially sustainable. Notably, with the future of fossil fuel and cars in flux, the sport may soon struggle for relevance despite its 'hybrid' focus. Furthermore, the machoism, bravado and risk-taking historically revered in Formula One and mythically evoked and exalted in contemporary Formula One mediations has been reconfigured and reassembled through technology. With a greater emphasis on driver safety, the encroachment of technologies mitigates against potential fatalities while literally taking elements of bravado and risk-taking out of the driver's control. Finally, societal shifts have ushered in a softening, diversified and more inclusive framework of and for different masculinities (Anderson, 2009; Gee & Jackson, 2017). Formula One cannot remain immune to these shifts, even if residual traces and cartoonish stereotypes attempt to retain and perpetuate hegemonic myths of the drivers as 'real men'.

Somewhat ironically, though, that is the point – Formula One, despite its attempts at progressive politics and positive transformations, remains welded to preserving a masculine fantasy and this hi-tech, 'glamorous' sport as distinctly male (Fleming & Sturm, 2011; Sturm, 2014). Thus, despite the gains of feminist movements, Formula One remains mired in gendered demarcations for men and women. Females are involved in Formula One but generally in subsidiary, supportive or submissive roles. However, women have run teams and do provide expertise through specialist design and technical roles, while the overt sexualisation of glamour has been vanquished with the banning of the grid girls since 2018.

Nevertheless, the focal point of Formula One, the prestigious role as driver, has evaded women since 1992, with only constrained test or development roles occasionally meted out. Thus, fundamentally, female drivers also fulfil largely ornamental roles – literally, via the photogenic mediated appearances of drivers like Carmen Jorda – or functionally, as rhetorical and symbolic figurines of progress – with no real change being enacted. Thus, despite its hi-tech vision and futuristic motorsport innovations, Formula One as a mega-event promulgates a blinkered vision of progressive gender politics. Fundamentally, the gendered role demarcations, the retention of appearance-based ornamental roles for females, however subtle or overt, and the limited opportunities for meaningful female involvement need to be addressed if Formula One wishes to remain relevant, sustainable or acceptable as a sporting mega event. Cognisant of contemporary gender relations, Formula One cannot afford to remain mired in its traditional practices and gendered performances of the past.

References

Anderson, E. (2009). *Inclusive masculinity: The changing nature of masculinities*. New York, NY: Routledge.

Anderson, B. (2014, October 1). De Silvestro's F1 career in jeopardy as Sauber deal hits trouble. *Autosport*. Retrieved from https://www.autosport.com/f1/news/116103/de-silvestro-f1-career-in-jeopardy

Anderson, E., & McCormack, M. (2018). Inclusive masculinity theory: Overview, reflection and refinement. *Journal of Gender Studies, 27*(5), 547–561.

Andrews, D., & Ritzer, G. (2018). Sport and prosumption. *Journal of Consumer Culture, 18*(2), 356–373.

Baudrillard, J. (2002). *Screened out* (C. Turner, Trans.). New York, NY: Verso. Original work published 2000.

Benigni, V., Porter, L., & Wood, C. (2014). The new game day: Fan engagement and the marriage of mediated and mobile. In A. Billings & M. Hardin (Eds.), *Routledge handbook of sport and new media* (pp. 225–236). New York, NY: Routledge.

Bernstein, A. (2002). Is it time for a victory lap? Changes in the media coverage of sport. *International Review for the Sociology of Sport, 37*(3–4), 415–428.

Bromber, K., & Krawietz, B. (2013). The United Arab Emirates, Qatar and Bahrain as a modern sport hub. In K. Bromber, B. Krawietz, & J. Maguire (Eds.), *Sport across Asia: Politics, cultures and identities* (pp. 189–211). New York, NY: Routledge.

Bruce, T. (2013). Reflections on communication and sport: On women and femininities. *Communication & Sport, 1*(1–2), 125–137.

Bustard, J., Bolan, P., Devine, A., & Hutchinson, K. (2019). The emerging smart event experience: An interpretative phenomenological analysis. *Tourism Review, 74*(1), 116–128.

Cairns, G. (2015). The hybridization of sight in the hybrid architecture of sport: The effects of television on stadia and spectatorship. *Sport in Society, 18*(6), 734–749.

Carah, N., & Dobson, A. (2016). Algorithmic hotness: Young women's 'promotion' and 'reconnaissance' work via social media body images. *Social Media and Society, 2*(4), 1–10.

Carmen Jorda and Formula One's money problem. (2015, February 27). AutoWeek. Retrieved from https://www.autoweek.com/racing/formula-1/a1864611/carmen-jorda-sexism-and-formula-one/. Accessed on December 18, 2020.

Chalip, L., & Fairley, S. (2019). Thinking strategically about sport events. *Journal of Sport & Tourism, 23*(4), 155–158.

Coad, D. (2008). *The metrosexual: Gender, sexuality, and sport*. Albany, NY: State University of New York Press.

Connell, R. (1995). *Masculinities*. St. Leonards, NSW: Allen & Unwin.

Connell, R., & Messerschmidt, J. (2005). Hegemonic masculinity: Rethinking the concept. *Gender & Society, 19*(6), 829–859.

Cooky, C., Messner, M., & Musto, M. (2015). "It's dude time!" A quarter century of excluding women's sports in televised news and highlight shows. *Communication & Sport, 3*(3), 261–287.

Couldry, N., Hepp, A., & Krotz, F. (Eds.). (2010). *Media events in a global age*. London: Routledge.

Crocket, H., Pringle, R., & Puddle, D. (in press). Masculinities in alternative sports: Ultimate frisbee and Parkour. In D. Sturm & R. Kerr (Eds.), *Sport in Aotearoa/ New Zealand: Contested terrain*. London: Routledge.

Dashper, K. (2018). Smiling assassins, brides-to-be and super mums: The importance of gender and celebrity in media framing of female athletes at the 2016 Olympic Games. *Sport in Society, 21*(11), 1739–1757.

Dayan, D., & Katz, E. (1992). *Media events: The live broadcasting of history*. Cambridge, MA: Harvard University Press.

F1. (2018, January 31). Formula 1 to stop using grid girls. Retrieved from www.formula1.com/en/latest/headlines/2018/1/formula-1-to-stop-using-grid-girls-.html

Fleming, D., & Sturm, D. (2011). *Media, masculinities and the machine: F1, transformers and fantasizing technology at its limits*. New York, NY: Continuum.

Fox, A. (Ed.). (2016). *Global perspectives on media events in contemporary society*. Hershey, PA: ICI Global.

Frandsen, K. (2020). *Sport and mediatization*. London: Routledge.

Frosh, P., & Pinchevski, A. (2017). Media and events after media events. *Media, Culture & Society, 40*(1), 135–138.

Fuller, L. (Ed.). (2006). *Sport, rhetoric and gender. Historical perspectives and media representations*. New York, NY: Palgrave.

Gee, S. (2014). Bending the codes of masculinity: David Beckham and flexible masculinity in the new millennium. *Sport in Society, 17*(7), 917–936.

Gee, S., & Jackson, S. (2017). *Sport, promotional culture and the crisis of masculinity*. London: Palgrave Macmillan.

Gill, R. (2016). Post-postfeminism? New feminist visibilies in postfeminist times. *Feminist Media Studies, 16*(4), 610–630.

Hall, M. (1992). *Hallmark tourist events: Impacts, management and planning*. London: Bellhaven.

Hamilton, L. (2019, May 20). F1 cars are not hard enough to drive. PlanetF1.com. Retrieved from https://www.planetf1.com/news/hamilton-f1-cars-are-not-hard-enough-to-drive/. Accessed on December 1, 2020.

Hargreaves, J. (1994). *Critical issues in the history and sociology of women's sports*. London: Routledge.

Hoksbergen, E., & Insch, A. (2016). Facebook as a platform for co-creating music festival experiences: The case of New Zealand's Rhythm and Vines New Year's Eve festival. *International Journal of Event and Festival Management, 7*(2), 84–99.

Horne, J. (2007). The four 'knowns' of sports mega-events. *Leisure Studies, 26*(1), 81–96.

Horne, J. (2010). Cricket in consumer culture: Notes on the 2007 Cricket World Cup. *American Behavioral Scientist, 53*(10), 1549–1568.

Hudson, S., & Hudson, R. (2013). Engaging with consumers using social media: A case study of music festivals. *International Journal of Event & Festival Management, 4*(3), 206–223.

Hutchins, B. (2016). "We don't need no stinking smartphones!" Live stadium sports events, mediatization, and the non-use of mobile media. *Media, Culture & Society, 38*(3), 420–436.

Jakubowska, H. (2018). No more grid girls at Formula One: The discourse analysis on hostesses' sexualized bodies, objectification, and female agency. *Society Register, 2*(1), 113–130.

Jeanes, R., Spaaij, R., Farquharson, K., McGrath, G., Magee, J., Lusher, D., & Gorman, S. (2020). Gender relations, gender equity, and community sports spaces. *Journal of Sport and Social Issues*. doi:10.1177/0193723520962955

John, A., & McDonald, B. (2020). How elite sport helps to foster and maintain a neoliberal culture: The 'branding' of Melbourne, Australia. *Urban Studies*, *57*(6), 1184–1200.

Kellner, D. (2003). *Media spectacle*. New York, NY: Routledge.

Kennedy, E. (2000). Bad boys and gentlemen: Gendered narrative in televised sport. *International Review for the Sociology of Sport*, *35*(1), 59–73.

Koivisto, E., & Mattila, P. (2020). Extending the luxury experience to social media–User-generated content co-creation in a branded event. *Journal of Business Research*, *117*, 570–578.

Lefebvre, S., & Roult, R. (2011). Formula One's new urban economies. *Cities*, *28*(4), 330–339.

Lenskyj, H. (2013). *Gender politics and the Olympic industry*. New York, NY: Palgrave Macmillan.

Lowes, M. (2002). *Indy dreams and urban nightmares: Speed merchants, spectacle, and the struggle over public space in the world class city*. Toronto, ON: University of Toronto Press.

Lowes, M. (2004). Neoliberal power politics and the controversial siting of the Australian Grand Prix motorsport event in a public park. *Loisir et Société/Society and Leisure*, *27*, 69–88.

Lowes, M. (2018). Toward a conceptual understanding of Formula One motorsport and local cosmopolitanism discourse in urban placemarketing strategies. *Communication & Sport*, *6*(2), 203–218.

Matthews, J., & Pike, E. (2016). 'What on earth are they doing in a racing car?' Towards an understanding of women in motorsport. *The International Journal of the History of Sport*, *33*(13), 1532–1550.

Messner, M. (1992). *Power at play: Sport and the problem of masculinity*. Boston, MA: Beacon.

Miller, T. (2017). *Greenwashing sport*. New York, NY: Routledge.

Mitu, B., & Poulakidakos, S. (Eds.). (2016). *Media events: A critical contemporary approach*. London: Palgrave Macmillan.

Morlidge, M. (2020, December 5). Romain Grosjean exclusive: Haas driver was 'at peace' with death as he recounts dramatic Bahrain crash. *Sky Sports*. Retrieved from https://www.skysports.com/f1/news/12433/12150934/romain-grosjean-exclusive-haas-driver-was-at-peace-with-death-as-he-recounts-dramatic-bahrain-crash

Muller, M. (2015). What makes an event a mega-event? Definitions and sizes. *Leisure Studies*, *34*(6), 627–642.

Newbold, J. (2015, May 6). Lotus sent the wrong message by signing Carmen Jordá. *Vice Sports*. Retrieved from https://www.vice.com/en/article/kbma5w/lotus-sent-the-wrong-message-by-signing-carmen-jord

Noble, J., & Hughes, M. (2004). *Formula One racing for dummies. An insider's guide to Formula One*. Chichester: John Wiley & Sons.

Pflugfelder, E. (2009). Something less than a driver: Toward an understanding of gendered bodies in motorsport. *Journal of Sport and Social Issues*, *33*(4), 411–426.

Pringle, R. (2018). On the development of sport and masculinities research: Feminism as a discourse of inspiration and theoretical legitimation. In L. Mansfield,

J. Caudwell, B. Wheaton, & B. Watson (Eds.), *The Palgrave handbook of feminism and sport, leisure and physical education* (pp. 73–93). London: Palgrave Macmillan.

Robeers, T., & Sharp, L. (2020). British and American media framing of online sim racing during Covid-19. In P. Pedersen, B. Ruihley, & B. Li (Eds.), *Sport and the pandemic: Perspectives on Covid-19's impact on the sport industry* (pp. 95–105). London: Routledge.

Roche, M. (2000). *Mega-events and modernity*. London: Routledge.

Roche, M. (2017). *Mega-events and social change: Spectacle, legacy and public culture*. Manchester: Manchester University Press.

Saward, J. (2013, January 7). Some ruminations on TV rights. *JoeblogsF1*. Retrieved from http://joesaward.wordpress.com/2013/01/07/some-ruminations-on-tv-rights/

Shackleford, B. (1999). Masculinity, hierarchy, and the auto racing fraternity. The pit stop as a celebration of social roles. *Men and Masculinities, 2*(2), 180–196.

Silk, M., & Manley, A. (2012). Globalization, urbanization and sporting spectacle in Pacific Asia: Places, peoples and pastness. *Sociology of Sport Journal, 29*(4), 455–484.

Smith, A. (2019). Justifying and resisting public park commercialisation: The battle for Battersea Park. *European Urban and Regional Studies, 26*(2), 171–185.

Spracklen, K., & Lamond, I. (2016). *Critical event studies*. London: Routledge.

Sturm, D. (2014). A glamorous and high-tech global spectacle of speed: Formula One motor racing as mediated, global and corporate spectacle. In K. Dashper, T. Fletcher, & N. McCullough (Eds.), *Sports events, society and culture* (pp. 68–82). London: Routledge.

Sturm, D. (2017). The Monaco Grand Prix and Indianapolis 500: Projecting European glamour and global Americana. In L. Wenner & A. Billings (Eds.), *Sport, media and mega-events* (pp. 170–184). New York, NY: Routledge.

Sturm, D. (2018). Formula E's 'green' challenge to motorsport events: The London e-prix as a case study. In H. Seraphin & E. Nolan (Eds.), *Green events and green tourism* (pp. 145–153). London: Routledge.

Sturm, D. (2019a). 'I dream of Genie': Eugenie Bouchard's 'body' of work on Facebook. *Celebrity Studies, 10*(4), 583–587.

Sturm, D. (2019b). Not your average Sunday driver: The Formula 1 Esports Series world championship. In R. Rogers (Ed.), *Understanding Esports: An introduction to the global phenomenon* (pp. 153–165). Lanham, MD: Lexington Books.

Sturm, D. (2021). From idyllic past-time to spectacle of accelerated intensity: Tele-visual technologies in contemporary cricket. *Sport in Society, 24*(8), 1305–1321.

Sylt, C. (2018, November 9). F1 audience crashes 5% on switch to pay TV. *Forbes*. Retrieved from https://www.forbes.com/sites/csylt/2018/11/09/f1-audience-crashes-5-on-switch-to-pay-tv/#22a10e3c4817

Thompson, A., Martin, A., Gee, S., & Guerin, A. (2017). Fans' perceptions of professional tennis events' social media presence: Interaction, insight, and brand anthropomorphism. *Communication & Sport, 5*(5), 579–603.

Thorpe, H., Toffoletti, K., & Bruce, T. (2017). Sportswomen and social media: Bringing third-wave feminism, postfeminism, and neoliberal feminism into conversation. *Journal of Sport and Social Issues, 41*(5), 359–383.

Tippett, A. (2020). Debating the F1 grid girls: Feminist tensions in British popular culture. *Feminist Media Studies, 20*(2), 185–202.

Toffoletti, K., & Thorpe, H. (2018). Female athletes' self-representation on social media: A feminist analysis of neoliberal marketing strategies in 'economies of visibility'. *Feminism and Psychology, 28*(1), 11–31.

Tremayne, D. (2012, July 8). The de Villota accident. *Grand Prix Plus, 106*, 24–25.

Turner, B. (2004). *The pits: The real world of Formula One.* London: Atlantic.

Wagg, S. (in press). 'It was ironic that he should die in bed': Injury, death and the politics of safety in the history of motor racing. In S. Wagg & A. Pollock (Eds.), *The Palgrave handbook of sport, politics and harm.* London: Palgrave.

Weaver, P. (2015, November 4). Susie Wolff quits after admitting F1 dream 'isn't going to happen'. *The Guardian.* Retrieved from https://www.theguardian.com/sport/2015/nov/04/susie-wolff-quits-f1-dream-williams

Wenner, L., & Billings, A. (Eds.). (2017). *Sport, media and mega-events.* New York, NY: Routledge.

Whannel, G. (2002). *Media sport stars. Masculinities and moralities.* London: Routledge.

Ytreberg, E. (2017). Towards a historical understanding of the media event. *Media, Culture & Society, 39*(3), 309–324.

Section 3
Gender, Disruption and Transformation at Mega-Events

Chapter 7

'Dare to Shine': Megan Rapinoe as the Rebellious Star of the FIFA Women's World Cup 2019

Riikka Turtiainen

FIFA Women's World Cup France 2019: From Marginal to Mainstream

Research findings have proved for decades that there is gender inequality in the sports world. Women's sport has a secondary status compared to male sports, and women's sports media coverage, especially in 'masculine' team sports, has failed to evolve much (e.g. Cooky, Messner, & Musto, 2015; Domeneghetti, 2018; Fink, 2015; Kian, Bernstein, & McGuire, 2013). However, there has been a lot of positive progress around media coverage of women's football recently.

In 2019, the FIFA Women's World Cup eventually turned into a mega-event. The official slogan of the tournament was 'Dare to Shine', reflecting the desire for the empowerment of girls and women through the sport. The viewing figures prove that the popularity of the women's game is truly growing: FIFA (2019) announced that over a billion people watched the event worldwide and over 82 million viewers watched the final game live. Coverage on digital platforms was accessed by 481.5 million people. Consequently, there is no longer room for excuses such as: 'there is no interest in women's football' or 'the quality of the game is poor' (see also Sherwood, Osborne, Nicholson, & Sherry, 2017). It seems that, finally, male sports followers also realise the true skills and athleticism of top female football players. One reason for that was the investment in the television broadcasting: in many countries the World Cup games were shown for the first time, with pre- and post-game programmes, and analysed closely by the studio hosts and guest specialists. The mainstream media has a responsibility for promoting women's sport and right now is the culturally relevant moment for a change in mentality. Furthermore, increasing numbers of followers and greater media coverage assist women's football to attract more sponsors (e.g. Finstad-Milion, Rethore, & Stengelhofen, 2019; Leberman & Froggatt, 2019). FIFA has now recognised the growing interest in female football and the commercial

Sport, Gender and Mega-Events, 133–148
doi:10.1108/978-1-83982-936-920211013

opportunity it offers. As FIFA President Gianni Infantino (FIFA.com, 2019) has articulated:

> More than a sporting event, the FIFA Women's World Cup 2019 was a cultural phenomenon attracting more media attention than ever before and providing a platform for women's football to flourish in the spotlight. The fact that we broke the 1 billion target just shows the pulling power of the women's game and the fact that, if we promote and broadcast world-class football widely, whether it's played by men or women, the fans will always want to watch.

In mainstream media, presentations of female athletes have long been trivialised by focussing on their personal lives and appearance emphasising femininity or by comparing their performance with men (Black & Fielding-Lloyd, 2019; Kane, LaVoi, & Fink, 2013; Petty & Pope, 2019; Ravel & Gareau, 2016). During the FIFA World Cup France 2019, female football players did not just gain widespread publicity but they were also treated in public with respectful interest based on their athletic performance. This is a significant improvement in contrast to the previous World Cup tournament in 2015 when Gordon Parks commented in the *Daily Record* that a mediocre version of the male game was being given a profile way beyond what it deserves. Among other things, FIFA published a profile of US forward Alex Morgan before the 2015 semi-final game and highlighted her physical appearance as 'very easy on the eye and good looks to match'. Moreover, the Football Association in England welcomed its bronze medallists home with a patronising tweet: 'Our #Lionesses go back to being mothers, partners and daughters today, but they have taken on another title – heroes' (Turtiainen, 2015).

In recent years, social media has served as a tool for more diverse (self-)representations for female athletes (Geurin-Eagleman & Burch, 2016; Hayes Sauder & Blaszka, 2018; Smith & Sanderson, 2015; Turtiainen, 2015), although many of them have taken advantage of it in quite conventional ways (Toffoletti & Thorpe, 2018a). It has been argued that, through social media, athletes can connect directly with their audience without the necessary presence of the mass media and without having their messages filtered through the public relations departments of sports organisations and mainstream-media outlets (e.g. Hambrick, Simmons, Greenhalgh, & Greenwell, 2010). Certainly, there are sport federations, organisations, clubs and sponsors who want to control athletes' online behaviour; however, social media may provide athletes with a chance to bring forth issues that are not covered by mainstream media.

During the FIFA Women's World Cup France 2019, one female player eclipsed others in terms of media attention. Megan Rapinoe was impossible to ignore: the US Women's National Soccer Team won the World Cup and she was awarded the most valuable player and top scorer of the tournament. She was also named Player of the Match in the World Cup final where she was the oldest (34) woman to score. Later the same year she was crowned the Best FIFA Women's

Player and Ballon d'Or winner. She was also named Sports Illustrated's Sports-person of the Year, only the fourth woman to win in the award's 66-year history, and honoured with the Glamour Woman of the Year award, together with Margaret Atwood and Greta Thunberg among others. In her speech at FIFA's The Best awards gala, she spoke out against racism, homophobia and the pay gap in football (Wrack, 2019). Before the FIFA World Cup tournament, 28 members of the United States team had sued the country's soccer federation over gender discrimination concerning pay equity and working conditions (see Cooky & Antunovic, 2020). At the World Cup itself, Rapinoe stole the show on and off the pitch and made repeated headlines for her athletic performance and fight for equality.

Rapinoe tends to be outspoken on multiple forums: she was the first white athlete to follow Colin Kaepernick's example and knelt during the national anthem before the National Women' Soccer League game 2016 in protest against racist injustice in the United States. Later, when Rapinoe had repeated the act of kneeling, the United States Soccer Federation instigated a policy to require players to stand during the national anthem (Schmidt, Frederick, Pegoraro, & Spencer, 2019; see also Clarke, 2019). After Rapinoe's first kneeling act, Schmidt et al. (2019) analysed 56, 402 user comments from Megan Rapinoe's Facebook page where she was labelled as anti-American, anti-military, and anti-nationalist. The common opinion in social media was that she should not mix sports and politics. But Rapinoe seems not to care about her controversial image. She is an unapologetic activist-athlete icon who, at the FIFA World Cup 2019, used her platform to act as a spokesperson for minorities and stand against discrimination in general.

Now that athlete activism – speaking out against perceived injustices, raising awareness and fostering dialogues around issues of inequality in and out of sports culture – has become more prominent due to the political movements like #metoo and #blacklivesmatter, it is relevant to examine how athlete activists use their social media platforms alongside physical acts as part of their protest activities to understand the new reality of activism in the digital age (Cooky & Antunovic, 2020; Galily, 2019; Schmidt et al., 2019). With that in mind, in this chapter I examine how Megan Rapinoe became 'the sportsperson of the year' in 2019. I do that by answering the following questions:

- What did she publish on her Instagram profile during the FIFA Women's World Cup France 2019?
- How did the mainstream media treat her performance on and off the football field?

Theoretical Framework

Previously, feminist sport studies has debated exclusion, marginalisation, trivi-alisation and sexualisation of female athletes, but a new kind of 'mainstream feminism' produces different articulations of femininity (Thorpe, Toffoletti, &

Bruce, 2017, p. 372). This post-feminism can be seen either as an anti-feminism – when feminism seems not to be needed anymore – or as an attempt to re-join femininity with liberal feminism when women want to be both feminine and politically active (e.g. Tredway, 2020). Postfeminist rhetoric emphasises women's autonomy, choice and empowerment. Consequently, as active subjects, female athletes are 'personally responsible for their own successes or failures' (Toffoletti, Francombe-Webb, & Thorpe, 2018, p. 7; see also Toffoletti & Thorpe, 2018a). Similarly, neoliberal ideologies value individual empowerment, personal respon-sibility and entrepreneurial subjecthood, and according to Kim Toffoletti et al. (2018), female athletes therefore adapt media-savvy, body-focussed and entre-preneurial strategies. Altogether, in neoliberal post-feminist ideology, women are encouraged to become individualised entrepreneurial agents: 'Simply, women who are able to individually overcome structural inequalities and obtain eco-nomic independence and success are celebrated as feminist subjects' (Thorpe et al., 2017, p. 372). These neoliberal feminist subjects are typically white, middle class, heterosexual and not concerned with equality, wage gaps and domestic violence (Tredway, 2020).

In this chapter, as my theoretical framework, I utilise Kim Toffoletti's and Holly Thorpe's (2018a) feminist thematic analysis of sportswomen's self-representation on social media. They explored how social media is used by female athletes to represent and promote themselves and their sport within a neoliberal and post-feminist context. As part of that, they discovered three strategies that female athletes adopt for constructing their identity and marketing themselves online: *self-love, self-disclosure and self-empowerment*. Toffoletti and Thorpe (2018a) analysed social media profiles of five top individual athletes: tennis players Serena Williams and Maria Sharapova, wrestler Ronda Rousey, racing driver Danica Patrick and surfer Alana Blanchard. In this chapter I test their results in the case of a team sport athlete, using the same thematic categories when analysing Instagram posts of football player Megan Rapinoe. Except for Maria Shaparova, all the athletes analysed by Toffoletti and Thorpe (2018a) are Americans, as is Rapinoe, but in other ways Megan Rapinoe's public profile seems to differ from the other athletes. Although Rapinoe is white, she is an openly gay female athlete with a non-heteronormative outlook. However, in the discussion below I consider to what extent Rapinoe uses the same strategies to promote her own agenda. Toffoletti and Thorpe (2018a) argue that less contro-versial and political female athletes who do not challenge gender norms have larger social media followings. Despite (or because of) their research findings, it is interesting to examine how Megan Rapinoe managed to achieve the status of the 'soccer superstar' and the sportsperson of the year while promoting her outspoken and, for some sports people, controversial statements against discrimination in social and mainstream media during the FIFA Women's World Cup France 2019.

Methodology

According to Toni Bruce and Dunja Abidin (2018), feminist sports media scholars are facing multiple methodological challenges when potential sites of research such as new apps and social media sites are expanding and changing rapidly. They require new methodological approaches (e.g. in-depth cases or digital ethnographies) for a more nuanced understanding of gender in digital sport environments. As a researcher of digital culture, I have employed and developed diverse methods to approach sports-related social media content – both user-produced and mainstream online media-centred. In this particular case, I introduce my method to collect and handle ephemeral Instagram stories. I follow Oren Soffer's (2016) argument about fading (audio)visual social media content as spoken communication. According to Soffer, instant-messaging application Snapchat represents the contemporary grammar of social media when it applies an oral paradigm to extremely visualised content. There is only limited time for viewing the content before it becomes inaccessible – like spoken words fade away and disappear. Similarly to Snapchat, Instagram launched (in 2016) its Stories feature which allows users to add text, drawings, emoticons, filters and augmented reality stickers to temporary (24 hour) images or video clips. I considered those Instagram stories as a part of an oral paradigm when I handled my research material, without downloading or recording the content itself anywhere. My material collection method respects the ephemeral social media content and maintains its authenticity by paying attention to the production context. I watched all the Instagram stories when they were available in the application. I wrote down ethnographic field notes about them without taking any screenshots or capturing moving images. I regard this as an ethical decision when Instagram stories are not originally meant to be permanent social media content. They have been created to be momentary glimpses impossible to return to after a certain time frame – not to be archived to the researcher's computer to watch again and again. That said, the privacy of public figures, such as Megan Rapinoe, can be considered to be narrower than other private individuals when posting publicly on social media, so it is ethically acceptable to include their publicly posted social media content within research, without gaining their explicit informed consent (see TENK, 3/2019, p. 57; Townsend & Wallace, 2016, p. 10).

Initially, I chose to follow eight players from the quarter-final teams attending the FIFA Women's World Cup France 2019. I observed their ephemeral Instagram stories published from the quarter-finals to the final game and for a couple of days after it (27 June–9 July 2019). The players were Caroline Graham Hansen (Norway), Lucy Bronze (England), Wendie Renard (France), Megan Rapinoe (USA), Sara Gama (Italy), Shanice Van De Sanden (Holland), Dzseinifer Marozsan (Germany) and Nilla Fischer (Sweden). The players I selected had significant roles in their teams, they represented different ethnicities and were at least relatively active on social media. I categorised their Instagram stories according to my own previous categorisation of female athletes' social media content (Turtiainen, 2016) to see what themes these football players were presenting overall in their posts. I asked how they were presenting themselves as professional female football players and what kind of topics they were dealing with in their Instagram posts. I was interested to see if they used social media as a tool for influence by speaking out for societal and political issues or raised awareness of equality among (sports) people.

Afterwards, I chose to focus in this study on Megan Rapinoe because she stood out from the other athletes with her outspoken posts. I have examined previously (Turtiainen, 2016) female team sports athletes who use social media to express their stance and values about gender (Finnish ice hockey player Noora Räty), sexual orientation (Swedish football player Nilla Fischer) and ethnicity (Māori rugby player Portia Woodman), so I wanted to perceive how Megan Rapinoe utilised the media attention – both social and mainstream media – during the FIFA World Cup to get her voice heard. In addition to Rapinoe's social media content, I went through online mainstream media publications which were framing her image and actions regarding the FIFA World Cup. At the beginning of the tournament (June 2019) Rapinoe had about 650, 000 followers on her Instagram profile (https://www.instagram.com/mrapinoe/) and at the end of the year 2019 there were over two million of them. She published 61 ephemeral Instagram stories in the time frame beginning from the FIFA World Cup quarter-finals and 27 still posts during the whole tournament. I also included those still Instagram posts in my research material when I analysed her pathway to becoming the respected rebel of the FIFA Women's World Cup France 2019.

From Self-love to Equal Love

The first of Toffoletti and Thorpe's (2018a) strategies by which female athletes construct the self online includes bodily self-esteem and acceptance. They discuss an Instagram selfie of Serena Williams as an example of making a Black female body visible in an empowering way. Williams brands herself as authentic and accepting by following the body-positive discourse (about the 'love your body' discourse, see Gill & Elias, 2014). Another example is photos where athletes pose without makeup, celebrating their 'real' and natural looks. When attached to this post-feminist discourse, the rules of bodily objectification and sexualisation of female athletes become redefined. These kinds of posts were common across Toffoletti and Thorpe's (2018a) research material and can be understood as branding the athletic self as a gender-progressive subject, challenging unrealistic body standards. But according to them:

> What is being 'sold', then, in a neoliberal marketplace is the female athletic body as a gendered product through which consumers can feel good about themselves without having to seriously challenge or question a sport culture that reproduces inequality on the basis of race and gender. For the followers of these athletes on social media, what they are being encouraged to relate to is not a highly trained, elite female athletic body that troubles the idea of male sporting superiority, but messages of women's self-esteem, self-worth and body confidence.
>
> (pp. 27–28)

Megan Rapinoe represents diverse femininity with her lavender dyed short hair that became her trademark during the FIFA World Cup. In her Instagram posts she seems a thoroughly self-confident athlete. Occasionally she gives a rather 'arrogant' impression of herself by not being afraid to take up space, express herself and be proud of her achievements, which is a part of her habitus and her way to express self-love. She breaks boundaries of traditional femininity by being slightly rough and loud and encourages her followers to 'be themselves'. During the FIFA World Cup, the discourse around her was less about her appearance than it was about the impression she gave through her behaviour. With her unapologetic attitude she certainly annoys some football followers, but that can be construed as an intentional message saying 'you do not have to please everyone' (see, e.g., Brockes, 2019). After the FIFA World Cup, the New York Post's Kyle Smith (2019) named Rapinoe as 'America's anti-sweetheart' and described her as 'arrogant, abrasive, sanctimonious, whiny, humourless, unpatriotic, self-important and immensely boring'. Rapinoe herself pointed out that there is a double standard for women in sports as male sports stars can be called arrogant in a positive way but female athletes should be humble in their success (Casey, 2019; see also Darvin & Pegoraro, Chapter 3).

One expression of Rapinoe's self-esteem is her signature pose, which became a symbol of her confidence and the fight for equality during the FIFA World Cup. She did the 'arms-wide goal celebration' with a satisfied expression on her face six times during the World Cup, and when she was asked about the origin of the pose in a *New York Times Magazine* interview, she explained:

> It was probably born out of a little arrogance. Like, are you not entertained? What more do you want? And it was sort of saying to Trump – but more to detractors in general – that you will not steal our joy from us as a team, as the L.G.B.T.Q. community, as America. It was kind of a [expletive] you, but nice.
>
> (Marchese, 2019)

After the victorious final game, Rapinoe's post-goal pose ended up on the covers of several newspapers and magazines (e.g. The Washington Post, L'Équipe, Sports Illustrated) and she re-posted those full-page pictures on her Instagram profile. She tends to draw attention to herself through both the pose and her outstanding athletic performance, but after doing so she takes advantage of this attention by using it to question the reproduction of inequality, e.g. homophobia, racism and underestimation of women's football. During the FIFA World Cup her individual actions were framed as catalysts for social change because beside her sport related statements she also used her publicity to raise awareness around issues affecting minorities. Apparently she has adopted the logic of neoliberal post-feminism when acting in a media-savvy way as a marketable role model, but instead of challenging only body standards, as some other female athletes have done, she wants to shake the standards of the whole sports culture and open public debate beyond the sports context as well. In the case of Rapinoe, loving herself means above all a statement on behalf of an equal love. As an openly gay footballer, her aim is to influence attitudes towards

LGBTQ+ people – to ensure that everyone has an equal opportunity to 'make the most of their lives'.

Self-disclosure as a Statement

The female team sports athletes I have examined previously present themselves primarily as professional athletes rather than wives, mothers or in other roles previously given them by mainstream media (Turtiainen, 2016; see also Barnett, 2013; Kristiansen & Broch, 2013). They mention their sports achievements on their social media profiles and their sport-related profile pictures are carefully considered self-presentations. The major part of their social media content concerns the team, games, training sessions, awards and sponsors. On the other hand, they also publish lots of selfies and through that practice, these athletes achieve 'subversive frivolity', the generative power caused by its ordinariness (Abidin, 2016). By publishing more sports career-related material, they differed from athletes in earlier studies (e.g. Geurin-Eagleman & Burch, 2016; Lebel, 2013; Sanderson, 2013; Smith & Sanderson, 2015). However, almost all athletes who are active on social media publish posts about their personal lives too, such as photos of family and friends from dinners and holidays, and social connections are expressed with greetings like birthday wishes or by thanking others for support.

Themes within Megan Rapinoe's Instagram posts and stories can be categorised in the same way as other female team sports athletes I have studied previously. She posted photos and video clips from the World Cup training sessions with her teammates, selfies with 'how many hours to the match?' counters, but also photos with her family and girlfriend, basketball player Sue Bird. In such ways she can be compared to football player Nilla Fischer who balances between authentic and strategic posts skilfully when revealing facts about her personal life on social media. When Fischer is on a tournament tour with her team, she dedicates her Instagram posts to her wife by tagging (@) her and writing: 'I miss you wifey – luckily we will be seeing soon'. But certainly, the posts are not targeted only for her wife because she posts them publicly on her Instagram profile, exposing both her private life and societal values to her fans and followers (Turtiainen, 2016). Megan Rapinoe acted in the same way at the end of the World Cup tournament when she posted a photo about herself and girlfriend Sue Bird with the caption 'I'm so in love with you. Thank you baby @sbird10'. She also shared the same picture on her Instagram story when 'introducing love of my life'.

One of the dominant features of athletes' social media use has been the opportunity to reveal aspects of their private lives to their followers – or at least create some sense of it. The posts are usually thoughtfully measured, but they should appear to be spontaneous so they can be considered as 'real'. These social media posts are expressions of contrived authenticity and reflexivity, as well as saleable objects (Abidin, 2016). Toffoletti and Thorpe (2018a) notice how in the case of Ronda Rousey, self-disclosure functions as a form of affective labour. They identify her as a symbol of 'a woman's capacity to strive for something better' (Toffoletti & Thorpe, 2018a, p. 25). She is an athlete who has taken responsibility for her own well-being by striving her way to the top of the sports world, coming from a working-class background. She operates in an affective way by revealing something 'authentic' and selling an idea of her own journey and her capacity to relate to other people's difficulties. Rousey is not the 'Do Nothing Bitch' (DNB), as she has branded herself with inspirational and motivational posts on social media. She invented 'DNB' to imply a woman who has no goals or ambitions in her life and is taken care of by someone else (Toffoletti & Thorpe, 2018a).

Megan Rapinoe can be compared to Ronda Rousey because of her background. She is from rural California where she grew up within a big working-class family. During the FIFA World Cup, she published a lot of posts related to her family. Most of her family travelled to France to see her play. They met in Paris during the early stage of the tournament and again two days before the final game on her and her twin sister's birthday, when Rapinoe published Boomerang posts (mini videos that loop back and forth) from a park picnic to her Instagram Stories. Right after the World Cup final, Megan Rapinoe wished 'happy birthday' to Brian on a live television interview. On the same day she posted a photo of him in her Instagram profile with the caption 'Happy Birthday to this rose (only a few thorns) I love you @calihound so proud of you!♥' Mainstream media reported that Brian was her brother who had just gotten out of prison to a rehabilitation facility to watch his sister win the World Cup (O'Kane, 2019). By revealing such things from her personal life on Instagram, Rapinoe makes herself more approachable. Her current life may seem glamorous, but distressing family circumstances make her more 'real' and easier to identify with. Through both social and mainstream media she is construed as an authentic fighter – fighting for herself and for others.

Self-empowerment and Politics

There are multiple ways to express self-empowerment present in the social media posts of female athletes. Toffoletti and Thorpe (2018a) focus mainly on sexualised empowerment when analysing their social media material. Athletes can now highlight their heterosexual femininity in the name of neoliberal post-feminism, when in the past, sexual images in male-dominant sports media were considered as objectification. Rather than passive and objectified, feminised selves are promoted as empowered and active subjects. That means Ronda Rousey can post her Sports Illustrated cover photo on her social media profile to celebrate the diversity of women's body types. On the other hand, racing driver Danica Patrick avoids posting sexually alluring photos on social media and performs her inner confidence with 'the right kind of visibility in a male-dominated sport' (Toffoletti & Thorpe, 2018a, p. 26). Athletes respond to the market for empowerment with their strong, muscular bodies which articulate assertive femininity – the kind that female athletes are expected to perform in the context of a neoliberal ethos where a flourishing sporting career can be seen as a personal choice (Toffoletti & Thorpe, 2018a).

Toffoletti and Thorpe (2018a) long for female athletic bodies that break heterosexy norms. As an openly gay, albeit white athlete Megan Rapinoe serves as this 'something else'. In her case, self-empowerment appears in her self-confident performance, as discussed above. Rapinoe promotes her own products on her Instagram profile, just like Serena Williams and Ronda Rousey. However, the life-style brand *re–inc* that she has co-founded with three other athletes is gender-neutral. During the World Cup she also promoted the *Love is Uninterrupted* hoodie she designed together with her partner Sue Bird. They launched a campaign to raise awareness and funds to protect Black and Brown queer youth against homophobic violence and bullying. Rapinoe published several posts and re-posts on Instagram with the hashtag #loveisuninterrupted. On one of the still posts she wrote: 'Sue and I designed this hoodie to acknowledge the history of pride and to end homophobic violence and bullying. We collaborated with @melodyehsani on this custom piece to acknowledge, empower and educate allies of #LGBTQ youth of colour'.

Megan Rapinoe mentions empowerment several times in her Instagram posts. Many of those posts are co-operation campaigns, such as the one with Microsoft where Reign FC (Rapinoe's club) players give advice to their younger selves. They explain how sport has shaped their lives as professional athletes, intending to inspire and encourage the next generation of female players. As Rapinoe retells in her post: 'Here's to empowering today for tomorrow'. She has also posted a video made in co-operation with Visa where she tells her story as a gay athlete and a female football player. On the video, marked with hashtags #dreambig and #betrue, Rapinoe makes clear how seriously she takes her responsibility as a role model. She calls it 'double earn' when female players have to do their best as athletes and at the same time help their sport to grow 'to leave the game in a better place'. Like other female athletes in this 'neoliberal post-feminist moment' (see Toffoletti & Thorpe, 2018a, p. 28), Rapinoe is balancing herself between individual empowerment and commercial self-promotion. She is undeniably producing her own brand but at the same time she is openly political in her statements. When Rapinoe was asked in a *New York Times Magazine* interview if she has any sympathy with the idea that sports should be a non-political oasis, she answered:

> I don't understand that argument at all. You want us to be role models for your kids. You want us to endorse your products. You parade us around. It's like, we're not just here to sit in the glass case for you to look at. That's not how this is going to go. Yeah, I don't [expletive] with that concept at all.
>
> (Marchese, 2019)

During the FIFA World Cup, Rapinoe became involved in national politics in a considerable way when then US President, Donald Trump, became irritated by her. Before the last 16-round game against Spain, an old video of Rapinoe went viral on online media. On the video she was asked whether the team would visit Donal Trump if they won the World Cup tournament and were invited. Rapinoe gave a laugh and responded: 'I'm not going to the fucking White House'. Donald Trump found it necessary to comment by tweeting: 'I am a big fan of the American Team, and Women's Soccer, but Megan should WIN first before she TALKS!' and 'Megan should never disrespect our Country, the White House, or our Flag, especially since so much has been done for her & the team'. The debate between Rapinoe and the US president resulted in international headlines. Rapinoe 'won the battle' by scoring two goals in the game against Spain and eventually winning the World Cup with the US team. As online memes and some media sites announced after the World Cup final, 'she made America great again' (see, e.g., Clarke, 2019; Keh, 2019).

Megan Rapinoe published several openly political posts on her Instagram profile during the FIFA World Cup. In one of her Instagram stories she re-posted sabre fencer Ibitihaj Muhammad's photo of a berry pie frosted with the US flag and with the text 'Close the camps' on it. Muhammad was the first Muslim American woman who wore a hijab while competing for the US in the Olympic Games. Rapinoe also re-posted numerous 'congratulations' in her stories and one of them was a tweet from Hilary Clinton who reminded followers about the significance of the US team's achievements: 'As we get ready to cheer on the #USWNT in Sunday's final, let's note that they're fighting for equal pay – and their advocacy could help all female athletes. I'm proud to stand with @mrapinoe and this team for fighting to win, on and off the field'.

For Megan Rapinoe empowerment is embracing who you are and simultaneously shedding light on issues to make the world a better place, whether that means fighting for LGBTQ+ and racial rights or pay equity for female athletes. She does not fear the consequences when she posts and says what she thinks. The neoliberal post-feminist discourse is clearly present in everything she does. She emphasises the potential of women who are capable, powerful and successful if they achieve change and have enough space and platforms to show who they really are. According to Rapinoe, the FIFA World Cup France 2019 was a turning point – the question is no longer *should* women be supported but *how* it can be done in general (see, e.g., Gregory, 2019; Parker, 2019). Rapinoe herself confirms she will continue to celebrate feminism by being loud and boisterous. As *the Washington Post* put it: '[S]he is an essential rebel: a defiant woman refusing to play by the antiquated be-cute-and-courteous rules that make many men feel better about female athletes' (Brewer, 2019).

Conclusion

As media coverage has an effect on public opinion, top athletes may have a strong impact through their acts on social and mainstream media (e.g. Galily, 2019; Turtiainen, 2015, 2016). Female athletes have become idols and role models within modern society (see Meier, 2015) and, if they want, they now have the opportunity to draw attention to wider issues and inequalities. During the FIFA Women's World Cup France 2019 Megan Rapinoe became the rebel who stood for something bigger than herself. The public discourse around her focussed on her athletic performances and the impression she gave with her social criticism. This is noteworthy as women athletes have long been defined primarily by their appearance and their traditional private life roles. The mainstream media raised Rapinoe to become the face of social change on and off the field and she deepened that image herself through her Instagram profile.

In the case of female athletes constructing representations of themselves online, all the self-attributes identified by Toffoletti and Thorpe (2018a) apply also to Megan Rapinoe. She has adopted the neoliberal post-feminist strategy to represent herself as *a self-loving* role model. On Instagram Rapinoe performs as a marketable, self-confident athlete who encourages her followers to express and be themselves, as the post-feminist ethos of acceptance announces. However, with her lavender dyed short hair she breaks boundaries of traditional femininity by being boisterous. She expresses self-esteem by taking up space (e.g. with her signature pose) and being proud of her achievements. She balances between authentic and strategic Instagram posts and follows the neoliberal strategy of *self-disclosure* by also revealing private matters from her personal life. This – together with things like her working-class background – makes her more 'real' and approachable. Furthermore, Rapinoe emphasises the importance of *self-empowerment* in her public performances and social media. She sure is a successful and celebrated person herself who has individually overcome inequalities and obtained economic independence, but as an openly gay activist-athlete she challenges heterosexual norms of this neoliberal feminist subject.

Megan Rapinoe is not afraid to put herself in the public eye and receive publicity, but as a team sports player, she is doing this at least partly in the name of her team, female sports, and non-discriminative sports cultures in general. Her team is not just the US World Cup winners or even just female athletes whose task is to help their sport to grow, but all marginalised groups – LGBTQ+, ethnic/racial minorities etc. – and people who support her values. There is certain complexity in Rapinoe's self-presentation and actions since, as a gay athlete, she is a member of a minority group herself, yet at the same time she acts in the name of solidarity, e.g. in support of people of colour. She promotes diversity and inclusion by raising awareness of Black queer youth's discrimination, and simultaneously promotes herself and sells products of her gender-neutral brand, but she does this in an unapologetic way without a need to please anyone. In the context of neoliberal post-feminist ideology this is a contradictory combination and therefore an interesting aspect to pay attention to in future research.

Furthermore, a more intersectional analysis is needed to address the whiteness of feminist athlete-activism since it is commonly available only to privileged white women (see McDonald & Shelby, 2018). Megan Rapinoe was the only player analysed for the project reported on in this chapter who drew attention to wider societal issues during the FIFA WWC, but as a white US player she also had better opportunity than most to gain the mainstream media's attention. As the US Women's National Team player and Rapinoe's National Women's Soccer League teammate, Crystal Dunn, has stated, the face of US women's soccer is that of a white woman. Dunn wants to change this narrative and demands her right as a black female athlete to be a star of campaigns, instead of just being a player

(Glass, 2021). Thus, even though Rapinoe was labelled America's anti-sweetheart during the FIFA WWC, she was still suitable for the role of a national hero thanks to her whiteness.

Although Megan Rapinoe is outspoken and challenging, she still contributes to neoliberal agendas through her promotion of corporations and sponsors in association with her views of equality. She utilises her position and strength of character in two ways: to gain attention to her societal message *and* to make her own living. That demands the ability to appear as agentic and confident, and to cause affective feelings of intimacy and inspiration. In sport-specific contexts, this can be understood through the concept of the athletic labour of femininity in order to make sense of complex dynamics and articulations of empowerment, entrepreneurialism, and individualisation (Toffoletti & Thorpe, 2018b). According to this perspective, Rapinoe's actions can undeniably be seen as a part of a neoliberal post-feminism, but at the same time there is something different in that arrogant and shameless way she acts – a way many male athletes have long acted. She is someone who really dares to shine.

This research was supported by the Academy of Finland project Centre of Excellence in Game Culture Studies (CoE-GameCult, 312396).

References

Abidin, C. (2016, April–June). "Aren't these just young, rich women doing vain things online?" Influencer selfies as subversive frivolity. *Social Media+ Society*, *2*(2). doi: 10.1177/2056305116641342

Barnett, B. (2013). The babe/baby factor. Sport, women, and mass media. In P. M. Pedersen (Ed.), *Routledge handbook of sport communication* (pp. 350–358). London and New York: Routledge.

Black, J., & Fielding-Lloyd, B. (2019). Re-establishing the 'outsiders': English press coverage of the 2015 FIFA Women's World Cup. *International Review for the Sociology of Sport*, *54*(3), 282–301.

Brewer, J. (2019). Megan Rapinoe isn't here to make you comfortable. *Washington Post*, 25 June. Retrieved from https://www.washingtonpost.com/sports/dcunited/megan-rapinoe-isnt-here-to-make-you-comfortable/2019/06/25/af08fda0-977c-11e9-8d0a-5edd7e2025b1_story.html. Accessed on February 12, 2021.

Brockes, E. (2019). Megan Rapinoe's 'egotism' is the perfect antidote to Donald Trump. *The Guardian*, 12 July. Retrieved from https://www.theguardian.com/commentisfree/2019/jul/12/megan-rapinoe-us-football-women-trump. Accessed on February 12, 2021.

Bruce, T., & Antunovic, D. (2018). Gender, media and new media methods. In L. Mansfiel, J. Caudwell, B. Wheaton, & B. Watson (Eds.), *The Palgrave handbook of feminism and sport, leisure and physicaleducation* (pp. 257–273). London: Palgrave Macmillan.

Casey, S. (2019). Megan Rapinoe is winning on and off the field. *Marie Claire*, 11 September. Retrieved from https://www.marieclaire.com/celebrity/a28940917/megan-rapinoe-interview-2019. Accessed on February 12, 2021.

Clarke, G. (2019). The fearless Megan Rapinoe embodies the best of America. *The Guardian*, 27 July. Retrieved from https://www.theguardian.com/football/2019/jun/27/megan-rapinoe-american-values-trump-criticism. Accessed on February 12, 2021.

Cooky, C., & Antunovic, D. (2020). "This isn't just about us": Articulations of feminism in media narratives of athlete activism. *Communication & Sport, 8*(4–5), 692–711. doi:10.1177/2167479519896360

Cooky, C., Messner, M. A., & Musto, M. (2015). "It's dude time!" A quarter century of excluding women's sports in televised news and highlight shows. *Communication & Sport, 3*(3), 261–287.

Domeneghetti, R. (2018). 'The other side of the net': (Re)presentations of (emphasised) femininity during Wimbledon 2016. *Journal of Policy Research in Tourism, Leisure and Events, 10*(2), 151–163.

FIFA.com. (2019, October). FIFA Women's World Cup 2019 watched by more than 1 billion. FIFA. Retrieved from https://www.fifa.com/womensworldcup/news/fifa-women-s-world-cup-2019tm-watched-by-more-than-1-billion. Accessed on February 12, 2021.

Fink, J. S. (2015). Female athletes, women's sport, and the sport media commercial complex: Have we really "come a long way, baby"? *Sport Management Review, 18*(3), 331–342.

Finstad-Milion, K., Rethore, C., & Stengelhofen, T. (2019). The Women's World Cup: A forum for denouncing sexism or promoting gender diversity? *The Conversation*, 15 September. Retrieved from http://theconversation.com/the-womens-world-cup-a-forum-for-denouncing-sexism-or-promoting-gender-diversity-123212. Accessed on February 12, 2021.

Galily, Y. (2019). "Shut up and dribble!" Athletes activism in the age of twittersphere: The case of LeBron James. *Technology in Society, 58*, 101109.

Geurin-Eagleman, A. N., & Burch, L. M. (2016). Communicating via photographs: A gendered analysis of Olympic athletes' visual self-presentation on Instagram. *Sport Management Review, 19*(2), 133–145.

Gill, R., & Elias, A. S. (2014). 'Awaken your incredible': Love your body discourses and postfeminist contradictions. *International Journal of Media and Cultural Politics, 10*(2), 179–188.

Glass, A. (2021). What's Soccer Pro Crystal Dunn's next chapter? Fighting for the recognition she deserves. *Forbes*, 25 January. Retrieved from https://www.forbes.com/sites/alanaglass/2021/01/25/whats-soccer-pro-crystal-dunns-next-chapter-fighting-for-the-recognition-she-deserves/?sh=359b7cf67562. Accessed on February 12, 2021.

Gregory, S. (2019). 'You will not silence us': Megan Rapinoe talks equal pay, World Cup celebrations and presidential tweets. *Time*, 10 July. Retrieved from https://time.com/5623543/megan-rapinoe-world-cup-trump-equal-pay/. Accessed on February 12, 2021.

Hambrick, M. E., Simmons, J. M., Greenhalgh, G. P., & Greenwell, T. C. (2010). Understanding professional athletes' use of twitter: A content analysis of athlete tweets. *International Journal of Sport Communication, 3*(4), 454–471.

Hayes Sauder, M., & Blaszka, M. (2018). 23 players, 23 voices: An examination of the US women's national soccer team on Twitter during the 2015 World Cup. *Communication & Sport, 6*(2), 175–202.

Kane, M. J., LaVoi, N. M., & Fink, J. S. (2013). Exploring elite female athletes' interpretations of sport media images: A window into the construction of social identity and "selling sex" in women's sports. *Communication & Sport, 1*(3), 269–298.

Keh, A. (2019). Trump criticizes Megan Rapinoe over refusal to visit White House. *The New York Times*, 26 June. Retrieved from https://www.nytimes.com/2019/06/26/sports/trump-megan-rapinoe-tweet.html. Accessed on February 12, 2021.

Kian, E. M., Bernstein, A., & McGuire, J. S. (2013). A major boost for gender equality or more of the same? The television coverage of female athletes at the 2012 London Olympic Games. *The Journal of Popular Television*, *1*(1), 143–149.

Kristiansen, E., & Broch, T. B. (2013). Athlete-media communication: A theoretical perspective on how athletes use and understand gendered sport communication. In P. M. Pedersen (Ed.), *Routledge handbook of sport communication* (pp. 97–106). London and New York: Routledge.

Lebel, K. (2013). *Professional athlete self-presentation on Twitter*. Thesis and dissertation repository. Paper 1303. The University of Western Ontario.

Leberman, S., & Froggatt, R. (2019, August 15). Busting the myth: No one watches women's sport. *Lockerroom*, 15 August. Retrieved from https://www.newsroom.co.nz/@lockerroom/2019/08/15/754187/busting-the-myth-no-one-watches-womens-sport. Accessed on February 12, 2021.

Marchese, D. (2019). Megan Rapinoe is in celebration mode. And she's got some things to say. *New York Time Magazine*, 29 July. Retrieved from https://www.nytimes.com/interactive/2019/07/29/magazine/megan-rapinoe-sports-politics.html. Accessed on February 12, 2021.

McDonald, M. G., & Shelby, R. (2018). Feminism, intersectionality and the problem of whiteness in leisure and sport practices and scholarship. In L. Mansfield, J. Caudwell, B. Wheaton, & B. Watson (Eds.), *The Palgrave handbook of feminism and sport, leisure and physical education* (pp. 497–514). London: Palgrave Macmillan.

Meier, M. (2015). The value of female sporting role models. *Sport in Society*, *18*(8), 968–982.

O'Kane, C. (2019). Immediately after World Cup win, Megan Rapinoe wishes Brian a happy birthday. Who is he? *CBS News*, 8 July. Retrieved from https://www.cbsnews.com/news/2019-womens-world-cup-team-usa-win-megan-rapinoe-wishes-brian-happy-birthday-who-is-he/. Accessed on February 12, 2021.

Parker, M. (2019). How soccer star Megan Rapinoe remains hopeful: 'Don't F*** with us'. *Parade*, 22 October. Retrieved from https://parade.com/940125/maggie_parker/us-womens-soccer-player-megan-rapinoe-self-care-women-empowerment/. Accessed on February 12, 2021.

Petty, K., & Pope, S. (2019). A new age for media coverage of women's sport? An analysis of English media coverage of the 2015 FIFA Women's World Cup. *Sociology*, *53*(3), 486–502.

Ravel, B., & Gareau, M. (2016). 'French football needs more women like Adriana'? Examining the media coverage of France's women's national football team for the 2011 World Cup and the 2012 Olympic Games. *International Review for the Sociology of Sport*, *51*(7), 833–847.

Sanderson, J. (2013). Stepping into the (social media) game: Building athlete identity via Twitter. In R. Luppicini (Ed.), *Handbook of research on technoself: Identity in a technological society* (pp. 419–438). Hershey: IGI Global.

Schmidt, S. H., Frederick, E. L., Pegoraro, A., & Spencer, T. C. (2019). An analysis of Colin Kaepernick, Megan Rapinoe, and the national anthem protests. *Communication & Sport*, *7*(5), 653–677.

Sherwood, M., Osborne, A., Nicholson, M., & Sherry, E. (2017). Newswork, news values, and audience considerations: Factors that facilitate media coverage of women's sports. *Communication & Sport, 5*(6), 647–668.

Smith, K. (2019). Megan Rapinoe wrongly thinks she's a preacher–Not a player. *New York Post*, 13 July. Retrieved from https://nypost.com/2019/07/13/megan-rapinoe-wrongly-thinks-shes-a-preacher-not-a-player. Accessed on February 12, 2021.

Smith, L. R., & Sanderson, J. (2015). I'm going to Instagram it! An analysis of athlete self-presentation on Instagram. *Journal of Broadcasting & Electronic Media, 59*(2), 342–358.

Soffer, O. (2016, July–September). The oral paradigm and Snapchat. *Social Media + Society, 2*(3). doi:10.1177/2056305116666306

TENK – The Finnish National Board on Research Integrity. (3/2019). The ethical principles of research with human participants and ethical review in the human sciences in Finland. TENK. Retrieved from https://www.tenk.fi/sites/tenk.fi/files/Ihmistieteiden_eettisen_ennakkoarvioinnin_ohje_2019.pdf. Accessed on February 12, 2021.

Thorpe, H., Toffoletti, K., & Bruce, T. (2017). Sportswomen and social media: Bringing third-wave feminism, postfeminism, and neoliberal feminism into conversation. *Journal of Sport and Social Issues, 41*(5), 359–383.

Toffoletti, K., Francombe-Webb, J., & Thorpe, H. (2018). Femininities, sport and physical culture in postfeminist, neoliberal times. In K. Toffoletti, H. Thorpe, & J. Francombe-Webb (Eds.), *New sporting femininities: Embodied politics in postfeminist times* (pp. 1–19). Cham: Palgrave Macmillan.

Toffoletti, K., & Thorpe, H. (2018a). Female athletes' self-representation on social media: A feminist analysis of neoliberal marketing strategies in "economies of visibility". *Feminism & Psychology, 28*(1), 11–31.

Toffoletti, K., & Thorpe, H. (2018b). The athletic labour of femininity: The branding and consumption of global celebrity sportswomen on Instagram. *Journal of Consumer Culture, 18*(2), 298–316.

Townsend, L., & Wallace, C. (2016). *Social media research: A guide to ethics.* Aberdeen: University of Aberdeen. Retrieved from https://www.gla.ac.uk/media/Media_487729_smxx.pdf. Accessed on February 12, 2021.

Tredway, K. (2020). *Social activism in women's tennis: Generations of politics and cultural change.* London and New York, NY: Routledge.

Turtiainen, R. (2015). Men's soccer? FIFA Women's World Cup in social media [Men's soccer? Naisten jalkapallon MM-kisat sosiaalisessa mediassa]. *WiderScreen.* 3/2015.

Turtiainen, R. (2016). Female team sports athletes in social media–Challenging gender, ethnicity and sexuality [Naisjoukkueurheilijat sosiaalisessa mediassa: sukupuolen, etnisyyden ja seksuaalisuuden esityksiä haastamassa]. In P. Berg & M. Kokkonen (Eds.), *Urheilun takapuoli–tasa-arvo ja yhdenvertaisuus liikunnassa ja urheilussa* (pp. 111–137). Helsinki: Nuorisotutkimusverkosto/Nuorisotutkimusseura. Retrieved from https://www.nuorisotutkimusseura.fi/images/urheilun_takapuoli_netti.pdf

Wrack, S. (2019, September 23). Lionel Messi and Megan Rapinoe named Fifa footballers of the year. *The Guardian*, 23 September. Retrieved from https://www.theguardian.com/football/2019/sep/23/the-best-fifa-awards-lionel-messi-megan-rapinoe-jurgen-klopp-jill-ellis. Accessed on February 12, 2021.

Chapter 8

Who Owns the Ball? Gender (Dis)Order and the 2014 FIFA World Cup

Jorge Knijnik, Rohini Balram and Yoko Kanemasu

Introduction

Nationalistic pride greeted the 2007 announcement that Brazil had been selected to host the 2014 (Men's) Fédération Internationale de Football Association (FIFA) World Cup, the 'Copa' (Cup) as Brazilians call it. The then-President Luiz Inácio Lula da Silva announced to the nation that the mega-event would strengthen Brazil as a 'first-world' state, and few uttered any disagreement. However, among those who did raise concerns about this mega-event were long-standing women's football activists, athletes and coaches who argued that the immense focus on and investment in men's football promoted by the men's World Cup would aggravate the already heavily unequal gender order within football and the broader sports realm in the country (Jourdan, 2019; Knijnik, 2018). Such inequity has roots in the country's sports history, where, due to draconian 1941 legislation, women were forbidden till the late 1970s to practice several sports (such as football, martial arts, water polo and others) deemed excessively 'masculine' for their fragile bodies (Bellos, 2002; Votre & Mourão, 2003).

These restrictions on women's sporting activities in Brazil have already been extensively examined in the past two decades. From historical, sociological and psychological angles, researchers have explained how these constraints have left their gendered mark over women's bodies and their involvement with sports. Rigo (2005) has shown that, as a direct outcome of the 1941 legislation, many good women's sides that had thrived throughout the country in the first half of the century, particularly in Brazil's South where they had attracted consistent crowds to their competition, were required to shut their doors. Women's football almost disappeared in Brazil from the early 1950s to the late 1970s. According to the author, it took 38 years for the ban to be lifted and Brazilian women to be permitted to openly play football in parks, schools and stadiums. Knijnik (2015) has discussed the psychosocial impact of these prohibitions over current female players, concluding that much of the distressful self-identity issues that these players presently carry originate from the prejudices and discriminations that started in the past century and are yet to be resolved in the country's psyche. The

Sport, Gender and Mega-Events, 149–162
Copyright © 2022 by Emerald Publishing Limited
All rights of reproduction in any form reserved
doi:10.1108/978-1-83982-936-920211014

same author has extensively examined the 'rotten roots' of women's football in the country, naming them the 'gendered twentieth-century legacy' of football that still blocks Brazilian women from freely enjoying the sport as they desire and deserve (Knijnik, 2014).

More recently, Elsey and Nadel (2019) have produced a comprehensive history of women and sports in Latin America. The authors have detailed the historical means of 'corporeal enactment of gender differences' (p. 23) that has been intensely engrained in the history of women and sports, particularly within football, in South America. Elsey and Nadel (2019) also present details on how, in a variety of ways, South American women, including Brazilian women, have found in-between spaces, amongst rigid patriarchal configurations, to organise and play their favourite sports, especially football.

From the brief summary of the research that has been undertaken in Brazil and South America about women and football, one can draw the conclusion that 'on-field' topics regarding women's football have already received some academic attention. On the other hand, other gendered issues that women still face to freely and equally participate in the Brazilian football context are yet to be examined. For example, da Costa (2007) has pointed out that, despite their extensive presence at football stadiums, studies on female supporters are scarce in the literature on Brazilian football. Haag (2018) has looked at women who ventured to work in leadership positions in professional football teams. However, to our knowledge, nothing has been said about women who tried to maintain their businesses, which is an integral part of local football match culture, during the 2014 Men's Copa. Specifically, we are yet to find studies that examine traditional groups of women having to face FIFA regulations that controlled all aspects of the game and tried to block them from making their living during the mega-event.

Hence, in this chapter, we analyse an 'off-field' case study to discuss how gender and multiple relations of power permeate all facets of the 'global game', and how gender conceptions were entrenched in the organisation of the 2014 FIFA Men's World Cup in Brazil. Our case study is centred on the gendered resistance that the *Baianas* (Bahia state native women, descendants of African slaves) demonstrated against FIFA's guidelines that banned them from selling their traditional hot spicy snacks (known as *acarajé*) at the new arenas that hosted the World Cup in Salvador, Bahia's capital city. We use the concept of 'everyday resistance' (Johansson & Vinthagen, 2020) to examine how, against the odds, the gender order was questioned and subverted during Brazil's Men's Copa. Our 'off-field' case study can substantiate the claim of gender disorder catalysed by the World Cup.

The case study becomes even more interesting if we consider that *Baianas* are Black women who have worked and sold their snacks daily for the past century during football matches inside and around football stadiums, as well as on the streets of Salvador, the 'more African city' in Brazil, where African religions have survived and Brazilian–African communities have sought to keep their cultural customs alive. Traditions such as selling street food in football stadiums are practices that have continued through generations, passed down from mother to daughter, empowering the families both economically and socially within their communities.

It is important to highlight that the first author of this chapter is a Brazilian feminist scholar who followed every single aspect of the cultural and social repercussions of the World Cup in his home country. The second and third author are also feminist scholars with a long-standing understanding and activism in relation to racial, colonial and gendered relations within a diverse range of contexts in sports.

We start by briefly discussing the role that football plays in shaping gender ideologies in South America and particularly in Brazil. Next, we introduce our theoretical framework and argue that the concept of everyday resistance can illuminate the daily struggles of ordinary people like Baianas. Then, after briefly discussing the emergence and the affirmation of Black feminism in Brazil, we present our case study, discussing how the Baianas defied the 2014 Men's Copa gender order, and what this resistance meant to the 'after-Copa' gender context within Brazilian sports.

Football: A Powerful Gender Metaphor in Brazilian Everyday Life

The 2014 Men's Copa permeated every single aspect of Brazilian life; it determined school contents and calendars, and the whole political scenario of the country. It also impacted the formation of ideologies, including gendered ones, within Brazilian culture. These ideologies, and the resistance to them, were seen in different aspects of the culture, for example, the language.

Football metaphors pervade the Brazilian Portuguese language and people's daily conversations – and not only during the World Cup. Football allegories permeate Brazilians' daily chats. Football tales are employed in Brazilians' sporting lives and also in their work or community life. You had better be cautious if you are 'on the penalty spot' in your employment – they might kick you out. Your love affair can be in 'extra time', approaching a conclusion, or even 'nil-all' if you are yet to have a sexual encounter with your lover.

This would not be different during the 2014 Men's Copa. The expression 'the ball's owner' is one of the supreme football metaphors in daily Brazilian Portuguese language. The ball's owner is the one who has the control. From the kid who has the one ball in a crowd and will go home if his peers don't play his way, to the chief who reins over everyone in the workplace, to the bouncer who decides who comes in and out of the discos – you had better be pleasant and keep an eye on the ball's owner.

However, the ball's owner is a male expression. That may sound peculiar to the monolingual English speaker, but nouns in Portuguese have genders. For example, 'the house' (*a casa*) is a female noun, 'the airplane' (the *avião*) is a male noun. One says '*o dono*' to indicate the male owner, or '*a dona*' to designate the female owner of any object. *O dono da bola* – the male ball's owner – has been conventionally used as an image of dominant men who control the government, trade and football. Of course, the ball's owner works as a compelling allegory as balls also denote phallic command, manhood and bravery that apparently only men have. The male ball's owner (*o dono da bola*) is indeed the one in charge.

However, a few months before the 2014 Men's Copa, a group of women photographers organised a photographic exhibition called '*As donas da bola*' – 'the female ball's owner' (Moura, 2014). This exhibition, which travelled across the country showing photos of diverse women playing football in a range of contexts, by subverting the traditional men's ownership of the ball, demonstrated that, as part of the overall gender struggle during mega sports events, gender resistance would continue during the 2014 Men's Copa – local women were not ready to conform without contestation of the hegemonic masculinity exacerbated by the Copa.

In the next section, we briefly present the principles of the concept of 'everyday resistance' as the analytical lens employed in this chapter. We show how this concept allows us to shed light on the daily struggles of ordinary people such as the Baianas as they go about their business of selling acarajé on the streets of Salvador.

Everyday Resistance

In exploring the socio-political significance of the Baianas' acts of defiance, we turn to the concept of 'everyday resistance', originally proposed by Scott (1985, 1989, 1990, 2012) and further refined by resistance studies scholars, especially Johansson and Vinthagen (2015, 2016, 2020; see also Vinthagen & Johansson, 2013). Scott (1985) formulated the concept to illuminate the hidden, oppositional nature of everyday, informal and non-organised acts of peasants in South East Asia. Scott showed everyday acts such as foot-dragging, dissimulation, false compliance, pilfering, feigned ignorance, slander, arson and sabotage to be 'disguised' resistance, which may involve little formal coordination or political articulation but may evolve into a pattern of oppositional actions – 'quiet unremitting guerrilla warfare' (Scott, 1989, p. 49) equally or even more effective in comparison with open, public revolts. By the fact of its embeddedness in daily life, everyday resistance constitutes 'the ordinary weapons of relatively powerless groups' (Scott, 2012), while often overlooked as trivial and pre-political by those who privilege organised political actions, it is 'the very basis of economic and political struggle conducted daily by subordinate classes' (Scott, 2013, p. 93).

Building on Scott's and resistance studies scholars' works (see e.g., Bayat, 2000, 2009; de Certeau, 1984), Johansson and Vinthagen (2020, p. 24) locate everyday resistance in 'a continuum between public confrontations and hidden subversion'. The analytical value of the concept lies in its capacity to 'capture the patterns of practices done by individuals or informal gatherings of groups, in which they engage with power relations or the effects of power in their ordinary lives' (Johansson & Vinthagen, 2020, p. 3). Notably, what separates everyday resistance from merely acting differently from the norm is how it relates to power; it has the potential to undermine, weaken, or destabilise power, if temporarily.

This is important also because resistance scholars have historically privileged political intent of actions and, thus, overlooked a whole array of creative oppositional tactics employed by subordinated individuals and groups. Johansson and Vinthagen (2020) stress that it is not oppositional intent but the agency of the subordinate itself and its transformative potential that constitutes resistance.

As many resistance scholars show, the concept is particularly useful in understanding the ways in which many oppressed individuals and groups in the Global South exercise their oppositional agency. Those who struggle against powerful mechanisms of domination may find space and medium for oppositional practices not limited to explicit political rhetoric or organised, formal political action. The claims that '"real resistance" is organised, principled, and has revolutionary implications ... overlook entirely the vital role of power relations in constraining forms of resistance. If we limit our attention to "real resistance", all that is being measured may be the level of repression that structures the available options' (Scott, 1989, p. 51). Harkness and Hongsermeier (2015, p. 1) show, for instance, in the Middle East and North Africa, '[o]pen social movements and intentional resistance can be dangerous activities ... particularly for women. In this setting, female activism often takes place as non-movements – mundane, collective actions taken by individuals ... commonplace activities such as working, attending college, or participating in sports'.

The Baianas' rebellion against FIFA's control over the 'Copa' stadiums can be fruitfully examined with insights from the concept of everyday resistance, especially its focus on mundane practices of the ordinary and their deeply political nature and potential. While, on the surface, the women's rebellion is an act motivated by self-interest and self-preservation, on closer examination, it emerges as a collective, repeated practice of disrupting the geopolitical, gender, class and racialised relations of power that subordinate them as Black working-class women of a postcolonial society.

Prior to analysing the everyday resistance staged by the Baianas during the 2014 Men's Copa, however, it is necessary to present the socio-historical context of Black women's activism in Brazil.

Black Feminism in Brazil: Incorporating Gender, Race and Social Class

As in other parts of the world, in the early 1970s, Black Brazilian women social activists struggled to fit and integrate into the agenda of the mainstream feminist movement (Da Silva, 2018). Early Black women social leaders and academics such as Lélia Gonzalez and Sueli Carneiro did not see themselves as Black feminists. Although, since the 1970s, their work had drawn extensively on the intersectionality of the oppression suffered by Black women – gender, race and social class – these leaders placed themselves, on the one hand, within the Black women social movement ('*mulheres negras*' movement), and on the other, within the broader feminist movement (Werneck, in Da Silva, 2018).

During those years, middle-class white women held hegemonic status in the Brazilian feminist movement. Hence, Black women's agenda was kept either invisible or patronised by white women (Ribeiro, 2016). The relationships between white and Black women were frequently mediated by a hierarchy and a condescending paternalism, and Black women's claims were constantly deemed as 'childish' by white feminist leaders (Da Silva, 2018). As noticed by Sueli Carneiro (one of the pioneer Black women leaders mentioned above), many of the white middle-class women who led the feminist movement at that time in Brazil had Black women domestic servants in their houses and workplaces (Carneiro, 2003). In some instances, these employment hierarchies reproduced the colonial relationships between masters and slaves that had been the norm in Brazil for more than three centuries of African slavery (Maranhão & Knijnik, 2011). Due to these rigid working connections, the otherwise progressive white feminist women could not see the oppression their housekeepers suffered not only as women but also as lower-class Black workers (Sepulveda Dos Santos, 2008).

As mentioned above, the pioneer Black women leaders spoke and wrote widely on the intersectionalities that oppressed women in Brazil. Lélia Gonzalez (1979) presented to the world the role of Black women in Brazilian society, whilst also discussing the social and educational conditions of Black people, particularly women, in the country (Gonzalez, 1981). However, due to the lack of effective means of dissemination at the time, her key writings were not well known by the new generations of Brazilian Black social activists and academic women. Hence, these young women later discovered the intersectionality concept through the works of Crenshaw that were initially translated to Portuguese and disseminated via the Internet at *Estudos Feministas (Feminist Studies)*, a leading Brazilian academic feminist journal and forum (Crenshaw, 2002).

During the 1980s and 1990s, a re-democratisation process took place in the country, and a range of new social and political associations and non-governmental organisations (NGOs) formed by Black people and particularly by Black women started to appear in the country (Da Silva, 2018). As discussed by Carneiro (2003), some of these organisations (such as the Geledes, founded and led by Sueli Carneiro) had as their pillars three clear strategies: first, they tried to occupy the institutional spaces that were responsible for the development and implementation of public policies directly related to women; in doing so, they would be able to push for the inclusion of Black women's agenda in public debates, guidelines and budgets; second, they sought a social acknowledgement of the African religions (particularly candomblé, which, as we will see later, is very important for the Baianas) that were professed by Black women; the Brazilian–African deities, or orishas (*orixas* in Portuguese) have also been of great relevance to Black women, and they wanted to stop discrimination against women devoted to them. Finally, these black NGOs continued to make a distinction between the broad feminist movement and the Black women social movement, which included women of lower-classes, peasants and domestic workers who did not feel represented in the mainstream feminist movement (Da Silva, 2018).

The recognition of Black feminism as a category where Black women could be fitted occurred in the early 2000s. A diverse range of Black women social movements created the *Association of All Black Brazilian Women* organisations and NGOs, to serve as an umbrella organisation and a point of unification for them. This Association made an explicit choice that they would be known as *Black feminists* (Ribeiro, 2016; dos Santos, 2009). With the advent of the Internet, a new generation of Black women social and political activists that belonged to this Association, as well as other academic Black women, started to gain visibility and momentum via their digital activism (Da Silva, 2018). Discussing the gender–race–social class conundrum, but also disseminating positive messages related to black aesthetics and culture, including rap music and black hairstyles, creating new forms of black parties and social events, these activists were successful in disseminating across the country and within their communities, the active voices of the Brazilian Black youth, specifically women (Lima, 2002). In early 2014, the then-President Dilma Roussef sanctioned the 25th of July as the *National Day of Tereza de Benguela and the Brazilian Black Woman*.[1] Coincidentally or not, the endorsement of the Men's Copa happened in the same year.

Next, we present the main heroines of this story: the Baianas, the Black Brazilian women who descend directly from African slaves; whose grandmothers continuously practiced their African religions despite strong persecution from the authorities and from whom they learned how to make a living on the streets – instead of remaining oppressed as domestic servants in affluent white households, enduring humiliations and daily violence as their ancestors had experienced during slavery times.

Baianas Lives Matter?

According to Ribeiro (2018), in the last decade the murder rate of white women in Brazil has decreased by nearly 10%; yet statistics show a completely opposite reality for Black women when considering their murder rate, which has increased by an alarming 54.2%. Ribeiro (2018) states that these numbers can only be understood in a social landscape where gender, race and social class are intertwined. Clearly, race is a relevant social category that determines which woman stays alive or dies in the country (Santos, Guimarães, & Araújo, 2007).

It is also useful to note that Brazil was the last country in the world to abolish African slavery (Prandi, 2000). It was only in the late 1800s that Black African slaves were set totally free. However, the same decree that set them free pushed them into miserable living conditions, as their former owners took even their clothes and let them wander in the streets of Rio de Janeiro and other cities. Soon, they climbed the surrounding hills and started to construct shantytowns (the favelas) to live in (de Menezes, 2009).

Nevertheless, the African communities across the country have kept and also reinvented their cultural traditions, including their religions. One of the most known of these African religions in Brazil is candomblé. During slavery times, slaves adopted into their own religion some practices of Catholicism (the major religion in the country) such as the worship of saints (Prandi, 2000). This mix of practices has coined the Afro-Brazilian religions. Candomblé has its origins in the

Yoruba traditions (Bastide, 2007), with its particular worldview, initiation rites and its own male and female deities (orishas).

In this chapter, we focus on the Baianas from Salvador, capital city of the Bahia state. Salvador has an important role in Brazil's history, as it was chosen by the Portuguese colonisers as the first national capital and remained the country's capital for more than 200 years (1549–1763). Salvador has the largest Black population in Brazil, and the Baianas discussed here are part of the candomblé tradition. They wear large white dresses, with several decorations including different layers of fabric. They take pride in keeping their costumes totally clean (Martini, 2007, p. 291); there are historical accounts of European tourists who were impressed by the neat and beautiful dressing of the Baianas (de Almeida Vasconcelos, 2016).

It is important to highlight that 'Baianas' is an umbrella label that encompasses a diverse group of women (Martini, 2007, p. 291). Diversity and plurality are a mark of Brazilian Black women (Ribeiro, 2018) and exist within the Baianas too. While we acknowledge this diversity, we employ the generic term in order to facilitate an understanding of their realities during the 2014 Men's Copa.

An important trait which unites all Baianas is that they are girls and women who have broken the cycle of working as domestic servants. In a country where 67% of children who work as housekeepers are Black, and among them, 97% are girls (Ribeiro, 2018) working under severe harsh conditions, the Baianas have fought to keep not only their family traditions alive but also their freedom and right to sell food on the streets. FIFA's attempt to control and forbid their street business is far from being the first challenge that the Baianas have battled. As early as in 1769, the Portuguese administration tried to implement an urban reform and 'clean' the streets of Salvador of all street food vendors, particularly women (de Almeida Vasconcelos, 2016). Over the following centuries, there were other initiatives to either abolish or regulate the street food businesses in Salvador, attempts that always targeted the Baianas. Behind the justification of urban reform to bring more organisation and hygiene to the streets, governments sought to privatise the food commerce, taking the Baianas out of business and transferring it to other types of contractors (de Almeida Vasconcelos, 2016). While a similar process was planned for the 2014 Men's Copa, the Baianas, as they had done in the past, fought against their elimination; however, this time the enemy was not a known local government, but a powerful global corporation.

Baianas, *Acarajé* and the Mega-Events Gendered Order

Acarajé is a dish made from peeled black-eyed peas formed into a ball and then deep-fried in dendê palm oil. It is a hot spicy snack that is found anywhere on the streets of Salvador. The Baianas dress in their typical all-white *candomblé* dresses, sit in their small street kiosks, and make and sell acarajé on the spot – charging around U\$2.00 each.

The Baianas used to make and sell acarajé in the *Fonte Nova* Stadium in Salvador – they had done so since its opening in 1951 (Bitter & BIitar, 2012). It is a tradition passed from mother to daughter through generations of families who make a living by selling this street food. When one visits a Brazilian city and walks its streets, one quickly notices how many Brazilians earn a living selling food and other goods on the streets. It is an important part of the local economy and culture that cannot be simply ignored.

However, during the World Cup, FIFA becomes the owner of the official stadiums and their surroundings. There is a 'FIFA zone' that extends two kilometres around the venues. Inside these 'occupied zones', FIFA only allows its sponsors' merchandise to be displayed and sold. No more acarajé or local food – if you are from overseas and travelled to lovely Salvador with its streets full of colonial history to watch the Netherlands beat Spain, instead of tasting delicious local food, FIFA would dictate that you can only eat a Big Mac or a Happy Meal – McDonald's was an official FIFA partner and had the monopoly of selling food within and around the stadiums.

However, FIFA would never have expected the reaction of the Baianas. When the Fonte Nova stadium was about to reopen after renovation for the 2013 Confederations Cup, Rita Maria dos Santos, the president of the Association of Baianas Acarajé and Porridge Vendors (ABAM), heard that FIFA would not allow them to work inside or close to the new stadium.

Rita and the other Baianas' leaders met as a matter of urgency and developed a collective strategy to fight against FIFA's decision that would implode their financial expectations for the World Cup tournament. They quickly started to email the authorities until they were contacted by Change.org. Working with the website, they put together an online petition which quickly garnered national and international attention.

The petition, which claimed Queremos baianas e acarajés na Copa de 2014 #baianasnacopa (We want Baianas e acarajés in the World Cup #baianasintheworldcup), gathered more than 17,000 signatures.[2] With this petition on their hands, Rita and the Baianas pushed the Brazilian government to help their cause. Members of the Federal Parliament stepped onto the stage to deliver speeches supporting the Baianas' cause. Ronaldo, the famous Brazilian striker who then was part of the World Cup Local Organising Committee, joined the movement. Influential international voices such as the German sports website *Sport.de* supported the Baianas' action; the website even compared the acarajé to the *currywurst*, the traditional German dish consumed in German street fairs, highlighting how both dishes were relevant to the local culture (Mendel, 2018). Dilma Rousseff, the first and so far only female Brazilian president in history, became personally involved with the acarajé issue. FIFA had to step back. Even with restrictions imposed by the FIFA standards – such as not using nail polish ('Is McDonald's under the same restrictions?' Rita ironically asked in several media interviews (Mendel, 2018)) – Baianas were allowed to sell their delicious acarajés in the new Arena Fonte Nova during the 2014 Men's Copa.

Acarajé and the Copa Race–Class–Gender Disorder

The Baianas' defiance and victory against the mighty power of the international football governing body was directly motivated by their immediate need to continue to make a living. To these working-class Black women for whom few viable livelihood alternatives exist, being able to continue to sell their snacks at mega-events like the World Cup was literally a matter of survival, as well as an opportunity to increase their income in the short term. In this sense, the mobilisation of national and international support for their cause was not formally framed in the Black feminist discourse. Yet, when contextualised in their long history of racial, class, and gender marginalisation as well as resistance against these multiple relations of power, their relentless actions against the FIFA control take on a new political dimension.

Making and selling acarajé as autonomous, independent entrepreneurs has historically offered the Baianas a primary medium of resistance – against the racial and class oppression that had previously confined them to the neo-colonial servitude of domestic work in white households; against the cultural imperialism that threatened to devalue their unique Afro-Brazilian heritage rooted in such critical daily practices as religious worship, clothing and food (acarajé being its principal example); and against patriarchy that doubly subordinates them as the 'marginalised of the marginal' – the experience that the mainstream Brazilian feminist movement had failed to acknowledge or address. In this context, the generations of Baianas selling acarajé became an infrapolitical practice of economic, cultural and social empowerment and grassroots insurgence against the intersectional power relations that Brazilian Black feminists had battled in political and academic arenas.

Furthermore, in this particular instance involving the World Cup, the women were taking on more than the class, racial and gender order of their society; they were faced with one of the most powerful international sporting bodies, which, despite its officially 'non-profit' status, vigorously acts to protect the investments of its transnational corporate sponsors and generates billions of dollars in annual revenue. In this case, they challenged not only the transnational food megacorporation that is one of FIFA's major sponsors (McDonald's) – their struggle represented the resistance of the local food culture, with its own taste, tradition and history, against the standardisation and unsustainable practices of the global food industry. Their insistence on selling their snacks at the World Cup stadium directly challenged the hegemony of the geopolitical power of the sport-industry complex. Their relentless grassroots campaign, aided by the medium of Change.org and an alliance with global civic activism, developed into an 'unremitting guerrilla warfare' of consequential magnitude, moving the initially unresponsive local officials and eventually pressuring the World Cup local committee and FIFA itself into concession.

This illuminates the power of everyday resistance as conceptualised by Johansson and Vinthagen (2020). Subordinated individuals and groups, even if they have considerably limited access to economic, cultural or symbolic capital, find within their everyday circumstances ways to exercise their oppositional agency, and through the historical, sustained nature of their actions, turn them into a formidable counter-hegemonic force that may weaken hegemonic power, even if marginally or temporarily. Simultaneously, this shows that, hidden behind the all-powerful appearance of sporting mega-events and the international sport-industry complex that occupies the attention of critical sport researchers, countless women and men daily resist such power in a multitude of creative, 'ordinary' ways that may escape scholarly attention.

Particularly in Brazil, these daily acts of resistance had their visibility increased as the 2014 mega-event approached. On the gender side, in the years that preceded the World Cup and in addition to the aforementioned '*as donas da bola*' display, a range of exhibitions highlighted the history of football in different Brazilian communities. Prepared by local museums and universities across the country, these events were well-attended by families and school children who learned about the diverse identities of multiple actors within Brazilian sports history. Moreover, these events allowed the students to participate in an array of football games and activities that challenged the mainstream (male) way of playing the game (Klanovicz & Siqueira Joras, 2016). Brazilian teachers, particularly in public schools, also resisted the FIFA event by introducing in their classes debates and pedagogical activities to show that football was much more than what the World Cup was bringing to the country (Knijnik, 2018).

The resistance also took the form of massive political protests against FIFA standards and the Brazilian government that allowed FIFA to take over the country. During the 2013 Confederations Cup (the trial event that FIFA puts together in the hosting country a year before the World Cup), thousands of Brazilians took over the streets to demonstrate their angst against FIFA's corrupt practices, such as massive funding of stadiums while the country's hospitals and schools were defunded. Fenced in their five-star hotel rooms, FIFA top officials even considered postponing or moving the game venues to another country (Müller, de Oliveira Junior, Feltes, & Sanfelice, 2013). It remains to be seen whether these types of daily resistance and protests against the sporting global powers can occur in other societies where civil society is not as diverse and organised as it is in Brazil.

While the power of FIFA, as well as the fundamental gender, class and racial hierarchies, may remain intact in the final analysis, such power is never total or unchallenged; the Baianas, by seizing the ball and asserting themselves 'as donas da bola' (female ball's owner), demonstrated the inherent contingency of hegemonic power and transformative scope in even the most unequal relations of power.

Then almighty FIFA's general secretary, Jérôme Valcke, who was the key officer designated to protect FIFA sponsors' interests during the mega sport event, and who initially was adamant against the sale of acarajé, was forced to retreat: with a wry smile, he appeared before the media and conceded that 'nobody can fight a Baiana'.

Everyday women – 1; FIFA – 0.

Notes

1. Tereza de Banguela was a Brazilian slave who escaped from slavery and led a 'quilombo' (a community of fugitive slaves) with her husband during the

eighteenth century in Brazil. She became a symbol of black resistance among Black Brazilian women.
2. https://www.change.org/p/queremos-baianas-e-acaraj%C3%A9s-na-copa-de-2014-baianasnacopa/u/2389830

References

Bastide, R. (2007). *The African religions of Brazil: Toward a sociology of the inter-penetration of civilizations.* Baltimore, MD: Johns Hopkins University Press.

Bayat, A. (2000). From 'dangerous classes' to 'quiet rebels': Politics of the urban suberltern in the Global South. *International Sociology, 15*(3), 533–557.

Bayat, A. (2009). *Life as politics: How ordinary people change the Middle East.* Standford, CA: Standford University Press.

Bellos, A. (2002). *Futebol: The Brazilian way of life.* London: Bloomsbury.

Bitter, D., & BIitar, N. P. (2012). Comida, trabalho e patrimônio: notas sobre o ofício das baianas de acarajé e das tacacazeiras. *Horizontes antropologicos, 18*(38), 213–236.

Carneiro, S. (2003). Enegrecer o feminismo: a situação da mulher negra na América Latina a partir de uma perspectiva de gênero. *Racismos contemporâneos, 49*, 49–58.

Crenshaw, K. W. (2002). Documento para o encontro de especialistas em aspectos da discriminação racial relativos ao gênero. *Revista Estudos Feministas, 10*, 177.

da Costa, L. M. (2007). O que é uma torcedora? Notas sobre a representação e auto-representação do público feminino de futebol. *Esporte e sociedade, 2*(4), 1–31.

Da Silva, C. (2018). Feminismo negro. De onde viemos: aproximacoes de uma memoria. In H. B. Hollanda (Ed.), *Explosao feminista: arte, cultura, politica, diversidade* (pp. 252–260). São Paulo: Companhia das Letras.

de Almeida Vasconcelos, P. (2016). *Salvador: Transformações e permanências (1549–1999).* Ilheu: Editus.

de Certeau, M. (1984). *The practice of everyday life.* Berkeley, CA: University of California Press.

de Menezes, J. M. (2009). Abolição no Brasil: a construção da liberdade. *Revista HISTEDBR On-Line, 9*(36), 83–104.

dos Santos, S. B. (2009). As ONGs de mulheres negras no Brasil. *Sociedade e cultura, 12*(2), 275–288.

Elsey, B., & Nadel, J. (2019). *Futbolera: A history of women and sports in Latin America.* Austin, TX: University of Texas Press.

Gonzalez, L. (1979). O papel da mulher na sociedade brasileira. In *Apresentado no Spring Symposium the Political Economy of the Black World.* Los Angeles, CA: Center for Afro-American Studies:UCLA.

Gonzalez, L. (1981). *A Questão Negra no Brasil.* Rio de Janeiro: Global: Cadernos Trabalhistas.

Haag, F. R. (2018). "O futebol pode não ter sido profissional comigo, mas eu fui com ele": trabalho e relações sociais de sexo no futebol feminino brasileiro. *Mosaico, 9*(14), 142–160.

Harkness, G., & Hongsermeier, N. (2015). Female sports as non-movement resistance in the Middle East and North Africa. *Sociology Compass, 9*(12), 1082–1093.

Johansson, A., & Vinthagen, S. (2015). Dimensions of everyday resistance: the Palestinian Sumūd. *Journal of Political Power*, *8*(1), 109–139.

Johansson, A., & Vinthagen, S. (2016). Dimensions of everyday resistance: An analytical framework. *Critical Sociology*, *42*(3), 417–435.

Johansson, A., & Vinthagen, S. (2020). *Conceptualizing 'everyday resistance': A trandisciplinary approach*. New York, NY: Routledge.

Jourdan, C. (2019). *2013: memórias e resistências*. Rio de Janeiro: Circuito.

Klanovicz, J. M., & Joras, P. S. (2016). Silvana Vilodre Goellner. *Motrivivência*, *28*(49), 242–243.

Knijnik, J. (2014). Gendered barriers to Brazilian female football: 20th century legacies. In J. Hargreaves & E. Anderson (Eds.), *Handbook of sport, gender and sexuality* (pp. 120–128). New York, NY: Routledge.

Knijnik, J. (2015). Femininities and masculinities in Brazilian women's football: Resistance and compliance. *Journal of International Women's Studies*, *16*(3), 54–70.

Knijnik, J. (2018). *The World Cup Chronicles: 31 Days that Rocked Brazil*. Balgowlah Heights, NSW: Fair Play Publishing.

Lima, A. (2002). Funkeiros, timbaleiros e pagodeiros: notas sobre juventude e música negra na cidade de Salvador. *Cadernos Cedes*, *22*(57), 77–96.

Maranhão, T., & Knijnik, J. (2011). Futebol Mulato: Racial constructs in Brazilian football. *Cosmopolitan Civil Societies*, *3*(2), 55–71.

Martini, G. T. (2007). *Baianas do Acarajé: A uniformização do típico em uma tradição culinária afro-brasileira*. Doctoral thesis, Universidade de Brasilia, Brasilia, p. 291.

Mendel, D. S. D. S. (2018). Nas ruas com as baianas de acarajé: desafios, lutas e representatividade. *História Oral*, *21*(1), 95–119.

Moura, D. (2014). *As donas da bola*. São Paulo: Syn Editora.

Müller, I. D., de Oliveira Junior, L. L., Feltes, A. F., & Sanfelice, G. R. (2013). Manifestos sociais e Copa das Confederações na cobertura da Folha de São Paulo. *Motrivivência*, *41*, 85–100.

Prandi, R. (2000). African gods in contemporary Brazil: A sociological introduction to Candomblé today. *International Sociology*, *15*(4), 641–663.

Ribeiro, D. (2016). Feminismo negro para um novo marco civilizatório. *Revista internacional de direitos humanos*, *13*(24), 99–104.

Ribeiro, S. (2018). Quem somos: mulheres negras no plural, nossa existência é pedagógica. In H. B. Hollanda (Ed.), *Explosão feminista: arte, cultura, politica, diversidade* (pp. 261–286). São Paulo: Companhia das Letras.

Rigo, L. C. (2005). Memórias de corpos esportizados: a natação feminina e o futebol infame. *Revista Movimento*, *11*(2), 131–146.

Santos, S. M. D., Guimarães, M. J. B., & Araújo, T. V. B. D. (2007). Desigualdades raciais na mortalidade de mulheres adultas no Recife, 2001 a 2003. *Saúde e Sociedade*, *16*, 87–102.

Scott, J. C. (1985). *Weapons of the weak*. New Haven, CT: Yale University Press.

Scott, J. C. (1989). Everyday forms of resistance. *Copenhagen Papers*, *4*, 33–62.

Scott, J. C. (1990). *Domination and the art of resistance: Hidden transcripts*. New Haven, CT: Yale University Press.

Scott, J. C. (2012). *Everyday forms of peasant resistance*. Retrieved from https://libcom.org/history/everyday-forms-peasant-resistance-james-c-scott. Accessed on February 12, 2021.

Scott, J. C. (2013). *Decoding subaltern politis: Ideology, disguise, and resitance in agrarian politics*. New York, NY: Routledge.

Sepúlveda Dos Santos, M. (2008). The repressed memory of Brazilian slavery. *International Journal of Cultural Studies*, *11*(2), 157–175.

Vinthagen, S., & Johansson, A. (2013). "Everyday resistance": Exploration of a concept and its theories. *Resistance Studies Magazine*, *1*, 1–46.

Votre, S., & Mourão, L. (2003). Women's football in Brazil: Progress and problems. *Soccer and Society*, *4*(2/3), 254–267.

Chapter 9

I Gotta Feeling … Let's Turn to the People! The 2018 Football World Cup in Russia

Katarzyna Raduszynska

I Gotta Feeling

The 2018 FIFA Men's World Cup (FWC) was a real game changer, a subversive coupling, a moment of transition from the artificially created FIFA world to an authentic international community. I call this the *human return* from commercialisation to togetherness, which is created by means of carnival, tech-performance, organisational performance and, of course, participants – football players, referees, FIFA authorities, politicians, stewards, sponsors, artists and celebrities, journalists, and, most important of all here, fans. Fans are not only spectators but primarily performers and crucial actors, in the stands and in front of the TV. This whole performance called the FWC is created for them. But it is also created by them, which is far more interesting and is the topic I will address in this chapter.

I have been a football fan for as long as I can remember, and watching sport was, in my family, a father-daughter ritual and one of my most important memories. It was my father who introduced me to watching my first ever Winter Olympic Games in Sarajevo in 1984. Thanks to him I will never forget Jayne Torvill and Christopher Dean's legendary Bolero's performance in the ice skating. Soon after, he was telling me why the 1984 Summer Olympic Games in Los Angeles was being boycotted by 14 Eastern Bloc countries and patiently explaining what the offside rule was. Then we were celebrating France as Olympic Champions and admiring the great second-placed Brazil after a thrilling final game. I was seven years old back then and that is how my mega-events adventure began – an adventure that continues to this day. I owe my passion for sport mega-events to my father, who introduced me to this world; a world that is largely owned and dominated by men. Although I have never felt out of place in this masculine world, from the very beginning it was absolutely clear that I am merely a guest here and it is mandatory that I obey the rules if I wanted to be allowed in. However, my father never took me to the football game because, as he said, the stadium was not the place for girls. So back then I learned this: sport mega-events belong to men and have always belonged to them. Yet also back then, holding my

Sport, Gender and Mega-Events, 163–183
doi:10.1108/978-1-83982-936-920211015

father's hand, I started to dream that one day I would go and watch the FIFA Football World Cup (FWC) live, by myself – a woman. It was my dream.

It took me a while but fortunately, the dream came true and I went to the FIFA World Cup 2018 in Russia to watch, study, explore and experience spectacles and performances of fans from all over the world. As a participating observer, I witnessed all the madness of the carnival. During my one-month trip to Russia I visited five cities – Kaliningrad, Moscow, St. Petersburg, Kazan and Volgograd. I went to FIFA Fan Zones in those cities and attended four games: Poland–Senegal; Argentina–Iceland; Germany–Mexico and Poland–Colombia. I listened, I watched, I took notes, I interviewed fans and I recorded video material. Based on this, this chapter is a reflection on performance, fandom and gender at this mega-event.

The chapter's aim is to explore the fan experience 'from the ground' considering how some of the controversial issues associated with this event affected fan experiences, and how gender and identity played out, questioning if and how fans can disrupt dominant narratives in the context of sport mega-events. I would like to describe moments of transition from the artificially created FIFA world to a more authentic international community – *human return* from commercialisation to togetherness. This is achieved by means of catharsis and creating a unique kind of community. I consider how phenomena that occurred before, during and after the FWC are connected. This mega-event is vast and marvellous and glittering, providing something we desperately lack in everyday life – catharsis. This is why, I argue, such sport mega-events are so sought-after and longed-for, attracting people from all over the world, regardless of gender, race, ethnicity, age, social status, religion, nationality or geographical area.

Sounds chaotic so far? It's not. It is just performativity, methodology necessary to depict this extraordinary phenomenon. My area of expertise is theatre and performance, which I draw on here to explore fan experiences at the 2018 FWC in Russia.

Let's Get It Started

As a PhD candidate I am investigating football fan performances, including spectacles and show, on and off the pitch. My background is theatre, which provides many helpful tools for understanding fan performances. Yet performances themselves are complex, textured and formed from different disciplines, where lines between them are vague and difficult to assign. Jon McKenzie proposed the thesis that modern culture, or post-culture, is destined to perform, and that 'performance will be to the twentieth and twenty-first centuries what discipline was to the eighteenth and nineteenth, that is, an onto-historical formation of power and knowledge' (McKenzie, 2002, p. 18). His influential book '*Perform or else: From discipline to performance*' proposes a broad conception of performance; one that is not limited to well-known theatre concepts but extended to interdisciplinary research and open to further interpretations and modifications. This general theory of performance may be used to explore the reality we live in, with its vague boundaries and unpredictability. In other words, McKenzie's concept does not provide any solutions, but rather makes performances problematic, multiplying questions. McKenzie (2002, p. 3) writes that 'Perform or Else initiates a challenge, one that links the performances of artists and activists with those of workers and executives, as well as computers and missile systems'. What, then, is performance? I do not have any clear definition, but explain here how I understand it and how, through this lens, I try to read the FIFA World Cup 2018 as I witnessed it.

Performance comes from perform and is inevitably linked to action – providing, staging, rendition, creating, execution, competition, racing, gathering, answering, establishing, asking and many more. Performance is always connected with an act of doing and as such is subject to interpretation. The raison d'être of performance is the performers themselves; artists and their shows, spectacles, happenings, performances and painting, body art, video art, events and non-artistic performances in everyday life, secular and religious rituals, social practices, manifestos, political protests, leisure time performances, games and play, tech-performances and many more. Performances are one of the most important behavioural forms and can be seen as the exemplification of behaviour, its ultimate manifestation.

Jon McKenzie is aware of the intricacy of these diverse displays of action. From the very beginning, he proposes to face the challenge of recognising and acknowledging that nothing happens by itself, nothing is in isolation and thus cannot be considered separately. McKenzie (2002) goes on to argue that not only is everything connected, but also things effect other things. McKenzie names those things, organises them and distinguishes them with care and understanding – in other words, he proposes his own performance theory.

Still sounds chaotic? Well, this is performativity, it is inherently variable. Yet it is not really chaos at all, and performance may be structured into three basic paradigms and their challenges, as McKenzie (2002) explains.

The first is the Efficiency of Organisational Performance, the origins of which McKenzie traces to after the Second World War in the United States. I interpret this paradigm as relating to all actions taken to improve our efficiency, like restructuring, reengineering, reinvention, downsizing, performance reviews, outsourcing, evaluation processes, human relations, decision-making, appraisal, benefits and communication. All these actions taken to achieve efficiency start with individual performances. If the goal is to understand and improve organisational performance, then individuals matter, both separately and in collaboration. This can be understood as: 'How much is this individual's performance contributing to the organization?' yet also 'How much is the organization contributing to this individual's performance?' (McKenzie, 2002, p. 57).

The second paradigm is the Effectiveness of Technological Performance, where 'performance has no existence per se, (…) what is meant is its effectiveness in a given task' (Borovits & Neumann, 1979, p. 3). McKenzie (2002, p. 97) argues: 'Other terms frequently employed as synonyms of performance are capability, operation, function, and efficiency. The performance of a technology refers to its technical effectiveness in a specific application or set of applications undertaken in a particular context'. What might this particular context be? In relation to mega-events, we can imagine the effectiveness of messages sent by authorities, based on tech-performance of surveillance cameras around the host city. Their mere presence, not even performance, helps prevent possible violations and misconduct.

And last but not least is the Efficacy of Cultural Performance. This refers to its subversive potential, revolutionary lines, and ability to sustain or to be the game changer in social and personal transformation. This may involve blending activities from different, often seemingly exclusive, spheres such as theatre, drama, rituals, ceremonies, carnivals, storytelling, games and plays. Cultural performance has always had the power to cross borders, to establish new orders, to undermine and re-define statuses:

> Cultural performances are 'occasions in which as a culture or society we reflect upon and define ourselves, dramatize our collective myths and history, present ourselves with alternatives, and eventually change in some ways while remaining the same in others'. This citation of a citation identifies three functions which scholars have regularly attributed to cultural performance: 1) social and self-reflection through the dramatization or embodiment of symbolic forms, 2) the presentation of alternative arrangements, and 3) the possibility of conservation and/or transformation. Given the imperative of social efficacy, theorists have largely concentrated on performance's transformational potential.
>
> (McKenzie, 2002, p. 31)

Transformation is an indispensable quality of liminality and may establish the paradigm of cultural performance – action makes/evokes new actions, which ultimately make change. This is a profoundly political approach to performance, as shifting from transgression to resistance presumes at least two strategies. The first seeks to overthrow authority/ies and the second to contest the existing order. This often leads to further steps, such as the formation of new communities or mass protests.

McKenzie (2002) thus distinguishes three kinds of performance and claims they operate together to create powerful and contradictory layers of society and its diversity. The three combine insights from anthropology, sociology, philosophy, art, psychology, electronics, politics, ethnography, cultural studies, gender studies, software laboratories, industry and many other fields. In this view of performance, allegedly distinct disciplines combine in endless variations to inform research objects, their connections and interactions. Shall we begin, then?

We Got the Beat That Power

In simple terms, performance can be a device to perpetuate an existing order or to change it. This is what I was looking at during my stay in Russia, drawing on Jon

McKenzie's (2002) three basic types of performance. First is Organisational Performance, the challenge of which is Efficiency. Here we can position the actions of Russia and FIFA, i.e., organising and running the tournament. Second, is Technological Performance and its Effectiveness – this again relates to FIFA, alongside the global media. Third, and perhaps most importantly, is Cultural Performance, the challenge of which is Efficacy, and here the focus is on the fans – soccer fans from all over the world who, over the course of one month, came together to create a monumental cultural performance.

To understand what kind of shift might have happened in Russia to enable this cultural performance, we need to consider the contexts of the event; place, time, the law, politics, and – perhaps most significantly – the role of the Russian state and that of FIFA.

The FIFA Men's World Cup is the biggest single-sport event in the world and every four years it becomes a somewhat controversial topic – this never changes. Every four years there are numerous challenges in relation to economic, political and human rights issues. Human rights and climate change organisations often highlight problems and challenge FIFA and the host nation on a variety of issues from exploitation of workers, to destruction of the environment. Yet they always lose – despite all the protests, calls for boycotts, appeals, the FWC goes ahead. To date, the only sport mega-event that has ever been cancelled was the 1940 Summer Olympic Games, originally to be held in Tokyo, rescheduled for Helsinki, but ultimately cancelled because of the outbreak of the Second World War. No other sport mega-event has yet been cancelled (2020's UEFA Euro Championships and the Tokyo Summer Olympics are, at the time of writing, postponed but not cancelled). The 2018 FWC was the third mega-event hosted by Russia, following the Summer Olympic Games in 1980 in Moscow and the 2014 Winter Olympics in Sochi. All three of these mega-events were marked by controversy and protest from different groups, yet all went ahead and were considered successful by key stakeholders. What makes these events so controversial? Let's take a closer look at what happened in Russia in relation to these events.

It is widely recognised that sport events have long been used for propaganda purposes by nation states, and Russia is certainly no exception to this. In February 1980, American president Jimmy Carter called for a boycott of the Summer Olympics in Moscow, in response to the Soviet Army's invasion of Afghanistan at Christmas 1979. As a result of Carter's call, 63 countries did not send their athletes to Moscow, an event that Soviet authorities wanted to use to present the power of the Soviet Union to the world. In response to the 1980 boycott, the 1984 Olympic Games in Los Angeles was boycotted by a total of 14 Eastern Bloc countries – all of the Soviet Union and East Germany.

Ten years later, after the fall of the Soviet Union, Vladimir Putin entered the political stage as Russian Prime Minister. It was clear from the very beginning that his aim was to restore Russia's reputation as a global powerhouse, and sport mega-events were an important part of this. The first mega-event was the Winter Olympics 2014 in Sochi, reputedly Putin's favourite resort. The event was preceded by controversy in relation to the signing of discriminatory laws, banning the promotion of non-traditional sexual relations. This violates not only the Olympic spirit but also international human rights and might have resulted in dangerous outcomes for visitors and locals, by restricting freedom of speech, of expression and of association. Amnesty International called on Putin to repeal the laws, which have led to increases in violence against LGBTQ+ people in Russia, and demanded the release of all prisoners of conscience, like the female music group, Pussy Riot. Several organisations around the world took action like sending letters, protesting in front of the Russian Embassy in Helsinki, a flash mob in Cambridge in the United Kingdom, protests in New York, and many more.

LGBTQ+ rights was not the only issue plaguing the 2014 Winter Olympics. The Circassian peoples called for cancellation or postponement of the event until Russia apologised for the nineteenth century Circassian genocide. In January 2013, Human Rights Watch published a report based on interviews with 66 migrant workers, who were facing exploitation in construction sites in Sochi (HRW, 2013). Russian authorities also resettled 2000 families to make way for Olympic venues, without proper compensation. And the last, but not least, controversy – the massive doping scandal, involving many sport disciplines and Russian authorities (BBC, 2019). Yet the 2014 Winter Olympics still took place. The International Olympic Committee declared them a resounding success (Olympic.org, 2015), even if some Western media suggested the Games lacked atmosphere (Walker, 2014). Perhaps unsurprisingly, Russia also declared the 2014 Winter Olympics to be successful (Walker, 2017) and began looking forward to FWC 2018.

Towards the end of the Winter Olympics, which took place from 7 February to 23 February, the Russian Federation annexed the Crimean Peninsula with the use of armed force, between 20 February and 26 March 2014. International response to the annexation of Crimea has been unequivocal yet eventually powerless: it was considered to be the most serious breach of European borders since the Second World War and authorities from all over the world sent letters condemning Russia and assuring support for Ukraine's sovereignty. Sanctions were enacted, the EU-Russia summit was cancelled, the G8 Meeting was moved from Sochi to Brussels and has become the G7 since then, as Russia has not been allowed to re-enter. However, despite this international condemnation, preparations for the 2018 FWC continued.

As with the 2014 Winter Olympics, there were protests from human rights groups in the run up the 2018 FWC. Yet despite protests, FIFA continued to support Russia's efforts to host the mega-event. Human Rights Watch's Deputy Executive Director Phillipe Bolopion (2018) said: 'There is a reason why autocrats aggressively seek to host mega sporting events. They offer publicity and a veneer of respectability – two things Russia is desperately in the market for'. As is FIFA, which was mired in scandals and allegations of corruption. In 2015, seven FIFA officials were arrested in Zurich and charged with receiving $150 million in bribes for broadcasting and marketing rights in the Americas. It was the culmination of an investigation that had been going on for several years, also encompassing the bidding processes for the 2018 and 2022 FIFA World Cup hosts (see Ritz & Mather, 2015).

Concerns about racism in Russia have long been an issue in relation to international football. Russian football supporters' racist behaviour was investigated by UEFA in 2013 following CSKA Moscow's home Champions League game against Manchester City, whose player Yaya Touré alleged he was racially abused by CSKA fans (BBC, 2013). The idea was proposed that Black football players might boycott the 2018 World Cup finals if Russia was not capable of dealing with the violence and racism in its stadiums. The topic was raised again after a friendly Russia-France game in March 2018 in St. Petersburg, when FIFA charged World Cup host Russia with fan racism following chants aimed at Black French players (The Guardian, 2018). These kind of racist incidents were connected with 'anti-gay' or 'gay propaganda' laws, and some international politicians and media outlets warned of possible racist attacks, harassment, threats, and acts of violence towards LGBTQ+ fans (e.g., Wintour, 2018).

International relations became even more difficult after the Skripal poisonings in the United Kingdom. The bungled assassination attempt appeared to have the Kremlin's fingerprints all over it, and on 15 March 2018, the UK Prime Minister Theresa May publicly blamed Russia and expelled 23 Russian diplomats, who were suspected of spying (BBC, 2018). Twenty more countries followed, expelling over 100 public officials. In this extraordinary gesture of solidarity with British authorities, consecutive governments threatened boycotts of the World Cup – Iceland, Japan, Sweden, Denmark, Australia and Poland. By April 2018, 60 members of the European Parliament called for the boycott. At the time no one knew or could even predict what was going to happen to the mega-event.

The situation facing the Russian FWC looked even more serious than a decade earlier when disquiet in the international community surfaced about human rights issues in China prior to the Summer Olympic Games in Beijing in 2008 (Brownell, 2012). In May 2018, Human Rights Watch published a report which detailed human rights abuses linked to preparations for the FWC 2018 (HRW, 2018). These included labour issues like working in extreme cold, deaths and injuries, retaliation and intimidation against workers. The HRW Guide also addressed existing discriminatory laws and human rights crises in Russia – including the crackdown on political opponents of the government, violence towards LGBTQ+ people and racism.

The global political situation was thus largely hostile to Russia, but the event went ahead. Circumstances leading up to the World Cup were not favourable, but for Vladimir Putin, this was no obstacle. He wanted to win this challenge and show that his country is safe and can host the best and greatest sporting carnival in the world.

It was a daring mission from the very beginning. Would Russia be able to pull off a successful mega-event in the context of such international hostility? One could argue, following performativity's criteria: yes, they did; mission impossible accomplished. How was it done? By what means or methods? Did we miss something? What really happened in the country, where human rights can often appear to be just an empty statement? What does this tell us about decision-makers and their actions? About our actions as fans and consumers of this mega-event?

Go out and Smash It

Following McKenzie, I would like to initiate a challenge, one that links the performances of all actors, human and non-human, who were part of, worked on, attended or were involved in whatever way in the FIFA World Cup – fans, ticket holders, national teams, referees, stewards, venues, stadium infrastructure and equipment, stands, national anthems, fan zones, labour practices, police procedures, artists, activists and so on.

Now, let us start with Organisational Performance and its Efficiency – both Russia and FIFA have given priority to the World Cup above all other events. It is the largest single-sport event in the world, FIFA's flagship event. It was important for Russia in terms of global and domestic reputation, coming soon after the Sochi Olympics in 2014, which is why it is not surprising Russia spent over $15 billion on the event. Twelve stadiums were built or modernised, and a fan passport called 'Fan ID' was introduced for the first time. About 64 games were played by 32 national teams and 736 players from 311 football clubs scored 169 goals. For those 32 teams, 215 domestic flights were organised. 445 training sessions were held at Team Base Camps, 55 at Venue Specific Training Sites, 85 official training sessions took place at the stadiums and 2 of them were open-to-public sessions and were watched by almost 40,000 spectators and 3,220 media representatives.

For over a month, 17,040 volunteers from 112 countries and 85 Russian regions were working at and around the stadiums with 18,000 more in host cities. 1,290 cars and 736 buses were used to drive players, referees and journalists. 1,827,678 Fan IDs were released to people from 181 countries, and a quarter of them were women. 7,707,400 people were registered in 11 Fan Zones and were able to attend 754 live musical performances. 3,031,768 people attended games in 12 stadiums and 17,440 stewards looked after them, with 20,850 security guards watching over. 10,967 people were hired to sell snacks and beverages. 1,500 security specialists from 160 federal and regional administrative entities watched over everything. 13 airports handled 15.8 million people, while 5.5 million arrived by train (see FIFA, 2018a).

Both the opening and closing ceremonies required 1,500 artists, 1,500 show production staff and 350 hair and makeup stylists. 980 lights were used for the lighting design and 2,000 meters of fabric were used for costumes. Safety was secured by 172 medical stations at all FIFA World Cup venues and 314 ambulances, 343 mobile medical teams onsite, 13 medical helicopters on stand-by and 6,455 accredited healthcare professionals at the stadiums. FIFA and Russia put in motion a great organisational machine, albeit a somewhat ambiguous one, as it consisted of thousands of undercover agents policing all public places, like the Red Square in Moscow, alongside over 100,000 policemen all over the country (see FIFA, 2018b). This created an extremely efficient organising apparatus.

The second aspect of McKenzie's (2002) framework, Technological Performance, is evident in a set of new world records, the effectiveness of high-performance elite sport. Sixty-four games were watched by over 3 billion people, of whom 22% watched it on mobile devices, rather than television (FIFA, 2018a). There was a record-breaking 7.5 billion web interactions, 580 million between-user actions, 1.25 billion watched videos. 270,000 accreditations were released in 14 Accreditation Centres for 14,044 broadcasters, of whom 78 were based in the International Broadcast Centre (IBC) in Moscow, where 7 professional TV studios were built. Just next to IBC HQ, American FOX TV built their own Russian HQ, twice as big as IBC, from where all the games were broadcast to the United States and watched by 16 million Americans, which is a record result given the fact that the US National Team did not qualify for the finals in Russia, and (men's) football is not one of the most popular sports in the United States. 64 games were judged by 35 referees, 62 assistant referees and outside the pitch 133 VAR (video assistant referees) who judged 455 VAR incidents, from which nine penalties were awarded. This was the first World Cup to use VAR technology, and this significant development has become an important contribution to football discourse.

All possible online actions were monitored in IBC. Since FIFA is the rights holder and the only organisation able to award broadcasting rights, there were strict restrictions on filming and broadcasting any video materials from inside of any stadium. Three separate rooms were created, where on dozens of LED screens global broadcasters and their online and offline media activities were surveilled around the clock. If there was any media activity without FIFA consent, the broadcaster was heavily fined and sometimes access revoked. Even unauthorised use of the official World Cup font 'Dusha' was strictly prohibited. Interestingly, the greatest transgression was unauthorised depictions of the pitch and grass – this was strictly forbidden and controlled by FIFA, using a hierarchical network of managers, supervisors and bodyguards, located in specially built dock hangars around the stadiums.

Technical Performance was thus highly effective, and Organisational Performance efficient. The final aspect to consider is Cultural Performance and here I turn to the fans, who performed amazing, international, diversified and peaceful actions.

Tonight's Gonna Be a Good Night (Turn to the Fans)

Cultural Performance is perceived as an engagement of social norms, as an ensemble of activities with the potential to uphold societal arrangements or as a phenomenal driver of personal and social transformation. While Cultural Performance's Efficacy to reaffirm existing structures and console or heal people has consistently been recognised as an ability to sustain, it is its transgressive, resistant or game-changing potential that has come to dominate the study of cultural performance. Questions about the efficacy of ceremonies and rites as cultural performances might be expressed as: What is actually happening here? When is it happening? Where does it lead to? What is the liminal stimulus, necessary to trigger change?

The Football World Cup brings fans from all around the world together in a cultural performance stretching from high to pop/mass culture. Fan actions can be considered transformative, if only we are ready to see them that way. I believe what might help here is to see the mega-event as a carnival, a month-long ball, where everything is turned upside down. Mikhail Bakhtin (1999) wrote about four carnival categories: profanation, carnivalistic mesalliances, eccentric behaviour and familiar, free interaction between people. The last category is especially interesting for us, and Bakhtin says:

> Carnival is a pageant without footlights and without a division into performers and spectators. In carnival everyone is an active participant, everyone communes in the carnival act. Carnival is not contemplated and, strictly speaking, not even performed; its participants live in it, they live by its laws as long as those laws are in effect; that is, they live a carnivalistic life. Because carnivalistic life is life drawn out of its usual rut, it is to some extent 'life turned inside out', 'the reverse side of the world'. (...) The laws, prohibitions, and restrictions that determine the structure and order of ordinary, that is noncarnival, life are suspended during carnival: what is suspended first of all is hierarchical structure and all forms of terror, reverence, piety, and etiquette connected with it – that is, everything resulting from socio-hierarchical inequality or any other form of inequality among people (including age). All distance between people is suspended (...) People who in life are separated by impenetrable hierarchical barriers enter into free familiar contact on the carnival square (...).
>
> (pp. 122–123)

In other words, carnival is a special time, where all the rules, gestures, behaviours and discourses of everyday life are suspended. It is an act of creation of new temporary principles, which may become non-temporary by being performed, accepted and respected.

A significant element is resistance, understood not by rough or violent actions, but as soft power performances. One of the first acts of resistance was the reactions of international fans to the warnings communicated through the global media. Due to Russia's discriminatory anti-gay propaganda laws, discussed above, a lot of media attention was justifiably paid to BAME (Black, Asian and minority ethnic) and LGBTQ+ fans' safety. For example, a number of potential risks to UK nationals were named explicitly by the Foreign and Commonwealth Office (FCO, 2018).

Despite these concerns, 12,637 people from London alone, and almost 35,000 from the wider United Kingdom travelled to Russia for the event. Fans who did travel to Russia were in agreement about the hospitality, excellent organisation, and ease of accessing information and emphasised the level of safety, which had been a huge concern before the event kicked off (see Skivington, 2018). These concerns were justified, because of the violent incidents in Marseille during the

European Championships in 2016, when Russian and English hooligans clashed (see Sly, Chapter 5). But, despite fears of violence, something completely different happened during the 2018 World Cup finals. Gary Neville, former Manchester United star and football coach, wrote on Twitter:

> This tournament is the best I've ever seen. This country has risen to the occasion!! Come and enjoy it if you can.
>
> (@Gnev2, 2 July 2018)

An England fan, Matt Maybury tweeted:

> Back from 2 weeks in Russia alive. I wasn't attacked by blood thirsty hooligans, I wasn't eaten by a bear & I haven't been poisoned or killed. The British media should be ashamed of themselves for their clear propaganda against the Russian people. Absolutely class country.
>
> (@ChezzerMaybury, 29 June 2018)

This transformation in perceptions of Russia was most evident when I visited Volgograd, where I met fans mostly from Japan, Iceland, Poland and England, because of the games that were played in the Volgograd Arena. For English supporters their national team's match in Volgograd proved to be an excellent opportunity to review not only Russian-English relations, but also to revisit the 1943 Battle of Stalingrad, to remember what happened then and throughout the Second World War – known as the Great Patriotic War to Russians – to pay tribute to the fallen and to make the slogan 'no more war' resound even more strongly. I watched them making the pilgrimage to Mamayev Kurgan, the great ensemble monument to heroes of the Battle of Stalingrad, where visitors climb 200 steps, symbolising 200 days of battle, to reach the tallest statue in Europe, The Motherland Calls. I witnessed moments of silence and reflection, I saw people crying, genuinely touched by the colossal sculpture park, representing not only Mother Motherland, the personification of Russia, but also the fallen soldiers, reminding us of the horrors of war. In those moments all the animosities and national footballing rivalries were put aside and one could feel unity and seriousness, separate from the tournament. Visiting Volgograd was one of the most startling points of my trip to Russia for the World Cup, personally and scientifically. Watching people paying tribute, observing reactions of Poles, English, Icelanders and Japanese, it was obvious that, for these football fans, nothing was the same anymore after visiting Mamayev Kurgan. It was an excellent example of cultural performance, where the age-old custom of honouring the dead is mixed with the carnival – the two co-existing perfectly side by side. It was football that was behind the reunion of former allies, performative action establishing this unique connection above all divisions. Travelling fans denied hostility and instead recognised hospitality as a core element of Russian culture. This is the embodiment of transformation, substituting hostility for hospitality.

Harder, Faster, Better, Stronger

In Russia in 2018, the famous national pride, so often portrayed as hooliganism, was instead transformed into a pretext to build international relationships and tell the whole world about these connections via social media – according to FIFA's reports, these actions were performed a record-breaking 7.5 billion times. And here tech-performance meets cultural performance – social media became the platform of cultural exchange. Usually we should exercise caution depending on TV coverage of mega-events, because the media creates the dominant, often restrictive, narratives. Yet this time it was the fans, celebrating together by chanting, dancing and marching, and broadcasting these actions to the rest of the world through social media. Unexpectedly, and unlike during previous FIFA World Cups or UEFA European Championships, there were no major nationalistic incidents, violence or hostility based on politics, and the fans could feel safe, surrounded by thousands of previously verified volunteers, police and invisible secret services. Led by hospitable Russians, fans were able to enjoy the carnivalistic World-Upside-Down Cup, being secretly guarded and guided by silent Russian state machinery. In such an artificially created world, all shifts and role-reversals of this kind are welcomed, up to certain limits, but still, it was a huge step for Russia at this time. (Subsequent events, such as the detention of Putin's opponent Navalny in early 2021, suggest that this huge step was nothing but a façade, at least on a political level.)

I was to able to observe this in Kazan, where the carnival character was also emphasised by the costumes and fan disguises. I met a young Colombian male fan, dressed as a woman, dancing, singing and attempting to attract Polish fans, so they would not support the Polish national team during the Poland-Colombia game in the evening. I also met a father with his little son, who was wearing a shirt with both Polish and Colombian colours on it. This little boy was trying to pronounce Polish players' surnames, which is not easy, but his struggling attempts were moving. It was a great lesson in respect for one's opponents, that a father taught his son. On the same occasion I watched thousands of Colombian fans wearing yellow afro wigs in tribute to former player, Carlos Valderrama, who was actually present at the stadium during the game and fans chanted his name in a gesture of honour. Colombian fans were also wearing T-shirts with the slogan 'It is Colombia, not Columbia!' and were eager to explain linguistic errors, and of course build relations. Kazan, the Muslim capital of Tatarstan, turned out to be an extremely hospitable and open city.

However, the biggest challenge was my trip to Moscow, Russia's capital. This 20-million inhabitant city was under the siege of fans and overcrowded for a month. The Red Square as a central meeting point became an enormous stage for performing fans, who were not spectators anymore, but empowered actors, performers telling their own stories: stories of their origins, traditions, fighting spirit and courage. It resembled all we have been taught about medieval theatre – everything looked like a moveable stage without a pageant wagon, placed anywhere, just to be seen. Fans were like actors or mime artists, wearing strong war paint and jester hats, carrying instruments like flutes and tabors, performing a unique show made of chants, rhymes, battle cries – all for fans of the opposing team. Fans-actors would perform their roles over and over for the changing audiences and would wait for a rejoinder. I watched Poles' 'dance spectacle', where part of a large group sang a song whose lyrics consisted of the names of Polish football players to the tune of 'No limit' by 2 Unlimited, and the second half was dancing a kind of waltz to the music. Suddenly Poles invited an old Russian couple into the circle and encouraged them to dance. Something magical happened – young Poles clapping Russians, having fun and being genuinely happy. I witnessed a number of meetings between Senegalese and Poles on the Red Square and on the subway – it seemed like a joyful contest, a festival of chants and bizarre stadium poetry. Usually distrustful Poles were apparently charmed by Senegalese fans and responded with nonnatural grace. What happened there was an extraordinary dialogue of two completely different cultures, dialogue based on mutual listening and of a genuine desire to learn something new about the others. The carnivalistic atmosphere suspended biases, invisible resentments stayed invisible, and mutual understanding uncoerced and genuine.

To make this all happen and maintain the carnival, Moscow changed its colours every day. Perfectly working security apparatus watched over the safety of the fans around the clock. You could meet police everywhere and their role was versatile. They were the first line of contact, Russia's visiting card – and it was amazing to watch them trying to manage and fulfil their duties. We could feel something like cordiality from those policemen. They welcomed us obeying the rules, the conversation between us all was clear, and everyone wanted to keep things safe. It was a big gesture of maturity on both sides – police and spectators. This maturity was also evident in the behaviour of the fans. I observed it especially on the Moscow Metro: thousands of fans entering this underworld of sculpture, painting, architecture and socialist classicism were charmed by the beauty of these underground palaces. It was an absolutely wondrous experience to watch fans from all over the world – noisy at street level, getting quieter as they walked downstairs, silently admiring the works of art. According to subsequent fan reports and narratives, it was in those very moments that change happened. Permanent change. A change of perspective, of how they perceive Russia, themselves, each other. This peculiar breakthrough into performance was also what all the fans came for, their ultimate agenda – for catharsis, that was expected to occur during the game. I witnessed this rite of passage, the exact moment of liminality, a time society's deepest values emerge. McKenzie is right when writing:

> Like theater, liminality would become a pervasive model of cultural performance itself: separated from society both temporally and spatially, liminal activities allow participants to reflect, take apart, and reassemble symbols and behaviors and, possibly, to transform themselves and society.
>
> (McKenzie, 2002, p. 36)

It sounds like Bakhtin, doesn't it? When separated from society, participants – here known as fans – are allowed to re-establish, transform, transcend, sometimes transgress, and definitely turn their own world upside down, if only for a month.

Look at Her Dancing

If sport mega-events are situated in the world of men, the question is whether in the twenty-first century there is now room for women as well? And not only women, but all people, including those who do not fit with binary sex classifications. Is everyone entitled to be equal? According to Lange (2020), 37% of World Cup fans in Russia in 2018 were female. But we should not think only about numbers, but whether these 37% were equal to men, the 63%? What does it even mean – equal? As sportswomen or female fans, or stewardesses or WAGS (wives and girlfriends)? How can women recognise themselves in men's world, where all the rules are set by organisations run by men, where men dominate sport, where it is men's competitions which are broadcast and watched by billions of fans, mostly men?

So, what is the picture? Are women really suppressed? Are they allowed to enter this world and make themselves comfortable? Who decides that? And how do women actually do it? How do they enter men's various worlds and how do they make themselves comfortable? Out of many issues I have been able to choose only a few to address here that illustrate the ambiguity of gender transgression and fan performances at the mega-event.

Many people take their rights for granted, such as the right to watch soccer in the stadium. For example, you are a huge fan of your local team and on Saturday – game day – just like everybody else, you are holding your Season Ticket, taking your umbrella and walking to the venue, meeting your friends on the way. You do not have to think about the steps you will have to take to reach your goal, which is to watch the game. It is just an ordinary Saturday, isn't it? Now, please imagine, this opportunity is not open to everyone, including women in some countries.

Let us rewind again to 1 December 2017, when the Final Draw was about to be held in Moscow, at the State Kremlin Palace, where the most famous artists and singers have performed. There were two hosts: Maria Komandnaya, Russian sport journalist, and Gary Lineker, former England football player. Komandnaya announced her role on Twitter on 17 November 2017. Reaction was immediate. Dozens of Iranians replied, asking the journalist to dress 'properly' for the ceremony – to cover her body – otherwise the Draw would be prohibited/cancelled on Iranian state TV. The Russian journalist did what was asked – she wore a black, modest dress. Iranians were able to watch the Final Draw, and afterwards Komandnaya asked on Twitter: *Iran, are you happy?*, initiating a debate, where under the pretext of discussing the dress, mostly Iranian citizens discussed their human rights, compulsory hijabs, censorship, politics, dictatorship, patriarchy and the Draw itself. For example:

> In Iran, we're fighting against compulsory hijab law and acts of
> violence against women, but you're just making it harder for us so,
> the answer is NO, we are not.
>
> (@PimpAlolama, 1 December 2017)

or

> We will never be happy, until have hijab by force, and censorship
> in our country.
>
> (@biya_baghalam, 1 December 2017)

or even

> I understand that you meant well, but that move just made you an
> accessory to a system of censorship and suppression against
> women. I wish you had worn what you wanted to wear. Unlike
> Iranian women who don't have personal freedom, you do. Don't
> give in to patriarchy.
>
> (@Elaheh_Ela, 1 December 2017)

Iranian women were prohibited from attending stadiums following the 1979
Islamic Revolution. Over the years women have been punished for even
attempting to attend games in the stadium – in March 2018, 36 women were
detained for trying to enter the Azadi stadium in Tehran. Ironically, Azadi means
freedom. Nothing could change it – signing petitions, official letters, or attempts
to influence Iranian authorities to repeal the regulation. Then suddenly, just
before the official kick-off for the 2018 FWC, the ban was lifted and for the first
time since 1981, women were allowed to enter the stadium and watch a live
broadcast of Iran's World Cup match against Spain. This was a game changer; in
2021, Iranian women are now allowed to watch football games from the stands
(albeit still with restrictions).

I met many Iranian women in St. Petersburg, where I was when the tournament started. I watched the opening game between Russia and Saudi Arabia in a
pub with Russians and Iranian men. Iranian women were not in there, but they
were outside, in the streets – chanting, dancing, meeting fans from around the
world. I saw joyful women carrying Iranian flags proudly and supporting their
national team, just like their male compatriots. I watched women having the time
of their lives, shouting out the names of famous footballers, predicting the winner
of the World Cup, talking about the intricacies of the offside rule. It was clear that
change had already happened and they would not let that freedom be taken away
from them. They were determined to take hold of this incredible power and
strength and bring it back to Iran, their homeland, which they could represent
with pride.

However, many actions in relation to the World Cup were ambiguous in terms
of gender performances. The head of FIFA's diversity programme, Federico
Addiechi, has called on broadcasters to stop showing closeups of attractive

women in the stands at World Cup matches. Addiechi said that although the common practise is not yet banned, he believes it will be in the future. However, the feminist Anna Fedorova was critical of the motivations behind this move and saw them as an attempt to deflect criticism from the next World Cup hosts, Qatar. She addressed her followers in her Facebook post:

> FIFA has asked TV channels to show fewer beautiful female fans as part of their match coverage. (…) And FIFA believes that sexism, not racism, is the main problem of the World Cup. And so 'as part of its anti-discrimination policy' FIFA is calling for a reduction in the number of attractive women on the staff. So if you are shown on TV sitting in the stands, FIFA will find you rather unattractive. (…) Except that I have a theory as to where this ridiculous gibberish comes from. It seems that the next championship will be held in Qatar. Women's freedom is really not respected there. It seems that FIFA is trying to adapt to the Islamic country's measures beforehand. And that is the real evil, of course. We are all against verbal discrimination, but let us respect the traditions of societies, where the woman is a piece of meat and the property of the man.
>
> (Fedorova, 2018, translated by the author)

Public debate in Russia around the World Cup was often filled with sexist and misogynistic discourse, supposedly in the name of defending Russian women's honour. Ordinary Russian women faced sexist and vulgar criticism for dating foreign football fans, coming to Russia for the mega-event. Platon Besedin, a columnist for the Moskovsky Komsomolets newspaper in Russia, was explicit and wrote: 'Russian women are bringing shame to themselves and their country' under the headline 'Time of whores: Russian women at the World Cup are disgracing themselves and their country'. In response, journalist Snezhana Gribatskaya posted a petition that collected more than 53,000 backers demanding apologies from the newspaper for insulting Russian women. Gribatskaya also called for criminal prosecution for incitement of hatred and hostility to women. 'Enough is enough, you've gone too far!' she said (Associated Press, 2018).

MP Mikhail Degtyaryov came out in support of Russian women saying: 'The more love stories we have connected to the World Cup, the more people from different countries fall in love, the more children are born, the better (…) Many years from now these children will remember that their parents' love story began during the World Cup in Russia in 2018' (Walker, 2018).

The Kremlin weighed in reluctantly on the controversy. President Putin's spokesman, Dmitry Peskov, was diplomatic and replied that Russian women are the best in the world and should make their own judgements. However, this issue made many Russian women angry and their furious comments flooded the Internet. The feminist blogger Alena Popova said: 'In a country where the majority of the population are women, it's crazy that there are no equal rights and that there is such a dangerous attitude toward women'. 'We were outraged by the fact that they decided they can actually control our sex life – who we kiss or go on dates with', said Snezhana Gribatskaya. Yulia Skulkina wrote: 'I don't understand why a woman can't chose herself who she should have sex with...' and Svetlana Zhukova explained, why she signed Gribatskaya's petition: 'I am signing this because every woman has a right to be in charge of her own body' (Walker, 2018).

Subjugated to patriarchy for centuries, this time Russian women were not going to give up fighting for themselves. They started to describe foreigners' cordiality, critiquing Russian men's unhealthy lifestyles which lead to short average life expectancy. Women were self-confident, assertive, brilliant and witty when speaking out against so-called 'traditional values' that have become government policy under Vladimir Putin. This opposition culminated in the band Pussy Riot invading the pitch during the final match between France and Croatia. This was a performance to draw attention to human rights violations, interrupting for a moment the most important festival of football. As the game was being played to decide who would lift the trophy that night, Pussy Riot wanted to draw the world's attention to the problems faced by Russia's political prisoners. A few minutes after the trespass, Pussy Riot released a statement, which I believe should be quoted in full:

> NEWS FLASH! Just a few minutes ago four Pussy Riot members performed in the FIFA World Cup final match – 'Policeman enters the Game'.
>
> Today is 11 years since the death of the great Russian poet, Dmitriy Prigov. Prigov created an image of a policeman, a carrier of the heavenly nationhood, in the Russian culture.
>
> The heavenly policeman, according to Prigov, talks with God Himself. The earthly policeman gets ready to disperse rallies. The heavenly policeman gently touches a flower in a field and enjoys Russian football team victories, while the earthly policeman feels indifferent to Oleg Sentsov's hunger strike. The heavenly policeman rises as an example of the nationhood, the earthly policeman hurts everyone. The heavenly policeman protects babies' sleep, the earthly policeman persecutes political prisoners, imprisons people for 'reposts' and 'likes'.
>
> The heavenly policeman is the organiser of this World Cup's beautiful carnival, the earthy policeman is afraid of the celebration. The heavenly policeman carefully watches for obeying the game rules, the earthly policeman enters the game not caring about the rules.
>
> The FIFA World Cup has reminded us of the possibilities of the heavenly policeman in the Great Russia of the future, but the earthly policeman, entering the rule-less game breaks our world apart.

When the earthly policeman enters the game, we demand to:

(1) Let all political prisoners free.
(2) No imprisonment for 'likes'.
(3) Stop Illegal arrests at rallies.
(4) Allow political competition in the country.
(5) Don't fabricate criminal accusations and don't keep people in jail for no reason.
(6) Turn the earthly policeman into the heavenly policeman.

(@pussyrrriot, 15 July 2018)

It was the 52nd minute of the game, when three women and one man invaded the pitch and the game was interrupted for about a minute. Although the invaders were later jailed for 15 days, what is important here is that it was women who were brave enough to perform this act of transgression, using the World Cup as an opportunity to draw the world's attention to fundamental issues. It was rough intrusion into men's world and profanation of one of the greatest male rituals – the ultimate game.

The whole world held its breath as sanctity was desecrated and disorder reigned. The game ended in a win for France over Croatia 4-2, but the real winner of the FWC was Croatia's first-ever woman president Kolinda Grabar-Kitarović. During the medal ceremony, Grabar-Kitarović, wearing a red and white Croatia soccer shirt, stood on the podium with Vladimir Putin and French president Emmanuel Macron. When Putin was handed an umbrella, she stood soaked by the heavy rain, but clearly delighted by Croatia's excellent performance. Stewards eventually handed her an umbrella as well. As one commentator on social media expressed:

Best scene at the World Cup. Pouring Rain, no umbrella and Kolinda Grabar Kitarović hugs every single player from Croatia and France, even if Croatia has just lost. That's pure emotional and so warmly. No politics, only sport! Congrats to both teams!

(Reuters, 2018)

I Wanna Scream and Shout and Let It All Out!

The quotation above encapsulates what we crave when attending sport mega-events – pure emotions, no politics, only sport! This is what we are looking for, what makes us human, shows the better side of ourselves, the one we like. I call this catharsis – derived from Aristotle's ideas of purification of fear and pity, understood psychologically as an intellectual clarification and as social sharing of emotions. Shared experience is one of the strongest emotional triggers, powerful and unifying. Properly directed, this could be the beginning of a new balance of power, the beginning of resistance, which could lead to actual change. Just like

Cultural Performance, this extraordinary exchange of actions and reactions is supported by tech-performance and organisational performance. These couplings induce catharsis, which induces *human return*, which in turn induces and creates a community, capable of performing actions.

Remembering that performances may act through symbolic forms, present alternative arrangements and/or be the game changer in social and personal transformation, we can look at the FWC as a gigantic performance, complex and versatile, that had the power to produce change. The month-long carnival was full of gestures and performances, which move from the symbolic sphere to reality.

What I witnessed in 2018 continues to take effect today. I watched thousands of people experiencing a rite of passage and for different people there were different important moments, not necessarily scoring goals. My experiences suggest that we should never underestimate the importance of sport mega-events, because they allow us to find and experience what we often lack in our everyday lives. This feeling that makes us think, the sky is the limit! That strengthens our self-identity, sense of purpose, sense of belonging and self-efficacy, maintains our dignity and helps us to endure and strive. It was not a single moment of transition, a moment of becoming, but a sequence of events and performances leading through catharsis to creating a genuine and powerful community, one that is aware of and respects differences between individuals, but acknowledges and recognises the power of the group.

I felt genuinely safe in Russia in 2018; among them all – women and men. I felt shameless expressing my emotions; nobody judged anyone, people showed cordiality and support to each other, regardless of gender, race, age and nationality. It was a great display of humility and tolerance. Being together at the mega-event, we became closer, more forgiving and thus more understanding and more aware.

You'll Never Walk Alone

When I was a little girl I had a dream to go to the World Cup. My father tried to protect me, saying it is 'not for girls'. But he was wrong, and 30 years ago our world looked very different. I am happy I did not believe him and I did things my own way and never gave up trying. Being present at the FWC in 2018, I learned much more than I could ever have hoped. I met people I would never have met under any other circumstances. I understand more and I feel more, I can give more, because I received so much and saw the power of sharing. Sport mega-events are phenomenal cultural performances and deserve recognition as such. These mega-event performances are not just reflections of changes occurring elsewhere. They are part of the complex feedback process that brings about change.

In 2020–2021, Polish women took to the street in protests against increasingly right-wing government policies that threaten women's rights and freedoms. Do you know what they were chanting?

'You'll never walk alone!'

Does it sound familiar? I hope it does.

References

Associated Press. (2018). Russian women push back at shaming over World Cup dating. *Star Advertiser*, July 15. Retrieved from https://www.staradvertiser.com/2018/07/15/features/russian-women-push-back-at-shaming-over-world-cup-dating/. Accessed on February 17, 2021.

Bakhtin, M. (1999). *Problems of Dostoevsky's poetics* (C. Emerson, Ed. and Trans.). (Vol. 8). Minneapolis, MN: University of Minnesota Press.

BBC. (2013, October 24). CSKA Moscow: UEFA opens racist chants case after Man City Match. *BBC Sport*. Retrieved from https://www.bbc.co.uk/sport/football/24654499. Accessed on January 19, 2021.

BBC. (2018, March 14). Russian spy: UK to expel 23 Russian diplomats. *BBC News*. Retrieved from https://www.bbc.co.uk/news/uk-43402506. Accessed on January 19, 2021.

BBC. (2019, December 9). Russia doping scandal: Athletes face potential ban from global sport. Retrieved from https://www.bbc.co.uk/news/world-europe-50708495. Accessed on January 19, 2021.

Bolopion, P. (2018, March 21). Are you ready for the World Cup of shame? Human Rights Watch. Retrieved from https://www.hrw.org/news/2018/03/21/are-you-ready-world-cup-shame. Accessed on January 19, 2021.

Boroitz, I., & Neumann, S. (1979). *Computer systems performance evaluation: Criteria, measurements, techniques, and costs.* Lexington, MA: Lexington Books.

Brownell, S. (2012). Human rights and the Beijing Olympics: Imagined global community and the transnational public sphere 1. *The British Journal of Sociology*, *63*(2), 306–327.

FCO. (2018, June 8). *The FCO's preparations for the 2018 World Cup in Russia: Government's response to the committee's 9th report: Thirteenth special report.* Retrieved from https://publications.parliament.uk/pa/cm201719/cmselect/cmfaff/1507/150702.htm. Accessed on January 29, 2021.

Fedorova, A. (2018, July 12). Facebook post. Retrieved from https://www.facebook.com/anna.october/posts/10217507705303982. Accessed on February 16, 2021.

FIFA. (2018a, August 15). The 2018 FIFA World CupTM in numbers. Retrieved from https://www.fifa.com/worldcup/news/the-2018-fifa-world-cuptm-in-numbers. Accessed on January 19, 2021.

FIFA. (2018b). 2018 FIFA World Cup RussiaTM. Retrieved from https://www.fifa.com/worldcup/archive/russia2018/. Accessed on January 19, 2021.

HRW. (2013). Race to the bottom: Exploitation of migrant workers ahead of Russia's 2014 Winter Olympic Games in Sochi. Human Rights Watch. Retrieved from https://www.business-humanrights.org/en/latest-news/pdf-race-to-the-bottom-exploitation-of-migrant-workers-ahead-of-russias-2014-winter-olympic-games-in-sochi/. Accessed on January 19, 2021.

HRW. (2018). Human rights guide for reporters: 2018 FIFA World Cup in Russia. Human Rights Watch. Retrieved from https://www.hrw.org/sites/default/files/news_attachments/reporters_guide_world_cup0518_pdfweb_0.pdf. Accessed on January 19, 2021.

Lange, D. (2020, November 26). FIFA World Cup: Global fans by gender 2018. *Statista*. Retrieved from https://www.statista.com/statistics/872302/world-cup-fans-gender/. Accessed on January 17, 2021.

McKenzie, J. (2002). *Perform or else: From discipline to performance.* New York, NY: Routledge.

Olympic.org. (2015, February 7). Success of Sochi 2014 lives on. Retrieved from https://www.olympic.org/news/success-of-sochi-2014-lives-on. Accessed on January 19, 2021.

Reuters. (2018). Croatia president Kolinda Grabar-Kitarovic wins admirers at World Cup final. *Hindustan Times*, July 16. Retrieved from https://www.hindustantimes.com/football/croatia-president-kolinda-grabar-kitarovic-wins-admirers-at-world-cup-final/story-gwvCWxvXrIqptqgifERSMP.html. Accessed on February 18, 2021.

Ritz, R. R., & Mather, V. (2015). The FIFA scandal: What's happened and what's to come. *The New York Times*, September 25. Retrieved from https://www.nytimes.com/2015/09/26/sports/soccer/the-fifa-scandal-whats-happened-and-whats-to-come.html. Accessed on January 19, 2021.

Skivington, K. (2018). What the World Cup has taught us about cultural understanding and fandom. *Illume Stories*. Retrieved from https://www.illumestories.com/2018/08/what-the-world-cup-has-taught-us-about-cultural-understanding-and-fandom/. Accessed on January 29, 2021.

The Guardian. (2018). World Cup hosts Russia charged with fan racism during France friendly. *The Guardian*, April 17. Retrieved from https://www.theguardian.com/football/2018/apr/17/world-cup-russia-charged-fan-racism-france-friendly. Accessed on January 19, 2021.

Walker, S. (2014). The Sochi Olympics legacy: 'The city now feels like a ghost town'. *The Guardian*, December 17. Retrieved from https://www.theguardian.com/sport/2014/dec/17/sochi-olympics-legacy-city-feels-like-a-ghost-town. Accessed on January 19, 2021.

Walker, S. (2017). 'Collaborators and traitors': Russia goes to war with Winter Olympics ban. *The Guardian*, December 10. Retrieved from https://www.theguardian.com/sport/2017/dec/10/russia-reaction-winter-olympics-ban-sochi-2014-putin-mutko. Accessed on January 19, 2021.

Walker, S. (2018). 'Have sex, make babies': Russian MP tells nation to welcome foreign fans. *The Guardian*, June 14. Retrieved from https://www.theguardian.com/world/2018/jun/14/have-sex-make-babies-russian-mp-tells-nation-to-welcome-foreign-fans. Accessed on February 17, 2021.

Wintour, P. (2018). World Cup: England fans' safety at risk in Russia, say MPs. *The Guardian*, June 8. Retrieved from https://www.theguardian.com/uk-news/2018/jun/08/world-cup-england-gay-lgbt-fans-safety-risk-russia-say-mps. Accessed on January 19, 2021.

Section 4
Gender, Sport and Mega-Events: Moving towards Equality?

Chapter 10

Sport Mega-Events as Drivers of Gender Equality: Women's Football in Spain

Celia Valiente

Introduction

This chapter explores the potential of sport mega-events to foster gender equality in sport. The empirical case of women's football in Spain is analysed with the help of secondary sources, press clippings, and statistics and documents from sport governing institutions and the main football management organisation (the Spanish Football Federation). In comparison with Spanish men's football, the development of Spanish women's football is clearly modest. Nonetheless, women's football large-scale events have recently taken place. Women's football mega-events (and other factors) are contributing to the advancement of professional women's football in Spain. Dimensions of this progress include, among others, the relaunch of major competitions and the establishment of new women's football teams. Moreover, thanks in part to large-scale women's football events, the number of girls and women playing football continues to increase. Notwithstanding the aforementioned positive impacts of women's football mega-events, Spanish football is still an arena where gender inequality is pervasive. For instance, the salary and working conditions of most professional female players are precarious, and women's presence in highly ranked positions of football management is very low.

Sport Mega-Events and the Search for Gender Equality

Research has identified negative impacts of sport mega-events. These include, among others, the detrimental consequences for the environment from the construction of sport facilities, the forced eviction of sectors of the population to build sport mega-facilities, or the high costs which the host country incurs (Hayes & Karamichas, 2012). Regarding gender, negative consequences of sport large-scale events also exist, such as the increase in prostitution and the trafficking of women for sexual exploitation to satisfy the demands by attendees of such large gatherings (Lenskyj, 2013). Not surprisingly, the celebration of sport mega-events produces protests (Boycoff, 2014).

Sport, Gender and Mega-Events, 187–200
Copyright © 2022 by Emerald Publishing Limited
All rights of reproduction in any form reserved
doi:10.1108/978-1-83982-936-920211016

However, as Dashper, Fletcher, and McCullogh (2015) argue, sport mega-events often have both positive and negative impacts. In spite of the negative consequences of sport mega-events, this chapter argues that sport large-scale events can function as a driver of (and key resource for) gender equality and this is so for at least three reasons. First, women's participation in sport mega-events sends society and policymakers the message that women can take part in and win important sport tournaments. Furthermore, women's participation in large-scale events associated with traditionally male sports sends the signal that these sports can be ably practiced not only by men but also by women. In current times characterised by globalisation and the pervasive use of new technologies of information and communication, sport-related messages can reach audiences around the world in seconds (Wenner & Billings, 2017).

Second, as historical research shows, in past times, elite female sporting pioneers generated an interest in their own sports among girls and women through various activities (Callan, Heffernan, & Spenn, 2018; Day, 2012, 2018; Valiente, 2019b, 2020b). Subsequently, in current times, female athletes participating in sport mega-events might foster girls' and women's interest in sport, which is often lower than boys' and men's interest in sport. Interest in sports is important if only because it correlates positively with sport practice (Cooky, 2018).

Lastly, female sport mega-events may foster higher mass media coverage of women's sporting events. This higher coverage is relevant because it could contribute to disentangling the vicious circle that associates low coverage of women's sport and small audiences of women's athletic competitions (Cookey, Messner, & Musto, 2018).

To examine the potential of sport mega-events to foster women's sport (and consequently gender equality in sport), this chapter examines the fast-changing status of women's football in contemporary Spain. It is to the presentation of the empirical case and sources that I now turn.

Selection of the Empirical Case and Sources

Regarding football in general, Spain is surely a first-class player. Some of the best men's football teams in the world are from Spain, such as *Real Madrid* and *Barcelona*. Football is the national sport with a massive following. The Spanish Football Federation is by far the sport federation with the highest number of federation licences: 1,095,604 licences, that is, slightly above 2% of the Spanish population. The next sport federation in terms of number of licences is basketball with approximately three times fewer licences than football (385,635) (2019 data; Ministerio de Cultura y Deporte, 2020). When the principal men's football teams play, stadiums are full. The presence of men's football in the mass media is overwhelming. Male football players are celebrities. Across Spain, with their pocket money, boys (but very rarely girls) buy cards with photographs of male football players. In school playgrounds, streets and squares, those boys eagerly exchange cards to complete their cards albums.

In contrast, the status of Spanish women's football is considerably more modest than men's football. The Spanish Football Federation only has 71,276 licences held by girls and women. Three other federations have a higher number of licences held by girls and women than football: basketball (132,927), mountaineering and climbing (84,118) and golf (76,243) (2019 data; Ministerio de Cultura y Deporte, 2020). In the recent past, the presence of women's football in the mass media was minimal. Most of the time, even the main women's teams trained at night and on dirt fields. Even when the principal teams competed, stadiums were nearly empty. However, and somewhat unexpectedly, women's football mega-events are now taking place in Spain, the most famous of which was the March 2019 match between *Atlético Madrid* and *Barcelona* at the Wanda Metropolitan Stadium in Madrid, watched by over 60,000 spectators (Gómez, 2019).

What are the impacts, if any, of these large-scale events on the evolution of women's football? The sources in this chapter to answer this question include press clippings and statistics and documents from sport governing institutions and the Spanish Football Federation.

Gender Inequality in Spanish Sports (and Football)

Before analysing the contribution of women's football mega-events to gender equality in football, it is important to note that in Spain, sport is a domain where gender inequality is pervasive (Valiente, 2019a). Let me illustrate this point with some statistics. Interest in sport is lower among women than men. In 2015, on a scale of 0–10, the average level of interest in sport in general for men aged 15 years or older was 7.1 while the parallel figure for women of the same age group was 5.8. Moreover, a quarter (25%) of men of that age group were very interested in sport in general (positions 9–10 of the scale), while the parallel figure for women was 10 points lower at 15% (Ministerio de Educación, Cultura y Deporte, 2015, pp. 69–71).

Girls and women participate in sport to a lesser extent than boys and men. In 2015, three out of five (60%) men aged 15 or older reported having practised sport in the previous year, whereas only 48% of women of the same age group had participated in sport in the previous year. Half of the men (50%) aged 15 or over reported having participated in sport at least once a week, that is, eight points higher than the parallel figure for women (42%). Furthermore, the average time these men and women reported having participated in sport weekly was 348 minutes for men and 269 minutes for women, that is, 79 minutes more for men (Ministerio de Educación, Cultura y Deporte, 2015, pp. 79–80). In addition, girls and women account for just 23% of holders of sport federation licences (2019 data; Ministerio de Cultura y Deporte, 2020).

The lower presence of women (in comparison to men) among sport practitioners starts in youth, since girls and female adolescents exercise considerably less than boys and male adolescents. Several studies have shown that on average a significant proportion of children and adolescents of both sexes do not comply with the international recommendations to do at least an hour a day of physical exercise of moderate or high intensity. Participation in this type of physical exercise diminishes as children become adolescents, and pronounced sex differences exist for all age groups. For instance, in 2013, 39% of boys aged 9–12 years did not meet the aforementioned international recommendation in comparison to 62% of girls of that age. The parallel figures for male and female adolescents aged 13–17 years were higher, at 50% for males and 86% for females (Roman, 2016, p. 6).

Women are also less numerous than men among spectators of sport competitions (live or from a distance, that is, through audio-visual media – television, radio and Internet) or those who obtained information on sport from newspapers and audio-visual media. In 2015, slightly less than half (46%) of men aged 15 or over reported having watched a sport competition last year whereas only just over a quarter (28%) of women of the same age did so. The difference between the proportion of men and women aged 15 or over who last year watched a sport competition from a distance (through audio-visual media) was also pronounced, at 90% for men and 70% for women. On the other hand, while three out of four (76%) men aged 15 or over obtained information on sports from newspapers or audio-visual media, less than half of women (43%) of the same age did so (2015 data; Ministerio de Educación, Cultura y Deporte, 2015, pp. 163–165).

A caveat is necessary at this point. Although gender undoubtedly influences sport practice and other sport-related behaviours, it is by no means the only influencing variable. Socioeconomic characteristics also influence sporting practices. For example, in Spain, other things being equal, the higher the education and occupational status of individuals, the higher is their sporting practice (García & Llopis, 2017; Kokolakakis, Lera-López, & Panagouleas, 2012).

As in many other European countries, football in Spain has always been principally a male sport (Puig & Vilanova, 2017; Vaczi, 2015). Currently, the overwhelming majority of people who play football are still boys and men. As stated above, only 6% of holders of football federation licences are girls and women – or 71,276 out of 1,095,604 (2019 data; Ministerio de Cultura y Deporte, 2020). As can be seen in Table 10.1, this proportion has varied minimally in the last 10 years, since it has oscillated between 4 and 6%.

Women's Football Mega-Events

In spite of the relative weakness of Spanish women's football (in comparison with men's football), several women's football large-scale events have recently taken place in Spain. For example, in January 2019, a match between *Athletic Bilbao* and *Atlético Madrid* at the San Mamés stadium in Bilbao was watched live by over 48,000 spectators (Rivas, 2019). The aforementioned March 2019 match between *Atlético de Madrid* and *Barcelona* at the Wanda Metropolitan Stadium in Madrid was watched by over 60,000 spectators (Gómez, 2019).

Large women's football events have begun to take place in Spain at approximately the same time as Spain participated in and achieved some successes at

Table 10.1. Holders of Licences from the Royal Spanish Football Federation by Sex, 2009–2019.

Year	Total	Men	Women	Percentage of Female Holders of Licences (%)
2009	779,829	749,089	30,74	4
2010	805,707	771,963	33,744	4
2011	834,458	798,176	36,282	4
2012	869,32	830,297	39,023	4
2013	855,987	815,381	40,606	5
2014	874,093	829,22	44,873	5
2015	909,761	869,237	40,524	4
2016	942,674	898,551	44,123	5
2017	1,027,907	967,578	60,329	6
2018	1,063,090	997,999	65,091	6
2019	1,095,604	1,024,328	71,276	6

Note: Ministerio de Cultura y Deporte (2020). *DEPORTEData: Base de datos* [SPORTData: Data base]. Retrieved 20 June 2020, from http://www.culturaydeporte.gob.es.

mega-scale events at the international level. These competitions are commonly characterised as mega-events because of visitor numbers, media coverage, costs and impacts. These competitions have been watched by ever-increasing mass media audiences. For instance, in May 2019, *Barcelona* was a finalist in the Union of European Football Association (UEFA) Women's Champions League in Budapest in a match against the *Olympique Lyonnais* watched live by nearly 20,000 spectators (Irigoyen, 2019). In summer 2019, Spain participated in the International Federation of Football Associations (FIFA) Women's World Cup in France. The Spanish team made it to the last 16 in this tournament. Twenty-two mass media from Spain went to France to cover the event, whereas only four mass media had gone in 2015 to Canada to cover the previous Women's World Cup. Gol, the TV chain that broadcast the matches, reached its highest audience milestone (12.8% for the Spain vs. United States match in the last 16) (Calonge, 2020a). Undoubtedly, the Women's World Cup is an international competition of paramount importance. The 2019 tournament was watched by more than a billion viewers (*The Economist*, 2019, p. 55).

The Positive Impacts of Women's Football Mega-Events in Spain

As shown next, one of the positive impacts of women's football mega-events (along with other factors) is the improvement of professional women's football. This improvement is being achieved through the relaunch of women's football main leagues, the establishment of women's teams by major football clubs, and other measures to promote women's teams and women's football in general. Another important positive impact of women's football mega-events is that the number of girls and women playing football continues to increase.

Improvements in Professional Women's Football

The relaunch of Spanish women's football main leagues: One of the manifestations of the current improvements in professional women's football is the relaunch of national women's football leagues. On 1 August 2019, some weeks after the occurrence of the Women's World Cup, Luis Rubiales, president of the Spanish Football Federation, announced a relaunch of major competitions for women's football, managed by the Federation. Sixteen teams would compete in the first league, which is called *Primera Iberdrola* after its main sponsor, *Iberdrola*, a utilities company. After each season, two teams would be relegated to the second league, which is called *Reto Iberdrola*. The second league comprises 32 teams. Teams competing in the first and second leagues must have at least three teams in non-professional categories, in order to promote the young players who come up through the clubs' youth and reserve teams. President Rubiales explicitly stated that in the next six years the objective would be to convert football into the most popular sport in terms of participation among Spanish girls younger than 14 years of age.

Additionally, a fourth female referee would arbitrate matches of the *Primera Iberdrola* (all referees in that league are women). Also, in the relaunched league, it would be mandatory for the names of female players to appear on their T-shirts worn during matches, in order to foster name recognition by fans and the general population (ABC, 2019; Moñino, 2019). When discussing the relaunch of Spanish women's football leagues, the major Spanish newspaper *El País* made reference to Spain's participation and relative success in recent women's football mega-events, thus establishing a relationship between the latter and the former (Moñino, 2019). In an illustrated report on Spanish women's football published in the major Spanish newspaper *El País* the day before the Spain vs. United States match of the FIFA Women's World Cup, *Iberdrola* (the utilities company sponsoring women's football leagues) argued that women's football reached a record level of development thanks to the occurrence of large-scale events (Iberdrola, 2019).

The establishment of women's football teams: The improvements in professional women's football are also achieved through decisions made by football clubs. Football clubs that previously had only men's teams can strengthen women's football by establishing their own women's teams. Of importance is the decision taken by *Real Madrid* to engage in women's football for the first time ever. *Real Madrid* was an exception among major European teams because it did not have any women's teams. On 25 June 2019, that is, the day after Spain played (and lost) against the United States in the Women's World Cup in France, the board of *Real Madrid* approved the purchase of an existing women's club, *Club Deportivo Tacón*. In this way, *Real Madrid* contributed to the improvement of women's football by dedicating part of their infrastructure and money to their female teams. For the 2019–2020 season, *Club Deportivo Tacón* retained its name. From

1 July 2020, that club became *Real Madrid* women's section (Giovio, 2019). Since *Valladolid* and *Getafe* later announced that they would establish their own women's teams, by the autumn of 2019, it could be stated that all clubs competing in the men's first league bar one (*Celta*) had (or would soon have) female teams (Cudeiro, 2019).

Other measures to promote women's football: Other measures, albeit of smaller importance, are also promoting women's football. For example, after the afore-mentioned (and other) large-scale events, some football clubs such as *Barcelona* started selling T-shirts with names of their female players in their official shops (Álvarez, 2019). Basque team *Real Sociedad* has done the same from October 2019 onwards (*El Diario Vasco*, 2019). This is important because this helps increase the visibility of these women players. It also gives fans an option to identify with them more through buying and wearing the T-shirts.

More Girls and Women Playing Football

A major positive impact of women's football mega-events (and other factors) would be a substantial increase in the number of girls and women playing foot-ball. That girls and women increasingly practice football means that messages in favour of women's football sent by women's football mega-events have been received by society. Girls and women playing football regularly reflects the fact that at least some sectors of the population no longer believe that football is exclusively a male sport.

As women's football mega-events have only taken place in Spain mainly in 2019, it is still too soon to know for sure whether, in part as a result of them, more girls and women are playing football. As Table 10.1 shows, between 2009 and 2019, the number of female holders of football federation licences has increased slowly but continuously (with the exception of 2015). As a result, the total number has been doubled, from 30,740 in 2009 to 71,276 in 2019. Most of these female holders of football licences are amateur players. But some of them may eventually become future professional female players, highly ranked female referees, female football coaches and senior football decision-makers.

Limits of Progress

Notwithstanding the positive impacts of mega-events on women's football in Spain, the improvements in Spanish women's football have important limits. As explained below, limitations can be illustrated by examining two realms: mini-mum pay and working conditions of female professional players and women's presence in football management.

Minimum Pay and Working Conditions of Female Professional Players

A chapter on women's football mega-events in Spain may project the view that major advances have already taken place regarding women's football, and subsequently, the status of Spanish women's football is, if not equal to that of men's football, at least comparable to the status of women's football in European countries situated to the north of Spain (if not the United States). However, nothing could be more wrong. To show the limitations in the progress achieved, let me focus on the issue of minimum pay and working conditions of female professional players competing in principal tournaments.

For the first time ever, a collective agreement will regulate minimum pay and working conditions of all female professional players in Spain. Negotiations between unions and the employer, the Association of Women's Football Clubs (*Asociación de Clubes de Fútbol Femenino*, ACFF) started in 2018 but stalled in 2019 around two issues: minimum salary and minimum working time. For instance, in August 2019, unions demanded a minimum salary of 17,000 euros per year but the ACFF offered 14,000 euros. In addition, many female football players were being hired for reduced working time. Unions demanded that women players are hired for at least 75% of the full-time week, but the ACFF offered only 50% (Moñino, 2019). As a result of the impasse in the negotiations, no collective agreement was signed and female players went on strike in the third weekend of November 2019 (Calonge, 2019b). It was only on 18 February 2020 when an agreement was signed. The agreement established a minimum salary of 16,000 euros per year for full-time players. Players had to be hired for at least 75% of the full-time week (with a minimum salary of 12,000 euros per year). The collective agreement would be binding retroactively from 1 July 2019 onwards once it is published on the official state bulletin (*Boletín Oficial del Estado*).

It is a paradox that in Spain, a country where women's football mega-events have taken place and proven to be popular, professional women players could not secure a minimum salary considerably above the general minimum wage (12,600 euros per year for full-time workers in 2019). To illustrate the huge distance between women's and men's professional football, it is worth mentioning that the 2015 four-year collective agreement for (men's) professional football established for 2016–2017 season a minimum salary of 155,000 euros per year in the first league and 77,500 euros per year in the second league (in both cases for full-time players as men players are not hired part-time). These amounts would be updated according to inflation in the subsequent three seasons (Resolution of 23 November 2015, of the General Directorate of Employment, which registers and publishes the collective agreement regarding professional football).

The long duration of the negotiations preceding the agreement for women's professional football, the final blockade of these negotiations in autumn 2019, and the modest pay conditions finally set for female players are manifestations of the shortcomings of women's professional football that still characterise Spain. Notwithstanding these shortcomings, the collective agreement means an improvement (however modest) in professional women's football. The major Spanish newspaper *El País*, among other media, and actors relevant to women's football, interpreted this collective agreement as a result of the development of female football thanks in part to the occurrence of large-scale events (Calonge, 2020a).

Women in Football Management

Across the world, women are underrepresented among those who occupy decision-making positions in sport management. According to data from the Sydney Scoreboard, a web-based tool tracking women's presence in management of national sport organisations in 45 countries from five continents, globally on average women account for 20% of board directors, 16% of chief executives and 11% of board chairs (also named 'board members', 'board presidents' and 'general secretaries', respectively, in some countries such as Spain) (Adriaanse, 2015, p. 149). A significant proportion of women in highly ranked sport management positions is crucial because, in general and with some exceptions, women are more aware of gender inequality than men and more active at fighting against gender inequality than men. On average and with some exceptions, women are better than men at representing women's interests in the decision-making process within sport organisations and institutions, notwithstanding the fact that not all women are committed to gender equality and some men actively endorse gender equality (Adriaanse, 2013; Burton & Leberman, 2017; Elling, Hovden, & Knoppers, 2019; Evans & Pfister, 2020).

A manifestation of women's progress in Spanish football would be a significant female presence among those who occupy decision-making positions in football management. But this presence is still very small. As in other European countries, sport management in Spain is organised through national sport federations (NSFs) (Burton & Leberman, 2017). Sixty-five NSFs exist in Spain. Regarding the football federation, very few women have reached decision-making positions within it. The president is a man, and only one of the eight vice-presidents is female. The board consists of 3 female members and 26 male members (Real Federación Española de Fútbol, 2020). The fact that three board members of the football federation are women complies with the law, as in 2014, in Spain, a gender quota was introduced for the boards of NSFs, whereby a minimum of three board members or 33% of board members have to be female (Valiente, 2019a, 2020a). However, the proportion of women on the board of the football federation (10%) is considerably lower than the average comparable figure for all NSFs (25%) (2018 data; Consejo Superior de Deportes, 2019).

Undoubtedly, in every football match, a principal figure is the referee. S/he is the highest (technical) authority during the match, and her/his task is to assure impartially that the rules of the game are followed strictly. Some Spanish women are now becoming referees at the highest level. In summer 2019, a Spanish woman, Guadalupe Porras, became the first female referee accredited to arbitrate the major men's football league. The major Spanish newspaper *El País* argued that Guadalupe Porras' accreditation was a manifestation of the improvement of women's status in football achieved in part thanks to mega-events such as the 2019 FIFA Women's World Cup in France (Calonge, 2019a). Again, Spain is no exception in this sense, as women in other European countries are working as highly ranked referees, although it is still unusual. Also, in summer 2019 (14 August), French female referee Stéphanie Frappart was the first woman to arbitrate a final of the UEFA (men's) Super Cup between Liverpool FC and Chelsea FC (Quixano, 2019).

That women become referees at the highest level and arbitrate the main matches played by women and men is important because it sends society the message that women can exercise the maximum (technical) authority in all types of matches, and by extension that football is not a male sport but a sport for both women and men. Notwithstanding the advancement in this area in Spain, much more progress is still needed, as the profession of football referee is still overwhelmingly a male profession and women referees often suffer harsh criticism and/or sexualisation.

Conclusion

Sport mega-events can promote gender equality. As the case of large-scale women's football in contemporary Spain shows, such large-scale competitions (and other factors) contribute to the advancement of professional women's sport and the increase in the number of girls and women practicing sport as amateur and elite athletes.

Granted, different definitions of gender equality exist. The definition used in this chapter refers to basic criteria such as participation numbers, pay and media coverage. This chapter concludes that women's football in Spain is now a step closer to (but still very far away from) gender equality because participation numbers, pay and media coverage have increased recently, in part due to sport mega-events. Critics would argue that this step is minuscule, and this definition of gender equality is very limited. Some critics would consider that gender equality could happen only after a radical transformation of football as a whole. These critics are right. However, it is safe to affirm that an increase in participation numbers, pay and media coverage means an improvement in women's football. This improvement is relevant for the most important women in the field, that is, women who play football as amateur sport practitioners or professional athletes, manage football (as managers or referees), and watch matches live or from a distance. But improvement is not synonymous with equality, as in comparison with the men's game, the women's game is nowhere similar in terms of popularity, visibility and resources.

Sport mega-events can foster women's sport (and by extension gender equality), especially if other factors are also working in the same direction. Let me pinpoint two of these factors regarding women's football in Spain: international factors and domestic gender equality measures in sport. As for international factors, women's football takes place not only in Spain but also in other comparable Western countries (as well as in other countries around the world) (Markovits, 2019). Sport is by definition an international arena, if only due to its cross-national contests. As Spanish women's teams compete with teams from other countries and in international competitions, it becomes clear that women's football in other countries (including but not limited to continental Europe, Scandinavia, the United Kingdom and the United States) has reached a level of maturity not comparable to that of Spain. This comparison signals that Spain needs to improve its women's football, as it improved men's football decades ago to reach the status of a global power. Thus, international factors play an important and mainly beneficial (if indirect) role in the Spanish context. As Florentino Pérez (2019), President of *Real Madrid*, stated, acknowledging international factors when explaining the club's decision to establish a women's team in the near future:

> Football played by women is a real, growing and non-stopping fact. It is a type of football that has been growing spectacularly. *Real Madrid* wants to be part of this world-wide phenomenon. It is now time that *Real Madrid* has its own team...to compete at the maximum level in all domestic and international contests [translation by author of this article].

As concerns domestic gender equality measures in sport, in Spain, policy-makers are pushing sport managers to be more active regarding the improvement of women's status in sport. For example, as explained above, since 2014, a gender quota exists for boards of NSFs by which three members of their boards (or 33% of their board members) have to be women. Sport federations are complying with this quota (Valiente, 2019a, 2020a). With this quota and other gender equality measures, sport authorities are indicating that gender inequality in sport is a pressing problem that needs to be solved.

The findings of this study open at least three areas for future research. First, this chapter has investigated the effects of women's football mega-events at the macro-level, analysing the issue for the whole country. Future studies may analyse such impacts at the meso- and micro-level. Such analyses would investigate the ways (if any) in which women's football large-scale events have changed ideas and behaviours of actors other than the main football clubs and the Spanish Football Federation, including less important football clubs and regional federations.

Second, national histories of women's sport in several countries over the last two centuries show that the increasing presence of women as sport amateur practitioners, elite athletes and sport managers is not always linear but rather a process punctuated by moments of stagnation and even steps backwards (Cahn, 2015; Hall, 2016; Hargreaves, 1994). In Spain regarding women's football, stagnation might occur, for instance, if people start believing that the measures already taken to improve women's football are sufficient, and no additional action in this regard is required. Backlash might happen, for example, if the presence of women on football fields is increasingly contested, and women players and female referees are insulted or criticised harshly when training, competing or arbitrating. The material analysed in this chapter does not suggest any strong and sustained negative reaction against women's sports after mega-events in Spain, but the possibility of such a stagnation or backlash exists and should be investigated.

Finally, in spring 2020, COVID-19 disrupted the sport world in an unprecedented way, as training, contests and mega-events were abruptly cancelled *sine die*. In early-May 2020, the Spanish Football Federation decided that the

2019–2020 women's football season had ended with the last matches played immediately before the outbreak of the pandemic (Moñino & Calonge, 2020). A similar decision has been taken for women's football major leagues in other countries with few exceptions such as Germany and the United States (Calonge, 2020b). In contrast, in Spain in June 2020, major leagues of men's football were resumed (Álvarez & Moñino, 2020). Thus, an impact of COVID-19 on Spanish women's football was the disappearance of large-scale events in the short run. The analyses of this and other effects of the pandemic would certainly be a major topic for future enquiry.

References

ABC. (2019). La nueva liga femenina estrena nombre y Supercopa [The new women's league has a new name and Supercup]. *ABC*, August 2, p. 44.

Adriaanse, J. A. (2013). The role of men in advancing gender equality in sports governance. In G. Pfister & M. K. Sisjord (Eds.), *Gender and sport: Changes and challenges* (pp. 50–70). Münster: Waxmann.

Adriaanse, J. A. (2015). Gender diversity in the governance of sport associations: The Sydney scoreboard global index of participation. *Journal of Business Ethics*, *137*(1), 149–160.

Álvarez, R. (2019). El Barça se lleva por delante al Tacón [Barça wins Tacón]. *El País*, 8 September, p. 35.

Álvarez, D., & Moñino, L. J. (2020). El Gobierno autoriza la vuelta de LaLiga desde el 8 de junio [Government permits the first League to resume from 8 June onwards]. *El País*, May 24, p. 37.

Boycoff, J. (2014). *Activism and the Olympics: Dissent at the games in Vancouver and London*. New Brunswick, NJ: Rutgers University Press.

Burton, L. J., & Leberman, S. (Eds.). (2017). *Women in sport leadership: Research and practice for change*. London: Routledge.

Cahn, S. (2015). *Coming on strong: Gender and sexuality in twentieth-century women's sport* (2nd ed.). Urbana, IL: University of Illinois Press.

Callan, M., Heffernan, C., & Spenn, A. (2018). Women's jujutsu and judo in early twentieth-century: The cases of Phoebe Roberts, Edith Garrud, and Sarah Mayer. *International Journal of the History of Sport*, *35*(6), 530–553.

Calonge, L. (2019a). Una árbitra de Primera [A female referee of major leagues]. *El País*, July 3, p. 48.

Calonge, L. (2019b). Seguimiento total de la huelga de las futbolistas [All female football players went on strike]. *El País*, November 18, p. 43.

Calonge, L. (2020a). La explosión del fútbol femenino [The explosion of women's football]. *El País*, January 2, p. 29.

Calonge, L. (2020b). Alemania también lidera la vuelta del fútbol femenino [Germany also heads the return of female football]. *El País*, May 29, p. 34.

Consejo Superior de Deportes. (2019). *Annual report 2018*. Retrieved from http://www.csd.gob.es. Accessed on February 13, 2021.

Cooky, C. (2018). "Girls just aren't interested": The social construction of interest in girls' sport. In C. Cooky & M. A. Messner (Eds.), *No slam dunk: Gender, sport, and the unevenness of social change* (pp. 113–138). New Brunswick, NJ: Rutgers University Press.

Cooky, C., Messner, M. A., & Musto, M. (2018). "It's dude time!" A quarter century of excluding women's sports in televised news and highlight shows. In C. Cooky & M. A. Messner (Eds.), *No slam dunk: Gender, sport, and the unevenness of social change* (pp. 209–234). New Brunswick, NJ: Rutgers University Press.

Cudeiro, J. L. (2019). El Deportivo femenino pega un estirón [The women's Deportivo grows]. *El País*, October 15, p. 49.

Dashper, K., Fletcher, T., & McCullough, N. (Eds.). (2015). *Sports events, society and culture*. London: Routledge.

Day, D. (2012). "What girl will now remain ignorant of swimming?" Agnes Beckwith, aquatic entertainer and Victorian role model. *Women's History Review*, *21*(3), 419–446.

Day, D. (2018). Swimming natationists, mistresses, and matrons: Familial influences on female careers in Victorian Britain. *International Journal of the History of Sport*, *35*(6), 494–510.

El Diario Vasco. (2019, October 14). Retrieved from https://real-sociedad.diariovasco.com/derbi-deja-record-20191014000821-ntvo.html. Accessed on February 13, 2021.

Elling, A., Hovden, J., & Knoppers, A. (Eds.). (2019). *Gender diversity in European sport governance*. London: Routledge.

Evans, A. B., & Pfister, G. U. (2020). Women in sport leadership: A systematic narrative review. *International Review for the Sociology of Sport*. Advance online publication. doi:10.1177/1012690220911842

García, M., & Llopis, R. (2017). *La popularización del deporte en España* [*The popularization of sport in Spain*]. Madrid: Consejo Superior de Deportes & Centro de Investigaciones Sociológicas.

Giovio, E. (2019). El Madrid se da un año para absorber al Tacón [Real Madrid will take over the Tacón in one year]. *El País*, June 26, p. 39.

Gómez, D. (2019, March 18). Women's soccer in Spain smashes turnout world record. *El País*. Retrieved from https://english.elpais.com/elpais/2019/03/18/inenglish/1552909015_525536.html. Accessed on February 13, 2021.

Hall, M. A. (2016). *The girl and the game: A history of women's sport in Canada* (2nd ed.). Toronto, ON: University of Toronto Press.

Hargreaves, J. (1994). *Sporting females: Critical issues in the history and sociology of women's sports*. London: Routledge.

Hayes, G., & Karamichas, J. (Eds.). (2012). *Olympic games, mega-events and civil societies: Globalization, environment, resistance*. Basingstoke: Palgrave Macmillan.

Iberdrola. (2019). La energía de la selección [The energy of the Spanish women's football national team]. *El País Semanal number*, June 23, pp. 20–23.

Irigoyen, J. I. (2019, May 18). Final de la Champions femenina: Europa todavía queda lejos [Final of the women's Champions: Europe is still far away]. *El País*. Retrieved from https://elpais.com/deportes/2019/05/18/actualidad/1558185320_329162.html. Accessed on February 13, 2021.

Kokolakakis, T., Lera-López, F., & Panagouleas, T. (2012). Analysis of the determinants of sports participation in Spain and England. *Applied Economics*, *44*(21). doi:10.1080/00036846.2011.566204

Lenskyj, H. J. (2013). *Gender politics and the Olympic industry*. Basingstoke: Palgrave Macmillan.

Markovits, A. S. (2019). *Women in American soccer and European football: Different roads to shared glory*. Torraza Piemonte: The Cody and Emma Golden Press.

Ministerio de Cultura y Deporte. (2020). DEPORTEData: Base de datos [SPORT-Data: Data base]. Retrieved from http://www.culturaydeporte.gob.es. Accessed on June 20, 2020.

Ministerio de Educación, Cultura y Deporte. (2015). Encuesta de hábitos deportivos 2015 [Survey on sport habits 2015]. Retrieved from http://www.culturaydeporte. gob.es/dam/jcr:ebf5ee1a-69c8-4809-9e7d-30ca5425e8d9/encuesta-de-habitos-deportivos-2015.pdf. Accessed on February 13, 2021.

Moñino, L. J. (2019). Nueva Liga, viejos problemas [New league, old problems]. *El País*, August 2, p. 33.

Moñino, L. J., & Calonge, L. (2020). "Playoff" exprés en 2°B y Tercera, y título para el Barça en la Liga femenina [Express playoffs in the second and third men's leagues, and title of champion for Barça in the women's first league]. *El País*, May 7, p. 34.

Pérez, F. (2019). Discurso íntegro de Florentino Pérez en la Asamblea General Extraordinaria 2019 [Discourse by Florentino Pérez to the 2019 Extraordinary general assembly]. Retrieved from https://www.realmadrid.com. Accessed on April 28, 2020.

Puig, N., & Vilanova, A. (2017). Sociology of sport: Spain. In K. Young (Ed.), *Sociology of sport: A global subdiscipline in review* (pp. 285–301). Bingley: Emerald Publishing Limited.

Quixano, J. (2019). El Liverpool sigue iluminado [Liverpool continues to be inspired]. *El País*, August 15, p. 28.

Real Federación Española de Fútbol. (2020). Junta directiva [board]. Retrieved from https://www.rfef.es. Accessed on April 20, 2020.

Rivas, J. (2019, February 1). Record-breaking turnout for women's soccer game in Madrid. *El País*. Retrieved from https://elpais.com/elpais/2019/01/31/inenglish/1548931453_913356.html. Accessed on April 20, 2020.

Roman, B. (Ed.). (2016). *Informe 2016: Actividad física en niños y adolescentes en España* [Report 2016: Children and adolescents' physical activity in Spain]. Barcelona: Fundación para la Investigación Nutricional.

The Economist. (2019). Global sports: Ahead of the game. *The Economist*, October 5, pp. 55–56.

Vaczi, M. (2015). *Soccer, culture and society in Spain: An ethnography of Basque fandom*. New York, NY: Routledge.

Valiente, C. (2019a). Spain: Social, political and organizational explanations. In A. Elling, J. Hovden, & A. Knoppers (Eds.), *Gender diversity in European sport governance* (pp. 36–45). New York, NY: Routledge.

Valiente, C. (2019b). Sport and social movements: Lilí Álvarez in Franco's Spain. *International Review for the Sociology of Sport*, 54(5), 622–646.

Valiente, C. (2020a). The impact of gender quotas in sport management: The case of Spain. *Sport in Society*. doi:10.1080/17430437.2020.1819244

Valiente, C. (2020b). Women pioneers in the history of sport: The case of Lilí Álvarez in Franco's Spain. *International Journal of the History of Sport*, 37(1–2), 75–93.

Wenner, L. A., & Billing, A. C. (Eds.). (2017). *Sport, media and mega-events*. New York, NY: Routledge.

Chapter 11

The Solheim Cup: Media Representations of Golf, Gender and National Identity

Ali Bowes and Niamh Kitching

Introduction: Women's Golf and the Solheim Cup

The increasing inclusion of women in sport has been mediated by societal gendered expectations. It is an oft-cited notion that sport is 'an institution created by and for men' (Messner & Sabo, 1990, p. 9), and sport is subsequently inherently rooted in assumptions of hegemonic forms of masculinity (Connell, 1987). This has historically made women's involvement in most sports problematic, constrained by gender norms and medical myths which symbolically rendered them unsuitable for participation in sport. Unsurprisingly, female golfers have struggled for equality in a golf culture that, like most sports, is 'widely regarded as male dominated and exclusionary' (Kitching, 2017, p. 404). Reis and Correia (2013, p. 324) highlight that the sport has a 'cultural tradition of for-gentlemen-only-clubs that has excluded women from clubhouses and from practising golf'. Despite women's involvement in the sport dating back to the sixteenth century, women were often symbolically excluded from golf; they could play, but not with the same freedom or flexibility as men. Where they were excluded from full membership and playing rights, women were forced to form ladies' sections, initiated by the St. Andrews Ladies' Golf Club in 1867 (George, 2009), and subsequently women's golf developed independently from the men's game, with the Ladies Professional Golf Association (LPGA) forming in 1950 and the Ladies European Tour (LET) in 1978. Scholars have highlighted several women throughout the 19th and 20th centuries that learned and played the sport, and subsequently excelled as golfers, challenging the male hegemony of the game (George, 2009; Reis & Correia, 2013).

Whilst feminist commentators have highlighted sport as a 'fundamentally sexist institution that is male dominated and masculine in orientation' (Theberge, 1981, p. 342), women have continued to engage with sport as both athletes and spectators. In the 21st century, Cooky and Messner (2018) highlight a gender transformation in the United States, noting that millions of girls are taking up sports such as football and basketball, and largely attribute this to shifts in the cultural expectation for and acceptance of girls' athleticism. In a UK context,

Sport, Gender and Mega-Events, 201–219
Copyright © 2022 by Emerald Publishing Limited
All rights of reproduction in any form reserved
doi:10.1108/978-1-83982-936-920211017

Velija and Malcolm (2009, p. 629) claim that 'it is widely accepted that there are now more opportunities for females to be involved in sports than ever before'. However, in golf – whilst acknowledged as one of the most successful (and lucrative) professional sports organisations for women – it has been noted by Kitching (2017) that exclusionary practices continue to impact the modern game, where women still struggle for equality of access, participation, employment and decision-making in golf. Female golfers are widely perceived as inferior to their male counterparts in driving distance, which is frequently used to frame women as less able golfers (McGinnis, McQuillan, & Chapple, 2005). Despite this, women continue to progress in the professional game, with increasing prize funds for the 2020 season on both the LPGA and the LET. The pinnacle of the game, however, golf's mega-event for women, is considered to be the Solheim Cup.

The Solheim Cup, a women's professional golf tournament, was founded in 1990 by Karsten Solheim[1] as a replica of the men's Ryder Cup, a biennial team golf tournament pitting 12 Americans against 12 Europeans in match-play format. Whilst not always the case, the current structure of the two events is exactly the same: the first two days involves players from each team competing in fourballs[2] and foursomes[3] matches, followed by a day of singles matches on the third and final day. The Ryder Cup has been claimed to be one of the most important and prestigious events in international sport. Dating back to 1926, it is considered 'the oldest competition of nations in professional golf, involving the two golf superpowers: the United States and Europe' (Kali, Pastoriza, & Plante, 2018, p. 102). Kali et al. (2018, p. 104) indicate that 'the halo of prestige surrounding the Ryder Cup derives not only from being the oldest competition of nations in professional golf and including most of the best professional golfers in the world, but also from the fact that no prize money is awarded for wining it'. The same is true for the Solheim Cup.

Similarly, the Solheim Cup, co-run by the LET and the LPGA, is subsequently considered to be the pinnacle of professional women's golf, and female golf's only 'mega-event'. Marketed as the biggest rivalry in women's golf, the Solheim Cup was first staged in Florida in 1990, and prior to the 2019 version has been dominated by the United States 10–5. In September 2019, the 16th edition of the event was held at the self-proclaimed home of golf, Gleneagles in Scotland, 19 years since the country last hosted the event and five years after the venue hosted the 2014 edition of the Ryder Cup. The first part of this chapter will critically discuss the tournament, in relation to literature on golf and national identity, and media coverage of sport and national identity, with a specific nod to work on women's sport and national identity. The second part of the chapter presents data collected from the British print media during the tournament, which will be analysed using a critical feminist framework to understand how female athletes are represented in women golf's only mega-event.

(Supra-)National Identity and Golf

International sport is often heavily linked with national identity, although golf is not often considered in the same way. Harris, Lee, and Lyberger (2017) describe how little research has considered the place of the nation in relation to golf. It has been claimed that the sport is often relatively insignificant in inculcating national sentiments. Owing to the lack of direct competition formats, nation versus nation contests and the absence of physical confrontation present in many other sports, golf is generally devoid of flags and nationalistic tendencies. Professional golfers playing on global tours are considered borderless athletes (Chiba, Ebihara, & Morino, 2001) who transcend national, racial and ethnic borders, de facto sports citizens of the world. For Liston and Kitching (2020, p. 869), 'golf is relatively inured from displays of nationalism that are more commonplace in international team sports'. Despite this, Bairner (2003) notes that the sport does have links to identity politics, and there have been instances where professional golfers have taken on cultural significance and become viewed as embodiments of the nation (Kitching & Bowes, 2020; Liston & Kitching, 2020).

There are some unique tournaments in golf that provide some avenue to consider the place of nationhood and national identity. Whilst Liston and Kitching (2020) explain that golf has little to do with national identity, they do note that golf's recent inception into the Olympic Games and the biennial Ryder Cup/Solheim Cup matches provide an exception. Team competitions within golf, with national or supra-national representation, provide an unusual instance where issues of national (and supra-national) identity in international golf settings might come to the fore. These events provide professional golfers with a unique opportunity for national representation: players representing (supra-)national teams, wearing (supra-)national uniforms, playing in front of thousands of fans waving (supra-)national flags, with their faces painted in (supra-)national colours. As Kali et al. (2018, p. 103) state:

> Playing for one's country is a great honor for which even very wealthy professional golfers vie. Being part of an elite groups of golfers who have the privilege of representing their countries, and not a direct monetary gain, is considered the Ryder Cup's own reward.

In researching the portrayal of national identities in sport, the examination of print or electronic papers has been widely used. In relation to the 2008 Ryder Cup, Harris et al. (2017) studied local and national print media in the United States and found that the tournament was an important site for framing narratives of the nation in media discourse. In examining print and electronic media accounts of the 2006 match in *USA Today* to assess how images of the US nation are presented, Harris and Lyberger (2008) found that the US loss was positioned within a broader narrative of a crisis in US sport and was attributed to the individualistic nature of US society and an overall cultural decline. These studies indicate the complicated nature of collective identity expressions in (men's) golf.

For both the players and fans of the Ryder Cup and Solheim Cup's European Teams, the notion of national identity is complex. Despite representing a Team

Europe, often there are overt displays of national allegiances, with fans getting behind this unique and convoluted tribalism in golf:

> ...while some fans of the European players in golf's Ryder Cup unfurl the flag of the European Union, many persist in waving their national flags despite the multinational composition of the European team.
>
> (Bairner, 2001, p. 2)

Maguire (2011) notes that the Ryder Cup and the Solheim Cup are central in the somewhat tentative emergence of a European sports identity, although the degree to which athletes feel any strong sense of identification to the geographical continent is as yet unexplored. The moveable geographical boundaries of the Ryder Cup event, along with the otherwise rare expressions of European identity articulated, have resulted in its derision in some quarters. Media examinations during the tournament have questioned the collective identity generated and Steen (2015, p. 349), in writing about the men's Ryder Cup, noted:

> With collective golfing success have come hints of a collective cultural identity; unfortunately, golf, lacking the passions, physical confrontation and tribal loyalties that underpin mass appeal, is probably the sport least likely to have a wider social impact.

Steen (2015, p. 348) further described the US–Europe match-play event as 'the oddest of major sporting competitions'; the United States in 'red-white-and-blue' competing against a team 'under a little-recognised flag...popularly referred to – and with no irony whatsoever – as "Team Europe", a multinational collective with little or no mutual identity to speak of beyond a professional rivalry with the Americans'. However, whilst the body of research on the Ryder Cup is scarce, it is even more stark for the Solheim Cup, with no published empirical work on it – despite an increasing body of academic literature that has interrogated press coverage of women in sport.

Gender and National Identity in the (Golf) Sport Media

In considering the significance of the Solheim Cup to national identity, there is an additional layer to consider in terms of gender. Clearly sport plays a central role in the formation of national identity; however, the sport that is central to recreating the national imagined community is often considered a male-only domain. Hobsbawm (1990, p. 143) had concluded that 'the imagined community of millions seems more real as a team of eleven named people', although it is hard to conceive that he thought those 11 people were anything other than men. Indeed, Hobsbawm argued that sport, at least for males, has proved uniquely effective in generating a sense of belonging to the nation. Sport, including golf, is also constructed as a male domain in the mass media, with Kane (2013) highlighting the symbiotic relationship between the sports media and hegemonic masculinity. Women's inclusion within the sports media is thus problematic; when women do find themselves on the sports pages of the popular press, they are often represented in ways that restrict our imagination about women's sport and retain the hegemonic position of men in sport (Bruce, 2016). However, Biscomb and Griggs (2013), Petty and Pope (2019) and Bowes and Kitching (2019) have all found shifts towards a greater awareness of, and coverage of, female athletes in the sports media.

Portrayals of female golfers in the sports media have an ambivalent history, where golf media has been shown to replicate the same exclusionary practices that are evidenced within the game. Although Billings, Angelini, and Eastman (2008, p. 65) highlight that rising audience interest in women's golf brought about challenges to golf's 'masculine hegemonic entrenchment', both televised and print media coverage of golf have continued to offer representations that reinforce divisions of gender, class, disability and race (Billings et al., 2006, 2008). There are, however, examples that offer some challenges to the gendered norms and traditional depictions of women in golf media. Research found that the media coverage of Annika Sorenstam's involvement in the 2003 PGA Colonial Tournament retained a gendered angle on the one hand, but on the other there were examples of non-gendered explanations of her successes too (Billings et al., 2006). More recently, Bowes and Kitching (2019) describe the print media representation of professional female golfers (again, when competing alongside men) as a double-edged sword, with positive informed coverage littered with gendered language. Kitching and Bowes (2020) then later describe how the print media framed Irish golfer Leona Maguire in non-gendered ways, as a model citizen representative of her nation.

There have been a few notable pieces of work that have considered the role of national identity in media coverage of women's sport. Wensing and Bruce (2003) note that coverage of female representatives during international sporting competition may follow different 'rules' than one would usually see in their representation. They explain that women competing for the nation 'may be less likely to be marked by gendered discourses or narratives than reporting on everyday sports' (Wensing & Bruce, 2003, p. 393). Bruce (2008, p. 62) later demonstrated, in the context of New Zealand, that 'women who win for the nation are highlighted as worthy of attention'. She notes that concepts of gender marking, compulsory heterosexuality, appropriate femininity, infantilisation, downplaying sports and ambivalence, fail to help us understand the way that female athletes are represented, drawing attention to the way 'nationalism almost completely overrode the usual ways that the sports media report on female athletes' (Bruce, 2008, p. 67).

Both authors have written on the topics of national identity and golf, gender and national identity and the media representations of female professional golfers, much of which informs this chapter. Bowes (2020) describes how international sporting competitions open up an avenue for sportswomen to be presented as legitimate national representatives, in both their media representations and their self-presentations. Further, Bowes and Bairner (2018) highlight that international sportswomen on the international sporting field *can* become active embodiments of their nation, fulfilling a role of proxy warriors in sport. Whilst Bowes and Bairner (2018; 2019) note that female athletes have a role to play in embodying the nation, this was in team sports that are often already closely aligned with a sense of national identity. This chapter aims to extend this work, and that on professional golfers (Kitching & Bowes, 2020; Liston & Kitching, 2020), to consider the ways in which female golfers in the 2019 Solheim Cup are represented in the sports media. Before doing so, it is important to present an overview of the competition itself.

The Story of the 2019 Solheim Cup

The 2019 teams were decided approximately a month before the tournament started. Team Europe was announced first, on 12 August 2019, and was made up of the top three players on the LET Solheim Cup points list, followed by the top five LET members on the Women's World Golf Rankings (WWGR) not already qualified, and four captains' picks (see Table 11.1). The team was captained by nine-time Solheim Cup player Catriona Matthew (Scotland), and assisted by former Solheim Cup players Dame Laura Davies (England), Kathryn Imrie (Scotland) and Mel Reid (England).[4] Team USA was announced on 26 August 2019 and consisted of the top eight players from the LPGA Solheim Cup points list, followed by the top two American players on the WWGR not already qualified, and two captains' picks (see Table 11.2). Team USA was led for the third time in a row by Juli Inkster, supported by assistants Pat Hurst, Nancy Lopez and Wendy Ward. As holders, Team USA needed 14 points to retain the Solheim Cup, with 14.5 required for Team Europe to take the trophy.

Prior to the tournament starting, Team USA were strong favourites: the average WWGR for Team USA was 31, with five of the world's top 20 players, compared to Europe's 103 (or 54, if you remove the anomaly of Suzann Pettersen's world ranking[5]), with only one player inside the WWGR top 20. The tournament started on Friday 13th September, with Team Europe winning the morning foursomes session 2.5–1.5, and the afternoon fourballs session shared 2–2. Saturday 14th September again started with a morning foursome session, also squared at two to two, with Team USA winning the afternoon fourballs 2.5–1.5. Starting eight to eight, it was a tense singles day on Sunday 15th September. The tournament came down to the last match left out on the course, where Suzann Pettersen for Team Europe had to hole a birdie putt on the 18th green to score the 14th and final point to win the Solheim Cup for Team Europe. She duly holed it, promptly followed by her unplanned, and surprising, retirement from the sport. The event was considered one of the closest of all time, with renowned women's golf journalist Ron Sirak proclaiming 'you'd have to search far and wide to find a more dramatic finish anywhere in the history of sports' (LPGA.com, 15 September 2019).

Table 11.1. Team Europe.

Player	Country	LET Points Rank	WWGR (12th August)	Solheim Cup Apps
Carlota Ciganda	Spain	1	13	3
Anne Van Dam	Netherlands	2	93	0
Caroline Hedwall	Sweden	3	116	3
Charley Hull	England	4	29	3
Georgia Hall	England	8	33	1
Azahara Munoz	Spain	N/A	36	3
Caroline Masson	Germany	N/A	52	3
Anna Nordqvist	Sweden	14	60	5
Celine Boutier	France	6	61	0
Jodi Ewart Shadoff	England	N/A	78	2
Bronte Law	England	N/A	25	0
Suzann Pettersen	Norway	N/A	644	8

A Critical Feminist Research Approach: Framework and Methodology

The event was hailed as a great success and saw significant press coverage in terms of print media, online media and television coverage. So, addressing a lack of academic attention to women's professional golf, and the Solheim Cup more specifically, this chapter aims to consider the intersection of gender and national identity using British media coverage of the Solheim Cup as a case study. As per some of the authors' previous work (Bowes & Kitching, 2019; Kitching & Bowes, 2020), this chapter adopts a critical feminist theoretical approach. A privileging of men and men's activities can result in the reproduction of institutionalised practices where women are excluded, marginalised and perceived as less important. While feminist perspectives that focus on equality and discrimination are criticised for oversimplifying females' diversified dispositions, critical feminisms write in relation to power, where gender relations are often defined by hegemonic

Table 11.2. Team USA.

Player	LPGA Points Rank	WWGR (26th August)	Solheim Cup Apps
Lexi Thompson	1	3	3
Nelly Korda	2	10	0
Danielle Kang	3	15	1
Lizette Salas	4	17	3
Jessica Korda	5	18	1
Megan Khang	6	46	0
Marina Alex	7	32	0
Brittany Altomare	8	40	0
Angel Yin	10	31	1
Annie Park	16	42	0
Morgan Pressel	20	55	5
Ally MacDonald[a]	9	57	0

[a]Ally MacDonald was initially a travelling reserve, but initial captain's pick Stacy Lewis had to withdraw due to injury.

masculinity and supported by cultural norms of male domination and female subordination. Thus, critical feminism as used in this chapter acknowledges the normalisation of patriarchal power relations in golf and media.

Data for this chapter were collected via the online electronic news database Nexis UK by the second author. The second author searched for full text newspaper articles from publications in the United Kingdom, using the keywords 'Solheim Cup' (anywhere in the text). Articles were collected between the dates of 12 August 2019, the day of the first Solheim Cup team announcement, until 22 September 2019, a week following the tournament (and thus the commencement of a new tournament week on the professional circuit). An initial search yielded 244 articles, but filtering for repetitive content, irrelevant content such as television schedules and articles under 50 words, this was reduced to 136. The following print media outlets were included: *Daily Mail* and *The Mail on Sunday*, *Daily Mirror* and *Daily Mirror (Ireland)*, *Daily Star*, *The Daily Telegraph* and *The Sunday Telegraph*, *The Express*, *The Guardian*, *The Independent* and *i-Independent*, *The Observer*, *The Sun*, *The Sun (Scotland)* and *The Sun (Ireland)*, *The Times*, *The Times (Scotland)* and *The Sunday Times*, and online articles from the same sources (that were not repeated in print versions). As part of the data collection, the authors recorded a number of particulars about the data, including the date, newspaper, page number and/or section (if provided), journalist and headline.

All articles were subject to a process of thematic analysis (Braun and Clarke, 2019). The lead author implemented a theoretical thematic analysis, a process which acknowledges the researcher's role in knowledge production (Braun and Clarke, 2019). The lead author went through the steps outlined by Braun and Clarke (2013), including familiarisation (an initial reading of the articles), reading and re-reading, coding, and then developing and reviewing themes. Following the development of themes, the second author was then consulted to verify the accuracy of these themes. Throughout this process, both authors adopted an explicitly feminist lens, acknowledging the gendered power relations that high-light the problematic ways women are represented in the sports press. The authors present four key themes from the data:

- The Solheim Cup *as golf*
- National proxy warriors
- Pettersen the 'Supermum'
- The Ryder Cup's Little Sister?

This chapter will draw upon both qualitative and quantitative measures to describe the above patterns of media coverage during the Solheim Cup. Furthermore, we present a discussion of the themes alongside extracts from the British print media's headline tournament coverage.

The Solheim Cup *as Golf*

One of the most obvious themes identified was that of a clear level of increased legitimacy of women's golf, in this instance the Solheim Cup, *as golf.* The press often took a non-gendered approach in how they wrote about the tournament, which we felt was evidenced in multiple ways. Firstly, of all the articles that were analysed, 116 of the 136 articles, over 85%, lead with the Solheim Cup as the key feature. This is significant because we have previously seen women's golf can be often written about as a sub text to a mainstream men's golf article (see Kitching & Bowes, 2020). For example, some early headlines described the make-up of each team:

> Van Dam seals a Solheim Cup spot.
> > (i-Independent, 12 August 2019)

> Cristie Kerr left out of US Solheim Cup team.
> > (Telegraph, 26 August 2019)

It was also noted that there was an obvious lack of gender marking of the coverage. Of the articles that were analysed, 97/136, or 71%, had no specific gender marking of the tournament itself. What we mean by this is there was no reference to the event as a *women's* event, or no reference to the players as *female* players. Later headlines demonstrate the lack of gender marking for the tournament, drawing on the official tournament name as well as key players:

> Hull blows chance to give Europe commanding lead.
> (Daily Telegraph, 14 September 2019)

> Europe stay level-headed as Hall and Boutier dig deep in Solheim Cup.
> (The Observer, 14 September 2019)

However, within these articles there were occasional mentions of other tournaments, whose official name was gender marked (15/136; 11%): Ladies Scottish Open, Women's British Open and CP Women's Open in Canada; the problem herein then is possibly not one of the media coverage, but of the organisational structures of professional golf. Like Bruce (2016) identified, there is a reduction in the gender marking of women's sport across the sport media landscape, of which this coverage seems to follow suit.

Further evidence of the legitimacy of the event *as golf* was noted in the purpose of the coverage. The content of the writing often focused on the event itself, rather than slipping into ambivalent coverage that juxtaposed sport content with irrelevant content (Bruce, 2016). An example here was Team Europe's Charley Hull's impending wedding, which featured in only 2/136 articles. Continuing to focus on the golf, almost half of all articles (64/136, 47%) mentioned team picks – either prior to the tournament or throughout their involvement at the tournament:

> Law and Ewart Shadoff earn wild cards for Solheim Cup.
> (Daily Telegraph, 13 August 2019)

> Juli calls Solheim Veterans.
> (The Sun, 27 August 2019)

Furthermore, 18% of articles published within a week of the event taking place mentioned the crowd numbers, which was positioned at between 80,000 and 100,000 spectators:

> Cup is crowd pleaser.
> (The Times Scotland, 17 September 2019)

This further served to legitimise the event as a significant sporting event and position the women as athletes.

National Proxy Warriors

The role of national identity has been identified as central in legitimating women's position as national representatives in sport (Bowes, 2020; Bruce 2008,

2016; Wensing & Bruce, 2003). Writing about the Ryder Cup, Steen (2015, p. 349) notes that the 'continental identity – hitherto unseen in any serious sporting arena and further witnessed in the camaraderie of participants in the women's Solheim Cup – is ripe for further investigation'. It was clear, then, that from the outset national identity was a key descriptor of the players in the tournament. The headlines from the tournament often led with a 'team' identity descriptor for either Team USA or Europe:

> US call up Cup vets.
> (Daily Mirror, 27 August 2019)

> Solheim Cup 2019: Europe and USA level at 8-8 going into final day.
> (The Independent, 14 September 2019)

> Europe on the level.
> (Daily Mirror (Ireland), 15 September 2019)

However, within the text of the articles, 67% mentioned the specific national identity of the European players. This demonstrates how important national identity is, as part of the supra-national European identity that being part of Team Europe instigates. The overtness of national identity descriptors for the European team members demonstrates that national identity is potentially more significant in describing athletes than the supra-national team identity. According to Wensing and Bruce (2003) and later Bruce (2008, 2016), for female athletes, media coverage of events where athletes are marked by their nationality may be less likely to be gender marked. Thus, the centrality of national identity is significant here in legitimising the 'bending of the rules' in terms of how gender was less likely to be used to frame female athletes.

Furthermore, Bowes (2020) describes how the media can draw upon a battle narrative to frame female athletes as proxy warriors in international sporting competitions. This was something that was evident here, with nearly half (47%) of all articles about the event containing some form of 'fight talk' or 'battle narrative'. Pre-tournament, the Sunday Times noted:

> Gleneagles can be a happy hunting ground for Europe again.
> (8 September 2019)

During the tournament week, there was a headline focus on the press conference 'quips' from American Danielle Kang, and European Suzann Pettersen. The Express (Ireland) went with the simple: 'War Cry' (13th September 2019), and the war/battle narrative from Kang and Pettersen's press conference discussions continued to hit headlines across a range of print media outlets:

> Kang looking to 'crush' Europe.
> (Daily Mail, 12 September 2019)

> Europe hit back at US in bitter war of words.
>
> (Daily Mail, 13 September 2019)

> Suzann going for the throat.
>
> (The Sun Scotland, 13 September 2019)

During the tournament, the headlines persisted with a battle focus in describing Bronte Law's performance after day one, and Celine Boutier and Georgia Hall's play following day two:

> Bronte in a battle.
>
> (Daily Star, 14 September 2019)

> Fightback from Boutier and Hall gives Europe hope.
>
> (The Sunday Telegraph, 15 September 2019)

Similarly, it was evident at the conclusion of the tournament, where the print media hailed Pettersen as 'heroic' after she holed the winning putt:

> Davies hails Norwegian heroic role but wants her to carry on.
>
> (The Daily Telegraph, 16 September 2019)

Here, the women are presented as legitimate athletes for their nation by framing them in warrior-like roles – or proxy warriors (Bowes & Bairner, 2018). These 'war like' metaphors can be associated with hegemonic notions of power and control and have been discussed in more detail in relation to the intersections of women, war and sport (Bowes, Bairner, Whigham, & Kitching, 2021). However, it is also possible that these narratives are part of the expanding frames of reference for female athleticism (Dashper, 2018) thereby positively influencing the formation of women athletes' multiple and evolving identities in and through sport.

Pettersen the 'Supermum'

Arguably the story of the event was the inclusion of Suzann Pettersen, via a captain's pick from Catriona Matthew, to Team Europe. It was noted as significant as it was less than two months after her return from maternity leave, following a near two-year absence from the sport. Of the articles that mentioned captains' picks, 75% of them noted the selection of Team Europe's Suzann Pettersen, despite the fact she was only one of seven players that were captains' picks during the tournament (when including both the withdrawn Stacy Lewis and her replacement Ally Macdonald for Team USA). The surprise element was drawn primarily from her world ranking at the time of the tournament, which framed her as a 'gamble' - despite her impressive history in the tournament as one of Europe's most decorated Solheim Cup players:

> World No 620 not a gamble, says Matthew.
>
> (The Times London, 13 August 2019)

> Captain Catriona rolls Solheim dice.
>
> (Daily Mail, 13 August 2019)

In this way, the framing of Pettersen prior to the tournament could be one that positions the role of athlete and mother in conflict and incompatible (McGannon, Curtin, Schinke, & Schweinbenz, 2015). Over half of all articles examined mentioned Pettersen in some form, but only 12 of these articles *did not* mention her role as a mother. Reference to her as a mother places Pettersen within familiar family networks (Dashper, 2018). This can also be read as problematic: it retains a framing of Pettersen embroiled with femininity and the appropriate roles of women. Pettersen's son Herman was often mentioned by name, which serves to construct the family unit as familiar and positions her in relation to heteronormative ideals (Dashper, 2018). This is a strategy the golf media has previously used in their coverage of Nancy Lopez (Team USA vice captain), where Jamieson (1998) positions the focus on marriage and motherhood as a modern-day apologetic that trivialised Lopez's athleticism. Furthermore, this can be seen as ambivalent coverage, in which the sport media focuses not explicitly on women's athletic achievements.

Much like McGannon et al. (2012) found with media representations of Paula Radcliffe post pregnancy, Pettersen's identities involve her being both a national athlete and a mother intertwined. However, as the tournament progressed and Pettersen played out the starring role, the media's pre-tournament fears over her suitability to play were negated. For example, the following headlines were published by *The Sun*:

> Mother of all wins: Solheim Cup heroes Pettersen and Matthew show the power of being a supermum after Europe beat America at Gleneagles.
> (The Sun, 16 September 2019)

> The legend of 'supermum' will continue to grow.
> (The Sun, 17 September 2019)

McGannon et al. (2015) described the 'athlete mother as superwoman' framing, with athlete mothers challenging the notion that women have to retire to have a family and shattering the myth that motherhood and sport are incompatible. Pettersen, after holing the tournament winning putt, enabled the media to shift the narrative into a supermum framing – a woman that can do it all, at the very top, although she had to prove herself first:

> Europe win Solheim Cup as Suzann Pettersen justifies inclusion by putting winner at Gleneagles.
> (mirror.co.uk, 15 September 2019)

The heteronormative aspect of this coverage also shines a light on the lack of attention given to the many more player identities on the teams. For example, at least half of the USA players were from multiracial backgrounds, and while the racial ambivalence here might be considered positively, it could also be seen as foreclosing on the many moving 'selves' of the players involved and linked to issues of quantity and quality of the coverage.

The Ryder Cup's Little Sister?

Despite a clear shift in how the print media presented both the athletes and the tournament, there was still some evidence of problematic media strategies. One such strategy involved the use of men's sport as a benchmark. In the articles examined, although 70% were not gender marked, 27% did make some point of reference to the Ryder Cup, the men's version of the event, and 17% likened female players to male equivalents. This was centred on American Danielle Kang, referred to as the Solheim Cup's Patrick Reed (a top male golfer who has represented Team USA in the Ryder Cup), and Europe's Bronte Law, likened to male European Ryder Cup players Francesco Molinari and Ian Poulter:

> Poulter helps Bronte give Europe advantage.
> (Daily Mirror, 14 September 2019)

> Law hoping to enjoy a repeat of her Molinari cup moment.
> (The Sunday Telegraph, 8 September 2019)

The articles that were gender marked (39/136; 29%) made distinctions that this was the best event in *women's* golf or featured the best crowds for a *women's* event. However, only two headlines from the data sample were specifically gender-marked, although these were both articles that highlighted the subordinate position of the women's game, in order to try to prompt some form of change:

> Women's golf never gets due credit.
> (The Times, 20 August 2019)

> Women's golf let down as 5 live snubs Solheim Cup.
> (Daily Mail, 10 September 2019)

There was some evidence that old habits die hard in the popular press regarding how they covered women's sport, although this was notably sparse including in more 'tabloid', sensationalist style papers. For example, *The Sun (Scotland)* led with the following headline going into the singles day:

> All the singles ladies.
> (The Sun (Scotland), 15 September 2019)

However, perhaps the worst example of gendered journalism was the following statement:

> They used to say the Solheim Cup was the 'Ryder Cup with lipstick'. These days, 'with stilettos' might be a better fit.
>
> (Daily Mail, 12 September 2020)

While comparing men's and women's sport has been critiqued in the past (e.g. Bruce, 2016), utilising the Ryder Cup a benchmark with which to build understanding might be a useful media strategy.

Conclusion: Evidence of Change?

> We're now watching so much women's sport they are no longer seen as women but as performers.
>
> (The Sunday Times, 15 September 2020)

This chapter has provided further evidence of positive media shifts in the representation of women's sport, and specifically in women's golf. On the whole, coverage focused on the Solheim Cup *as golf*, female golfers *as golfers,* and in the majority reporting on sporting content *as sport*. This framing in one of golf's 'mega-events' has potential to translate into consistency in the types of representations female athletes receive in the sport media, moving away from sexualisation and feminisation towards more legitimacy in their inclusion as *athletes*. Whilst it is important for female athletes to be seen in the sport media, perhaps of equal importance is the ways in which they are portrayed.

The significance of both national and supra-national identification in the Solheim Cup was clear and is one thing that marks out this mega-event as unique on the golfing calendar. The emphasis of both national and supra-national identification is obvious and could be evidence of why the reporting was not overly gendered (Bruce, 2008; Wensing & Bruce, 2003). The women were presented as proxy warriors doing battle – significant for women to be seen as legitimate athletes *and* legitimate national representatives.[6] It is clear that international team events in golf open up a space for more gender-neutral coverage (compared to previous discussions of media coverage in women's golf – see Bowes & Kitching, 2019), and for increased legitimacy of the women's game in the sporting press.

However, it is important to retain a critical focus in our analysis of the print media coverage. Whilst it is undoubtedly exciting for women's golf fans and feminist sport media scholars to see women dominating stories and headlines, it is worth noting that the extent of media coverage is contextual – the mega event of women's golf, played in the 'home of golf', with four British captains and four British players. It remains to be seen whether the global sport media can find a more permanent space for gender-neutral stories about the women's game outside of its showcase tournament. In terms of the type of coverage, it could be argued that the reduction of gender marking in the coverage of the Solheim Cup is specific to this tournament, as the Solheim Cup is a tournament specific to the women's game. Again – the challenge is to pay attention to whether or not media coverage of women's golf more broadly can and will follow similar patterns. In this vein, as the event continues to grow in stature and success in the future, it will be interesting to see if the print media continue to pay attention to the men's version of the competition as a point of reference.

However, as Dashper (2018) notes, the most likely consumers of the British sport media are men, reading stories written by male journalists for a male-dominated audience. For the sample of media analysed here, there were 30 different authors cited – of which only one (Molly McElwee writing for *The Times Scotland*) was female. It could be argued then that if the underrepresentation of female sport journalists continues, it will be hard to see more progressive and consistent change in print media coverage. Franks and O'Neill (2016) highlight that there is a trend of invisibility of female sports journalists in national UK papers – a finding supported here – and as Kian and Hardin (2009) note, it is male writers that are more likely to reinforce gender stereotypes. The wider implications of this have the potential to be significant – more equitable coverage in the sports media could have a noteworthy impact on the gendered culture of golf more broadly. The success of the Solheim Cup, including its strong presence in the sport media, could well be a springboard to shifting perceptions of women in golf cultures and challenging the male hegemony of the game.

Notes

1. Karsten Solheim (1911–2000) was a Norwegian-born engineer who creating the golf equipment company Ping in 1959 and, alongside his wife Louise, was a committed supporter of women's golf.
2. Fourballs involves four balls on the course: two players per team go head to head. The player that scores the lowest on each hole wins the hole for their team.
3. Foursomes involves two balls on the course: again, two players per team go head to head. However, each team only has one ball and players will hit alternate shots until the ball is holed. The team that scores the lowest on each hole wins the hole for their team.
4. The captain is able to select her own assistant captains and will often pick former Solheim Cup players whom she knows well. In this regard, there is often a strong influence from one of Europe's nations (in this regard, the United Kingdom).
5. Whilst on paper her world ranking might lead one to question her involvement, Suzann Pettersen was the most experienced player in the field and one of Europe's greatest ever Solheim Cup players.
6. The ideas were further developed for a special issue on war, peace and sport: Bowes, A., Bairner, A., Whigham, S. and Kitching, N. (Forthcoming). Women, war and sport: The battle of the 2019 Solheim Cup. *Journal of War and Culture Studies*.

References

Bairner, A. (2001). *Sport, nationalism, and globalization: European and North American perspectives.* Albany, NY: SUNY Press.

Bairner, A. (2003). Political unionism and sporting nationalism: An examination of the relationship between sport and national identity within the Ulster unionist tradition. *Identities: Global Studies in Culture and Power, 10*(4), 517–535.

Billings, A. C., Angelini, J., & Eastman, S. (2008). Wie shock: Television commentary about playing on the PGA and LPGA tours. *The Howard Journal of Communications, 19*(1), 64–84.

Billings, A., Craig, C., Croce, R., Cross, K., Moore, K., Vigodsky, W., & Watson, V. (2006). "Just one of the Guys?" Network depictions of Annika Sorenstam in the 2003 PGA Colonial Tournament. *Journal of Sport & Social Issues, 30*(1), 107–114.

Biscomb, K., & Griggs, G. (2013). "A splendid effort!" Print media reporting of England's women's performance in the 2009 Cricket World Cup. *International Review for the Sociology of Sport, 48*(1), 99–111.

Bowes, A. (2020). National identities and international sport: What about the women? In N. Villanueva (Ed.), *The athlete as national symbol: Critical essays on sports in the international arena.* (pp. 88–112). Jefferson, NC: McFarland and Company Inc.

Bowes, A., & Bairner, A. (2018). England's proxy warriors? Women, war and sport. *International Review for the Sociology of Sport, 53*(4), 393–410.

Bowes, A., & Bairner, A. (2019). Three lions on her shirt: Hot and banal nationalism for England's sportswomen. *Journal of Sport & Social Issues, 43*(6), 531–550. doi: 10.1177/0193723519850878

Bowes, A., Bairner, A., Whigham, S., & Kitching, N. (2021). Women, war and sport: The battle of the 2019 Solheim Cup. *Journal of War and Culture Studies, 13*(4), 424–443. doi:10.1080/17526272.2020.1829788

Bowes, A., & Kitching, N. (2019). 'Battle of the sixes': Investigating print media representations of female professional golfers competing in a men's tour event. *International Review for the Sociology of Sport, 55*(6), 664–684. doi: 10.1177/1012690219842544

Braun, V., & Clarke, V. (2013). *Successful qualitative research: A practical guide for beginners.* London: Sage Publications.

Braun, V., & Clarke, V. (2019). Reflecting on reflexive thematic analysis. *Qualitative Research in Sport, Exercise and Health, 11*(4), 589–597.

Bruce, T. (2008). Women, sport and the media: A complex terrain. In C. Obel, T. Bruce, & S. Thompson (Eds.), *Outstanding: Research about women and sport in New Zealand* (pp. 51–71). Hamilton: University of Waikato, Malcolm Institute for Educational Research.

Bruce, T. (2016). New rules for new times: Sportswomen and media representation in the third wave. *Sex Roles, 74*, 361–376.

Chiba, N., Ebihara, O., & Morino, S. (2001). Globalisation, naturalisation and identity: The case of borderless elite athletes in Japan. *International Review for the Sociology of Sport, 36*(2), 203–221.

Connell, R. (1987). *Gender and power.* Cambridge: Polity Press.

Cooky, C., & Messner, M. A. (2018). *No slam dunk: Gender, sport and the unevenness of social change.* New Brunswick, NJ: Rutgers University Press.

Dashper, K. (2018). Smiling assassins, brides-to-be and super mums: The importance of gender and celebrity in media framing of female athletes at the 2016 Olympic Games. *Sport in Society*, *21*(11), 1739–1757.

Franks, S., & O'Neill, D. (2016). Women reporting sport: Still a man's game? *Journalism*, *17*(4), 474–492.

George, J. (2009). 'An excellent means of combining fresh air, Exercise and society': Females on the fairways, 1890–1914. *Sport in History*, *29*(3), 333–352.

Harris, J., Lee, S., & Lyberger, M. (2017). The Ryder Cup, national identities and team USA. *Sport in Society*, *20*(3), 413–427.

Harris, J., & Lyberger, M. (2008). Mediated (re)presentations of golf and national identity in the United States: Some observations on the Ryder Cup. *International Journal of Sport Communication*, *1*(2), 143–154.

Hobsbawm, E. J. (1990). *Nations and nationalism since 1780: Programme, myth, reality*. Cambridge: Cambridge University Press.

Jamieson, K. M. (1998). Reading Nancy Lopez: Decoding representations of race, class, and sexuality. *Sociology of Sport Journal*, *15*(4), 343–358.

Kali, R., Pastoriza, D., & Plante, J. F. (2018). The burden of glory: Competing for nonmonetary incentives in rank-order tournaments. *Journal of Economics and Management Strategy*, *27*(1), 102–118.

Kane, M. J. (2013). The better sportswomen get, the more the media ignore them. *Communication & Sport*, *1*(3), 231–236.

Kian, E. M., & Hardin, M. (2009). Framing of sport coverage based on the sex of sports writers: Female journalists counter the traditional gendering of media coverage. *International Journal of Sport Communication*, *2*(2), 185–204.

Kitching, N. (2017). Women in golf: A critical reflection. In M. Toms (Ed.), *The Routledge handbook of golf science* (pp. 404–413). London: Routledge.

Kitching, N., & Bowes, A. (2020). 'Top of the tree': Examining the Irish print news portrayal of the world's best female amateur golfer during her transition to professional golf. In N. O'Boyle & M. Free (Eds.), *Sport, the media and Ireland: Interdisciplinary perspectives* (pp. 167–181). Cork: Cork University Press.

Liston, K., & Kitching, N. (2020). 'Our wee country': National identity, golf and 'Ireland'. *Sport in Society*, *23*(5), 864–879. doi:10.1080/17430437.2019.1584186

Maguire, J. A. (2011). Globalization, sport and national identities. *Sport in Society*, *14*(7–8), 978–993.

McGannon, K. R., Curtin, K., Schinke, R. J., & Schweinbenz, A. N. (2012). (De)constructing Paula Radcliffe: Exploring media representations of elite running, pregnancy and motherhood through cultural sport psychology. *Psychology of Sport and Exercise*, *13*(6), 820–829.

McGinnis, L., McQuillan, J., & Chapple, C. L. (2005). I just want to play: Women, sexism, and persistence in golf. *Journal of Sport & Social Issues*, *29*(3), 313–337.

Messner, M. A., & Sabo, D. F. (1990). Introduction: Toward a critical feminist reappraisal of sport, men, and the gender order. In M. A. Messner & D. F. Sabo (Eds.), *Sport, men, and the gender order* (pp. 1–16). Champaign, IL: Human Kinetics.

Petty, K., & Pope, S. (2019). A new age for media coverage of women's sport? An analysis of English media coverage of the 2015 FIFA women's world cup. *Sociology*, *53*(3), 486–502.

Reis, H., & Correia, A. (2013). Gender inequalities in golf: A consented exclusion? *International Journal of Culture, Tourism and Hospitality Research, 7*(4), 324–339.

Sirak, R. (2019). A Solheim Cup for the ages. *LPGA*, September 15. Retrieved from https://www.lpga.com/news/2019-final-recap-solheim-cup. Accessed on February 13, 2021.

Steen, R. (2015). Uneasy Ryder: The Ryder Cup, anti-Americanism and the 'Yoo-rop' phenomenon. *Sport in Society, 18*(3), 347–363.

Theberge, N. (1981). A critique of critiques: Radical and feminist writings on sport. *Social Forces, 60*(2), 341–353.

Velija, P., & Malcolm, D. (2009). 'Look, it's a girl': Cricket and gender relations in the UK. *Sport in Society, 12*(4–5), 629–642.

Wensing, E. H., & Bruce, T. (2003). Bending the rules. *International Review for the Sociology of Sport, 38*(4), 387–396.

Chapter 12

Flag before Gender Biases? The Case for National Identity Bolstering Women Athlete Visibility in Sports Mega-Events

Andrew C. Billings and Patrick C. Gentile

Introduction

In an overall sports media complex that tends to diminish women athletes both in terms of visibility (Cooky, Messner, & Musto, 2015) and depiction (Kane, LaVoi, & Fink, 2013), sports mega-events often provide a more progressive glimpse of what gender equity could entail. In an edited volume, Wenner and Billings (2017) position the sports mega-event as defining

> …significant moments inscribed in the collective cultural memory, resonating not only with rabid fans, but also for many less passionate about sport. Their appeal resides in transcending the ordinary and being recognized as extraordinary.
>
> (pp. 3–4)

In essence, the atypicality of such events forges new constructs for interpreting what constitutes sports media.

This chapter advances an argument built on the notion that the constructs on which sports mega-events are built are uniquely advantageous for advancing gender equity in terms of visibility, yet less so on more troubling dialogue-oriented terrain. Using the Olympics and FIFA World Cup as exemplars, the case is made that national identity becomes the central mechanism in which individuals advance heuristics of self-categorisation theory, blunting many of the common tropes frequently utilised in other everyday sports media renderings. While only one measure of gender equity (with divergent dialogues still often diminishing or differentiating women athletes), such mega-events will nevertheless be argued as progressive in comparison, offering useful constructs for advancing principles of gender equity within everyday sports media that do not rise to the level of a mega-event. Moreover, this chapter will identify possible mechanisms for then tackling

Sport, Gender and Mega-Events, 221–238
Copyright © 2022 by Emerald Publishing Limited
All rights of reproduction in any form reserved
doi:10.1108/978-1-83982-936-920211018

the more endemic elements of entrenched masculine hegemony within constructs and dialogues of sport as a whole.

Gender Differences in Sports Media: An Overview

This chapter will advance three metrics that have consistently shown troubling media depictions of and for women athletes. Each are described below to establish a baseline of media treatment beyond the realm of international sports mega-events before then determining differences that arise when the notion of nation becomes part of the depiction.

Disparity 1: Lack of Media Exposure

The amount of media coverage of men's and women's sports are significantly and historically unequal (Hansen, 2012). Sports represent big business, with viewership numbers suggesting audiences still are increasing. Between 2003 and 2013, viewership of sports in North America had increased a whopping 232%, with over 116,400 hours of annually consumable sports media being produced (Schmidt, 2016; Scibetti, 2014). Yet, between 3 and 5% of all newspaper coverage is about women's sports and less than 2% on programmes such as North American ESPN's *SportsCenter* (Messner & Cooky, 2010; Messner, Duncan, & Jensen, 2006; Schmidt, 2016). Other studies show similar statistics, if not worse, as Billings and Young (2015) found that *Fox Sports Live* on new ESPN-challenger FS1 had half the coverage of women's sports than ESPN's *SportsCenter* did: dropping from 2% to less than 1% of all clock-time. Women's sports coverage in the United States accounts for only 1.5% of television sports coverage and 5.7% of newspaper articles (Schmidt, 2018), and in the United Kingdom and Australia less than 10% of all sports media is devoted to women (Australian Sports Commission, 2014; Schmidt, 2018). Schmidt (2018) content-analysed 3,382 sport sections in popular newspapers in three nations (United States, United Kingdom, Australia) finding that 84% ($N = 2,841$) of all articles were devoted to men's sports, 3% ($N = 103$) of articles were dedicated solely to women's sports and the remaining 10.5% ($N = 356$) articles were about something other than specifically men's or women's sports (Schmidt, 2018). This sample is large enough to conclude that there is a significant disparity for how men's and women's sports are communicated in the media on an international scale.

There are three central reasons why women are disadvantaged through this metric. The first reason is that they are given limited coverage. Next, women's sports are perceived to be second to men's sports. The last factor is that there is constantly an emphasis on femininity for sports coverage of women (Lumpkin, 2009; Schmidt, 2016). In addition to these three inequities, sports have a long history of hegemonic masculinity, referring to the way behaviours and traits are typically associated with men, including toughness, competitiveness and aggression (Chandler & Munday, 2011; Lynch, 2009; Schmidt, 2018). This hegemony allows stereotypes to be formed, shaping a social and gender hierarchy that advantages men and marginalises women (Connell & Messerschmidt, 2005; Schmidt, 2018). Aside from hegemony, cultivation theory (Morgan, Shanahan, & Signorielli, 2009) also explains why women's and men's sports have unequal coverage (Schmidt, 2016), as it pertains to how mass media has narrow and restricted coverage of certain people and events that is repeated, causing people to develop a schema consistent with what is being presented in the media. This can reinforce gender roles; with the number of women's coverage compared to men's being staggeringly unequal, stereotypes and perceptions of women's sports are perpetuated.

Disparity 2: Visual Depiction

Previous research has shown that female athletes' athleticism is devalued, and often sexualised (Daddario, 1992; Duncan, 1990; Duncan & Sayaovong, 1990; Hardin, Lynn, Walsdorf, & Hardin, 2002). Bernstein and Kian (2013) conducted a study regarding female athleticism, finding frequent depictions of passivity and few depictions of power. This is problematic as sports tend to be perceived as a competitive landscape requiring aggressiveness and dominance for athletic success (Cranmer, Brann, & Bowman, 2014; Messner, 1988). Mediated passivity of women athletes is usually advanced when a female athlete is compared to male athletes in a variety of sporting situations, including basketball and tennis (Billings, 2003; Billings, Halone, & Denham, 2002; Cranmer et al., 2014). Additionally, marginalisation based on visual depictions is amplified via high sexualisation, further de-emphasising athletic abilities and accomplishments. Cranmer et al. (2014) conducted a study about how both male and female athletes are framed in ESPN's *The Body Issue,* discovering that females were framed as less athletic, more sexualised and generally devalued compared to men in the same issue. The sexualisation of women athletes in mass media also reinforces patriarchal structures (Alper, King, & Jhally, 2002), consistent with how society often views women (Daniels, 2009). Furthermore, Grow (2008) conducted a study regarding female athletes and Nike's branding of them, finding that femininity was highlighted over athleticism. Grow claims that 'in the patriarchal world of athletics and sports, which fundamentally shape Nike as an organization, there is a social order that further constrains women by privileging femininity over athleticism' (Grow, 2008, p. 316). Such findings align with previous studies on athleticism and the sexualisation of female athletes. Furthermore, female athletes who 'show more skin' are more sexualised in the media and, subsequently, perceived as less intelligent than athletes who wear more clothes during competitions and advertisements (Gurung & Chrouser, 2007).

Visual media portrayals of men and women athletes are also different because male athletes in advertisements are shown mostly by their faces only, while women athletes are usually shown in full-body photos. Archer, Iritani, Kimes, and Barrios (1983) suggest that face-only photos suggest power and superiority, while full-body photos demonstrate inferiority and indicate that women's bodies are more important than their faces, reinforcing gendered social norms. This disparity between male and female athletes is shown in how they pose for their social media, a platform seen as more athlete-controlled by allowing athletes to determine the degree of connection with fans and other public figures, decreasing social distance (Emmons & Mocarski, 2014; Kassing & Sanderson, 2010; Pegoraro, 2010). Social media also functions as a place where athletes can market themselves (Yan, 2011), yet the visual depictions of male and female athletes are strikingly different. Emmons and Mocarski (2014) performed a visual content analysis to explain gender differences in athletes' Facebook posts, discovering that female athletes were more likely to be smiling and looking at the camera, in contrast to stoic, candid shots more frequently offered by male athletes. This suggests that female athletes need to be seen (Grosz, 1994) in idealised, posed situations (Emmons & Mocarski, 2014). In all, visual depictions of women athletes are consistently troubling and endemically problematic.

Disparity 3: Linguistic Depiction

In sport, women are often described differently than their male counterparts. According to Stanley (1977), these asymmetrical gender differences in describing them tend to mark women as 'other', reinforcing gender hierarchies. In one of the first studies conducted on this disparity, Messner, Duncan, and Jensen (1993) found that women were marked as 'the other'; for instance, men college basketball teams participated in the 'NCAA National Championship' while women basketball teams participated in the 'NCAA Women's National Championship'. Names were also mentioned much more for male athletes than female athletes, likely a function of broadcaster familiarity and knowledge as it is difficult to know names without regular season media coverage. This study also found that the women were referred to as 'girls', aligning with Koivula's (1999) study which found female athletes are frequently referenced by broadcasters as 'girls' rather than 'women'.

Similar to the aforementioned research, an analysis of broadcaster commentary of a tennis match between Martina Navratilova and Jimmy Connors showed that Navratilova was not described as favourably as Connors. Navratilova was constantly referenced to as 'Martina' while Connors was acknowledged as 'Connors'. Connors was described as 'the best in tennis', while Navratilova was considered 'the best woman in tennis', further reinforcing gendered language (Billings et al., 2002; Halbert & Latimer, 1994). Other striking differences reveal that broadcasters tend to talk about men in terms of athleticism, while women often had comments directed at them regarding their personality, appearance and background (Billings et al., 2002), showing that men are described as superior, 'natural' athletes, with women described by traits that are not associated with athletics. Eastman and Billings (2000) found similar points of demarcation; on *SportsCenter*, commentators used phrases for men like, 'He's a monster', 'don't mess with him' and 'he is THE MAN'. Men were also compared to Jesus Christ, by terms like 'messiah' and 'saviour' (p. 208). Women were not described in similar manners (partly because they were rarely described at all). In addition, the dating lives of women were mentioned frequently with athleticism downplayed. The collective findings illustrate clear differences in how men and women athletes are described divergently in a variety of media outlets.

The Intermingling of Gender/Nationality: Social Identity Theory in Action

Communication research includes a collection of theories that relate to group membership, ranging from the tacitly joined to the explicitly identified. This programme of theories is based in the belief that there are two ways to define oneself: by who one *is*, and by who one *is not*. For instance, social comparison theory (Festinger, 1954) advances the position that similarities within a preferred group or diminishing dissimilarities with an undesired group are both part and parcel of one's self-concept and identity. Sometimes these choices seem hard-wired within societal norms; for instance, a teen wishing to age-identify with a senior citizen group would have a very difficult time doing so. Other times, the group affiliations are more fluid; for instance, selecting a favourite English Premier League football team is largely something that can be decided without others denouncing the affiliation. Nevertheless, social comparison is all about groups in which one can embrace or reject: the desired (via upward contacts) and the undesired (via downward comparisons; see Taylor & Lobel, 1989).

Tajfel and Turner (1986) undergird social comparison theory to advance social identity theory, which formalises in-group and out-group identification. Social identity highlights the malleability of one's identity, as a person occupies multiple in-groups simultaneously and opts to activate an affiliation based on time, circumstance and surroundings. A woman might elevate their gendered identity when attending a feminist seminar; a sports fan might make their favourite team transcendent to all other affiliations when the big game is on. Differing from self-categorisation theory (Turner, Hogg, Oakes, Reicher, & Wetherell, 1987), which functions as a social identity of the group, social identity is based on individual group affiliation (or lack thereof) rather than entire groups affiliating with similar heuristics. However, each of these theories highlight how one often subconsciously opts to define oneself within a group in which they identify (in-group), or (again also without cognisance) neglect affiliation with a group in which they do not consider themselves to be similar (out-group).

In-groups and out-groups collectively form 'us vs. them' dichotomies in society based on anything from political affiliation to sexual identity to the academy which one attends. However, sport fandom seemingly operates on some of the most overt dichotomies in all of society. Cialdini, Borden, Thorne, Walker, Freeman, and Sloan's (1976) seminal work found personal pronoun use increasing as the result of a win and then decreasing as the result of a loss (e.g. 'we won' vs. 'they lost'). Cialdini et al. dubbed the concept BIRGing, or Basking in Reflected Glory, to explain the social identity connections that were not yet formally theorised by Tajfel and Turner (1986).

However, sport functions in a manner in which a multiplicity of affiliations occur within the same athletic contest. Seemingly part of a psychology that transcends cultural boundaries (see Mehus & Kolstad, 2011; Smith & Schwarz, 2003) it appears that

> ...the nature of the social relations in the intergroup context for both groups was such that it functioned, in part at least, to shape the normative dimensions of the social category driving collective action.
>
> (Stott, Hutchison, & Drury, 2001, pp. 375–376)

In a desire for group bonding within sport, self becomes less critical to the aims of the group, with the connection with the in-group creating a motivation for certain directions, forms and types of fandom. As Voci (2006) noted in a study of sport fan identity:

> The more the in-group was perceived as homogeneous and, at the same time, distinct from the out-group, the more the self was depersonalized...the more the self was depersonalized – that is, the more the self was perceived as different from the out-group and similar to other in-group members – the stronger were group phenomena.
>
> (p. 86)

Voci (2006) highlights how in the desire for group partitions ('my group is demonstrably different than the other group(s) because...'), self-interests are often sacrificed in the process. As Bruner, Dunlop, and Beauchamp (2014) observe:

> Due to shared group membership (and the positivity extoled toward those categories with which an individual possesses membership), fans of a team will be more likely to interpret the behaviors of that team favorably relative to fans of an opposing team.
>
> (p. 52)

The blunting of schisms for a common sport-based cause is well documented. Melton and Cunningham (2014) identified how sport helped to counteract negative feelings about stigmatised demographic groups, such as people within the LGBTQ community. Delia (2015) described the sport fanship shuffling of the identity deck, noting that (at least temporarily) the groups in which people divide are trumped by sporting interests, via

> ...blasting friends and family who are supporters of rival universities (i.e., not strangers); although they share group identities with these individuals (e.g., same hometown, gender,

social class), these commonalities are pushed aside when engaging
in blasting behaviours.

(Delia, 2015, p. 402)

Even before formally advancing social identity–based theoretical constructs, Turner (1975) noted that sports often function as an exception to most societal rules for connection and disconnection with other groups.

Not all sports function in the same manner; the greater the stakes, the more power in-group identification and out-group derogation have to shape conversations, attitudes and desires (Dimmock & Grove, 2005, p. 44). It appears that the temporary loss of the here and now that Morse (1990) references leads one to critically evaluate less and focus more on the overt divisions of the sporting event: the clash of the teams, the different colours of the uniforms. Devlin and Billings (2016) found that there were many overlapping forms of identity fused within an international sporting competition (the men's FIFA World Cup), with allegiance to sport, nation and team all unfurling in significantly different manners. Brown, Billings, Devlin, and Brown-Devlin (2020) uncovered similarly overlapping yet distinctive functions of fandom in the 2018 Winter Olympics, finding that sport, Olympic, team and home nation each altered the viewing experience and motivations in different ways, forging 'rings of fandom' that warranted further scholarly exploration.

Enter: International, Mixed-sex Sports Competitions

International sports mega-events such as the Olympics or the FIFA Women's World Cup ultimately play an intriguing role in social identity as they move nationality from a variable that is largely seen as a constant (all from the same country) to one that often is viewed as a binary ('us' vs. 'them'). As an exemplar of how one variable grows to supersede another, consider the findings from Bruce (2014) who studied Paralympic athletes to find that many of the schisms previously found in other studies of disability (Cherney, Lindemann, & Hardin, 2015; Hardin, 2006; Hardin & Hardin, 2003) were somewhat dissipated in the light of the 'us/them' dichotomy. Not only were a nation's athletes more visible because of a home nation affiliation, but they were also depicted with more depth and nuance than what was typically found in media. Bruce argued that such a finding could be a viable path forward towards positive representations of underrepresented or under-described groups.

This chapter argues that such social identity theoretical principles are present when nationality mixes with a different variable: gender. Much as Bruce (2014) did not claim any level of long-term panacea through this combining of variables, we acknowledge that wrapping women's sports in a national flag is not any sort of solution. However, the fact that women's sports can be wrapped in a national flag with the result being demonstrably different representations cannot be ignored. As such, we contrast the problematic gender differences in sport highlighted earlier in this chapter with the gender representations now found in international mega-sporting competitions. Again, we use the same three metrics as before, albeit with now significantly different results.

Augmented Disparity 1: Lack of Media Exposure

To reiterate the baselines involved in everyday sport, North American sports television networks typically offer women's coverage roughly two percent of the time or less (Billings & Young, 2015; Cooky et al., 2015). Other nations fare a bit better, but with typically less than 10% of all available time (Australian Sports Commission, 2014; Schmidt, 2018). Thus, international sports have always provided stark comparisons, but never more so than the Olympic Games.

Consider the longitudinal work in the United States synopsised in the book by Billings, Angelini, and MacArthur (2018). Over a 20-year period, women Olympians always received demonstrably more clock-time within NBC's prime-time coverage, with an absolute baseline of 33% in a Winter Games and 46% in a Summer Games. The same US sports media ecosphere offering frames of exclusion in much of its annual content highlighted women athletes exponentially more in the Olympics. For the sake of brevity, we include just one snapshot of the Olympic exception here, using just the Summer Games as exemplar. The combined work of Billings et al. (2018) is offered in Table 12.1.

As Table 12.1 shows, not only did women athletes receive far more coverage than any daily sports media outlet would offer, the women's share *grew* gradually over the 20-year composite of time. In both of the last two Summer Olympics (London [2012] and Rio [2016]), women received the majority of coverage. While many reasons could be postulated (and this table provides sound reference for the metrics that follow), Billings and Angelini (2019) argued that the number of medals won by each gender was likely a predictive role in projecting the amount of media coverage each gender would receive. Since women earned the majority of the US medals in these two Summer Games, for instance, the network producers seemingly blunted any notion of gender division in favour of showing home nation athletes succeeding. Fig. 12.1 shows the strong correlation between these two variables, medals won and clock-time received in the prime-time coverage.

Of course, this is a mere exemplar and is one specifically focused on the United States. However, this appears to be an overt strategy for commercial companies, prioritising home athletes doing well (Billings, 2006).

Other international sporting exemplars must utilise different metrics. The FIFA Women's World Cup, for instance, is now often shown in its entirety as even preliminary rounds featured no more than four matches per day. Thus, exposure becomes a trickier variable, dictated more by whether something airs for free, broader access (for instance, France's TF1) or relegated to less accessible pay media providers (for instance, France's Canal+). However, ultimate audience attainment illustrates the 'flag over gender' model in action; the 2019 FIFA Women's World Cup broke audience records, with a global audience of 1.12

Table 12.1. Clock-time for Women in the Summer Olympic Games (1996–2016).

Event	1996 (Atlanta)	%	2000 (Sydney)	%	2004 (Athens)	%	2008 (Beijing)	%	2012 (London)	%	2016 (Rio)	%	Total	%
Archery	0:00	0.0	0:00	0.0	<0:01	<0.1	0:00	0.0	0:00	0.0	<0:01	<0.1	<0:01	<0.1
Badminton	0:00	0.0	0:00	0.0	<0:01	<0.1	0:00	0.0	0:00	0.0	0:00	0.0	<0:01	<0.1
Basketball	0:17	1.7	0:15	1.6	0:03	0.2	0:00	0.0	0:02	0.1	0:02	0.1	0:39	0.5
Beach Volleyball	0:00	0.0	0:00	0.0	2:00	9.8	3:35	15.3	3:39	15.3	4:46	20.0	14:00	11.4
Boxing	n.a.	n.a.	n.a.	n.a.	n.a.	n.a.	n.a.	n.a.	<0:01	<0.1	<0:01	<0.1	<0:01	<0.1
Canoeing	0:13	1.3	0:00	0.0	0:15	1.2	0:00	0.0	0:00	0.0	<0:01	<0.1	0:28	0.4
Cycling	0:43	4.3	0:00	0.0	<0:01	<0.1	0:11	0.8	0:16	1.1	0:03	0.2	1:13	1.0
Diving	2:35	15.3	2:04	14.0	3:08	15.4	2:54	12.4	2:44	11.4	1:38	6.8	15:03	12.2
Equestrian	0:06	0.6	0:00	0.0	<0:01	<0.1	0:00	0.0	0:00	0.0	0:00	0.0	0:06	0.1
Fencing	0:00	0.0	0:00	0.0	0:05	0.4	0:04	0.3	<0:01	<0.1	<0:01	<0.1	0:09	0.1
Field Hockey	0:00	0.0	0:00	0.0	<0:01	<0.1	0:00	0.0	<0:01	<0.1	<0:01	<0.1	<0:01	<0.1
Golf	n.a.	n.a.	n.a.	n.a.	n.a.	n.a.	n.a.	n.a.	n.a.	n.a.	0:01	0.1	0:01	<0.1
Gymnastics	9:34	57.2	5:04	34.3	6:09	30.2	8:04	34.4	6:57	29.0	6:37	27.7	42:25	34.5
Handball	0:00	0.0	0:00	0.0	<0:01	<0.1	0:00	0.0	0:00	0.0	0:00	0.0	<0:01	<0.1
Judo	0:00	0.0	0:00	0.0	<0:01	<0.1	0:00	0.0	0:00	0.0	0:01	0.1	0:01	<0.1
Modern Pentathlon	n.a.	n.a.	0:00	0.0	0:00	0.0	0:00	0.0	0:00	0.0	0:00	0.0	0:00	0.0

Table 12.1. (Continued)

Event	1996 (Atlanta)	%	2000 (Sydney)	%	2004 (Athens)	%	2008 (Beijing)	%	2012 (London)	%	2016 (Rio)	%	Total	%
Rhythmic Gymnastics	0:02	0.2	0:00	0.0	<0:01	<0.1	0:00	0.0	<0:01	<0.1	0:00	0.0	0:02	<0.1
Rowing	0:00	0.0	0:07	0.8	0:14	1.1	0:12	0.9	0:15	1.0	0:04	0.3	0:52	0.7
Rugby	n.a.	n.a.	n.a.	n.a.	n.a.	n.a.	n.a.	n.a.	n.a.	n.a.	<0:01	<0.1	<0:01	<0.1
Sailing	0:00	0.0	0:00	0.0	<0:01	<0.1	0:00	0.0	0:00	0.0	0:00	0.0	<0:01	<0.1
Shooting	0:00	0.0	0:00	0.0	0:00	0.0	<0:01	<0.1	0:01	0.1	0:02	0.1	0:03	<0.1
Soccer	0:23	2.3	0:00	0.0	0:14	1.1	0:00	0.0	0:16	1.1	0:02	0.1	0:55	0.8
Softball	0:30	3.0	0:00	0.0	0:00	0.0	0:02	0.1	n.a.	n.a.	n.a.	n.a.	0:32	0.4
Swimming	0:55	5.5	2:06	14.2	3:00	14.7	3:15	13.9	4:04	17.0	5:04	21.2	18:24	15.0
Synch. Swimming	0:21	2.1	0:00	0.0	0:19	1.6	0:00	0.0	<0:01	<0.1	0:00	0.0	0:40	0.5
Table Tennis	0:00	0.0	0:00	0.0	<0:01	<0.1	0:00	0.0	0:00	0.0	<0:01	<0.1	<0:01	<0.1
Taekwondo	n.a.	n.a.	0:04	0.5	<0:01	0.0	0:00	0.0	0:00	0.0	<0:01	<0.1	0:04	<0.1
Tennis	0:03	0.3	0:02	0.2	0:01	0.1	0:00	0.0	0:02	0.1	<0:01	<0.1	0:08	0.1
Track and Field	1:02	6.2	3:39	24.7	4:05	20.0	4:59	21.3	4:24	18.4	5:20	22.4	23:29	19.1
Trampoline	n.a.	n.a.	0:00	0.0	0:11	0.9	0:10	0.7	<0:01	<0.1	0:00	0.0	0:21	0.3
Triathlon	n.a.	n.a.	0:40	4.5	0:22	1.8	0:00	0.0	0:01	0.1	0:04	0.3	1:07	0.9
Volleyball	0:00	0.0	0:46	5.2	0:12	1.0	0:00	0.0	1:13	5.1	0:02	0.1	2:13	1.8

	C1	C2	C3	C4	C5	C6	Total
Water Polo	n.a.	0.0 / 0:00	0.0 / <0:01	0.1 / 0:02	0.1 / 0:02	0.1 / 0:04	<0.1
Weightlifting	n.a.	0.0 / 0:00	0.0 / <0:01	0.0 / <0:01	0.0 / <0:01	0.0 / <0:01	<0.1
Wrestling	n.a.	n.a.	0.0 / 0:00	0.0 / 0:00	0.0 / 0:00	0.0 / 0:00	<0.1
Women's Total	100.0 / 16:44	100.0 / 14:47	100.0 / 20:22	100.0 / 23:26	100.0 / 23:56	100.0 / 23:52	100.0 / 122:59
% incl.men	49.3	47.5	47.7	45.8	54.8	53.7	49.8

*Taekwondo, Trampoline and Triathlon were added to the Olympic programme starting at the 2000 Games. Golf and rugby were added to the Olympic programme starting at the 2016 Games. Women's events were added to the Olympic programme for Modern Pentathlon, Water Polo and Weightlifting starting at the 2000 Games, Wrestling starting at the 2004 Games and Boxing starting at the 2012 Games. Softball was removed from the Olympic programme as of the 2012 Games in London.

Women Athlete (%'s)

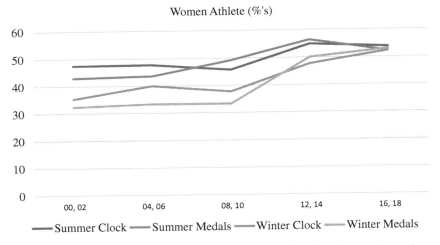

Fig. 12.1.   Percentage of Women's Medals Won by Proportion of
Received Clock-time.

billion viewers (Glass, 2019). Many nations witnessed virtual night-and-day differences in interest. For instance, the winning team in the 2019 World Cup was
the United States, garnering a national audience of 15.6 million for the championship match in July (Battaglio, 2019). Just five months later, the National
Women's Soccer League (NWLS) Championship registered 166,000 viewers
(Michelis & Nwulu, 2019), the highest NWLS rating in three years, but just
slightly more than 1% of the audience in the World Cup Final, where nations (not
cities within a single nation) were competing. Thus, from the Olympics to the
World Cup, women athletes manage to move from being bit players to starring
roles when donning the colours and flag of their home nation.

Augmented Disparity 2: Visual Depiction

Visual representation of women athletes within international sporting events is a
double-edged sword as media representations often depict dichotomies for women
athletes, such as the pretty vs. the powerful (Smallwood, Brown, & Billings, 2014).
Dashper (2018) notes this tension, finding that Olympic 'coverage is now rarely
overly sexual, but continues to be framed by narrow heteronormative ideals of
acceptable sporting femininity' (p. 1753). When considering the troubling findings
in the aforementioned non-international visual depictions, women Olympians are
less likely to have disproportionate highlighting of femininity over athleticism
(Grow, 2008) and overt sexualisation (Cranmer et al., 2014) or be rendered in
staged, non-athletic, passive poses (Emmons & Mocarski, 2014). Nevertheless, as
Dashper (2018) highlights, frames for women Olympians still are fairly limited,

ranging from a focus on celebrity to other ways in which the female body is important from the vantage point of the male gaze.

However, the actual media coverage dedicated to international women's athletics rarely features these poses. Coche and Tuggle (2016) showed that Olympic women's depictions were predominantly in competition rather than staged, passive elements, and McCann (2019) reports on how women athletes in the World Cup were able to highlight athleticism and attractiveness in equal measure, arguing that 'muscles and make-up mix just fine' (para. 1).

It is fair to refer back to Table 12.1 and conclude that the Olympics features women in sports that often include young females in swimsuits and leotards, as Coche and Tuggle (2016, p. 121) conclude that more 'socially acceptable' women's sports are highlighted. Nevertheless, these offerings inordinately highlight women athletes in action, playing the sports in which they excel. That single feature makes international sport depictions progressive when compared to most other aspects of women's sport media.

Augmented Disparity 3: Linguistic Depiction

A final metric on which to consider women's athletics within international mega-sporting competitions is the language used to describe the athletes, which, as previously documented, often disparages women's accomplishments and legitimacy (see Koivula, 1999). Here we again fail to witness equality in all forms, yet scholars now find there is less overt stereotyping and more notions of difference and divergence of dialogue.

Within the Olympic Games of the 1990s, for instance, women athletes received a heightened number of comments about their attractiveness when compared to their male athlete counterparts, but then these differences failed to emerge in any twenty-first century analysis (Billings et al., 2018). Differences continue to emerge in ways that likely reflect slight differences in the actual athletes competing more than any hard-wired gender stereotyping. For example, the US coverage of the 2016 Summer Games featured more comments about men athletes succeeding due to intelligence, yet also showed that women athletes were disproportionately more likely to have their strength and courage highlighted (Billings et al., 2018). Even when some findings could be seen as skewing towards a stereotype (such as a finding of highlighting men's experience and reducing women to novice status), those must be mitigated with the sport being enacted. For instance, men gymnasts tend to peak at an older age than women gymnasts, who often retire by their early 20s, meaning that a comment about the heightened experience of a male might be more of an age descriptor than one about the perceived lack of expertise of women gymnasts.

Beyond the Olympics, scholars continue to find that media outlets depict women's sports and the athletes that play them both positively and with affirming language (Petty & Pope, 2019). Of course, there is much more work to be done in this regard. Black and Fielding-Lloyd (2017), for instance, contend that English media still use events such as the Women's FIFA World Cup to re-establish women as outsiders. The claim being made here is not one resembling cures, fixes and solutions but rather of progress, advancement and moves towards equity that the international sports mega-event seems to be facilitating, at least somewhat, for women athletes.

Conclusion

Previous research on female and male athlete disparities suggested a significant gender difference regarding female athletes' lack of media exposure, visual overt sexualisation and femininity was highlighted over athleticism when being described. However, the findings in this chapter suggest that the marginalisation of female athletes is being mitigated and is not as common as it once was. Women's coverage on NBC has grown in the last 20 years and the home nation is shown to be more important over the gender of the athlete. Women (in the United States) have also won more medals in recent Olympics, and their success is at the forefront, rather than their gender. International female athletes in events like the Olympics and the World Cup are also not overly sexualised visually as previous investigations into this issue suggested. Olympic women's depictions are also beginning to show them in competitive environments, rather than staged elements. Lastly, scholars are concluding that female stereotyping is diminishing, and their strength and courage in beginning to be emphasised. While progress still needs to be made, these findings are positive because they suggest that female athletes are starting to get the credibility and respect they deserve.

References

Alper, L., & King, K. (Producers), & Jhally, S. (Director). (2002). *Playing unfair: The media image of the female athlete* [Motion picture]. Northampton, MA: Media Education Foundation.

Archer, D., Iritani, B., Kimes, D. D., & Barrios, M. (1983). Face-ism: Five studies of sex differences in facial prominence. *Journal of Personality and Social Psychology*, *45*(4), 725–735.

Australian Sports Commission. (2014, April). Women in sport broadcasting analysis. Retrieved from https://secure.ausport.gov.au/__data/assets/pdf_file/0007/615913/Wom en_in_Sport_Broadcasting_Analysis_April_2012_-_March_2014.PDF. Accessed on January 15, 2020.

Battaglio, S. (2019). Women's World Cup final draws 15.6 million viewers as the U.S. scores a big win. *Los Angeles Times*, July 8. Retrieved from https://www.latimes.com/business/hollywood/la-fi-ct-women-soccer-ratings-20190708-story.html. Accessed on January 15, 2020.

Bernstein, A., & Kian, E. M. (2013). Gender and sexualities in sport media. In P. M. Pedersen (Ed.), *Routledge handbook of sport communication* (pp. 319–327). London: Routledge.

Billings, A. C. (2003). Dueling genders: Announcer bias in the 1999 U.S. Open tennis tournament. In R. S. Brown & D. J. O'Rourke, III (Eds.), *Case studies in sports communication* (pp. 51–62). Westport, CT: Praeger.

Billings, A. C. (2006). *Olympic media: Inside the biggest show on television*. London: Routledge.

Billings, A. C., & Angelini, J. R. (2019). Equity achieved?: A longitudinal examination of biological sex representation in the NBC Olympic telecast (2000–2018). *Communication & Sport*, 7(5), 551–564.

Billings, A. C., Angelini, J. R., & MacArthur, P. J. (2018). *Olympic television: Broadcasting the biggest show on Earth*. London: Routledge.

Billings, A. C., Halone, K. K., & Denham, B. E. (2002). 'Man' that was a 'pretty' shot: An analysis of gendered broadcast commentary of the 2000 men's and women's NCAA final four basketball tournaments. *Mass Communication & Society*, 5(3), 295–315.

Billings, A. C., & Young, B. D. (2015). Comparing flagship news programs: Women's sport coverage in ESPN's *SportsCenter* and FOX Sports 1's *FOX Sports Live*. *Electronic News*, 9(1), 3–16.

Black, J., & Fielding-Lloyd, B. (2017). Re-establishing the 'outsiders': English press coverage of the 2015 FIFA Women's World Cup. *International Review for the Sociology of Sport*, 54(3), 282–301.

Brown, K. A., Billings, A. C., Devlin, M. B., & Brown-Devlin, N. A. (2020, in press). Rings of fandom: Overlapping motivations of sport, Olympic, team, and home nation fans in the 2018 Winter Olympic Games. *Journal of Broadcasting & Electronic Media*, 64(1), 20–40.

Bruce, T. (2014). Us and them: The influence of discourses of nationalism on media coverage of the Paralympics. *Disability & Society*, 29(9), 1443–1459.

Bruner, M. W., Dunlop, W. L., & Beauchamp, M. R. (2014). A social identity perspective on group processes in sport and exercise. In M. R. Beauchamp & M. A. Eys (Eds.), *Group dynamics in exercise and sport psychology* (2nd ed., pp. 38–52). New York, NY: Routledge.

Chandler, D., & Munday, R. (2011). *A dictionary of media and communication*. Oxford: Oxford University Press.

Cherney, J. L., Lindemann, K., & Hardin, M. (2015). Research in communication, disability, and sport. *Communication & Sport*, 3(1), 8–26.

Cialdini, R. B., Borden, R. J., Thorne, A., Walker, M. R., Freeman, S., & Sloan, L. R. (1976). Basking in reflected glory: Three (football) field studies. *Journal of Personality and Social Psychology*, 34, 366–375.

Coche, R., & Tuggle, C. A. (2016). The women's Olympics?: A gender analysis of NBC's coverage of the 2012 London Summer Games. *Electronic News*, 10(2), 121–138.

Connell, R. W., & Messerschmidt, J. W. (2005). Hegemonic masculinity rethinking the concept. *Gender & Society*, 19(6), 829–859.

Cooky, C., Messner, M. A., & Musto, M. (2015). "It's dude time!": A quarter century of excluding women's sports in televised new and highlight shows. *Communication & Sport*, 3(3), 261–287.

Cranmer, G. A., Brann, M., & Bowman, N. D. (2014). Male athletes, female aesthetics: The continued ambivalence toward female athletes in ESPN's the Body Issue. *International Journal of Sport Communication*, 7, 145–165.

Daddario, G. (1992). Swimming against the tide: 'Sports Illustrated's imagery of female athletes in a swimsuit world'. *Women's Studies in Communication*, 15, 49–64.

Daniels, E. A. (2009). Sex objects, athletes, and sexy athletes: How media representations of women athletes can impact adolescent girls and college women. *Journal of Adolescent Research, 24*(4), 399–422.

Dashper, K. (2018). Smiling assassins, brides-to-be and super mums: The importance of gender and celebrity in media framing of female athletes at the 2016 Olympic Games. *Sport in Society, 21*(11), 1739–1757.

Delia, E. B. (2015). The exclusiveness of group identity in celebrations of team success. *Sport Management Review, 18*(3), 396–406.

Devlin, M. B., & Billings, A. C. (2016). Examining the world's game in the United States: Impact of nationalized qualities on fan identification and consumption of the 2014 FIFA World Cup. *Journal of Broadcasting & Electronic Media, 60*(1), 40–60.

Dimmock, J. A., & Grove, J. R. (2005). Relationship of fan identification to determinants of aggression. *Journal of Applied Sport Psychology, 17*(1), 37–47.

Duncan, M. C. (1990). Sports photographs and sexual difference: Images of women and men in the 1984 and the 1988 Olympic Games. *Sociology of Sport Journal, 7*(1), 22–43.

Duncan, M. C., & Sayaovong, A. (1990). Photographic images and gender in *Sports Illustrated for Kids. Play & Culture, 3*, 91–116.

Eastman, S. T., & Billings, A. C. (2000). Sportscasting and sports reporting: The power of gender bias. *Journal of Sport and Social Issues, 24*(2), 192–213.

Emmons, B., & Mocarski, R. (2014). She poses, he performs: A visual content analysis of male and female professional athlete Facebook profile photos. *Visual Communication Quarterly, 21*(3), 125–137.

Festinger, L. (1954). A theory of social comparison processes. *Human Relations, 7*(2), 117–140.

Glass, A. (2019, October 21). FIFA Women's World Cup breaks viewership records. *Forbes.* Retrieved from https://www.forbes.com/sites/alanaglass/2019/10/21/fifa-womens-world-cup-breaks-viewership-records/#66688f921884. Accessed on January 15, 2020.

Grosz, E. (1994). *Volatile bodies: Toward a corporeal feminism.* Bloomington, IN: Indiana University Press.

Grow, J. M. (2008). The gender of branding: Early Nike women's advertising a feminist antinarrative. *Women's Studies in Communication, 31*(3), 312–343.

Gurung, R. A. R., & Chrouser, C. J. (2007). Predicting objectification: Do provocative clothing and observer characteristics matter? *Sex Roles, 57*, 91–99.

Halbert, C., & Latimer, M. (1994). "Battling" gendered language: An analysis of the language used by sports commentators in a televised coed tennis competition. *Sociology of Sport Journal, 11*, 298–308.

Hanson, V. (2012). The inequality of sport: Women < men. *The Review: A Journal of Undergraduate Student Research, 13*, 15–22.

Hardin, M. (2006). Disability and sport: (Non)coverage of an athletic paradox. In A. Raney & J. Bryant (Eds.), *Handbook of sports and media* (pp. 625–635). New York, NY: LEA.

Hardin, B., & Hardin, M. (2003). Conformity and conflict: Wheelchair athletes discuss sport media. *Adapted Physical Activity Quarterly, 20*, 246–259.

Hardin, M., Lynn, S., Walsdorf, K., & Hardin, B. (2002). The framing of sexual difference in *SI for Kids* editorial photos. *Mass Communication & Society, 5*, 341–359.

Kane, M. J., LaVoi, N. M., & Fink, J. S. (2013). Exploring elite female athletes' interpretations of sport media images: A window into the construction of social identity and 'selling sex' in women's sports. *Communication & Sport*, *1*(3), 269–298.

Kassing, J. W., & Sanderson, J. (2010). Fan-athlete interaction and Twitter: Tweeting through the Giro: A case study. *International Journal of Sport Communication*, *3*(1), 113–128.

Koivula, N. (1999). Gender stereotyping in televised media sport coverage. *Sex Roles*, *41*(7–8), 589–604.

Lumpkin, A. (2009). Female representation in feature articles published by Sports Illustrated in the 1990's. *Women in Sport & Physical Activity Journal*, *18*(2), 45.

Lynch, A. (2009). Hegemonic masculinity. In J. O'Brien (Ed.), *Encyclopaedia of gender and society* (pp. 411–413). Thousand Oaks, CA: Sage.

McCann, A. (2019). World Cup players say muscles and makeup mix just fine, thanks. *The New York Times*, June 20. Retrieved from https://www.nytimes.com/2019/06/20/style/world-cup-women-hair-gender.html. Accessed on January 15, 2020.

Mehus, I., & Kolstad, A. (2011). Football team identification in Norway: Spectators of local and national football matches. *Social Identities*, *17*(6), 833–845.

Melton, E. N., & Cunningham, G. B. (2014). Examining the workplace experiences of sport employees who are LGBT: A social categorization theory perspective. *Journal of Sport Management*, *28*(1), 21–33.

Messner, M. (1988). Sports and male domination: The female athlete as contested ideological terrain. *Sociology of Sport Journal*, *5*(3), 197–211.

Messner, M., & Cooky, C. (2010). Gender in televised sports: News and highlights shows, 1989–2009. *USC Center for Feminist Research*, p. 4.

Messner, M. A., Duncan, M. C., & Jensen, K. (1993). Separating the men from the girls: The gendered language of televised sports. *Gender & Society*, *7*(1), 121–137.

Messner, M., Duncan, M. C., & Williams, N. (2006). The revolution is not being televised. *Contexts*, *5*(3), 34–38.

Michelis, B., & Nwulu, M. (2019, December). National Women's Soccer League Championship on ESPN is the most-viewed NWSL match in three years. *ESPN Press Room*. Retrieved from https://espnpressroom.com/us/press-releases/2019/10/national-womens-soccer-league-championship-on-espn-is-the-most-viewed-nwsl-match-in-three-years/. Accessed on January 15, 2020.

Morgan, M., Shanahan, J., & Signorielli, N. (2009). Growing up with television: Cultivation processes. In J. Bryant & M. B. Oliver (Eds.), *Media effects: Advances in theory and research* (3rd ed., pp. 34–45). New York, NY: Routledge.

Morse, M. (1990). An ontology of everyday distraction: The freeway, the mall, and television. In P. Mellacamp (Ed.), *The logics of television*. Bloomington, IN: Indiana University Press.

Pegoraro, A. (2010). Look who's talking - athletes on Twitter: A case study. *International Journal of Sport Communication*, *3*(4), 501–515.

Petty, K., & Pope, S. (2019). A new age for media coverage of women's sport?: An analysis of English media coverage of the 2015 FIFA Women's World Cup. *Sociology*, *53*(3), 486–502.

Schmidt, H. C. (2016). Women's sports coverage remains largely marginalized. *Newspaper Research Journal*, *37*(3), 275–298.

Schmidt, H. C. (2018). Forgotten athletes and token reporters: Analyzing the gender bias in sports journalism. *Atlantic Journal of Communication*, *26*(1), 59–74.

Scibetti, R. (2014, February 6). Retrieved from https://www.thebusinessofsports.com/2014/02/06/nielsen-year-in-sports-media-report-2013. Accessed on January 15, 2020.

Smallwood, R., Brown, N., & Billings, A. C. (2014). Female bodies on display: Attitudes regarding female athlete photos in *Sports Illustrated's* swimsuit issue and *ESPN: The Magazine's* body issue. *Journal of Sports Media, 9*(1), 1–22.

Smith, R. A., & Schwarz, N. (2003). Language, social comparison, and college football: Is your school less similar to the rival school than the rival school is to your school? *Communication Monographs, 70*(4), 351–360.

Stanley, J. P. (1977). Gender-marking in American English: Usage and reference. In A. P. Nilsen, H. Bosmajian, H. C. Gershuny, & J. P. Stanley (Eds.), *Sexism in language* (pp. 43–74). Urbana, IL: National Council of Teachers.

Stott, C., Hutchison, P., & Drury, J. (2001). 'Hooligans' abroad? Inter-group dynamics, social identity and participation in collective 'disorder' at the 1998 World Cup Finals. *British Journal of Social Psychology, 40*(3), 359–384.

Tajfel, H., & Turner, J. C. (1986). The social identity theory of inter-group behavior. In S. Worchel & L. W. Austin (Eds.), *Psychology of intergroup relations*. Chicago, IL: Nelson-Hall.

Taylor, S. E., & Lobel, M. (1989). Social comparison activity under threat: Downward evaluation and upward contacts. *Psychological Review, 96*(4), 569–575.

Turner, J. C. (1975). Social comparison and social identity: Some prospects for intergroup behaviour. *European Journal of Social Psychology, 5*(1), 1–34.

Turner, J. C., Hogg, M. A., Oakes, P. J., Reicher, S. D., & Wetherell, M. S. (1987). *Rediscovering the social group: A self-categorization theory*. Oxford: Blackwell.

Voci, A. (2006). Relevance of social categories, depersonalization and group processes: Two field tests of self-categorization theory. *European Journal of Social Psychology, 36*(1), 73–90.

Wenner, L. A., & Billings, A. C. (Eds.). (2017). *Sport, media, and mega-events*. London: Routledge.

Yan, J. (2011). Social media in branding: Fulfilling a need. *Journal of Brand Management, 18*(9), 688–696.

Chapter 13

Conclusions: Sport, Gender and Mega-Events: Looking to the Future

Katherine Dashper

The chapters collected in this book represent a broad range of approaches to studying gender and mega-events and illustrate the diversity of issues and challenges that sport mega-events face in the twenty-first century. In relation to gender, sport mega-events can be best understood as paradoxical as they both contribute to reinforcing *and at the same time* provide challenge to traditional gender norms, discourses and practices.

In many ways, sport mega-events are conservative entities that help reinforce gender norms and delineate what is acceptable and praiseworthy in relation to gender, race, (dis)ability, sexuality and nationality. One of the most injurious aspects of contemporary mega-events is the policing of bodies through ongoing sex testing which, as Anna Adlwarth explained in Chapter 2, marginalises – often excludes – inter* and trans* athletes, as well as othering athletes through racial and colonial norms and discourses. Athleticism and power continue to be considered incompatible with femininity (see Darvin & Pegoraro, Chapter 3), with women still often considered more as ornamental appendages than serious athletes (see Sturm, Chapter 6). Hegemonic forms of masculinity still celebrate heroism and stoicism for athletes (see Smith, Chapter 4), and aggression and violence in many male fan cultures (see Sly, Chapter 5). Sport mega-events, as major capitalist ventures, often exacerbate inequalities, further marginalising those already on the side-lines of wealth and power in sport, as happened when the FIFA Men's World Cup was hosted in South Africa and then Brazil (see Knijnik, Balram & Kanemasu, Chapter 8). In these and other ways, sport mega-events reinforce the status quo of global sport, supporting and even strengthening gendered discourses that marginalise and discriminate against many groups and individuals.

However, at the same time, sport mega-events offer highly visible and potent opportunities to challenge and disrupt the norms of global sport. The example of the *baianas* in Brazil, as discussed by Knijnik, Balram and Kanemasu in Chapter 8, illustrates the power of marginalised groups to challenge the might of organisations like FIFA and to win. The extraordinary acts of everyday resistance by

Sport, Gender and Mega-Events, 239–246
Copyright © 2022 by Emerald Publishing Limited
All rights of reproduction in any form reserved
doi:10.1108/978-1-83982-936-920211019

these Black Brazilian women indicate that possibilities for change persist, even in the face of the seemingly impenetrable power of global sport organisations. Raduszyńska's (Chapter 9) performance-based analysis of football fans at the 2018 FIFA Men's World Cup in Russia also shows the power of everyday resistance to reclaim sport mega-events as celebrations of friendship and unity. Athletes also contribute to reimaging sport mega-events in less oppressive ways, as the disruptive self-presentation of US footballer Megan Rapinoe illustrates (see Turtiainen, Chapter 7). In a less overtly disruptive manner, the willingness of male athletes to openly discuss their mental health crises also begins to rework gender norms in the context of sport mega-events (see Smith, Chapter 4). Even efforts to increase visibility of female sporting performance, as in the case of women's football in Spain (see Valiente, Chapter 10), or to use national allegiance as a way to shift focus away from gender and onto sporting achievement (see Bowes & Kitching, Chapter 11 and Billings & Gentile, Chapter 12), show that narrow gendered discourses can be shifted, if only temporarily, in the context of sport mega-events.

This is the paradox of sport mega-events, which are both heavily implicated in maintaining current limited discourses and practices around gender, race, class and nationhood, and may also be one highly visible mechanism through which marginalisation and discrimination may be challenged and reworked. In the 21st century, sport mega-events have become a hugely significant phenomenon, impacted by increased globalisation, mediatisation and commercialisation. They are often beset with conflict – around access, human rights, gender and racism, for example – but still attract enormous audiences to watch and celebrate the extremes of human bodies and, in many ways, minds. Yet nothing stands still, and the ongoing dominance of sport mega-events in both the elite sport and planned event worlds is not assured. This final chapter considers some of the potential challenges and opportunities that may face sport mega-events in the coming years, and some of their implications for gender (in)equality.

Global Health

The writing of this book has been completed in the shadow of the COVID-19 pandemic of 2020–2021, which has forcefully highlighted just how fragile our globalised networks really are. 2020 saw the postponement of several mega-events, including the Tokyo Summer Olympic Games. At the time of writing, the International Olympic Committee (IOC) and Tokyo Organising Committee are still saying the event will go ahead in July 2021, but the ongoing devastation of the virus puts this in doubt. Measures such as athlete passports are being explored but there is a real possibility that this will be the second time that Tokyo has had its Olympics cancelled, the last time being in 1940 with the outbreak of World War II.

While COVID-19 has had a far bigger effect than any other health issue on mega-events, it is not the first time that global health has come into conflict with mega-event programming. Before the 2016 Summer Olympic Games in Rio the

Zika virus caused widespread concern, especially due to the virus' effect on pregnant women. Global health crises pose an enormous threat to the future of mega-events.

Mega-events may be particularly vulnerable to global health crises, due to the large numbers of people they involve, travelling from all over the world to congregate in a relatively small area for an intense period of time. As planning for mega-events begins many years beforehand, global health crises have potential to completely derail mega-events, often at the last minute. The economic ramifications are enormous, affecting host cities, rights holders, media partners, sponsors and insurers, among others. Insurers are facing a $2–3 billion loss if the Tokyo Olympics are cancelled in 2021 (Hussein & Cohn, 2021). There are numerous other implications, such as harm to athletes' mental health when the goal they have been focusing on for years is suddenly gone, with consequences for coaches and support teams as well (Smith, Chapter 4; Taku & Arai, 2020; see also Reardon et al., 2020). Given that mega-events are often rare opportunities for female sports and athletes to experience widespread media attention and its associated rewards (see Billings & Gentile, Chapter 12; Bowes & Kitching, Chapter 11), cancellation of mega-events will likely impact women's sport considerably. Following the COVID-19 pandemic, there are already signs that men's elite sports events will return before women's, with long-term implications for gender equality (Valiente, Chapter 10).

Emerging evidence about COVID-19 suggests that the impacts of the pandemic are gendered. Globally, women are taking on the brunt of unpaid caring responsibilities (Bahn, Cohen, & van der Meulen Rodgers, 2020), are more likely to reduce their working hours (Collins, Landivar, Ruppanner, & Scarborough, 2020) or lose their jobs and incomes (Gezici & Ozay, 2020), and rates of domestic violence against women have increased (Taub, 2020). These, and other factors, will impact on women's ability to engage with sport, as athletes, fans, coaches and in other roles. Elite athletes are already expressing concern that the pandemic will increase gender inequalities. Pre-pandemic, women's sports were experiencing growth, with increased media attention and bigger attendance at live events, but there is concern that this momentum will now be lost (Williams, 2021). There is thus potential that the pandemic may widen gender inequalities in sport.

Public perception is an important issue, and mega-event organisers will need to ensure that they are cognisant of public opinion and respond appropriately in response to global health crises that may derail mega-events (see Wang, Wang, & Yoon, 2021). It will also be important to consider the gendered implications of different health crises and efforts to mitigate those effects in relation to sport mega-events.

Ongoing Discrimination

Some of the contributions to this collection suggest that there are signs that sport mega-events may contribute to improvements in gender equality in sport (Billings & Gentile, Chapter 12; Bowes & Kitching, Chapter 11; Raduszynska, Chapter 9;

Valiente, Chapter 10). This is promising, but there are also many examples which indicate that discriminatory practices continue, from the governing of sport mega-events (Adlwarth, Chapter 2) to media framing of sports and athletes (Darvin & Pegoraro, Chapter 3).

Sport mega-events are conservative, traditional entities based on masculine, colonial-racist logics (Sykes, 2017). This was illustrated plainly when Yoshiro Mori, the head of the Tokyo 2020 organising committee, made sexist remarks in February 2021 about problems with 'talkative' women in sports organisations. Although he did eventually resign, he initially refused to do so until public pressure forced his hand. The IOC condemned Mori's comments as 'inappropriate' but did not call on him to quit (Sky Sports, 2021). In a more positive move, Mori was replaced by Japan's Olympic minister, Seiko Hashimoto, who has represented Japan at seven Olympics and is one of only a few prominent female politicians in Japan, and who acted swiftly to add more women to the Games' organising board (McCurry, 2021). This example illustrates the pervasive sexism at the heart of powerful organisations like the IOC. Discrimination continues at all levels of sport mega-events and will require ongoing efforts to address.

The Shift from the West

As noted in Chapter 1, while many Western nations are increasingly stepping back from mega-event hosting, nations in the Global South recognise mega-events as opportunities to pursue political, cultural, social and economic objectives on a global scale (see also Graeff & Knijnik, 2021). When mega-events are hosted outside of the Global North, and particularly in Muslim countries and/or those with very different social and cultural traditions to the Western Judeo-Christian societies in which mega-events originally developed, this may lead to change and (re)negotiation around numerous factors at the heart of mega-event ideologies, practices and representations (Russell, O'Connor, Dashper, & Fletcher, 2014). This may raise questions around the preparedness of some developing nations to deliver mega-events (Dowse & Fletcher, 2018), but also may have implications for gender (in)equality.

The next iteration of the FIFA Men's World Cup will take place in Qatar in 2022. Although relatively liberal in comparison to some of its neighbours, questions have been asked about the position of women in the Middle East and female fans' freedom and safety if they attend the mega-event in Qatar (Shapiro, 2016). Issues may also arise for female officials, as Sheikh Joaan bin Hamad bin Khalifa Al-Thani, brother of Qatar's ruler, recently refused to even acknowledge female officials at a FIFA Club World Cup awards ceremony, despite 'fist bumping' with male officials (Carr, 2021).

When Beijing hosted the 2008 Summer Olympic Games there was widespread international condemnation in relation to China's alleged human rights abuses, with the IOC receiving harsh criticism as the event rights holder (Brownell, 2012). Kidd (2010) suggested that the IOC needed to rethink its position on human rights, but this has largely failed to manifest. Whether in relation to indigenous and ethnic minority community rights (Knijik, Balram & Kanemasu, Chapter 8), LGBTQ + rights (Van Rheenen, 2014), forced evictions and police brutality (Talbot & Carter, 2018), worker rights (Ganji, 2016) or a variety of other issues, mega-events remain sites of struggle in relation to human rights (Horne, 2018).

Human rights abuses are not confined to emerging nations. The mistreatment of women athletes like South African runner Caster Semenya at the hand of global organisations like the IOC and World Athletics (see Adlwarth, Chapter 2), displacement of poor communities in host cities (Watt, 2013), conflicts with indigenous communities (O'Bonsawin, 2010) and athlete abuse and exploitation in numerous countries, including the United States (Smith & Pegoraro, 2020), illustrate the pervasiveness of human rights abuses in mega-events in the Global North. Issues of human rights abuses in relation to sports mega-events look set to continue.

The 'shift from the West' is only partial, however, as the next two Summer Olympic Games have been awarded to traditional Global North powers – Paris in 2024 and Los Angeles in 2028 – and the next FIFA Women's World Cup will be co-hosted by Australia and New Zealand in 2023. However, it is clear that the ambulatory nature of mega-events means that the local context of the host will impact on the event itself. These impacts prompt (re)negotiation of the underlying norms and traditions of mega-events, leading to changes which could either contribute to or hinder progress towards greater gender equality.

Mediatisation

Sport mega-events are global media spectacles, and the importance of mediatised reproduction and dissemination is not likely to diminish (see Sturm, Chapter 6). Changes in the media landscape, such as the explosion of social media, open up possibilities for fans and athletes to present their own narratives, disrupting long-established norms repeated in the mainstream media (Raduszyńska, Chapter 9; Turtiainen, Chapter 7). Fan communities may appropriate social media for less progressive means as well, such as building and sustaining hooligan communities (Sly, Chapter 5) or spreading hate and misogynistic abuse aimed at female athletes and officials (Kavanagh, Litchfield, & Osborne, 2019). Whether as a force for transformation or violence (symbolic and physical), social media has changed the media landscape and the ways in which people around the world engage with sport mega-events.

Traditional media remain an important stakeholder group in sport mega-events, however, as they continue to be the means through which most people will consume these global tournaments. As with social media, traditional media remains an ambivalent player in relation to gender equality and mega-events. Although still under-reporting women's sports, and resorting to limiting and often discriminatory frames of reference (see Darvin & Pegoraro, Chapter 3), traditional media reporting on sport mega-events represents one of the few opportunities for women's sports and athletes to receive widespread media coverage, which may be an important step towards greater gender equality (Billings & Gentile, Chapter 13; Bowes & Kitching, Chapter 11).

Environment and Climate Change

Climate change is an issue that sport mega-events will not be able to ignore for too much longer. Mega-events have major environmental impacts, related to building new infrastructure and the enormous amount of travel they entail (athletes, officials, workers, volunteers, spectators etc.). Environmental impacts are starting to receive more media and popular attention (Yoon & Wilson, 2019) and this is likely to continue to grow. The 2022 Qatar FIFA Men's World Cup has the goal of being the first carbon-neutral World Cup, and green technologies and sustainable development concepts are being deployed. This is promising, but additional efforts will be needed to reduce negative impacts on environmental, as well as some social, levels (Meza Talavera, Al-Ghamadi, & Koç, 2019).

While the impacts of climate change will be felt by everyone, these impacts will not be equal and will exacerbate existing inequalities related to gender, class, poverty and race (MacGregor, 2010). Some regions in the Global South are likely to experience the worst extremes of environmental damage and change, which will potentially clash with growing ambitions to host mega-events. The ways in which climate change and changing attitudes to environmental impacts of sports tournaments will intersect with gender and other axes of power to influence the future of sport mega-events require further investigation.

Conclusion

These and many other factors will shape the future of sport mega-events and the ways in which these global media spectacles act as sites for both the (re)production of restrictive and limiting gender norms *and* for disrupting and transforming those same practices. The chapters in this collection have explored different elements of this paradox at the heart of mega-events and illustrate the need for further critical research on the interrelationships between sport, gender and mega-events.

References

Bahn, K., Cohen, J., & van der Meulen Rodgers, Y. (2020). A feminist perspective on COVID-19 and the value of care work globally. *Gender, Work & Organization*, *27*(5), 695–699.

Brownell, S. (2012). Human rights and the Beijing Olympics: Imagined global community and the transnational public sphere 1. *The British Journal of Sociology*, *63*(2), 306–327.

Carr, J. (2021). Sheikh snubs shake: Qatari royal refuses to acknowledge female officials with a fist bump during FIFA Club World Cup awards ceremony. *Mail Online*, 12 February. Retrieved from https://www.dailymail.co.uk/news/article-9254141/Qatari-royal-refuses-acknowledge-female-officials-FIFA-Club-World-Cup-awards-ceremony.html. Accessed on February 17, 2021.

Collins, C., Landivar, L. C., Ruppanner, L., & Scarborough, W. J. (2020). COVID-19 and the gender gap in work hours. *Gender, Work & Organization*, *28*, 101–112.

Dowse, S., & Fletcher, T. (2018). Sport mega-events, the 'non-west' and the ethics of event hosting. *Sport in Society*, *21*(5), 745–761.

Ganji, S. K. (2016). Leveraging the World Cup: Mega sporting events, human rights risk, and worker welfare reform in Qatar. *Journal on Migration and Human Security*, *4*(4), 221–259.

Gezici, A., & Ozay, O. (2020). How race and gender shape COVID-19 unemployment probability. SSRN 3675022. 16 July. Retrieved from https://papers.ssrn.com/sol3/papers.cfm?abstract_id=3675022. Accessed on February 18, 2021.

Graeff, B., & Knijnik, J. (2021). If things go South: The renewed policy of sport mega events allocation and its implications for future research. *International Review for the Sociology of Sport*. doi:10.1177/1012690220981342

Horne, J. (2018). Understanding the denial of abuses of human rights connected to sports mega-events. *Leisure Studies*, *37*(1), 11–21.

Hussein, N. Z., & Cohn, C. (2021). If Tokyo Olympics cancelled, loss for insurers would be 'mind-blowingly' big. *Insurance Journal*, 27 January. Retrieved from https://www.insurancejournal.com/news/international/2021/01/27/599039.htm#:~:text=Subscribe-,If%20Tokyo%20Olympics%20Canceled%2C%20Loss%20for%20Insurers,Be%20'Mind%2DBlowingly'%20Big&text=LONDON%20%E2%80%94%20Insurers%20are%20facing%20a,event%20cancellation%20market%2C%20brokers%20say. Accessed on February 17, 2021.

Kavanagh, E., Litchfield, C., & Osborne, J. (2019). Sporting women and social media: Sexualization, misogyny, and gender-based violence in online spaces. *International Journal of Sport Communication*, *12*(4), 552–572.

Kidd, B. (2010). Human rights and the Olympic Movement after Beijing. *Sport in Society*, *13*(5), 901–910.

MacGregor, S. (2010). 'Gender and climate change': From impacts to discourses. *Journal of the Indian Ocean Region*, *6*(2), 223–238.

McCurry, J. (2021). Tokyo 2020: Japan to appoint female Olympic head after sexism row. *The Guardian*, 18 February. Retrieved from https://www.theguardian.com/sport/2021/feb/18/tokyo-2020-japan-to-appoint-olympic-seiko-hashimoto-sexism-row. Accessed on February 18, 2021.

Meza Talavera, A., Al-Ghamdi, S. G., & Koc, M. (2019). Sustainability in mega-events: Beyond Qatar 2022. *Sustainability*, *11*(22), 6407.

O'Bonsawin, C. M. (2010). 'No Olympics on stolen native land': Contesting Olympic narratives and asserting indigenous rights within the discourse of the 2010 Vancouver Games. *Sport in Society*, *13*(1), 143–156.

Reardon, C. L., Bindra, A., Blauwet, C., Budgett, R., Campriani, N., Currie, A., … Hainline, B. (2020). Mental health management of elite athletes during COVID-19: A narrative review and recommendations. *British Journal of Sports Medicine*, *55*(11), 608–615. doi:10.1136/bjsports-2020-102884

Russell, K., O'Connor, N., Dashper, K., & Fletcher, T. (2014). Sports mega events and Islam: An introduction. In K. Dashper, T. Fletcher, & N. McCullough (Eds.), *Sports events, society and culture* (pp. 189–204). London: Routledge.

Shapiro, S. (2016). What Qatar 2022 means for female fans. *Soccer Politics*. 10 April. Retrieved from https://sites.duke.edu/wcwp/2016/04/10/what-qatar-2022-means-for-female-fans/. Accessed on February 17, 2021.

Sky Sports. (2021). Yoshiro Mori: Tokyo Olympics president resigns after making sexist remarks about women. *Skye Sports*, 12 February. Retrieved from https://

www.skysports.com/olympics/news/15234/12215656/yoshiro-mori-tokyo-olympics-president-resigns-after-sexist-remarks-towards-women. Accessed on February 17, 2021.

Smith, L. R., & Pegoraro, A. (2020). Media framing of Larry Nassar and the USA gymnastics child sex abuse scandal. *Journal of Child Sexual Abuse*, 29(4), 373–392.

Sykes, H. (2017). *The sexual and gender politics of sport mega-events: Roving colonialism*. Abingdon: Routledge.

Taku, K., & Arai, H. (2020). Impact of COVID-19 on athletes and coaches, and their values in Japan: Repercussions of postponing the Tokyo 2020 Olympic and Paralympic Games. *Journal of Loss and Trauma*, 25(8), 623–630.

Talbot, A., & Carter, T. F. (2018). Human rights abuses at the Rio 2016 Olympics: Activism and the media. *Leisure Studies*, 37(1), 77–88.

Taub, A. (2020). A new COVID-19 crisis: Domestic abuse rises worldwide. *The New York Times*, 6 April. Retrieved from https://chescocf.org/wp-content/uploads/2020/04/Domestic-Abuse-Rises-Worldwide-New-York-Times.pdf. Accessed on February 17, 2021.

Van Rheenen, D. (2014). A skunk at the garden party: The Sochi Olympics, state-sponsored homophobia and prospects for human rights through mega sporting events. *Journal of Sport & Tourism*, 19(2), 127–144.

Wang, Y. Y., Wang, T. D., & Yoon, K. (2021). A methodology for the sport industry to capture public perceptions and responses in the time of COVID-19. *Journal of Emerging Technologies in Accounting*, 18(1), 205–211. doi:10.2308/JETA-2020-058

Watt, P. (2013). 'It's not for us': Regeneration, the 2012 Olympics and the gentrification of East London. *City*, 17(1), 99–118.

Williams, R. (2021). Women's sport: 80 per cent of female athletes say growth hindered during pandemic by inequalities with men's sport. *Sky Sports*, 10 February. Retrieved from https://www.skysports.com/more-sports/news/29877/12212884/womens-sport-80-per-cent-of-female-athletes-say-growth-hindered-during-pandemic-by-inequalities-with-mens-sport. Accessed on February 17, 2021.

Yoon, L., & Wilson, B. (2019). Journalism, environmental issues, and sport mega-events: A study of South Korean media coverage of the Mount Gariwang development for the 2018 Pyeong Chang Winter Olympic and Paralympic Games. *Communication & Sport*, 7(6), 699–728.

Index

Acarajé, 150, 156–157
   and Copa Race–Class–Gender
      disorder, 157–159
Adams, Nicola (British boxer),
   14–15
Advantage theory, 47–48
Africa Cup of Nations, 1
Androgen Insensitivity Syndrome,
   33–34
Asian Games, 1, 6
Asociación de Clubes de Fútbol
      Femenino (ACFF), 194
Athlete. *See also* Male elite athletes
   activism, 135
   elite, 36–37
   female, 33–34, 134–136
   Inter* athletes, 239
   in particular, 33–34
   passports, 240
   Trans* athletes, 37, 239
Athletics South Africa (ASA), 39
Australian Grand Prix. *See*
      Formula One

Baianas, 15, 17, 150, 156–157,
   239–240
Baianas Lives Matter,
   155–156
Barcelona, 188
Barr body test, 36
'Biological men', 47
Biological passport, 37
Black, Asian and minority ethnics
   (BAME), 172
Black Brazilian women, 239–240
Black feminism, 17
   in Brazil, 151, 153, 155
Black feminists, 154–155
Blanchard, Alana (surfer), 136

Brazil
   Black feminism in, 151, 153, 155
   gender metaphor in Brazilian,
      151–152
Bronze, Lucy (England), 137

Carneiro, Sueli, 154
Carnival, 172
Chand, Dutee (Indian sprinter),
   38–39
Climate change, environment and, 244
Club Deportivo Tacón, 192–193
Colonial/Modern Gender System, 45
Combat sports, 8–9
Commonwealth Games, 1, 6, 12
Competition, 2–3
Competitive sports, 9
Copa Race–Class–Gender disorder,
   157–159
Coping strategies, 77
Cost, 3
Court of Arbitration for Sport (CAS),
   38–39
COVID-19 pandemic, 1, 240–241
Critical feminist research approach,
   207–209
Cultural performance, 171
   efficacy of, 166

Dean, Christopher, 163–164
Dichotomous sex, 35
Differences of sexual development
   (DSD), 34, 39
   women with, 40
Direct costs, 3
Discrimination, ongoing, 241–242
Diversity, 156
Do Nothing Bitch (DNB), 140–141

Elaborated Social Identity Model
   (ESIM), 94–95, 103
Elite athletes, 36–37
Elite sport, 33
Ellie Soutter (snowboarder), 74
Emotion management, 76
English disease, 93
Environment and climate change, 244
Equality, 39–40
   gender, 21–22
Equestrian sport, 14
Estudos Feministas (*Feminist Studies*),
   154
Ethical relativism, 59, 63–64
European Athletic Championships, 35
Events, 2–3
'Everyday resistance' concept, 152–153

Fair competition, 33
Fair fights, 98
Fairness, 39–40
   promise of fairness and inclusive
      policies, 49–50
   in sport mega-events, 37–39
Familiarisation, 209
Fan ID, 170
Fan(s)
   Fan zones, 170
   at football mega-events, 93–94
   presence and absence of, 99–101
   violence, 7
Fédération Internationale de Football
      Association (FIFA), 1, 149
   FIFA Men's World Cup, 4, 6–7
   FIFA Women's World Cup, 6–7
   General, 143
   Rights, 141
   Scandal, 168
Female
   athletes, 33–34, 134–136
   sport mega-events, 188
   sports and athletes, 9
Feminism
   black, 17
   liberal, 17
   multiple, 18

multitude of, 16–17
neoliberal, 11, 18
post-feminism, 8–9, 18, 135–136
postcolonial, 17–18
Third-wave feminism, 11
Feminist
   commentators, 201–202
   sport studies, 135–136
   sports media scholars, 136–137
   thematic analysis, 136
FIFA Men's World Cup, 163
   Brazil (2014), 21
   in Qatar (2022), 242
   Russia (2018), 10–11, 106–107
FIFA Women's World Cup, 57
   'Dare to Shine', 133–134
   France (2019), 133–135
   methodology, 136–138
   Rapinoe, Megan, 134–135
   self-disclosure as statement,
      140–141
   self-empowerment and politics,
      141–143
   from self-love to equal love,
      138–139
   theoretical framework, 135–136
FIFA Women's World Cup Now
      (live Twitter show), 57
Fischer, Nilla (Sweden), 137
Flintoff, Freddie (cricket player), 74
Flints Crew at Spartak Moscow,
      97–98
Fluidity, 17
Football
   cultural role, 93
   fan violence at, 93–94
   FIFA Men's World Cup, Russia
      (2018), 106–107
   football-related disorder, 98
   gender (dis)order and, 151–152
   historical, 93
   masculinity, football and violence,
      92
   mega-events, 91
   participation, 1–2
   pay, 134–135

presence and absence of fan violence
at football mega-events,
99–101
UEFA Championships, France
(2016), 101–106
Football Association (FA), 74
Football Banning Orders
(FBOs), 94
Football hooliganism, 93,
107–108
evolution in England, 92
at mega-events, 94–95
policing and policy, 94–95
in Russian Federation,
96–99
subcultural violence and
nationalism, 95–96
Football World Cup (FWC), 92,
163–164, 221–222
Carnival, 172
cultural performance, 171
diversity programme, 177–178
effectiveness of technological
performance, 165–166
efficacy of cultural performance,
166
efficiency of organisational
performance, 165
feeling, 163–164
getting power, 166–169
harder, faster, better, stronger,
174–176
investigating football fan
performances, 164–165
Iranian women, 177
organisational performance and
efficiency, 170
perceptions of Russia, 173
public debate in Russia, 178
in Russia, 164
shared experience, 180–181
sport mega-events, 176, 181
technological performance,
170–171
traditional values, 179–180
Forest fights. *See* Fair fights

Formula One, 113–114
as (gendered) 'glamorous' event,
116–117
drivers, 113
grid girls, 120
macho racers, 117–120
as mega-event, 113, 115–116
ornamental females, 120–124
and spectacle, 115–116
Fox Sports, 57
Free testosterone (fT), 43–44

Gama, Sara (Italy), 137
Gender, 33, 45, 47, 239
binary, 118
differences in sports media,
222–225
equity, 221–222
gender equality, sport mega-events
and search for,
187–188
gender trouble and sport
mega-events, 13–15
gender/nationality, intermingling of,
225–227
identity in (Golf) sport media,
204–206
(in)equality, 16
inequality in Spanish sports,
189–190
lack of media exposure,
222–223
linguistic depiction,
224–225
marking, 13
metaphor in Brazilian,
151–152
sexism, 120
sport and, 6–10
sport mega-events, gender and
mediatisation, 10–13
stereotypes, 45–46
theorising gender and sport
mega-events, 15–18
verification, 39–40
visual depiction, 223–224

Gender (dis)order
    Acarajé and Copa
        Race–Class–Gender
        disorder, 157–159
    Baianas, *Acarajé* and mega-events
        gendered order, 156–157
    Baianas Lives Matter, 155–156
    black feminism in Brazil,
        153–155
    everyday resistance, 152–153
    football, 151–152
Gender stereotypes, 59–60
    in sport media, 60–61
Gendered dynamics, 113
Gendered evaluations of dominant
    play, 64–66
'Gladiators' of Spartak Moscow,
    99–100
Glamour, 20, 113, 116–117
Global Health, 240–241
Global North, 242
Global South, 242, 244
Golf
    Ryder Cup, 202–204
    Solheim Cup, 6, 209–210

Hansen, Caroline Graham (Norway),
    137
Hashimoto, Seiko (Japan's Olympic
    minister), 242
Hegemonic masculinity, 7, 18
Hi-tech racing, 113
Hooligan(s), 91
Hooliganism, 7, 91
    England/'Old Skool', 100
    football hooliganism evolution in
        England, 92
    Russian Style, 98
    violence, 95–96
Human rights, 243
'Hybrid' technology, 120
Hybridity, 17
Hyper-masculine nationalist identity,
    100
Hyperandrogenism, 38, 43–45, 47

IAAF Policy on Gender
    Verification, 38
Inclusive masculinity, 74, 118
Inclusive policies, 34, 49–50
Indianapolis 500, 115–116
IndyCar, 120–121
Infantino, Gianni (FIFA President),
    133–134
Inter* athletes, 239
Inter*sex, 37–38
Inter*sex athletes, 37–38
Inter*sex people, 33–34
International Association of Athletics
    Federation (IAAF), 9, 33
International Broadcast Centre (IBC),
    170–171
International crises, 1
International Federation of Football
    Associations (FIFA),
    190–191
International Olympic Committee
    (IOC), 4, 33, 168, 240
International sport, 202–203
    competitions, 227–234
Intersex, 39–40
    sports competitions, 227–234
Iranian women, 177

Kellner, 115
Kelly Catlin (cyclist), 74
Kłobukowska, Ewa, 36
"Known hooligans" movement, 94–95

Ladies European Tour (LET), 201
Ladies Professional Golf Association
    (LPGA), 201
Lambert, Elizabeth (University of New
    Mexico soccer player), 61
Le Mans, 120–121
Lesbian, gay, bisexual, trans, queer
    (LGBTQ+), 15
    rights, 168
Liberal feminism, 17
Liberal feminist approach, 16–17
Linguistic depiction, 224–225, 233–234

Macho racers, 117–120
Male elite athletes, 73
    athlete role models and recovery,
        84–87
    displaying vulnerability, 80–82
    interpretative analysis, 75–76
    mental health suffering as antithesis
        of sport, 77–80
    methods and approach to study,
        75–77
    nuance of suffering in sport, 75
    sport and mental health, 74–75
    sport as coping mechanism,
        82–84
Marozsan, Dzseinifer (Germany), 137
Masculine hegemonic entrenchment,
    205
Masculinity, 75
    aggressive, 91
    football, violence and, 92
    hegemonic, 117–118
    hyper, 7
    inclusive, 74, 118
Masculinity in sport, 57–58
McKinnon's theory, 49–50
Media
    coverage, 11
    framing of sports, 12
    lack of media exposure,
        222–223, 228, 232
    mediatisation, 10–13
    representation, 11
    Social media, 11–12, 60, 134,
        223–224
    traditional–print and TV, 243
    women athletes in, 59–60
Mediated reach, 3
Mediatisation, 10, 13, 243
    of sport events, 116
Medico-scientific foundation,
    40–45
Mega-event(s), 1–3, 12, 241
    gendered order, 156–157
    hosting, 3
    masculine hegemony in, 13–14
    meaning, 6

Mental health, 75–76
    and male elite athletes, 74–75
    suffering as antithesis of sport,
        77–80
Mental toughness, 75
Minimum pay of female professional
    players, 193–194
Monaco Grand Prix, 115–116
Montreal Summer Olympics (1976), 4
Morgan, Alex, 64–65
Motor-racing events, 115–116
Motorsport, 119
'*Mulheres negras*' movement, 153
Multiplicity, 17

National identity
    in (Golf) sport media, 204–206
    gender differences in sports media,
        222–225
    intermingling of gender/nationality,
        225–227
    international, intersex sports
        competitions, 227–234
National proxy warriors,
    210–212
National sport federations (NSFs), 195
Nationalism, 91, 93, 95–96
Nationality, 239
Neo-colonial fetishism, 35
Neoliberal feminisms, 18
'New' media, 11
Nongovernmental organisations
    (NGOs), 154
Nuance of suffering in sport, 75
NVivo software, 77

'Off-field' case study, 150
Okolofutbola, 98
'Old Skool' typologies of hooligan
    violence, 100
Olympic Games, 5–7, 9–10, 34, 39–40,
    58–59, 221–222
Olympic Games–Summer, 35
    general, 1
    Rio (2016), 10–11
    Tokyo (2020/21), 39, 240

Olympic Games–Winter
  general, 1
  Sochi (2014), 167
Olympique Lyonnais, 190–191
Olympique Marseille (OM), 101
Olympism, 5
Online academic databases, 39–40
Organisational performance, efficiency
    of, 165
Organised sport, 6–7
Ornamental females, 120–124

Pan American Games, 1, 6
Patrick, Danica (racing driver), 136
Perfectionism, 74–75
Performance
  cultural, 171
  gender, 1
  organisational, 165
  technical, 171
Plurality, 156
Polycystic ovary syndrome, 38
Post-feminism, 8–9, 18, 135–136
Postcolonial feminisms, 17–18
Primera Iberdrola, 192
Professional sport, 48–49
Public perception, 241
PubMed, 39–40

Qatar FIFA Men's World Cup (2022),
    244

Race, 45, 47, 239
Racial hierarchies, 46
Racism
  in football, 107, 139–140
  Megan Rapinoe and, 134–135
  in Russia, 169
Rapinoe, Megan (US footballer),
    14–15, 64–65, 134–135,
    137–139, 141, 239–240
  empowerment, 142–143
  most valuable player and top scorer
    of tournament in FIFA
    Women's World Cup,
    134–135

in national politics, 142–143
outspoken on multiple forums, 135
#USWNT, 143
Real Madrid, 188
Red-Blue Warriors at CSKA, 97–98
Renard, Wendie (France), 137
Resistance concept, 152–153
Reto Iberdrola, 192
Rights, scandal, 4
Rio Games (2016), 13
Role congruity theory (RCT), 59, 62
Rousey, Ronda (wrestler), 136
Rubiales, Luis (president of Spanish
    Football Federation), 192
Rugby World Cup, 6
Russia
  Controversy, 167–168
  Putin, 99
  Russian Federation, football
    hooliganism in, 96–99
  Russian football hooliganism, 108
  USSR, 97–98
Ryder Cup, 202–204

Sanden, Shanice Van De (Holland),
    137
Sarajevo Winter Olympics (1984), 4
Scopus, 39–40
Self-categorisation theory, 221–222
Self-disclosure, 136
  as statement, 140–141
Self-empowerment, 136
  and politics, 141–143
Self-love, 136
Semenya, Caster (African athlete), 9,
    39
Separatism, 98
Sex, 35
  verification tests, 33
Sex biology, 46
Sex integration, 14–15
Sex regulation, 39–40
Sex segregation, 39–40
Sex testing, 33–34, 39–40
  analysis, 40
  author's position, 35

current debate on sex testing and
fairness in sport mega-
events, 37–39
history of, 35–37
hyperandrogenism, race and gender,
45–47
level playing field, 47–48
medico-scientific foundation and
(bio)ethical considerations
of current regulations, 40–45
methods, 39–40
promise of fairness and inclusive
policies, 49–50
reviewed articles by themes, 41–43
in sport mega-events, 33
Sexuality, 9–10, 239
'Sexually empowered' female, 8–9
Sharapova, Maria (tennis players), 136
Shared experience, 180–181
Snapchat (instant-messaging
application), 136–137
Social comparison theory, 225
Social identity theory in action,
225–227
Social media, 11–12, 60, 134, 223–224
Social role theory (SRT), 59, 62–63
Socioeconomic characteristics, 190
Sociology of sport, 1–2
Solheim Cup, 202
critical feminist research approach,
207–209
gender and national identity
in(Golf) sport media,
204–206
as Golf, 209–210
national proxy warriors, 210–212
Pettersen the 'Supermum', 212–214
Ryder Cup's little sister, 214–215
story of 2019 Solheim Cup, 206
(supra-)national identity and golf,
202–204
Women's Golf and, 201–202
Spanish Football Federation,
187–188
Sport media, 12
gender differences in, 222–225

Sport mega-events. *See also* Football
World Cup (FWC), 1–2, 6,
33–34, 58–59, 221, 239,
242–243
current debate on sex testing and
fairness in, 37–39
gender, mediatisation and, 10–13
gender trouble and, 13–15
history of sex testing in, 35–37
and search for gender equality,
187–188
theorising gender and, 15–18
Sport(s), 1, 39–40
as coping mechanism, 82–84
and gender, 6–10
in Latin America, 150
male elite athletes in, 74–75
mental health suffering as antithesis
of, 77–80
nuance of suffering in, 75
SPORTDiscus, 39–40
Stockholm Consensus, 37
Stylized exoticism, 122–123
Subcultural violence, 95–96
Summer Olympic Games. *See also*
Winter Olympics Games, 1,
4, 6, 12
in Beijing (2008), 242–243
Los Angeles in 2028, 243
Paris in 2024, 243
in Rio, 240–241
(Supra-)national identity and golf,
202–204
Sydney Games (2000), 13
'Symbolic politics', 4–5

T-talk, 46
Technological performance, 170–171
effectiveness of, 165–166
Televisual techniques, 115–116
Thematic analysis, 209
Third-wave feminism, 11, 18
Thorpe, Ian (swimmer), 74
Tokyo Olympics (2020/21), 240–241
Tokyo Organising Committee, 240
Torvill, Jayne, 163–164

Traditional media, 243
Traditional values, 179–180
Trans*athletes, 37, 239
Trans*men, 37
Trans*people, 33–34
Trans*persons, 37–38
Trans*women, 33–34, 37, 40, 47
Transgender, 39–40
Tweddle, Beth (British female
    gymnast), 8
Two-sex model, 33

UEFA Championships, France (2016),
    92, 101, 106
Union of European Football
    Associations (UEFA), 6,
    190–191
United States Women's National team
    (USWNT), 57, 64–65
Urban transformation, 3–4
US Women's National Team
    (USWNT), 19
Ustawki, 98

Video assistant referees (VAR),
    170–171
Violence
    fan violence at football, 93–94
    football and, 92
    'Old Skool' typologies of hooligan,
        100
    subcultural, 95–96
Visitor attractiveness, 3
Visual content analysis, 223–224
Visual depiction, 223–224, 232–233
Visual media portrayals,
    223–224
Visual representation of women
    athletes, 232–233
Vulnerability, displaying, 80–82

Well-being, 75–76
Western notion of binary sex, 34
Whiteness, 9–10

Williams, Serena (tennis players),
    11–12, 136, 138
Wimbledon Tennis Championships,
    2–3
Winter Olympics Games. *See also*
    Summer Olympic Games
    in PyeongChang(2018),
        10–11
    in Sarajevo (1984), 4
    in Sochi (2014), 167–168
Women, 63
    athletes in media, 59–60
    barriers for women in sport,
        60–64
    category in elite sport, 33
    with DSD, 40
    ethical relativism, 63–64
    football in Spain, 187
    in football management,
        195–196
    in Formula One, 120
    gender inequality in Spanish sports,
        189–190
    gender stereotypes in sport media,
        60–61
    gendered evaluations of dominant
        play, 64–66
    improvements in professional
        women's football,
        192–193
    with inter*sex variations,
        33–34
    limits of progress, 193–196
    more girls and women playing
        football, 193
    participation rates in sport, 57
    position in sport, 8
    positive impacts of women's
        football mega-events in
        Spain, 191–193
    role congruity and social role
        theory, 62–63
    selection of empirical case and
        sources, 188–189

sport mega-events and search for
gender equality, 187–188
and sports in Latin America,
150
football mega-events,
190–191
Women's Golf and Solheim Cup,
201–202
Women's World Golf Rankings
(WWGR), 206

Working conditions of female
professional players,
193–194
World Anti-Doping Agency
(WADA), 37
World Athletics. *See* International
Association of Athletics
Federation (IAAF)
World Athletics Championships,
1, 34